JOSEP MANUEL PERAMÀS

A Treatise on the Guaraní System of Government in Comparison with Plato's Republic (1793)

TEXTS *from the* EARLY AMERICAS

JOSEP MANUEL PERAMÀS

A Treatise on the Guaraní System of Government in Comparison with Plato's Republic (1793)

edited and translated by

Michael Brumbaugh

DUMBARTON OAKS, TRUSTEES FOR HARVARD UNIVERSITY, WASHINGTON, D.C.

Printed in the United States of America by Sheridan Books, Inc.

LIBRARY OF CONGRESS CATALOGING-IN-PUBLICATION DATA

NAMES: Peramás, José Manuel, author. | Brumbaugh, Michael Everett, editor, translator. | Peramás, José Manuel. De administratione guaranica comparate ad Rempublicam Platonis commentarius. | Peramás, José Manuel. De administratione guaranica comparate ad Rempublicam Platonis commentarius. English.

TITLE: A treatise on the Guaraní system of government in comparison with Plato's Republic (1793) / Josep Manuel Peramàs ; edited and translated by Michael Brumbaugh.

DESCRIPTION: Series: Texts from the early Americas | Includes bibliographical references and index. | Text in Latin with English translation on facing pages ; introduction and notes in English. | Summary: "The Guaraní-Jesuit communities of greater Paraguay, in existence from 1609 until 1767, represent a unique collaboration between Indigenous and European peoples in the history of the Americas. Reports of these communities were met with fascination in Europe, where readers imagined the Guaraní and Jesuits as starting from a clean slate, unconstrained by the customs that guided social, religious, economic, and political life in Europe. European intellectuals mythologized these communities, using ancient Greek paradigms to characterize (and caricature) the communities within the context of a broader ideological conflation of antiquity and the Americas. Josep Manuel Peramàs's *De Administratione Guaranica Comparate ad Rempublicam Platonis Commentarius* [A Treatise on the Guaraní System of Government in Comparison with Plato's Republic (1793)] emerges as a response to this European intellectual tradition. Written by a leading humanist scholar who lived among the Guaraní, the treatise offers a systems-level analysis of how the Guaraní-Jesuit communities were structured, focusing on twenty-five formative aspects of the civic experience (e.g., weddings, public festivals, clothing, political offices). In making this groundbreaking treatise available to English audiences, this bilingual edition offers new perspectives on the Guaraní and new avenues for exploring the complex legacy of classical literature in the Americas"—Provided by publisher.

IDENTIFIERS: LCCN 2024006835 | ISBN 9780884025191 (hardcover)

SUBJECTS: LCSH: Plato. Republic. | Jesuits—Missions—Paraguay—Early works to 1800. | Guarani Indians—Paraguay—Early works to 1800.

CLASSIFICATION: LCC F2230.2.G72 P458 2024 | DDC 989.2/03004983822—dc23/eng/20240403

LC RECORD available at https://lccn.loc.gov/2024006835

GENERAL EDITOR: Frauke Sachse
ART DIRECTOR: Kathleen Sparkes
DESIGN AND COMPOSITION: Melissa Tandysh
MANAGING EDITOR: Sara Taylor

www.doaks.org/publications

CONTENTS

ACKNOWLEDGMENTS

I come to this text as a specialist in the languages, literatures, and cultures of ancient Greece and Rome. Much of my work investigates ways in which ancient cultural products, particularly literary texts, become relevant anew in settings that are chronologically, geographically, and culturally removed from their original contexts. Some of the most stimulating and intriguing examples of this phenomenon take place in multicultural contexts that implicate diverse priorities and ways of knowing. I do not pretend to possess all the many competencies necessary to fully command the diverse contexts and academic disciplines at stake in this kaleidoscopic text. My efforts here are intended to make this important source available and intelligible to a wider audience as a witness to its times. It is my hope that this edition will serve as a foundation for further critical inquiry and investigation.

This project began in 2008 with a fortuitous encounter with the title of Peramàs's treatise (but not the text itself) in the Archivo General de la Nación in Buenos Aires. Over the subsequent sixteen years working on this text, I have enjoyed incredible generosity and support from colleagues and friends across the globe—far more than can be adequately chronicled here. Before I began my own studies in this area, conversations with John Gallucci and David Lupher opened my eyes to a vast world of Latin that lay outside the curriculum of most Classics departments in the United States at that time. At the University of California, Los Angeles (UCLA), Kathryn Morgan, Amy Richlin, Shane Butler, Giulia Sissa, Anthony Pagden, and Peter Stacey encouraged my initial efforts to understand this text, the classical traditions on which it draws, and the early modern world from which it emerged. Opportunities to speak about this text at the Universidad de los Andes, American Society for Eighteenth-Century Studies, University of Maryland, Ohio State University, UCLA, Universidad Nacional de Córdoba, Society for Classical Studies, and Democritus University of Thrace have contributed to broadening my perspectives on this material and helped me better understand how I can make it accessible to a variety of constituencies.

Institutional support from UCLA, Reed College, and Princeton University allowed me to obtain images of the original edition and transcribe the Latin text, with invaluable assistance from Laura Moser at Reed College and Anne Brown at Princeton University. Tulane University has been a tremendous champion of this work, and I am indebted to the Department of Classical Studies, the Provost's Office, Hortensia Calvo and the Latin American Library, Thomas Reese and the Stone Center for Latin American Studies, Carol Lavin Bernick and her crucially important Faculty Investment Fund, and, especially, Brian Edwards and the School of Liberal Arts for providing support for site visits and archival research in Italy, Paraguay, and Argentina, as well as a generous subvention for the beautiful map created by Gene Thorp. The majority of the project was completed with the support of a National Endowment for the Humanities Summer Stipend, a Loeb Classical Library Fellowship, and a sabbatical from Tulane University.

I am indebted to Àngels Rius i Bou of the Biblioteca de l'Abadia de Montserrat and Diana Kohnke of the Sutro Library, who offered crucial assistance and invaluable photographs when it was impossible for me to consult their collections in person; Francesc Costa, who became my guide to Peramàs family records in Mataró and led me to the work of Xavier Clavell of the Museu Arxiu de Santa Maria de Mataró; Paolo Campana, who generously shared his deep knowledge of publishing and bookmaking in eighteenth-century Faenza; Leonardo Waisman and Julián D'Avila, whom I consulted to better understand the musical landscape of the Guaraní-Jesuit communities; and fellow scholars of Peramàs, especially Maya Feile Tomes, Marcela Suárez, Fabrizio Melai, and Daniel Silverman, who have shared their work in progress and been thoughtful interlocutors over the past several years. I also wish to thank the staff at the Rare Book and Special Collections Reading Room at the U.S. Library of Congress, the Biblioteca Comunale Manfrediana di Faenza, the Chiesa di Santa Maria dell'Angelo, the Museo Regional Aníbal Cambas, the Centro de Investigaciones y Estudios sobre Cultura y Sociedad at the Universidad Nacional de Córdoba, the Colegio Nacional de Monserrat, and the Archivum Romanum Societatis Iesu. I owe special thanks to Federico Sartori for serving as my intrepid guide to Jesuit Córdoba and the *estancias*; his energy and generosity are matched only by his enviable expertise.

I am grateful to Kris Lane, Ryan Boehm, Emilia Oddo, Nihar Mathur, and Nancy McIntyre for reading drafts of the introduction and offering valuable feedback from a variety of perspectives. I wish to thank members of my Tulane seminars on Plato, Latin in the Americas, and early modern utopianism for hours of lively discussion and for calling my attention to mistakes in the text and translation. I thank Andrew Laird for his support and for alerting me to this exciting new series; the team at Dumbarton Oaks, particularly Frauke Sachse and Sara Taylor, who have been ideal publishing partners; and the anonymous referees for their helpful suggestions and critiques. Here at Tulane University, logistical and administrative support from Liz Reyna and Tara Hamburg has been essential to obtaining research materials, undertaking research travel, and funding the whole endeavor.

The greatest source of support throughout the most difficult (and the most enjoyable) stages of this project has undoubtedly been my wife, Elaine Kao, who accompanied me on research trips to Europe and South America, offered useful feedback on the readability of the translation, workshopped countless drafts of the introduction with me, and welcomed endless discussion about every rabbit hole I got lost in along the way. Without her encouragement, patience, and thoughtfulness, this project might never have reached completion. It is to her that I dedicate this volume.

INTRODUCTION

The Guaraní-Jesuit communities of greater Paraguay, in existence from 1609 to 1767, represent a unique collaboration between Indigenous and European peoples in the history of the Americas. Over a period of one hundred and fifty years, some thirty-three towns came to represent the joint efforts of several hundred thousand Guaraní and a few hundred Jesuits. Each of these communities typically had between two and five thousand Guaraní and two Jesuit priests. To describe these settlements as communities is not to suggest that all involved had the same goals nor, indeed, to deny that they emerged within a broader historical context of pervasive inequality and coercion. What is worth emphasizing, however, is the multiplicity of perspectives and agendas that coexisted within these communities as well as the agency of the men and women who invested their labor and, in many cases, their lives in establishing and sustaining large sedentary communities over several generations (Sarreal 2014; Wilde 2009, 2018a).[1]

News of these communities spread like wildfire among the Indigenous peoples of the Río de la Plata Basin in the heart of South America and throughout Europe. The oral reports are lost to us, but many of the written accounts circulated widely and remain accessible today. Particularly for those far away in Europe, America and the communities taking shape in Paraguay were the stuff of fantasy.[2] Because European readers were generally ignorant of the cultural and political dynamics in these communities prior to European contact, they often assumed that the Americas closely resembled some "originary" state of human existence; the Jesuits and Guaraní were imagined as starting from a clean slate, a concept that would come to be closely associated with Descartes's and Locke's theories about human psychology. As viewers, removed from the subjective realities of subtropical mission life, Europeans presumptuously (and naively) projected their political and cultural desires onto this American "heterotopia" (Foucault 1984). This New World appeared to them to be unconstrained by the norms and customs that guided and controlled social, religious, economic, and political life

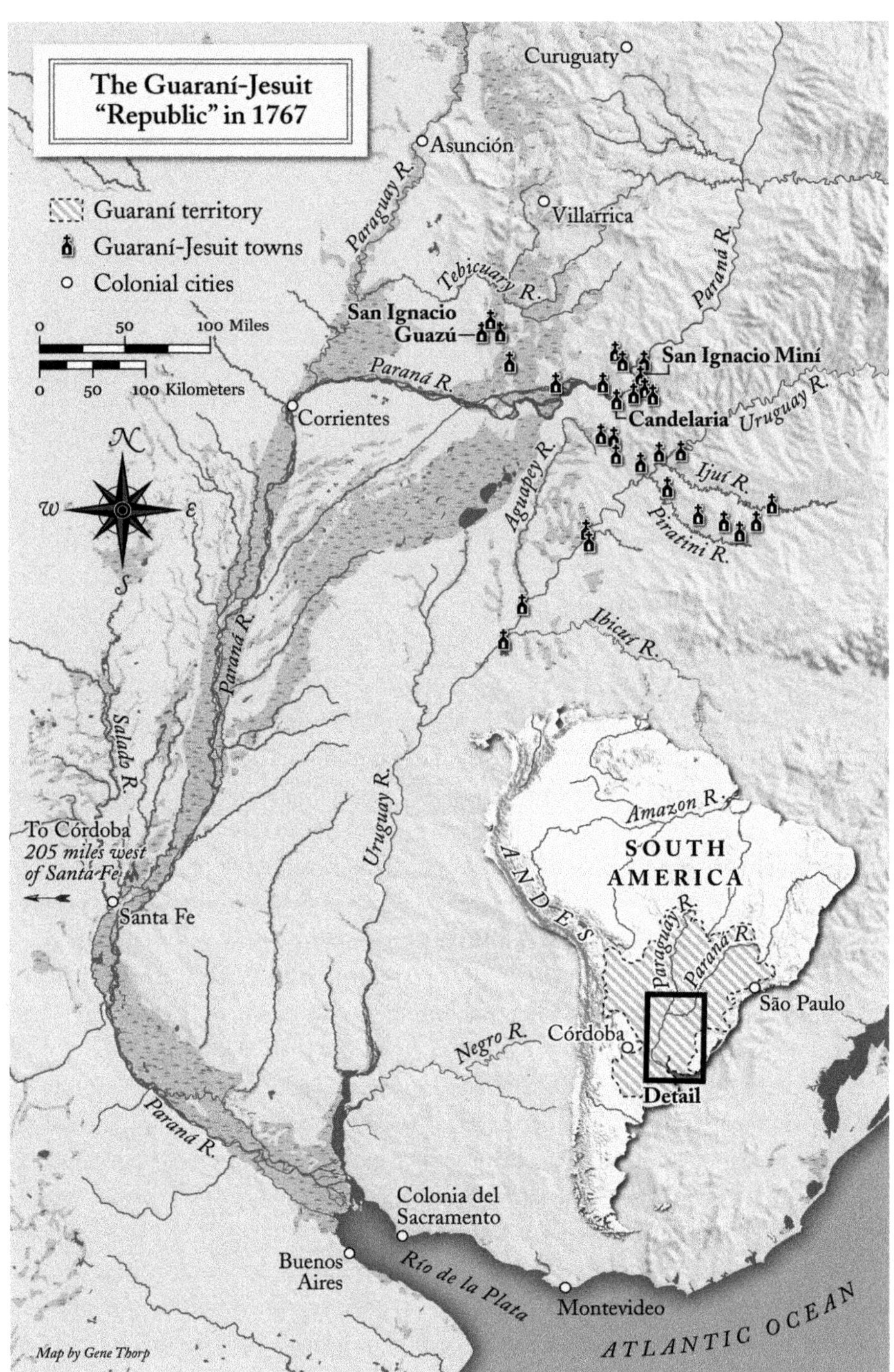

Map showing the extent of Guaraní territory prior to European contact, alongside the location of Guaraní-Jesuit towns of the "Republic" of Paraguay in the year of the Jesuit expulsion. Map by Gene Thorp.

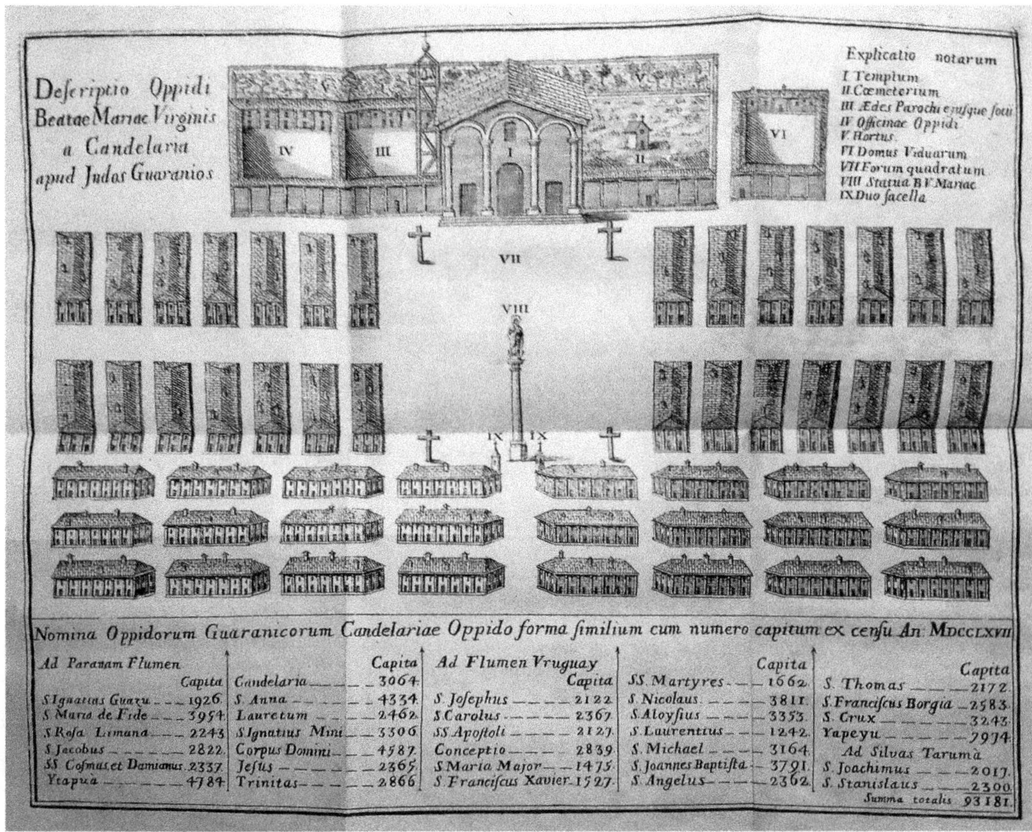

Folded plate bearing a site plan of Candelaria, the administrative hub of the Guaraní republic, along with a list of thirty-two Guaraní towns and their populations in 1767. This large-format plate was published as part of Peramàs's 1793 volume of biographies at great expense and referred to in the De Administratione Guaranica. Photograph by Michael Brumbaugh.

in Europe. But if that was so, how did it function? Most consumers of mission tales were too impatient or uninterested in learning the answers from the Americans themselves and instead invented their own solutions by probing the wisdom traditions of the ancient Mediterranean. Rome, Greece, Egypt, and the Near East enjoyed a privileged place in early modern Europe because of their connections to Christianity and because they had produced artifacts of culture that Europeans valued, including impressive architecture, art, and literature. As a result, Europeans viewed the ancient Mediterranean world as a repository of fundamental truths about humanity, and they endeavored to use this store of knowledge as a tool to understand newly encountered peoples the world over. In the European imagination, the mythologized Guaraní-Jesuit communities of Paraguay quickly came to be associated with ancient Greece.[3]

Josep Manuel Peramàs's *De Administratione Guaranica Comparate ad Rempublicam Platonis Commentarius* (hereafter, *DAG*) [A Treatise on the Guaraní System of Government in Comparison with Plato's Republic (1793)] emerges as a response, and in many ways a rebuttal, to this European intellectual tradition. The treatise offers a systems-level analysis of how the Guaraní-Jesuit communities were structured, focusing on twenty-five formative aspects of the civic experience (e.g., weddings, public festivals, clothing, political offices), each of which he presents as a unit of analysis. He proceeds systematically through these units by presenting his synthesis of Plato's thoughts on a particular topic and its role in structuring civic life, then offering an account of how the Paraguayan communities functioned in practice. This approach was born out of a persistent claim, made by proponents and detractors alike in Europe, that the Jesuits had established a Christo-Platonic political regime in Paraguay.[4] Implicit in this claim was a bias about the superiority of European over American knowledge as well as a false assumption that Guaraní culture and political norms did not contribute to shaping these emerging communities.

For the Platonic portion of each chapter, Peramàs brings together material from the *Republic* and the *Laws*.[5] Written in Athens during the first half of the fourth century BCE, each of these works presents a dialogue in which the participants build out a hypothetical political system. These systems are designed to overcome the limitations of human nature, as Plato saw them, in order to maximize certain kinds of human excellence for individuals and the community writ large. The two political systems have some features in common but are by no means interchangeable, as Peramàs himself acknowledges (e.g., *DAG* 68). These were Plato's most widely read works in the eighteenth century, and their popularity was almost certainly due to a pervasive interest in crafting new and improved political systems to revise or replace existing regimes. Peramàs's treatise speaks squarely to this interest and engages with Plato as a means of participating in this intellectual enterprise. For Peramàs, Plato's texts serve as a jumping-off point for inquiry and a means of engaging with contemporary discourse rather than a font of authoritative and sacrosanct knowledge. He variously offers amazement (e.g., for Plato's approach to the "inquisition," *DAG* 29), reproach (e.g., for Plato's failure to denounce polytheism, *DAG* 33, and his endorsement of wife sharing in the *Republic, DAG* 53), and even incredulity (e.g., at Plato's fascination with the highly composite number 5,040 in the *Laws, DAG* 17) as he synthesizes Plato's positions, demonstrating a deep knowledge of Plato's work and a familiarity with major figures who engaged with it, including Aristotle, Cicero, Thomas Aquinas, Marsilio Ficino, Thomas More, Francis Bacon, and others.[6]

The Guaraní sections typically respond to one or more aspects emphasized in the Platonic material but then branch out into more detailed and expansive treatments of the subject under consideration. Though Peramàs himself spent time in several of these Guaraní-Jesuit communities, he stresses in the introduction that the accounts he provides are drawn from well-respected, published sources, which he dutifully footnotes.[7] This, as it turns out, is a defensive posture designed to hedge against accusations of embellishment; in reality, his writing bears the unmistakable traces of his own personal experiences, which he only makes explicit for rhetorical effect when it renders his account more vivid or authoritative. Thus, he offers eyewitness anecdotes on the Guaraní invention of *fútbol* (*DAG* 105), the presence of Spanish citizens in the mission communities (*DAG* 188–192), the making and wearing of a Guaraní *Aovasy* or poncho (*DAG* 199–201), the profound emotional and spiritual response he had to reading a book written by a Guaraní resident of Loreto (*DAG* 231–232), and the devastating assault in which the Guaraní took up arms to defend their community against "a strike force of Abipones or Guaicuruan looters" (*DAG* 340). While Peramàs does report some inconsistencies and anecdotal variations, he is primarily interested in the systemic, normative, and anonymized behavior of individuals and groups in terms of their sociopolitical rather than personal lives, much as Plato was.[8] Likewise, his analysis focuses on the dynamic interplay between the individual and the community as well as on the habituation of values and behaviors that structure civic life and render the system of government self-perpetuating.

In contrast to the straightforward methodology of comparison that he describes in his introduction (*DAG* 1–6), Peramàs weaves several threads of ambiguity throughout his treatise.[9] Chief among these is a tension present even in the work's title. In Latin, *De Administratione Guaranica* does not specify the relationship between the Guaraní and the act of governing much as in the following translation: "On the Governance [System] of the Guaraní." Does this work claim to describe a government that belongs to the Guaraní and in which they exercise agency, or is it about a regime imposed on the Guaraní by external agents seeking to control them?[10] Even in the context of a larger effort to defend the labors of his Order, Peramàs is circumspect in his characterizations of the Jesuit project and variously casts them as authors of the regime, members of the Guaraní community, or simply bystanders fulfilling a minimum advisory role mandated by the Spanish crown. In many ways, this lack of clarity mirrors the historical realities of the Guaraní-Jesuit communities, which anthropologist and historian Guillermo Wilde has characterized as made up of "spaces of ambiguity" driven by something in between coercion and consent (Wilde 2009).

Throughout the treatise, Peramàs seeks to bolster his analysis with evidence drawn from European wisdom traditions. Thus, prose and poetry from ancient Greek and Roman authors are made to sit alongside the Hebrew and Christian scriptures to form a unified corpus of knowledge about human psychology, behavior, and social structures. Far from a detached exercise in antiquarianism, his work represents a thorough and impassioned attempt to intervene in the most hotly contested debates of the day. A renewed emphasis on "happiness"[11] as life's primary objective led many to ask what type of government was best suited to that end. A perennial topic of interest for political theorists of every era, the issue had come to a head in the late eighteenth century at the dawn of the so-called Age of Revolutions. Should the old regimes be overturned and, if so, what should replace them? Many of those advocating for change sought a redistribution of power and property, often under the banner of "equality," "liberty," "democracy," and "republic"—notions closely associated with Graeco-Roman political thought (Velema and Weststeijn 2018).

For Peramàs, analyzing the Guaraní-Jesuit communities against the backdrop of Platonic political models offered invaluable evidence about the nature and limits of such ideas at a time when Europe needed it most. Writing on the eve of the French Revolution, he feared that pseudo-philosophical libertinism was drawing Europe into chaos (e.g., *DAG* 316) (Melai 2020). By no means an apologist for the excesses of the ancien régime, the author provides detailed discussions of egalitarianism and the community of goods, associating these governing principles with Plato, the ancient Christians, and the Guaraní-Jesuit communities. Though he praises these as constitutive of the ideal state, he is adamant that they are beyond the reach of stratified communities with deeply entrenched notions of individual property ownership, like those in Europe. In this way, he seeks to add a new American chapter to the European store of humanistic knowledge.

The Guaraní

> Guaraní territory is not a portion of the Earth's surface; territory is culture and culture is territory. Guaraní territory is not something prior to the Guaraní; it is their creation. Therefore, Guaraní territory is not occupied or conquered, but thought, spoken, and lived. To use a barbarism, you would have to say that it is *culture-tory*.
>
> —BARTOMEU MELIÀ (2015)

Today, Guaraní culture and language predominate in Paraguay, where over five million people (77 percent of the population, according to the most recent national census) speak at least one dialect of the language. People who identify as Indigenous Guaraní as well as those of mixed descent also live throughout neighboring regions of southern Brazil, northern Argentina, and southeastern Bolivia. Defining what it means to be "Guaraní," as well as the term itself, however, is inextricably bound up with the Luso-Hispanic invasion beginning in the early sixteenth century. Indeed, the ways that Europeans conceptualized the Americas, how they perceived the geography and its inhabitants, and their methods of organizing and transmitting that information have variously altered, displaced, and even effected the erasure of Indigenous ways of knowing, including self-definition. As a consequence, it is all but impossible to provide an account of the Guaraní that does not bear traces of this exogenous, uninvited influence.

The earliest European expeditions along the Pacific and Atlantic coasts of South America, as well as subsequent ventures to the interior of the continent, brought Europeans in contact with a variety of Indigenous peoples. Based on their own observations and information they gathered from the people they met, European outsiders spent the next century creating and refining ethnographic frameworks to distinguish between Indigenous groups based largely on geography and language—often with a limited understanding of a people's own cultural memory, conception of group identity, and systems of interethnic relationships. Beyond the limitations of their knowledge, the creation of these frameworks was driven by European priorities and pragmatic considerations (MacCormack 1999). In the face of such great linguistic diversity, Europeans sought to establish "general languages" that would serve as the lingua franca for each region and function as a central part of a strategy of colonial control. For the vast expanse of territory east of the Andes that would come to be known as Paraguay, Europeans selected Guaraní as the primary vehicle for communicating with Indigenous peoples, a choice that had extensive political and cultural ramifications for the various ethnic groups in the region (Avellaneda 2014; Estenssoro 2015; Ganson 2003; Lee 2014; Melià 2003).

Today, linguists working to trace the cultural phylogenetics, or evolutionary history, of Indigenous languages in South America view the situation differently (see, for instance, the approaches in Telesca and Vidal 2021). They understand Guaraní as a member of the Tupí language family, which originated in the Amazon Basin. Speakers of several languages in the Tupí-Guaraní subfamily, including ancient Guaraní, inhabited coastal Brazil from Paranaguá south and inland to the eastern Chaco and foothills of the Andes, primarily along the extensive river basins of the Paraguay, Paraná, Uruguay, and Río de la Plata rivers. This vast territory cuts through parts of present-day Brazil, Argentina, Uruguay, Paraguay, and Bolivia. While the date of this migration and the routes employed remain a topic of debate, patterns of settlement, economic activity, technology, and other material culture linked to the Guaraní offer some clues. One recent study hypothesizes two pulses of expansion: one taking place over the first three centuries of the Common Era as they moved from Amazonia into southeastern Brazil, and another larger expansion into the vast river systems of the La Plata Basin, which began around 1000 CE and continued up until European contact (Bonomo et al. 2015).

Prehistoric Guaraní peoples were horticulturists who lived in forested areas alongside rivers. There, they practiced slash-and-burn techniques, also known as shifting cultivation, to produce crops such as maize, manioc, tobacco, and cotton. This system of land use depleted the soil of its nutrients within a few years, and thus the Guaraní would develop a new plot of land for their crops. Since it could take as much as a generation for depleted plots to be ready for recultivation, Guaraní settlements would need to relocate periodically in the event they ran out of nearby land suitable for cultivation. In addition to overland travel, they expertly navigated the local river systems in canoes made from tree trunks and supplemented their diet with hunting, gathering, and fishing.

The material record left behind by these Pre-Columbian communities, including artifacts from daily life and traces of their settlements, further adds to our picture of Guaraní prehistory. The surviving objects most closely associated with the Guaraní are polished axes, *tembetá* (facial ornamentation with ritual and social significance), funerary urns, and ceramics (including dishes, shallow bowls, and large jars) that were distinctive for their corrugated and fingernail-incised surface decorations as well as their polychromy (red or black painted or brushed over a white slip) (Bonomo et al. 2015). Their large communal dwellings, textiles and woven baskets, and other objects made from organic materials have left fainter traces, which are largely supplemented by the later historic record.

With roots in the ancient past, the oral traditions of the Guaraní continue to the present day. This living form of cultural and historical memory offers glimpses at the precontact phases of the rich traditions developed by the Guaraní across more than two millennia. As with other oral and textual traditions around the world, it can be challenging to retrospectively separate out the original elements from subsequent interventions that have been incorporated into the tradition. As such, the details of prehistoric Guaraní religion, folklore, kinship and social dynamics, as well as inter- and intra-ethnic political relations, are now to a greater or lesser extent colored by European interpretation. Influential in this respect were the early chronicles of André Thevet (1557), Jean de Léry (1578), Claude d'Abbeville (1614), and Yves d'Évreux (1615) on encounters with Indigenous peoples of coastal Brazil (Garavaglia 1999; Monteiro 1999).

The Guaraní-Jesuit Republic

The earliest and most detailed ethnographic sources relating to the people the Europeans called "Guaraní" come from Jesuit authors beginning in the final decade of the sixteenth century (Melià 1981; Wilde 2018a). An elite religious order, the Jesuits (formally known as the Society of Jesus) were founded by a group of young men studying in Paris and were recognized by the pope in 1540. Known for their intense dedication to scholarly pursuits, the Jesuits joined the much older Catholic Orders of Franciscans, Dominicans, Augustinians, and Mercedarians as collaborators in the Portuguese and Spanish colonial enterprises in both the east and west "Indies" (i.e., Asia and the Americas). Highly trained polymaths with a talent for language learning, these priests were often called upon to engage with Indigenous populations, learn their languages, and establish settlements, known as missions or "reductions." The primary purpose of such settlements was to head off conflict between Indigenous peoples and the Europeans invading their territory. Where Europeans had taken Indigenous self-determination off the table, participation in the missions was seen by some as preferable to the horrors entailed by perpetual conflict with colonists and the military forces that supported them. The fate of these missions was determined by the Indigenous and European participants in the communities as well as the external forces exerting pressure on them.

Founded a half century after the first Europeans reached the Americas, the Society arrived in the New World in the late 1560s. By then, where conditions had been most conducive to establishing missions, the older orders had already done so. Thus, in 1607, the Jesuits moved deep into the heart of the South American continent, far from the major colonial capitals, and established the Province of Paraquaria [Paraguay]. A unit of religious administration rather than a geopolitical territory, the province had its headquarters in the university town of Córdoba and included present-day Paraguay, Argentina, Uruguay, and parts of Bolivia, Brazil, and Chile. Two years later, the Jesuits found a partner in the Indigenous leader Arapysandú and established San Ignacio Guazú on land he controlled on the banks of the Tebicuary River deep in Guaraní territory. Over the next four decades, they founded over thirty additional communities, each with one to two thousand Guaraní-speaking Indigenous residents drawn from various local tribal and ethnic groups.[12] Despite the proliferation of these communities, most Indigenous people in the region continued living outside of this network.

For both the Guaraní and Jesuits, participation in mission communities involved leaving behind one's ancestral home, committing to a life of hard work, and taking on tremendous risk. For the Jesuits, this choice was made freely, whereas the Indigenous participants faced more dire constraints. The establishment of these communities was fraught with difficulty and conflict, as various Guaraní stakeholders reacted differently to the threats and opportunities they associated with taking part in them. Some Guaraní leaders, incorrectly referred to as caciques by Europeans, saw these settlements as a means of consolidating power, while others, particularly spiritual leaders, saw that they would undermine their position in society. Non-elites were in an even more difficult position because they had to decide whether to follow these leaders or strike out on their own.

At its peak in 1732, the population of the Guaraní-Jesuit "Republic," as admirers and critics alike would call the collection of communities, topped 140,000, an estimated 85 percent of the entire Guaraní population. In a radical departure from their traditional way of life, the Guaraní built row houses, churches, and workshops first from wood and adobe and then ultimately in stone; these later structures were monumental in scale. In addition to the awe they inspired in viewers, these buildings served as virtually impenetrable fortresses designed to protect residents from threats posed by Spanish *encomenderos* (landholders granted extensive authority by the crown to exploit Indigenous labor) and Brazilian slave hunters known as *Paulistas* (from greater São Paulo) and Mamelukes (from *mamelucos*, a Portuguese term for Mestizo settlers), who constantly threatened to kidnap the Guaraní. While populations in these communities fluctuated, each town was generally home to two to four thousand Guaraní and just two Jesuits (the Cura, primarily engaged in political and logistical matters, and his colleague, devoted to religious matters) as well as any Jesuits there on a temporary basis. The pair of Jesuits directed religious life, oversaw external economic and political matters, and worked alongside Indigenous magistrates to manage civic affairs. The Jesuits in each community reported to a Superior in the Guaraní-Jesuit town of Candelaria, the administrative and geographic center of the "Republic."

The most substantial and detailed written accounts of these communities emerge from the Jesuit historiographical tradition itself. The Society's chief chroniclers in Paraguay include Antonio Ruiz de Montoya (1585–1652), Diego de Boroa (1585–1657), Nicole du Toit (1611–1685), Anton Sepp von Reinegg (1655–1733), Pedro Lozano (1697–1752), José Cardiel (1704–1782), José Guevara (1719–1806), Domingo Muriel (1718–1795), and Josep Manuel Peramàs (1732–1793), whose many books and letters were published and circulated in Europe and the Americas.[13] Moreover, the *Litterae Annuae* (Sp. *Cartas Anuas*), produced in every Jesuit province around the world and submitted to Rome, provide a wealth of data and narrative detail about both the Jesuits and the Indigenous members of mission communities. These "annual letters" served an administrative function but also had literary qualities and were intended as the first draft of history for Jesuit scholars (Friedrich 2008).

Ultimately, advanced literacy among the Guaraní elite began to provide new avenues for the expression and transmission of Indigenous perspectives and ideas (e.g., *DAG* 73, 231–232) (Cerno and Obermeier 2013; Neumann 2015; Neumann and Wilde 2014; Rodríguez-Alcalá 2010; Vega 2018; Wilde 2014). Perhaps more importantly, this literacy had far-reaching consequences for Guaraní efforts to secure self-determination and self-governance. Jesuits resisted this and obstructed Guaraní efforts to reform governance structures in their communities. This, in turn, gave rise to internal dissension and even insurrection, as in the case of the movement led by Pedro Mbaiugua, son of the Indigenous leader of Mission San Carlos. Other struggles saw Guaraní and Jesuits united against external foes, including disease and a drawn-out war over the Spanish-Portuguese border that cut through their territory. While Peramàs discusses some of the threats faced by the Guaraní-Jesuit communities (e.g., smallpox at *DAG* 18, and Paulista slave-raiders at *DAG* 106 and 259), he generally focuses macroscopically on civic institutions and how they should function with scant discussion of their acute or chronic shortcomings.

The Provincial, or head of the Jesuit province, was based some eight hundred miles to the south at the Collegium Maximum of Córdoba, the bustling administrative center of Jesuit Paraguay.[14] In tandem with the adjoining Monserrat school, the Collegium Maximum was the most important university east of the Andes and drew in students from throughout the region (Arbo 2016). From there, the Jesuits administered a complex apparatus of colleges and churches in dozens of Spanish settlements as well as a vast and ever-expanding network of missions. To sustain this massive operation, the Jesuits relied on a series of *estancias* (farming and ranching estates), which had been donated by wealthy patrons and were worked by thousands of enslaved Africans.[15]

In repeated attempts to replicate the dynamics of the Guaraní communities, the Jesuits engaged with dozens of other Indigenous groups (e.g., the Chiquitos, Ava Guaraní, Poya) to found scores of missions throughout the Southern Cone as well as in other provinces in the Americas and Asia.[16] No other project by any religious order or external colonial power approached the size, complexity, or longevity of the Guaraní-Jesuit communities. Indeed, the collaboration was unique the world over and, as a result, elicited intense reactions. Some of Europe's brightest and most adventurous young men were desperate to journey to Paraguay to take part in the much-mythologized project, just as twentieth-century youth would later become fascinated by space travel and aspire to be among the select few to explore the "final frontier." Sentiments were just as strong in the opposite direction, and anti-Jesuit detractors claimed that this "Republic" was, in fact, a powerful Jesuit kingdom that had enslaved the Guaraní (*DAG* 244–246), lived from hidden gold mines (*DAG* 294), and had designs on toppling European monarchs (*DAG* 279).[17] Fearful of the Jesuits' status as supranational, autonomous power brokers, the imperial courts of Europe serially banished the Order from their territories (e.g., Portugal in 1759, France in 1764, Spain in 1767), culminating in Pope Clement XIV's outright suppression of the Society of Jesus in 1773. Following the expulsion, the Guaraní did not rise up against the Spanish

(*DAG* 274), as the colonial powers had feared, instead pursuing a more pragmatic path by seeking to secure greater autonomy for their communities in the face of new political realities. Despite some limited successes, the Guaraní towns subsequently experienced a rapid demographic collapse, which has been attributed to Spanish-imposed administrative reforms, out-migration of male residents, epidemics, the rapid growth of non-Indigenous populations in the region, and a nexus of other sociopolitical and economic factors.[18]

Josep Manuel Peramàs i Guarro (1732–1793)

Josep Manuel, as he was known in his native Catalan, was baptized in Mataró on March 17, 1732, within a few days of his birth. Both of his parents, Rafael Peramàs i Vilapura and Theresa-Maria Guarro, hailed from prominent merchant families aspiring to nobility.[19] The fifth of ten children,[20] Josep Manuel spent his childhood at La Casa de la Por, the sixteenth-century Peramàs estate in the foothills northwest of the coastal city of Mataró. In 1743, royal service obligations forced Rafael and his family to leave behind their ancestral home and business affairs to relocate to Cartagena, near Murcia.[21] Whatever this royal service entailed, the family was sufficiently well situated that several of their children went on to prominent careers in the Americas. The eldest son known to have reached adulthood was Melcior (1729–1788), who pursued a military career, served as the private secretary to Antonio María de Bucareli while governor of Cuba (1766–1771) and viceroy of New Spain (1771–1779), was made a knight of the Order of Carlos III, and became a patron of the arts and sciences in Mexico (Costa Oller 2018:10–14). Next, "Count" Baltasar (1730–1791) became a wealthy land owner and coca producer in Cochabamba, Bolivia, where his activities included an attempt to establish a mission for the local Yuracaré in furtherance of his agricultural enterprise (Berg 2010:24–27, 251–255; Costa Oller 2018:14–20; Guzmán 1969; Meruvia Balderrama 2000:167–229).[22] Finally, Joaquim (1739–1790) also joined the military, rising to Commander of Engineers during the successful Siege of Pensacola (1781) and supervising several infrastructure projects while based in New Orleans as Lieutenant Colonel of the Royal Corps of Engineers (Costa Oller 2018:26–30; Cruz Freire 2013, 2016).[23]

Josep Manuel's American story was set in motion when he returned to Catalonia to enter the Jesuit Novitiate in Tarragona (1747) at the age of fifteen, several years younger than most others in his cohort.[24] After completing the two-year program, he did preparatory work at the Colegio de San Ignacio in Manresa for a year before moving on to the three-year Philosophy curriculum in Zaragoza. Around 1753, he obtained a post within the humanities faculty, teaching Latin literature at the Real y Pontificia Universidad de Cervera. The university was internationally renowned for Latin, and Josep Manuel used his position to refine his already considerable language skills and broaden his exposure to ancient literature.[25]

Though delighting in the world of humane letters, Josep Manuel was eager to join one of the Jesuits' overseas missions and submitted a petition to that effect. In

1754, Superior General Ignazio Visconti granted his wish and assigned him to the vast American province of Paraquaria [Paraguay]. The precocious young scholar traveled over six hundred miles to the Casa de Contratación in Cádiz, where he was registered on February 13, 1755, as "José Peramás. Student. Native of Mataró. Age 22. White, minimal beard, black eyes and hair." On April 8, he set out for the Americas with a cohort of seventy Jesuits, twenty-nine of whom were destined for Paraguay,[26] including the infamous Bernardo Ibáñez de Echavarri, who would later feature as a villain in Peramàs's treatise.[27] After a stopover in the Canary Islands, the ship arrived in Montevideo on July 17 and crossed over to Buenos Aires. Josep Manuel then traveled some five hundred miles inland to Córdoba.

Once in Córdoba, Peramàs began doctoral studies in Theology, took turns ministering to the incarcerated,[28] and was chosen to draft the 1756–1762 edition of the province's *Litterae Annuae*, which were by that time no longer published annually. Upon reading the copy sent to Rome, the Jesuit historian Giulio Cesare Cordara (1704–1785) was so impressed by the high-quality Latin coming from a student that he wrote to congratulate the young Peramàs, initiating a correspondence that appears to have been sustained for some time.[29] Over the next four years, Peramàs was ordained a priest (1758/1759), defended his doctoral thesis, and completed the year-long, final stage in Jesuit formation known as the Third Probation or Tertianship.

At nearly thirty years of age, Peramàs finally earned a coveted spot in the missions and "took up the Spartan lifestyle" in San Ignacio Miní (*Vitae Sinopsis* XXII), a community of 3,222 Guaraní.[30] Peramàs offers very little detail about this period in his life, owing no doubt to his stated concerns for preserving impartiality in the *De Administratione Guaranica* and his distaste for self-praise. Nonetheless, his extensive discussion of the Guaraní way of life is informed by his own experiences living among them and his personal observations can be found throughout his writing. In any event, his time among the Guaraní was limited, perhaps no more than a year and a half. A new cohort of students from Europe created a need for additional faculty, and Peramàs was summoned back to Córdoba to assume the chair in Rhetoric and, subsequently, the chair in Moral Theology.[31] During this period, Peramàs took his fourth and final vow in 1765 and published the *Laudationes Quinque* [*Five Praises*, 1766], an encomiastic work offering a history of the Jesuit-run Monserrat school and praises of its founder, Ignacio Duarte y Quirós.[32] Still in his early thirties and the youngest member of the faculty, Peramàs stood out among colleagues a generation or more his senior, a harbinger for the career that lay ahead of him.

This promising trajectory was interrupted in the middle of the night on Sunday, July 12, 1767, when Lieutenant Governor Fernando Fabro swept into Córdoba at the head of a detachment of eighty soldiers and unceremoniously dragged Peramàs and his fellow Jesuits from their beds. At bayonet point, the Jesuits and novices were ushered into the dining hall of the college, where Fabro read Carlos III's royal edict ejecting the Jesuits from Spanish-claimed territory, providing neither justification nor due process. Eager to find the vast troves of treasure rumored to exist in the territory, Fabro set about taking control of the Jesuit apparatus and ordered the Jesuits and their novices, all of whom volunteered to remain with their teachers, to set out on the perilous journey into exile. In his diary, Peramàs offers a vivid, day-by-day account of events in which he likens the expulsion to the fall of Troy, quoting the priest Panthus's lament from Vergil's *Aeneid*: "It has come—the final day, Troy's inescapable hour. We are Trojans no more; Troy is no more" (*Aeneid* 2.324–325, in Fúrlong 1952:47).

After six months in transit, the Jesuits of Paraguay arrived in Spain, where they were incarcerated with Jesuits from other provinces as they waited to learn their fate. Despite the difficult conditions, the priests established a prison college, in which Josep Manuel served as minister of Moral Theology (*Diario* 268). It was another year before these Jesuits would reach their final destinations, each province having been assigned to a different point of exile in the Papal States. The province of Paraguay was assigned to Faenza, a town not far from Bologna in the Emilia-Romagna region of present-day Italy. Within months of their arrival, the Jesuits, with the support of local Italian nobility, set about reestablishing their college in order to resume their scholarly and ecclesiastical mission. Four and a half years later, in 1773, Pope Clement XIV officially suppressed the Society of Jesus. While some of the Jesuit provinces in exile gradually disbanded, the Jesuits of Paraguay pooled their meager resources and practiced a form of communalism not unlike the one they advocated in the Guaraní communities (Batllori 1966; Guasti 2009, 2019; Melai 2011). Much maligned and all but destitute, they marshaled the only weapons at their disposal and set about writing voluminously against the anti-Jesuit detractors in hopes of vindicating and perhaps even reestablishing the Order.[33]

Peramàs joined in the effort and wrote works aimed at advancing the Jesuit cause and, more broadly, engaging with some of the most pressing political issues of the day. In addition to his exile diary, completed on Christmas Eve 1768, Peramàs produced a revised and expanded version of that diary in Latin known as the *Annus Patiens* [Year of Suffering], which concludes with a doleful elegiac poem.[34] Among his most important works from this period are the epic poem *De Invento Novo Orbe* [On the Discovery of the New World, 1777] (Feile Tomes 2015a, 2015b, 2015c, 2018; Feile Tomes and van der Velden n.d.); a shorter epic on the rare elevation of an ex-Jesuit, Domenico da Marchesi, to the bishopric of Faenza, entitled *Adveniente Faventiam Episcopo* [On the Bishop's Arrival in Faenza, 1787]; and two volumes of biographies, *De Vita et Moribus Sex Sacerdotum Paraguaycorum* [On the Life and Habits of Six Priests of Paraguay, 1791] and *De Vita et Moribus Tredecim Virorum Paraguaycorum* [On the Life and Habits of Thirteen Men of Paraguay, 1793]. This final work included the treatise *De Administratione Guaranica* and was published some months after Peramàs's death on May 23, 1793, likely due to the efforts of Ignasi [Ignacio] Peramàs i Mates, second cousin of Josep Manuel.

Throughout these works, Peramàs seeks to highlight the achievements of the Jesuits of Paraguay, whether implicitly or explicitly, in response to the political forces that led to the suppression as well as to the attacks mounted by philosophers and anti-clerical currents within the Iberian and broader European Enlightenment. Indeed, Peramàs sets up Enlightenment philosophes as his rhetorical opponents in the *De*

Administratione Guaranica, variously styling them as Epicurean, atheistic sophists enraptured by an insane pseudo-philosophy of unbridled hedonism and self-love bent on revolution (e.g., *DAG* 1, 29, 55, 307). He reserves his most pointed attacks for contemporaries such as the Dutch philosopher Cornelis de Pauw, decried as a fabulist and mentioned over thirty times by name, and Jesuits turned critics, including Guillaume Thomas Raynal and Peramàs's own one-time friend Bernardo Ibáñez de Echavarri. These undoubtedly belong to a larger discourse of Jesuit apologetics.

While Peramàs's engagement with these figures often focuses on refuting specific claims they have made, the conflict relates more broadly to fundamental ideological differences regarding matters of political and ethical philosophy, proto-anthropology, and proto-sociology. What does it mean to be human? What constitutes the good life? How do the needs and interests of the individual relate to those of the group? What practices and institutions can a society cultivate that will be conducive to producing the greatest human flourishing? These and other questions guide nearly every discussion throughout the text and, as such, implicate this work in a broader philosophical discourse relating to how humans should structure their societies and conduct their lives. Here, Peramàs sets his treatise in dialogue with early modern thinkers such as Bacon, Buffon, Burke, Büsching, Hervás, Montesquieu, More, and Rousseau, as well as over two dozen ancient authors including Plato, Aristotle, Philo, Cicero, Vergil, Seneca, Tacitus, and Plutarch.

History of the Text

De Administratione Guaranica was published in Faenza by Archi Press as a preface to a volume of biographies, *De Vita et Moribus Tredecim Virorum Paraguaycorum* (1793).[35] Reaching nearly five hundred pages, the volume contains: a biography of St. John of Nepomuk by Peramàs (III–XVI); an unsigned, posthumous overview of Peramàs's life (*Vitae Sinopsis* XVII–XXVII); the *De Administratione Guaranica* (1–162);[36] a declaration reserving the Holy Roman Church's authority to confirm the veracity of any miracles described in the biographies (*Protestatio*, 162); a foldout table providing the distances in Spanish leagues between each of the thirty Guaraní towns (163); the biographies of six priests, four students, and three laymen, half of whom perished as a result of the forced exile (163–460); and a table of contents listing the starting page of each chapter of the *De Administratione Guaranica* and each biography (461–462). It also includes the following items without pagination: a note explaining that a census of the Chiquitano missions has been added because they feature prominently in the volume; the *Vidit* (March 6, 1793) and *Imprimatur* (March 28, 1793) from the ecclesiastic authorities; a folded plate containing a census of Chiquitano towns from December 1766; and a much larger folded plate bearing a site plan of Candelaria, the administrative hub of the Guaraní republic, along with a list of thirty-two Guaraní towns and their populations in 1767. This large-format plate was nearly six times the size of a standard page and was produced at great expense using two different printing technologies: first, an intaglio engraving on a copper plate was used on a chalcographic press to create the image, and then the same page was run through the typographic press to add the Guaraní census (see above, page 3).

The author of the *Vitae Sinopsis* reveals himself as the party responsible for shepherding the book through to publication after Peramàs's death. The text of the *Vitae Sinopsis* suggests that its author was someone very close to Josep Manuel with intimate knowledge of his childhood and his time at the novitiate in Tarragona. An inscription in a now lost edition of the book is said to have indicated that the biography was written "by his most devoted brother Ignacio," whom scholars correctly identified as Ignacio Peramás [*sic*], S.J. While this attribution was widely accepted, the text of the *Vitae Sinopsis* made it clear that the author could not be one of Josep Manuel's siblings and that because Ignacio was ten years older than Josep Manuel, the two would not have been enrolled in the novitiate together. Thus, Ignacio's authorship was rejected (Feile Tomes 2015b:10n33). What scholars did not recognize is that Ignasi [Ignacio] Peramàs i Mates was not Josep Manuel's brother but rather his second cousin, whose delayed entry to the Jesuit Order makes it far more likely that the two overlapped in Tarragona.[37]

Though their age difference likely prevented them from being close as children in Catalonia,[38] Josep Manuel and Ignasi surely became well acquainted during the twenty-five years the two spent in Emilia-Romagna. Born in Mataró in 1722, Ignasi joined the Jesuits comparatively late at age twenty-one. He spent 1743–1745 in the novitiate at Tarragona and then studied at Manresa, a sequence Josep Manuel repeated almost immediately after his older cousin. Because Ignasi's journey to America was significantly delayed, the Order surely assigned him to a temporary post at one of their schools in the interim. While there is no evidence of how he was employed during this period, he could have been sent back to Tarragona where Josep Manuel was enrolled in the novitiate (1747–1749), a period covered in some detail in the *Vitae Sinopsis* (XVIII–XIX). Finally, in 1749, he set out on a year-long journey to Quito.[39] He ultimately rose to the position of procurator of the fledgling and short-lived Universidad Real y Pontificia de San Francisco Javier in Panama (Cid Labra and Casini 2021; Mateos 1960:150–151, 170–173). Following the expulsion, he was resettled in Ravenna (Astorgano Abajo 2004:257), not twenty miles from Josep Manuel in neighboring Faenza. The cousins corresponded and likely grew close over the years, culminating in Ignasi composing a biography of Josep Manuel for inclusion in the book he brought to publication. In 1798, a royal order allowed him to return home to Mataró, where he died in 1799.

In the *Vitae Sinopsis*, Ignasi writes: "In the last letter [Josep Manuel] sent me, when he said that he had already brought the second volume of illustrious men to its conclusion, and now has it ready for press; He added: 'When you read the book, you will be amazed at how indulgent the censors of this work have been with me.'"[40] It is left tantalizingly unclear what indulgence Peramàs felt the ecclesiastical censors had granted him. Censorship was highly political and works critical of the Church could be fatal for their author and disastrous for anyone associated with the publication, including the press and any financiers.[41]

While we will likely never be able to answer the question conclusively, one possibility is that Peramàs is referring to the inclusion of the *De Administratione Guaranica* together with the *Vitae Sinopsis*. Several details lend credence to this conjecture. First, Peramàs emphasizes in his letter that the indulgence is cause for amazement (*miraberis*). Life writing was popular among Jesuits, particularly in the post-suppression era, when such scholarship was seen as contributing to a larger project of justifying the Society's good works; the inclusion of a lengthy work in a different genre, however, was atypical for such volumes, and the humanistic learning and political theory on display in the *De Administratione Guaranica* is truly exceptional in contemporary Jesuit literature.[42] Furthermore, Peramàs describes it as a "precursor" (*prodromos*) to the biographies, emphasizing that "there is such frequent mention of these Indians [the Guaraní] in the biographies . . . that this topic seems in no way out of place" (*DAG* 2). While this claim appears perfectly reasonable to the casual observer, it is altogether untrue. In fact, none of the thirteen men featured in the volume spent a significant amount of time in the Guaraní communities examined in the treatise and, as a result, little mention of these towns is made in the biographies.[43] Peramàs goes on to emphasize the congruity of Platonic doctrine and Christianity, so that no one thinks the treatise is "useless" (*DAG* 3), and stresses that anyone reading Plato might be forgiven for thinking that he had been trained in Christian doctrine (*DAG* 35).[44] Despite these assurances, the treatise and the biographies are almost completely independent of one another, which likely reflects the fact that they were not originally conceived as components of a single work.

Sympathetic to the plight of the Jesuits, the Archi Press had also printed earlier works by Peramàs and numerous others by exiles resident in the region (Campana 2021). Although records relating to the size of print runs and the financing and distribution of such editions are rare, the *De Vita et Moribus Tredecim Virorum Paraguaycorum* (1793) was likely to have been privately financed and relatively small, as fewer than two dozen copies are known to be extant today. Despite the limited release and the chaotic political environment of the late eighteenth century, the book circulated in Europe and the Americas. We are fortunate to be able to trace the itinerary of one such copy, which was initially owned by fellow Jesuit biographer Juan Luis Maneiro (1744–1802), a contemporary who was hard at work memorializing the Jesuits of Mexico in nearby Bologna.[45] Though in failing health, Maneiro was able to return to Mexico in 1799, and among the few possessions he brought with him on the long voyage was *De Vita et Moribus Tredecim Virorum Paraguaycorum*. Sometime after his death in 1802, the evidently cherished volume then passed into the ownership of Agustín Pomposo Fernández de San Salvador (1756–1842), a prominent Mexican intellectual who claimed descent from European and Nahua nobility. Deeply involved in the ideological debates surrounding Mexican independence, Pomposo found Peramàs's treatise fascinating and, in an unrelated publication from 1821, previewed a Spanish translation of the *De Administratione Guaranica* in an effort to boost subscriptions. The advertised work never materialized.[46] This copy of Peramàs's volume, with the names of its former owners inscribed on the title page, was later purchased by Adolph Sutro at the turn of the next century, possibly when he bought the storied collection of the Abadiano family of publishers and booksellers in Mexico in 1889. The book was ultimately bequeathed to the California State Library in San Francisco, where it resides today.

More than a century after Pomposo's advertisement, the first translation of *De Administratione Guaranica* was published in Buenos Aires under the title *La República de Platón y los guaraníes* (1946). This Spanish edition included a translation of the treatise and notes by Juan Cortés del Pino, along with an introduction by the prolific Argentine historian Guillermo Fúrlong, S.J. This landmark publication, along with a raft of related works by Fúrlong, secured a prominent place for the treatise in Hispanophone scholarship on Indigenous history and ethnography as well as the history of the Jesuit Order. In 2004, Bartomeu Melià, S.J., the renowned linguist and ethnologist of the Guaraní, together with Father Francisco Fernández Pertíñez, S.J., published a new translation of the treatise, entitled *Platón y los guaraníes,* with a Jesuit press in Asunción, Paraguay. Inexplicably, these translations exclude some of Peramàs's lengthy footnotes. Stelio Cro, a scholar of utopianism, produced versions in Italian (1994) and Spanish (2018). None of these four translations is in wide circulation today, and no others are known to exist. Furthermore, though recently digitized, the Latin text has been largely inaccessible given that fewer than twenty copies of the 1793 publication are still extant.

Notes on the Latin Edition and English Translation

The present volume offers the first scholarly treatment of the Latin text of *De Administratione Guaranica,* along with a parallel English translation. It reproduces the 1793 edition as closely as possible with the goal of transmitting the Latin text as originally written. A few changes relating to aspects of the typography and format imposed by the original publisher have been made, however. Corrections have been introduced conservatively, with the text altered only where there is an obvious typographical error; for a list of these alterations, see below. The present volume does not, by contrast, "correct" forms such as *legesis* to *legeris* (e.g., *DAG* 238) or the adverb *comparatē* in the work's title to the participle *comparata* (as some have seen fit to do), in order to preserve the historical orthography and "Latinity." For ease of reading, the ampersand (&) has been replaced with "et" and the medial or long "s," in common use until the early nineteenth century, has been eliminated in favor of the round or short "s," familiar to modern readers (e.g., *Philosophia* instead of *Philoſophia*). The "z" with a swash tail (ʒ) has been retained to preserve the text's differentiation between that letter and the standard "z."

The original edition uses italics for non-Latin words, most book titles, and for shorter quotations in the main body of the text. Footnotes have the opposite formatting, using italics except for non-Latin words, book titles, and shorter quotations. In both the main text and the footnotes, quotations longer than ten lines are indicated by a low double comma („) at the beginning of every line of the quotation. This edition uses standard English quotation marks and only italicizes non-Latin words and book titles throughout the entire text.

In the original edition, the footnotes are indicated in the text with letters (e.g., a, b, c, etc.), the sequence of which begins anew with each page. The present edition prints these as endnotes with running numeration in superscript. Thus, the original edition's note "b" on page 13 is note 10 in this edition. It can be cited with reference to the corresponding paragraph as *DAG* 24n10. Instead, translator's notes appear beneath the main text.

Corrigenda

	PRINTED TEXT	CORRECTION
DAG 15n4	Pretoresque	Praetoresque
DAG 18n7	Cisuruayci	Cisuruguayci
DAG 24	Amaricaeque	Americaeque
DAG 30	picent	dicent
DAG 32	immittes	immites
DAG 41	ille	illae
DAG 50n19	Europeau	European
DAG 75	τέτραμπνὸν	τετράμηνον
DAG 84	iniquit	inquit
DAG 99	Prefecti	Praefecti
DAG 111	Mariti	Matriti
DAG 112	ritulo	titulo
DAG 117	agrestria	agrestia
DAG 126	aggregebantur	aggregabantur
DAG 135	Liberis	Liberi
DAG 144	dinstincti	distincti
DAG 186	Guananiorum	Guaraniorum
DAG 228	dependentqne	dependentque
DAG 269	esurentibus	esurientibus
DAG 279n119	Geograghiae	Geographiae
DAG 292	protuderetur	protruderetur
DAG 342	Discerint	Discernit
DAG 83	Peramàs periphrases Philo in the first sentence and then continues with his own analysis, but the printers used quotation marks for everything following "Musica, ait, . . . " and placed the citation at the end of the paragraph. The citation has been moved and the quotation marks removed.	
DAG 342	Footnote 153 was misplaced; it belongs after the St. Thomas quotation at paragraph end.	

Translation

This text is a veritable linguistic and cultural palimpsest. In it, a Catalan author who belongs to a Spanish community of Jesuits, residing among Italians (upon whose generous support they depend), uses the nuanced and rhetorically sophisticated Latin of Cicero (first century BCE) to write about Indigenous Guaraní communities and culture in comparison with ideas originally expressed in Athenian Greek of the fourth century BCE. Moreover, throughout the treatise, the author engages with literature and scholarship in all of these languages as well as in French, Portuguese, and German (though seemingly not in English, for which he relies on translations). Indeed, Peramàs's decision to write in Latin is central to his self-presentation as an authoritative source and signals his own aspirations for this work to be available to an international audience. The present edition identifies in brackets [ ] sources that Peramàs did not name, revealing for the first time his engagement with authors such as Edmund Burke, whom he cites as "an anonymous Englishman" (*DAG* 276–277).

As a Catalan, Peramàs was sensitive to the erasure of linguistic identity and drew parallels between the status of languages marginalized by imperial powers in Europe and the Americas (*DAG* 79). Additionally, in the Latin version of the *Annus Patiens* (*ARSI Paraq.* 21), he discusses his resistance to Latinizing surnames, preferring instead to present the vernacular spelling. Given both his practice and his explicit statement of preference, names, bibliographic references, and non-Latin words are presented in their vernacular whenever possible and English translations are provided where appropriate. This includes the author's own name, which is rendered in his native Catalan (Josep Manuel Peramàs) rather than in the adopted Spanish (José Manuel Peramás), as most scholars have done. For the Guaraní, Melià's spelling in the 2004 translation is followed. Weights and measures are translated from Latin to contemporary Spanish units and present-day imperial conversions are provided in brackets.

The *De Administratione Guaranica* is a rhetorically sophisticated work, and Peramàs's style incorporates vivid imagery, sarcastic humor, and a vast emotional range. These elements are embedded within the language of the text, and the act of translation necessarily disrupts the nuances of the original. The goal of this translation is both to make the *De Administratione Guaranica* available to an anglophone audience and to assist readers in using the original Latin text. Thus, fluidity in English is balanced against a desire to maintain syntactic parallels that will allow readers to move back and forth between the English and Latin text. Both literal and more idiomatic translations are widely used, as the text requires. For instance, Peramàs sarcastically calls into question the Enlightenment notion of "happiness" with the cutting parenthetical remark *si superis placet* (*DAG* 1), which is translated as "if you can call it that" rather than the more literal "if [that term] pleases those above." By contrast, Peramàs's practice of embedding the Jesuits within the agricultural idiom of his text, where he calls them "cultivators" (*cultores*), "caretakers" (*curators*), and "laborers" (*operarii*), is followed instead of the more familiar "missionaries" (*missionarii*, a neologism in Latin), which he only uses when quoting others. Thus, translations that may be unfamiliar to the modern reader are occasionally chosen in an effort to preserve Peramàs's idiom and broader ideological discourse, which emphasizes hard work, cultivation, and the provision of care as foundational to the well-ordered state. These translations allow the reader to see more readily the way that Peramàs draws parallels between the endeavors of the Jesuits and those of the Guaraní, particularly in the nexus of terminology linking culture and cultivation.

There are a variety of culturally embedded terms throughout the treatise for which no translation will be wholly adequate. To preserve the text as a witness to its times, terminology that is racialized and/or that unambiguously conforms to contemporary paradigms of inequality and cultural superiority (e.g., translating *Indi* as "Indians" despite the obvious historical inaccuracy) is retained. Elsewhere, however, the translation has attempted to avoid imposing assumptions about normative cultural attitudes in cases where the text is ambiguous. For instance, the Latin adjective *rudis* denotes the quality of being "raw," "unworked," or "simple," but in many contexts carries with it the additional connotation of being "ill-made," "awkward," and "ignorant." When something or someone is described in Latin as being *rudis*, the translator must interpret the term within a broader ideological context to accurately represent the author's perspective. In this text, ideologically neutral translations of such terms are preferred, unless otherwise indicated (e.g., as when Peramàs cites a detractor accusing the Jesuits of being "stupid and completely backward" [*stultos planeque rudes, DAG* 62]).

NOTES

1 Indeed, Peramàs reminds his readers to think about the Guaraní as independent agents rather than objects of agency, just as they would think about Europeans; see, for example, *DAG* 273.

2 For the European fascination with these communities as well as the cultural and intellectual contexts that gave rise to these Jesuit efforts, see Imbruglia 2017; Zantop 1997.

3 Brumbaugh 2021 examines the arc of the Greece/Paraguay analogy across a range of seventeenth- and eighteenth-century writers in Europe as the background to Peramàs's comparative project. Important studies of Peramàs and his treatise include Bustamante 2001; Caturelli 1992; Cornelli 2016, 2017; Feile Tomes 2018; Fúrlong 1925, 1952; Hudde 1983; Melai 2020; Morales 2010; Orta Nadal 1953; Romanato 2010; Suárez 2017a.

4 Indeed, these perspectives have long remained in circulation (e.g., Cunninghame Graham 1901; Lugon 1949); even today, Peramàs's work is often misconstrued as a straightforward endorsement of this claim.

5 Peramàs describes his methodology in *DAG* 4–5. A comparison of his translations of Plato with the published translations available to him makes it clear that Peramàs is working directly from the Greek text.

6 See the index for a full list of the sources cited by Peramàs.

7 Peramàs's approach to quotation is rather free; see, for instance, his extensive "quotation" of Giovanni Battista Noghera, *DAG* 305–306, in which he editorializes and expands upon the original Italian text as he translates it without signaling his interventions.

8 Sarreal 2014 uses a socioeconomic lens to outline the history of these communities through a careful analysis of the documentary evidence.

9 In the introduction (*DAG* 4), Peramàs explicitly calls on his readers to make up their own minds about the comparison he has performed—an invitation he repeats throughout the treatise.

10 Peramàs's use of the adjective *Guaranicus* throughout the rest of the treatise does little to clarify the issue, since it indicates Guaraní ownership (e.g., "Guaraní language") and refers to contexts with no Guaraní agency (e.g., calling the Jesuits in these communities "Guaraní Priests").

11 For early modern writers, "happiness" translated the ancient Greek term εὐδαιμονία and referred to human flourishing (e.g., "the pursuit of happiness" in the U.S. Declaration of Independence). Peramàs problematizes the concept in the treatise (e.g., *DAG* 1) and characterizes the more liberal enlightenment philosophers as conflating happiness with libertine hedonism; cf. Lodovico Antonio Muratori's *Il cristianesimo felice* (1743, 1749) and *Della pubblica felicità* (1749).

12 On the formation of these communities and their populations, see Armani 1994; Ganson 2003; Jackson 2021; Maeder 1996, 2013; Morales 1998; Sarreal 2014; Wilde 2009.

13 The Franco-Belgian du Toit, Austrian Sepp, and Catalan Peramàs are better known by their Hispanicized names: Nicolás del Techo, Antonio Sepp, and José Manuel Peramás.

14 The Spanish governor and Catholic bishops who exercised temporal and ecclesiastical authority over the province were located in the far-off cities of Buenos Aires and Asunción.

15 Peramàs stresses that the Jesuits of Paraguay went to great lengths to shield the Guaraní from Spanish and Portuguese enslavement (*DAG* 106 and 259); he emphasizes that slavery did not exist in the towns (*DAG* 170n65, 244–246, 254), yet fails to mention that the forced labor of Indigenous Africans was central to the broader Jesuit enterprise (see Austin 2020; Ganson 2016).

16 On the Chiquito missions, see Burgés and Tomichá Charupá 2008; Tomichá Charupá 2002.

17 Peramàs takes on many of these detractors throughout the *De Administratione Guaranica.*

18 Maeder 1992; Sarreal 2014:93–236; Whitehead 2015; Wilde 2001. Jackson 2019 demonstrates that the decline also had its roots in dynamics emerging at the end of the Jesuit era.

19 The baptism registry in the Museu Arxiu de Santa Maria de Mataró records the following entry: "Llorens, Sebastià, Joseph, Ignasi, Emanuel, Antoni, legitimate and natural son of Rafel Peramàs y Vilapura, merchant, and of Teresa Peramàs y Guarro" (B13F246I113, Museu Arxiu de Santa Maria de Mataró). On the Peramàs and Guarro families, see Molas i Ribalta 1973.

20 Nine of these children, including Josep Manuel, were baptized at the Basilica of Santa Maria in Mataró; the tenth was baptized at the Church of Santa María de Gracia in Cartagena. For a study of the Peramàs family based on the records in Mataró, see Costa Oller 2018. Costa Oller kindly provided me with an unpublished genealogical chart of the Peramàs family compiled by Xavier Clavell, as well as facsimiles of the baptism records from the Museu Arxiu de Santa Maria de Mataró. Fúrlong (1925:379), followed by all scholars outside of Mataró, incorrectly reports that Josep Manuel had only two brothers, Miguel and Ignacio [*sic*]. Of these, Ignacio (1722–1799)—or Ignasi—was actually the son of Rafael Peramàs i Plegamans, a second cousin of Josep Manuel's father. I have discovered no trace of a Miguel/Miquel, though several more distant Peramàs relatives bear the name. One of the children is known to have died in childhood (Rafael, 1733–1737) and several of the others leave behind faint documentary evidence beyond their baptism: Gaspar (born 1725), Gaspar (born 1726), Maria (born 1735), Jaume (born 1737), and Anna (born 1743).

21 *Vitae Sinopsis* XVIII. His mother and father baptized their tenth child, Anna, on April 19, 1743, at Santa María de Gracia, Cartagena, where their own funerals would later be held in 1748 and 1766, respectively.

22 Several of Baltasar's descendants remain influential figures in Bolivia today.

23 Joaquim died at Plaquemines' Turn, where he was supervising the construction of a pair of fortifications along the Mississippi River; he was interred October 5, 1790, in the cemetery of Ignacio de la Veliza following a funeral mass in the newly rebuilt St. Louis Church, New Orleans (Archdiocese of New Orleans, St. Louis Cathedral, Funeral Records, vol. 1784–1793, p. 28, no. 631).

24 Jesuit Novices were rarely younger than sixteen in that period, and most of Josep Manuel's cohort would have been in their late teens or even early twenties.

25 *Vitae Sinopsis* XX–XXI. On the importance of classical sources in the Jesuit educational tradition, see Bertrán-Guera 1984; Dainville 1978.

26 The expedition was led by José de Vera Saravia of Santiago (1697–1774) and Balthasar Hueber of Tyrol, who would later become Provincial of Chile (1762–1768) (Müller 2011:224–225).

27 Having already been dismissed once from the order, Ibáñez de Echavarri would be ejected again before reaching his destination. He subsequently published several works defaming the order.

28 In his biography of Manuel Querini, Peramàs reports that on one occasion Querini, then rector of the college, advised him to give a prisoner a Spanish translation of Carlo Gregorio Rosignoli's *Verità eterne* (1699), *Sex* p. 82.

29 This correspondence is not known to be extant, but it is mentioned in the *Vitae Sinopsis* (XXI) and corroborated by a copy of Peramàs's first published work, *Laudationes Quinque,* which bears a handwritten private dedication to Cordara in Latin (transcribed in Fúrlong 1921:350).

30 This is the figure recorded in the 1762 census reported in the *Literae Annuae,* which further breaks down the population by demographic.

31 This was an honor usually reserved for those who had previously held the chair in Philosophy (*Vitae Sinopsis* XXIII).

32 The importance of this work is underlined by the fact that it was the very first work published on the newly installed printing press in Córdoba; today, it occupies a special place in Argentine book history (Silverman and Garone Gravier 2021; Suárez 2005).

33 From at least the early 1790s, rumors were circulating that Pope Pius VI was on the verge of reinstating the order. He never did, but eventually the order was restored by

Pope Pius VII in 1814, over two decades after Peramàs's death. See Wilde 2018b on Jesuit efforts during the period of the suppression.

34 Neither manuscript appears to have been published, but they were likely made available to his contemporaries (Suárez 2017a, 2017b).

35 This second volume of *Vitae* is far more dramatic than the one published two years earlier. In it, Peramàs highlights the Jesuits who died tragically during the forced march to exile and, in many instances, at an unusually young or old age. Most of the thirteen men featured are representative of the unsung Jesuits, laboring in obscurity rather than the six famous provincials, rectors, and missionaries featured in the 1791 volume. These and other contemporary Jesuit publications are an outgrowth of the practice of including detailed biographies for deceased priests in the *Litterae Annuae*.

36 There is a concluding paragraph at the end of the *De Administratione Guaranica* numbered CCCXLV, which indicates two corrections the author wanted to register for his 1791 volume of *Vitae*: the omission of a minor detail in the life of Manuel Vergara, and an incorrect date in the life of Vincente Sans.

37 Fúrlong, in several publications, incorrectly reported on the handwritten and difficult to read archival records in Mataró, likely because both Peramàs men had fathers named Rafael (Peramàs i Vilapura vs. Peramàs i Plegamans).

38 The *Vitae Sinopsis* (XVII–XVIII) gives what feels like a firsthand account of Josep Manuel's childhood home—details that Ignasi would have known from his own childhood.

39 Bernardo Recio, S.J. (1714–1791), recounts their travels together (Recio 1947:II.26, 30, 358).

40 *In postrema, quam ad me dedit, epistola, cum dixisset, perduxisse se se jam ad terminum secundum illustrium virorum volumen, praeloque paratum habere; adjunxit: miraberis cum librum legeris, quanta mecum indulgentia usi sint operis hujus censores* (XXVI). On the politics of writing and publishing during this period, see Donato 2014.

41 For example, Bruno Martí (1728–1778), a contemporary of Peramàs, died in captivity after receiving a life sentence for criticizing Pope Clement XIV and the suppression of the Jesuit Order in print.

42 Perhaps the closest parallel is Francisco Jarque, *Insignes misioneros de la Compañía de Jesús en la Provincia del Paraguay* (Pamplona, 1687), the final third of which is entitled "El estado que al presente gozan las misiones de la Compañía de Jesús en la provincia del Paraguay, Tucumán y Río de la Plata" (284–424).

43 Instead, of all the men memorialized, only four (Mesnser, Chome, Pallozzi, and Schmid) worked closely with Indigenous communities; these were priests who spent the bulk of their careers in Bolivia among communities the Jesuits referred to as the Chiriguano, the Zamuco, and, especially, the Chiquitano. Only Ignace Chome spent time living among the Guaraní; he was initially posted to the Guaraní towns before being reassigned to the Chiriguano.

44 The first six paragraphs lay out the rationale and methodology for the work more generally, but the references to Christian doctrine seem aimed at the censors, to whose criticism Peramàs was especially attentive (*Vitae Sinopsis* XXVI).

45 Born in Vera Cruz, New Spain (Mexico), Maneiro lived in Bologna and Rome during the exile. In total, he published approximately forty biographical works praising Jesuits of Mexico in Latin. Thirty-five of these are contained in the three-volume *De vitis aliquot Mexicanorum aliorumque, qui sive virtute, sive litteris Mexici imprimis floruerunt* (Bologna, 1791–1792). It is not known whether the two men were acquainted, but there is a high likelihood that they were given their proximity and the similarity of their projects.

46 A prolific author and pamphleteer, Pomposo sought subscribers to help finance his serialized publications. Part one, volume two of his edition of *Las cartas americanas* (Mexico, 1821) begins with an unnumbered, four-page advertisement soliciting subscriptions and teasing future publications. Later in that same volume, between pages 88 and 89, there is a one-page insert meant to further entice subscribers; it consists of a sample title page for Pomposo's translation of the *De Administratione Guaranica* (verso) and a paragraph describing it in connection with topics covered in *Las cartas americanas* (recto) (Ferrante 2021).

LATIN EDITION AND ENGLISH TRANSLATION

DE ADMINISTRATIONE GUARANICA COMPARATE AD REMPUBLICAM PLATONIS COMMENTARIUS

I. Siquando tempus ullum fuit celebrem illam Rempublicam Platonis in usus deducendi, hoc est profecto, cum insanientis Philosophiae Epicureus grex, exosus majorum nostrorum sancta instituta, rectumque gubernandi modum, omnia susque deque vertit, atque aliud ex alio in dies comminiscitur, ut felices (si superis placet) populos efficiat. Cur ergo illam eximii Philosophi, quem totius graeciae doctissimum appellat Tullius, Reipublicae formam non adoptant sibi? Sunt ibi quaedam, quae non probes; id equidem scio, et fateor; sed pleraque sunt pulcherrima et optima. Haec sumant, in his se se exerceant, et quandoquidem nobiscum, et nostro more nolunt vivere, a nobis tandem secedant novarum rerum studiosi, interpositoque Oceano in ultimas migrent terras, ubi soli regnent: id multo erit melius, quam tot deliria, et somnia philosophica in vulgus spargere, e quibus tanta fit rerum perturbatio, ut suae quemque fortunae nunc maxime poeniteat.

II. Sed numquam vani homines commenta sua, utpote inimica Religioni, et contraria felicitati publicae, sapientibus probabunt; neque ex eorum impiis decretis Respublica ulla, quae cum Platonica comparari possit, stabit in Europa. Quid vero? Stat illa, aut stetit aliquando alibi gentium? Id nunc quaere instituimus, subitque animum ostendere in America quiddam simile extitisse Platonicis inventis inter Guaranios Indos, quorum ita frequens nobis mentio est in vitis virorum Paraguaycorum, ut argumentum hoc, tamquam prodromus, haud alienum proposito nostro esse videatur.

III. Accedit huc (nequis inutilem putet Commentarium hunc) quod a nobis dicenda sic conjuncta sint cum mysteriis Christianae institutionis, ut plane constet ab hac una pendere bonum publicum, tantoque beatiores esse populos, quanto obsequentiores sunt Christi praeceptis, ac divini cultus veraeque fidei tenaciores; qua re nihil validius est ad refutanda hujus temporis Philosophorum-o temeraria atque irreligiosa molimina.

A TREATISE ON THE GUARANÍ SYSTEM OF GOVERNMENT IN COMPARISON WITH PLATO'S REPUBLIC

1. If ever there has been a time to put Plato's famous Republic into use, surely this is it. The Epicurean flock of Philosophy gone-mad hates the sacred institutions of our ancestors and the proper way of governing, and so turns everything upside-down and on a daily basis fabricates one falsehood after another to make the people "happy" (if you can even call it that). So why then do they not adopt that form of Republic proposed by the Philosopher *par excellence*,* whom Cicero calls the most learned man of all Greece? There are certain things in his Republic of which you will not approve. Indeed, I know this and confess it up front. But in fact, most of its contents are quite admirable and excellent. Those zealous for revolution should take up these things and busy themselves with implementing them; seeing as they do not want to live with us or according to our customs, they ought to break off from us, at long last, and emigrate to the ends of the earth leaving an ocean in between us. There they can be their own rulers. This will be much better than spreading so many philosophical dreams and flights of fancy among the masses, from which so much disruption comes about that now everyone is completely dissatisfied with his lot in life.

2. But, seeing as they are hostile to religion and contrary to public happiness, these deceptive people will never convince the wise of their schemes. Nor will any Republic, which could be compared with Plato's, function in Europe if it is based on their impious decrees. And what about the Platonic Republic? Does it function, or has it ever functioned anywhere in the world? This is what we now propose to investigate, and it occurs to me to point out that in America something somewhat similar to that Platonic invention existed among the Guaraní Indians. There is such frequent mention of these Indians in the biographies of the men of Paraguay [contained in the present volume] that this topic seems in no way out of place and is thus a precursor, so to speak, for my project.

3. It is appropriate to add here (so that no one thinks this treatise is useless) that what I am going to say is so connected to the mysteries of the institution of Christianity that there can be no doubt that the public good depends on this alone. Likewise, the more blessed the people are, the more compliant they are with Christ's precepts and, indeed, the more steadfast they are in divine worship and the true faith. There is nothing more powerful than this fact to refute the foolhardy and irreligious endeavors of today's Philosophers.†

* i.e., Plato.

† *Philosophes* [Fr.], public intellectuals of the eighteenth-century Enlightenment whom Peramàs associates with the burgeoning revolution in France.

IV. Is autem nobis scribendi erit modus: ponam compendio quid quaque in re voluerit Plato;[1] dein dicam quid inter Guaranios fieret, ac tuum esto denique, collatis capitibus, pronunciare, convenirent ne invicem utraque instituta, an contra discreparent. Ceterum ad rem hanc digne tractandam opus esset justo volumine, quod nec hujus est loci, nec temporis. Hac causa medium tenentes delibabimus dumtaxat aliqua, e quibus fiat conjectura de reliquis.

V. Nequis vero putet a nobis hic quicquam fingi, quo magis emineat comparatio ista, profiteor me, quae dicam (tametsi inter Guaranios diu fui) ex editis jampridem monumentis producturum, ex scriptis scilicet Cl. V. Ludovici Antonii Muratorii, qui cum alios, tum testem citat Hippolytum Angelitam, Coenobitam Conventualem, versatum quondam in Paraguayca regione. Utar item libris Jacobi Vannierii, Galli, et Galli etiam Petri Francisci Xaverii Charlevoixii, cujus historiae adjecta est pulchra descriptio Josephi Cardielis Hispani *de moribus Guaraniorum.*

VI. Sunt etiam plures alii, qui hac agunt de re, ut Montesquieu, ut Haller, ut Busching, ut terni Antistites, qui oppida Guaranica pro munere suo lustrarunt, Petrus Faxardo Ordinis SS. Trinitatis, Josephus Peralta Ordinis PP. Praedicatorum, et Josephus Palos Ordinis S. Francisci. Episcopus etiam e Clero Emanuel Antonius de la Torre (quem nos superstitem Bonisauris reliquimus) post aditos primo (his adiit) Guaranios an. MDCCLIX. litteras cum insigni commendatione Guaranicae administrationis ad Aulam Matritensem misit: sed hae litterae editae in publicum non sunt. At jam gravissimum et disertissimum Graecorum Philosophorum audiamus.

De Situ Urbis condendae.

PLATO

VII. Urbs, quoad ejus fieri poterit, semota a mari, condatur in media regione, ubi et copia silvae sit, et fertilis ager, qui omnia ferat, quibus civitati opus est; nec tamen abunde ferat omnia, ne luxus ex nimia ubertate irrepat in cives. Quippe si situs urbis portui sit proximus, et indigeat supra modum peregrinis rebus, fiet, ut incolae induant dissonos, et varios mores, eosque pravos, instituto cum externis commercio, quo (auctis mercibus et pecunia) aperietur locus fraudibus et dolis, receptaeque consuetudines erunt instabiles incertaeque, importatis aliunde aliis atque aliis vitae et victus et vestium modis usibusque. E contrario, non debet locus urbis distare nimium a mari, ut possit illa merces, quibus eget, sibi facile comparare. (Lib. IV. et V. de Legg.)

4. This, then, will be my method of writing: I will summarize what Plato had in mind on each topic;[1] then I will say what happened among the Guaraní, and finally it will be up to you, having compared the sections, to pronounce whether the two systems are in agreement with one another or, conversely, there are discrepancies. Otherwise, it would require an entire volume to discuss this matter in the way it deserves, but this is neither the place nor the time for that. For this reason, taking a middle path, I will just touch on some things, so that from them it will be possible to make a conjecture about the rest.

5. So that no one thinks I have fabricated anything here in an effort to embellish the comparison, I promise that what I say (although I spent a long time among the Guaraní) will be drawn from previously published works, namely from the writings of the most famous Ludovico Antonio Muratori, who cites various witnesses including Ippolito Angelita, a Conventual Franciscan who used to reside in the region of Paraguay. Likewise, I will use the books of the Frenchman Jacques Vanière, and also those of the Frenchman Pierre François Xavier de Charlevoix, to whose history the Spaniard José Cardiel's beautiful description *On the Customs of the Guaraní* has been appended.

6. There are many others in addition who treat this topic, like Montesquieu, Haller, Büsching; as well as three Bishops, who, in their official capacity, examined the Guaraní towns: Pedro Fajardo, of the Order of the Most Holy Trinity [Trinitarians], José Peralta of the Order of Preachers [Dominicans], and José Palos of the Order of St. Francis [Franciscans]. Also from the secular Clergy is the Bishop Manuel Antonio de la Torre (who was still alive when we left him in Buenos Aires), who after encountering the Guaraní for the first time in 1759 (he visited them) sent a letter to the Court in Madrid with an extraordinary recommendation of the Guaraní system of government; however, this letter was not published. But let us now listen to the most authoritative and eloquent of the Greek Philosophers.

On the Placement of the City to Be Founded

PLATO

7. The city, so far as it is possible, should be set off from the sea and founded in the middle of a region where there are abundant forests and the sort of fertile land that produces everything a community needs. However, it should not produce everything in excess lest luxury born from overabundance should creep into its citizens. For if the site of the city is near a port and it develops a dependence on foreign goods it will happen that the inhabitants assume discordant and diverse values—and perverse ones at that, once commerce has been established with outsiders, on account of which (with the rise of merchandise and money) the place will be open to crime and deceit. The usual customs will be unstable and unreliable; for when things have been introduced from other places so too are other ways and practices of living and eating and dressing introduced. On the other hand, the location of the city ought not be too far from the sea so that it can easily buy for itself the goods it needs (*Laws* Book 4 and 5).

GUARANII.

VIII. Guaranica regio procul a mari distat, quo fit, ut a nautis variarum gentium corrumpi non possint indigenarum mores. Merces tamen, quibus Guaranii indigent, haud difficiliter illuc invebuntur; patientes enim navium sunt amnes Parana, et Uruguay, per quos Indi descendunt Bonasauras, sibique necessaria emunt. Regio autem silvosa est, atque ita distincta partim collibus, partim campis, ut poene omnia ad victum apta gignat.

De forma costruendae urbis.

PLATO

IX. Urbs sublimi posita loco in orbem ducatur, ut et munitior sit, et mundior. Templa struantur circa forum. Sunto etiam ruri aliae aedes sacrae, ut eo convenientes cives colonique inter se noseant, et ament.[2] Muri urbis ne extollantur; si enim alti sunt, purae aurae flatus prohibent; et munimentis praeterea confisi cives, satis se se ab externa vi tutos putant, neque armis assuescunt. Ceterum privatae domus ita condantur, ut earum aequabilitate, et forma structurae, urbs tota sit quodammodo murus. (Lib. VI. Legg.)

GUARANII.

X. Oppida Guaraniorum commodissimae aedificationis erant. Struebantur, si fieri poterat, celso in loco. Fori (quadrati ad CL. circiter ulnas) partem unam occupabat templum, et coemeterium cum aede curionis, et artificum officinis. In tres alias partes distributae erant Indorum domus e caemento omnes, et tectae imbricibus. Earum autem justum numerum intersecabant paria inter se viarum spatia. Quippe fori aedes excipiebantur aliis atque aliis aedibus a tergo, partitis aequa portione vicis: atque hac causa in forum et in templum facilis undique erat aditus. Ad quattuor vero fori angulos locabantur quaternae excelsae Cruces, quae divini Redemptoris, et Redemptionis humanae mysteria oppidanorum occulis et animis objicerent cum grata memoria. Erant item ruri sacella quaedam pro colonorum viatorumque usu. Vide, quam initio posuimus, oppidi Candellariae formam aere incisam.

THE GUARANÍ

8. The Guaraní region is far from the sea in a place where the customs of the native people cannot be corrupted by the sailors of various nationalities. However, it is scarcely difficult for the goods the Guaraní need to be brought there. For the Paraná and Uruguay rivers are open to ships and it is along these that the Indians reach Buenos Aires and buy necessities for themselves. Moreover, the region is forested and divided into areas with hills and others with plains in such a way that virtually everything is suitable for providing nourishment.

On the Layout of the City to Be Built

PLATO

9. The city should be built in a circle on a high spot so that it is more orderly and easier to defend. Temples should be erected around the *agora*.* There ought to be other sacred shrines in the countryside so that when they meet each other there the citizens and colonists come to know and love one another.[2] City walls should not be erected; for, if they are tall, walls prohibit the flow of pure air; and moreover, citizens trusting in the fortifications consider themselves sufficiently safe from external threat that they do not accustom themselves to using weapons. As for the rest, private houses should be built in such a way that in their uniformity and in the manner of their construction the entire city is essentially a wall (*Laws* Book 6).

THE GUARANÍ

10. The towns of the Guaraní consisted of buildings that were very appropriate. They were built, to the extent possible, on high ground. The town square (measuring approximately 150 *varas* [approx. 411 ft] per side) had on one side a church and a cemetery together with the priest's residence and the artisans' workshops. All of the Indians' houses, made of rough-hewn stone and tile roofs, were distributed along the other three sides. However, a grid of parallel streets separated off a fixed number of these houses. For the residences on the town square were distinct from the various others behind them, with the blocks spaced equally apart; and for this reason, there is easy access to the town square and the church from all sides. At the four corners of the town square are located four raised crosses, which cast the mysteries of the divine Redeemer and human Redemption upon the eyes and souls of the townsfolk along with grateful remembrance. Likewise, there are in the countryside certain small sanctuaries for the use of colonists and travelers. See the town plan of Candelaria, etched in bronze, which we placed at the beginning [of this book].†

* A gathering place at the center of civic life in any Greek polis.

† See page 3.

De servando modo in aedibus et suppellectili.

PLATO

XI. Domus ne sint sumptuosae: satis est, si contra frigus aestumque habitatorem tueantur. Supellex esto simplex, nec aurea, nec argentea,[3] sed talis, quae neque impediat cives bonos esse, neque addat spiritus et vim cuiquam ad alios laedendos. Victus paratu facilis, ut assa caro sine condimentis, et bellariis. Vasa, mensae, reliqua utensilia intra modum: nec quisquam quicquam possideat nisi certa mensura. Primorum autem urbis aedes, et penus ad alendam plebis benevolentiam omnibus pateant civibus. (Lib. III. de Repub. et V. de Legg.)

GUARANII.

XII. Guaraniorum aedes erant simplices, sed satis illae munitae contra anni tempestates. Una domibus mensura ambitu quadrato septem circiter ulnarum. Dividebantur autem in insulas, quarum singulae senas, septenasve (numeri satis non memini) aedes continebant, interjectis (ut dictum est) aequis viarum spatiis. Domorum omnium ostia, et frontem tutabatur a sole, et pluvia, trium ulnarum porticus, qua tectus circumire oppidum posses.

XIII. Supellex Indorum parca admodum; lectus pensilis, quem *Hamacam* vocant; ollae aliquot patellaeque fictiles, et amphorae; pro cyathis, cassae nucleo cucurbitae; arcae, binae ternaeve condendis vestibus; sediculae, nec multae, et rudes. Haec omnia omnibus oppidanis fere paria. Auri argentive ne semuncia quidem inter Guaranios praeterquam in templo. Victus e carne assa elixave, atque ex agri frugibus; puls e *mandioca*; nullum condimentum praeter indigenum piper. Salem regio non fert: importatus tamen aliunde dividebatur aliquoties patribus familias. Claves, vel serae aedium nullae; nihilo tamen minus tuta erant omnia; adeo oppidani re aliena abstinebant.

On the Limits to Be Observed Regarding Households and Household Goods

PLATO

11. Houses should not be extravagant; it is enough if they protect the inhabitant against the cold and heat. Let the furnishings be simple—neither gold nor silver[3]—but such that they neither prevent citizens from being good nor supply anyone with the inspiration and incentive to harm others. Nourishment should be easy to prepare, like roasted venison without seasonings or confections. Dishes, tables, and the remaining utensils should be within limits: no one should possess anything aside from what was standard. Moreover, the households of the city's leaders and stored provisions for nourishing the well-being of the masses should be open to all citizens (*Republic* Book 3; *Laws* Book 5).

THE GUARANÍ

12. The homes of the Guaraní were simple, but they were sufficient defenses against the year's seasons. There was a single size for houses: about seven *varas* [approx. 19 ft] per side. Moreover, these were distributed into blocks, each of which contained six or seven (I cannot remember the exact number) houses with equal spaces for streets interspersed (as mentioned above). The entrances and the front of all the houses were protected from both sun and rain by a portico three *varas* [approx. 8 ft] wide so that you would be under a roof while moving around town.

13. The household goods of the Indians were extremely frugal; a hanging bed, which they call a *Hamaca*;* some pots, plates, and jars made of clay; instead of cups, gourds hollowed out inside; chests—two or three for storing clothes; little seats, not many, and simply made.† All these things are essentially equal for all the townspeople. Regarding gold and silver, there's not so much as half an ounce among the Guaraní, except in the church. Nourishment comes from meat that is either roasted or boiled and the produce of the field; there is porridge made from *mandioca*‡ and no seasoning beyond indigenous pepper. The region produces no salt, yet on occasions when it was imported from elsewhere it was distributed to the heads of households. The houses had neither keys nor bolts; yet everything was no less safe. Indeed, the townspeople kept away from the property of others.

* Hammock.

† Given the "simpler is better" ideology of this text, the term *rudis* does not carry the negative connotations often associated with it.

‡ Yuca.

De gente coalitura in urbem.

PLATO

XIV. Gens sit una, et lingua; eaedem leges sint, eadem sacra, his enim mirifice coalescit civium amicitia. Qui e variis confluunt populis linguae variae, ii prae desiderio morum et legum, quibus antea assueverunt, non probant urbis, in quam adsciscuntur, leges, et mores, qui tamen mutandi temere non sunt, receptis usibus peregrinis. (Lib. IV. de Legg.)

GUARANII.

XV. In triginta Guaraniorum priscis oppidis[4] (his bina adjecta fuerunt aetate nostra) gens una omnino erat, atque una lingua, quae viguit, atque etiam num viget, in maxima Americae meridialis parte ab Oceano Brasilico ad amnim usque Maranonium, atque hunc etiam ultra, usui enim est in Cayena. Qui terrarum tractus multo est amplior, quam quanto obtinuit olim lingua vel Graeca vel Latina, quibus Guaranica nihil cedit artificio et elegantia, de qua re dicemus in vita Ignatii Chomae.[5] Amicitia autem inter Guaranios post suscepta christiana sacra tam erat solida et constans, ut solidior et constantior esse nusquam possit: nam *societate gentis, et linguae* (adde religionis) *quam maxime homines conjunguntur,* ait praeclare Tullius. (De officiis lib. I. c. XVI.)

De numero civium et domorum.

PLATO

XVI. Qua civium frequentia constitura sit civitas dici recte non potest nisi e regionis amplitudine,[6] et vicinitate aliarum urbium, a quibus locus arctetur, vel unde oriri queat bellum. Ceterum ager tantus esse debet, quantus satis sit alendis moderatis hominibus. Justus civium numerus esto quinque milia et quadraginta, neque amplius minusve. Cives describuntur in duodecim tribus; ager in totidem partes dividitur; domus autem pari sunto civium, sive familiarum numero. Quot vero commoditates habeat numerus is prae aliis numeris explicat Plato ipse. (Lib. V. de Legg.)

On the Group of People That Will Come Together to Form the City

PLATO

14. There should be a single cultural group* and a single language. The laws and the sacred rites should all be the same. For it is from these things that friendship between citizens miraculously takes shape. Those who come together from different populations with different languages, out of a desire for the customs and laws to which they had previously been accustomed, do not approve of the laws and customs of the city with which they are still becoming acquainted. Nevertheless, these must not be altered rashly, resulting in the admission of foreign practices (*Laws* Book 4).

THE GUARANÍ

15. In the thirty early towns[4] of the Guaraní (in my time, two had been added to these) there was a single cultural group to be sure, and a single language, which flourished, and flourishes even now, in the majority of South America from the Brazilian Ocean all the way to the Marañón River,† and even beyond this since it is in use in Cayenne.‡ This portion of the earth is much greater than the amount of territory either the Greek or Latin language once occupied, and the Guaraní language cedes nothing to these in terms of refinement and elegance, on which I shall say more in the biography of Ignacio Chomé.[5] However, after the Christian religion had been adopted, friendship among the Guaraní was so firm and steadfast that something firmer and more steadfast could not exist anywhere. For "humans are yoked together most of all by the bonds of a shared identity and language" (you might add religion), as the illustrious Cicero said (*On Duties* 1.16 [1.17]).

On the Number of Citizens and Houses

PLATO

16. It is not possible to say precisely what quantity of citizens should constitute the state except from the size of the region[6] and the proximity to other cities from which the site should be kept distant; otherwise war could break out. That aside, the land ought to be extensive enough to sustain people in modest conditions. The right number of citizens should be 5,040, no more no less. The citizens are assigned to twelve tribes and the land divided into as many parts; the houses, however, should be equal to the number of citizens or, rather, families. Plato himself explains how many advantages this number has over other numbers (*Laws* Book 5).

* *Gens*—which here translates Plato's γένος—refers to people who would self-identify as a group on the basis of shared descent, culture, or another commonality.

† Known today as the Amazon River.

‡ The capital of French Guiana on the northern coast of South America.

XVII. In Guaraniorum oppidis nullus certus numerus virum domorumve, neque una agri mensura pro omnibus. Amplissimi singulis oppidis erant fines in praedia, et armenti pascua: idque commodius certe est ad deducendas colonias; dabatur enim novis colonis, quod satis ipsis esset sine aliorum detrimento. At Plato, qui totum agrum aequis partibus in singulas civium familias ita dividit, ut nihil vacet, quo, quaeso coloniam (quam deducendam ait, cum supra numerum illum quinque millium et quadraginta, soboles succrescit) quo, inquam, coloniam mittet? Non video; neque ipse nodum hunc solvit. Adde huc, si quispiam locus cetera habeat bona, quae Plato requirit; sed ager aptus solum sit binis civium millibus, quingentis, et viginti (quae dimidia pars est definiti ab eo numeri) relinquetur ne ager iste desertus, prohibita urbis aedificatione, vel si aedificetur, civitas perfecta non erit, deficiente justo numero? Durius id dictu videtur, hominisque nimium decreta sua probantis.

XVIII. Oppidum SS. regum (vulgo *Yapeyu* vocant) omnium Guaraniorum maximum constabat an. MDCCLXVII. familiis mille quingentis unde viginti, capitibus autem septem mille nongentis septuaginta quattuor. Oppidum vero S. Laurentii omnium minimum habebat eo anno familias tercentum undecim, capita mille ducenta quadraginta duo. Reliquorum oppidorum status, et numerus intra ista summi et insimi census extrema: oppidis aliis erant quattuor millia capitum, aliis tria millia, aliis alia. Crescebat autem, aut minuebatur Indorum soboles, prout crebrius rariusve saeviebant alibi atque alibi pustulae illae, quas medici vocant variolas. Haec lues genti Indicae capitalis est.[7] Equidem sic puto, si malum istud (quo caruerunt olim Americani) ea loca identidem non invaderet, ita Guaranios propagatum iri, ut regio illa ceteroquin amplissima vix ipsis suffectura esset. Verum pauci menses multorum annorum stirpem poenitus extinguunt.

THE GUARANÍ

17. In the towns of the Guaraní there is no fixed number of men or houses nor a measure of agricultural land for every individual. In each of the towns there was very ample territory for farms and pastures for livestock; indeed, it was certainly more than sufficient for the colonies that had to be established; for the new colonists were granted what they needed so long as there was no detriment to the others. But given that Plato divided up all the land into equal parts for the individual families of citizens so that nothing would be left vacant, where, pray tell, will he send the [new] colony, which he says must be dispatched once the progeny cause the citizenry to grow beyond that figure of 5,040? Where, oh where? I do not understand. He did not untie this knot. Additionally, if a certain place should have the other good qualities that Plato requires, but the land is only suited to 2,520 citizens (which is half of the number designated by him), should that land be left deserted because the construction of a city is prohibited, or if it is constructed, will the state be imperfect because it lacks the correct number of citizens? It seems fairly stubborn to say this, and characteristic of a person who puts too much stock in his own doctrines.

18. In 1767, the Guaraní's largest town, Santos Reyes (commonly called Yapeyú), contained 1,519 families but 7,974 individuals. Yet San Lorenzo, the smallest of all, had in that year 311 families and 1,242 individuals. The situation and population of the rest of the towns were between these extremes of the maximum and minimum census. There were four thousand individuals in some towns, three thousand in others, and so on. The Indians' progeny would wax and wane depending on whether those pustules that doctors call smallpox were raging more frequently or more rarely in one place or another. This plague is fatal for the Indian race.[7] Certainly I believe that if this evil (from which the Americans were formerly free) had not invaded these places over and over again, the Guaraní would have increased such that the region, which is otherwise extremely spacious, would hardly have met their needs. The reality is that a few months utterly extinguishes a lineage of many years.

De templo et sacrificiis.

PLATO

XIX. DEUM ante omnia ad statuendam urbem invocemus, qui utinam invocatus audiat, et audiens nobis dexter adsit, et nostrae civitati leges serat; norma enim boni Deus, qui est ipsa bonitas. Haec sapienter Plato, qui nihil antiquius religione haberi vult, sine ea enim nec respublica, nec genus humanum stare queunt. Quippe hoc differunt homines a belluis, quod hae creatorem rerum, et Numen, nec colunt, nec noscunt, nec nosse possunt; homo autem et noscit, et colere debet, et colit tamquam patrem, et dominum, et Deum, a quo mentem accepit; et accipere assidue pergit bona cetera ab ejusdem providentia, omnium moderatrice. Quapropter (ait Tullius)[8] *haud scio, an pietate adversus Deos sublata, societas etiam humani generis tollatur.* Qui dicendi modus vi latinae linguae respondet huic; arbitror tollendam societatem sublata pietate.

XX. Ceterum de rebus sacris sic jubet Plato. Fiant quotannis sacrificia tercentum sexaginta quinque (id est quotidie sacrificetur.) Sollemnitates sunto duodecim (id est singulae singulis mensibus) quot sunt civium tribus, quae alternis celebriores hos agent dies. Summus Pontifex unus esto. Nutrices magistraeque pueris et puellis praefectae, quotidie cum alumnis suis ab anno tertio ad sextum usque intersint Sacrificio; et siquis sibi creditorum immodeste quid agat, vel peccet irreligiose, eum dein puniant. Hymni non alii sint, quam deorum, nec laudationes aliae, quam optimorum virum, feminarumque. Poetae procul ab urbe, totaque regione pelluntor. (Lib. IV. X. de Rep. et IV. V. VI. VIII. XII. de Legg.)

GUARANII.

XXI. Nulla in oppidis Guaranicis major cura quam de Deo divinisque rebus. Templum magnificum tribus constans alis, trisque in forum ostiis. Eximia ibi omnia, vixque in urbibus etiam maximis melior et gravior sacrorum apparatus. Laquearia, tholus, columnae, altaria partim picta, partim inaurata. Candellabra, vasa, totumque sacrificandi instrumentum ex argento. Indumenta Sacerdotum e tela Damascena, aurove textili. Mappae, pallae, alba vestis, amictus tegens littantis Umeros et guttur e bysso subtilissima.

On the Church and Sacrifices

PLATO

19. First of all let us call on GOD to establish the city; hopefully he listens once called upon, is favorable to us as he listens, and sows the seeds of law for our state. For God, who is goodness itself, is the measure of the good. So says Plato wisely, who wants nothing to be considered of greater importance than religion, for without it neither the republic nor the human race can endure. Certainly, in this regard humans differ from wild beasts, since the latter neither worship nor recognize the creator of things and his Divinity nor are they capable of recognizing it. A human, on the other hand, recognizes and ought to worship God, through whom he receives his cognitive ability, just as he worships his father and lord. Unceasingly he keeps receiving other goods through God's providence, the moderator of all things. For this reason, Cicero says,[8] "I hardly know whether, if piety toward the Gods were abolished, humankind's society would be abolished." This way of speaking in Latin corresponds to the following meaning: I judge that society would be abolished if piety were abolished.

20. Besides this Plato prescribes as follows regarding sacred matters: There ought to be three hundred and sixty-five sacrifices annually (that is, a sacrifice should be offered daily). There should be twelve Festivals (that is, one each month), which is the same as the number of citizen tribes, which will take turns acting as the primary celebrants on these days. There should be one chief priest.* Nurses and teachers put in charge of boys and girls should attend sacrifices daily with their students aged three all the way to six years old; if anyone of those entrusted by the citizens should do anything improperly or transgress against religion, then they should punish him. There should be no hymns except those for the gods and no praises other than for the very best men and women. Poets should be banished far from the city and the entire region (*Republic* Books 4 and 10; *Laws* Books 4, 5, 6, 8, and 12).

THE GUARANÍ

21. There is no greater concern in the Guaraní towns than God and divine matters. The church with its three aisles and its three doorways onto the town square is magnificent. Everything there was exceptional and the splendor of the sacrificial apparatus in even the greatest cities is scarcely better or more dignified: coffered ceilings, cupola, columns, and altars—some painted, some gilded. Candelabra, vessels, and every instrument of sacrifice made of silver. The priests' garments were of damask or gold textile. The purificator, the pall, the albs, the amice covering the shoulders and neck of the celebrant were made of the finest linen.

* Translating ἀρχιερεύς (Plato, *Laws* 12.947a).

XXII. Singularis omnino erat illic splendor aedis sacrae, qua re plurimum detinentur Indorum animi, ut libentius, religiosiusque piis mysteriis intersint. Atque eo domus Dei magis eminebat, quo cetera aedificia humiliora erant et simpliciora, etiam Curionis aedes sine ulla superiore contignatione, sed structis plano in solo aliquot cubiculis sex ulnarum ambitu. Unum illorum pro Parocho, aliud pro ejus collega, reliqua pro hospitibus; omnia autem non alio cultu, quam qui decet virum religiosum, et ei erat similis, quo utebatur eliseus vates, id est, *lectulus, et mensa, et sella, et candelabrum.*[9]

XXIII. Sacrificabatur quotidie a Curione, ejusque collega. Quaterni minimum pueri optime instituti aderant facienti ad aram maximam cum rubra, vel violacea, vel nigra (pro diei officio) tunica, quam super pendebat circum brevius e lino amiculum. Minoribus aris ministrabant bini dumtaxat acolythi, sed eodem ornatu. Dum fiebat res divina pulsabant semper Musici instrumenta varii generis cum Organo pneumatico. Sollemnitates celebrantur majori caerimonia. Dominicis autem aliisque diebus festis cantabat Sacerdos; et cum cantu itidem litabat feria II. pro vita jam functis, ac Sabbatis in honorem B. V. MARIAE.

XXIV. Equidem magnam Europae, Americaeque partem peragravi, et nusquam pietatem majorem in templis vidi. Testes hujus rei appello sacros Antistites, qui oppida Guaranica saepe lustrarunt, publicisque laudibus cultum illum magnopere commendarunt. Quibus Episcopis auctoritate sua pondus addidit Benedictus XIV. Pontif Max. qui non semel Ecclesiam illam aliis ad exemplum proposuit.[10]

XXV. Philippus V. Rex Catholicus cum ex Antistitum, aliorumque testimoniis rescisset, quantus esset nitor et decus templorum Guaranicorum, *quibus* (ait) *religiosus, splendidius, cultiusque nequit quicquam fieri,* continere se se non potuit, quin (qua erat humanitate) hac super re moderatori provinciae Paraguaycae, et Sociis Guaranicis gratularetur, amorem in ipsos suum testatus, quod adeo eximie Dei domum curarent.[11] Norat videlicet pius Rex, quam Regi summo placeat magnificentia in rebus sacris, quidquid enim in has opum effunditur instar est debiti tributi pro auro, argentoque, et gemmis, ornandique corporis cetero instrumento in hominum usus ab eodem conditis: id quod vel a solo Salomonis studio pro templo illo, quo nihil terrarum Orbis vidit augustius, abunde constat.

22. Moreover, the splendor of the sacred shrine there was completely unique, and that is what most engaged the Indians' spirits so that they more cheerfully and scrupulously attend to the holy mysteries. Indeed, the house of God stood out all the more given that the rest of the buildings were more diminutive and more basic; even the priest's house was without any upper story, with the various rooms of six *varas* [16 ft] per side arranged on a single floor. One of these rooms was for the parish priest, another for his colleague, and the rest for guests; all, however, with no decoration other than what is proper for a religious man, and it was similar to what the prophet Elisha used, namely "a little bed, a table, a seat, and a candlestick."[9]

23. Daily mass was offered by the Priest and his colleague. Each time, at least four excellently trained boys would be involved in the activity at the highest altar with red, purple, or black cassocks (according to the day's ceremony), and a shorter linen mantle would hang down over this. Acolytes tended the lesser altars, just two at a time, but in the same attire. While the mass was taking place, the musicians always played instruments of various kinds alongside the pneumatic organ. Festivals were celebrated with greater ceremony. On Sundays and other feast days the Priest would sing and likewise there were services with song on the second day of the week for the deceased and on the Sabbath in honor of the Blessed Virgin Mary.

24. Indeed, I have traversed the better part of Europe and America and I have never seen greater piety in churches. As witnesses to this fact, I call on the sacred Bishops, who have examined the Guaraní towns many times and zealously commended their ritual with public praise. And Pope Benedict XIV, who more than once set forth that church* as an example for others, has added the weight of his own authority to these Bishops.[10]

25. When the Catholic King, Felipe V [of Spain], had learned from the testimony of the Bishops and others how great the brilliance and glory of the Guaraní churches was, he said "none could be more scrupulous, more splendid, or more elegant than these"; he was unable to contain himself, nay he even (such was his humanity) congratulated the Superior of the province of Paraguay and the Guaraní Jesuits for this, having testified to his own love for them because they were caring for the house of God so very excellently.[11] Evidently the pious King knew how much the magnificence of sacred objects pleases the heavenly King. For whatever wealth is lavished on these is equivalent to the tribute owed taking the place of gold, silver, gems, and other means of adorning the body all of which God fashioned for human use. That this is the case is abundantly clear from the example of Solomon's singular zeal for that temple, which is more majestic than anything the World has ever seen.

* i.e., the Guaraní church, understood collectively.

XXVI. At vero pendendus magni non esset aedis sacrae apparatus, nisi internus animorum habitus, externaque corporis modestia sanctitati loci respondissent. Namque hic finis est externi cultus, quo nulla usquam gens caruit, illum quippe inspirat ipse instinctus naturae; quandoquidem et Deum palam colere, et alii alios vicissim ad eum colendum excitare debemus. Religiosae autem caerimoniae, oculis adspectantium objectae, vividam, vegetamque mysteriorum memoriam servant, aluntque, atque ad pietatem sublevant animos addictos nimium per se materiatis rebus, quae ipsos misere distrahunt, et avocant ab spiritus officiis. Et vero nisi extrinsecus obsequium in Deum signo aliquo profitearis, quis, quaeso, te ab Atheo discernet? Arae, preces, genuum submissio, poenae expiatoriae pro admissis noxis, accensi cerei in vivae indicium fidei, publicae supplicationes, sunt tamquam animata et spirans pietatis vox, et stimulus, quo mens ad coelestia sensim erigitur. Sane Christus ipse ad Sacramenta sensili materia usus est, aqua, pane, vino, oleo. Quapropter inde usque ab nascente Ecclesia ritus extimi, et templi functiones, et cantus, et effigies Divorum, et ejusmodi alia, maximi facta sunt: quod si alii deessent testes, vel solus Prudentius Hispanus tempori illi proximus fidem omnem rei huic (quam elegantissima ejus carmina passim praedicant) faceret. Quid? quod visa (exempli causa) Dei Mater MARIA vel picta, vel sculpta, cum divino puero, sacratiores aliquando sensus aspicienti movet, quam eloquens Orator multa de Virginis laudibus et dignitate disserens? quamquam de doctrina sacra, et de lege, necessaria omnino sunt ad fovendam retinendamque Religionem crebre conciones. Sed de hac re satis dictum est.

XXVII. Pueri Guaranici, puellaeque, et viri, matresque familias, et oppidi magistratus, quotidie ad sacrum Missae conveniebant. Summum omnibus silentium, atque instar fuisset monstri aliquem ibi cum aliquo quicquam loqui, vel oculos immodeste circumagere. Sacramenta Poenitentiae, atque Eucharistiae insigni pietatis sensu obibant frequenter multi, postque acceptum divinum panem omnes simul sub finem sacrificii gratias coelesti hospiti agebant e formula in hanc rem concepta, quam praelegebat flexis genibus ante aram maximam unus e cantoribus.

26. Certainly the grandeur of the sacred shrine should not have been of high regard unless the internal disposition of spirit and the external moderation of the body had corresponded with the sanctity of the place. For this is the epitome of external worship, which no cultural group has ever lacked; indeed, nature's very impulse inspires it. Since, indeed, we ought to both worship God publicly and rouse one another in turn to worship him. Moreover, religious ceremonies, set before the eyes of onlookers, nourish the memory of the mysteries and keep it vivid and lively; they raise up toward piety spirits that, on their own, are excessively devoted to material things, which lamentably distract them and divert them from the duties of the spirit. And certainly, unless you outwardly declare your allegiance to God with some sign, who, I ask, will distinguish you from an atheist? The altars, the prayers, the kneeling, the atonements for the offenses committed, the candles lit to indicate a lively faith, the public prayers—these are like a living and pulsating voice of piety, as well as an incitement by which the mind is aroused gently toward heavenly matters. By all means, Christ himself used materials that could be perceived by the senses in the Sacraments: water, bread, wine, oil. For this reason, ever since, the visible rites, the functions of the church building, the songs, the images of the Saints, and other such things, have been held in the greatest esteem by the nascent Church. And if these other testimonies were insufficient, indeed, all on his own the Spaniard Prudentius, very close to that period, would convince everyone of this fact (which his extremely elegant songs would proclaim far and wide). Why? Because whenever (for example) Mary Mother of God is seen, whether it is a painting or sculpture, with her divine son, doesn't she stir senses in the beholder that are more sacred than those the eloquent orator stirs up as he discusses the praises and dignity of the Virgin? Nevertheless, frequently preaching on sacred doctrine and law is altogether necessary to foment and preserve Religion. But enough has been said on this matter.

27. The Guaraní boys and girls, men and matriarchs, and town magistrates, would attend the sacred rite of Mass daily. Everyone remained perfectly silent, and it would be almost monstrous if anyone said anything to anyone else or let their eyes wheel around improperly. Many regularly received the sacraments of Penance and Eucharist with a feeling of extraordinary devotion. Once the divine bread was received, toward the end of the sacrifice, all would give thanks at once to the heavenly host with a formula composed for this purpose, which one of the cantors would read out on bended knee before the main altar.

XXVIII. Ingressuri longum iter expiabant se se salutari confessione, et sacrosancto Viatico muniebant; in oppidum autem regressi utrumque mysterium iterabant denuo. Praeter maximum in oppidis templum, erant ruri, ut dictum est, aediculae quaedam sparsim positae, quas Indi vel praedia, vel armentum curantes crebro adibant, recitandarum precum, exercendaeque Catecheseos causa. Ibi Sacerdotes iter agentes sacrificabant; ac si eos nox occuparat, hospitabantur in cubiculo ad id ipsum parato, quod haerebat aedi sacrae. Hymni non illic alii, quam de DEO, et JESUCHRISTO, et B. V. MARIA, et superis heroibus, quorum laude et compita, et viae, et agri, et silvae, et amnes, et montes resonabant. Carmina profana inter Guaranicos nulla, nedum impuri lascivique poetae.

De inquisitione in impios.

PLATO

XXIX. Nihil tam mihi mirum in Platone videtur, quam quod pro Republica instituerit tribunal Inquisitionis, et quidem tribunali nostro simillimum. Pessime res haec habeat necesse est liberioris, philosophiae epicureum, et atheum gregem, ac boni ordinis perturbatores, impatientes freni, quique in se, et sua inquiri nullo modo volunt, proscinduntque probris omnibus sacros Fidei judices. Sed bene factum: Plato ipse quales ejusmodi homines sint, graviter describit. Non parum, ait, refert, si ostenderimus, eos qui vanis, ineptisque argumentis abutuntur, ut alios ad impietatem trahant, prave et perverse philosophari ... Cum maxima autem statuta a sceleratis, et impiis corrumpantur, cujusnam potius, quam legislatoris, est illis obsistere, tuerique jus aequum et justum? Haec ille.

XXX. Quo autem modo tribunal Inquisitionis statuit? Si quis, inquit, impie quid agat, aut dicat, qui agentem, dicentemve audierit, videritve, magistratibus indicato. Quod si viderit, audieritve, et deferre rem nolit, ipse impietatis reus esto. Ubi vero constiterit de culpa, judices hominem sacrilegum pro singulis irreligiose admissis afficient singulis suppliciis. Omnes autem hujus generis rei arcta custodia coercentur. (Quid hic dicent, qui adeo sacrae Inquisitionis carcerem detestantur?) Deinde explicat Plato, quaenam et quot sint genera impietatis, atque alios impios impiis alii nocentiores esse affirmat. E nocentioribus sunt, ait quidam, qui rerum potiti neminem formidant, quidam qui exercitum ductant, quidam qui seditiose declamant, quidam qui templi sollemnitatibus illudunt, quidam qui inanibus sophismatum captiunculis infatuant populum ...

28. When they were about to go on a long journey, they purified themselves with a salutary confession and fortified themselves with the traveler's communion. Then after returning to town, they would go through both mysteries again. In addition to the town's main church, there were some chapels scattered here and there in the countryside, as has been said, where the Indians who took care of the farms and the livestock would go frequently to recite their prayers and practice the catechism. There, the priests who were traveling would offer sacrifices; and if the night fell upon them, they would be lodged in a room prepared for this purpose, attached to the chapel. There were no hymns there besides those for God, Jesus Christ, the Blessed Virgin Mary, and the heroic saints, with whose praises the crossroads, roads, fields, forests, rivers, and mountains resounded. There were no secular songs among the Guaraní, nor were there any impure or unrestrained poets.

On the Inquisition against the Impious

PLATO

29. Nothing in Plato is so amazing to me as the fact that he set up a tribunal of the Inquisition for the Republic, and, in truth, it is rather similar to our own tribunal. This must be most upsetting to the Epicurean and atheist flock of libertine* philosophy and the disturbers of good order who cannot endure restraint and who are unwilling for themselves and their own actions to be examined in any way and yet they defame the sacred judges of the faith with every sort of reproach. But, fortunately, Plato himself authoritatively describes the nature of this sort of people. It is no small matter, he says, if we show that those who misuse empty and absurd arguments to draw others toward impiety, are improperly and subversively playing the philosopher. When the highest institutions are corrupted by criminals and the impious, who else but the lawmaker has the responsibility to confront them and uphold the fair and just rule of law? This is what he says.

30. But how did he set up the tribunal of the Inquisition? If anyone, he says, does or says anything impiously, whoever hears or sees the one acting or speaking, must inform the magistrates. If he does not want to report the fact that he saw or heard something, he himself is guilty of impiety. Whenever there is agreement regarding guilt, the judges will punish the sacrilegious person for each of the individual things done irreligiously. Indeed, everyone of this sort is held in close confinement. (What will those who so detest the prison of the Holy Inquisition say to this?) Plato later explains what and how many types of irreligion there are and asserts that some of the impious are more harmful than others. Among the more harmful, he says, are those who take possession of things and then fear no one, those who lead an army, those who make seditious speeches, those who mock the solemnities of the temple, those who infatuate the public with the worthless fallacies of sophisms . . .

* Lit. "more liberal"; Peramàs uses the term broadly against the *philosophes*, whom he accuses of radicalism, self-love, hedonism, and all manner of licentiousness.

XXXI. Id praefatus pergit dicere, cum ita distinctus sit impiorum coetus eos quidem, qui non a pravis moribus, sed ab amentia quadam tales evaserint, hos judex in coercitionis carcere non minus quinquennio detineto, quo toto tempore nefas esto civium cuiquam eos adire, et adloqui. Ubi vero vinculorum tempus finitum fuerit, qui poena sanior, et modestior factus sit, is dein cum sanis et modestis habitato. Sin autem sacrilegii rursus damnabitur, plectatur morte.

XXXII. Causam tanti supplicii hanc reddit: nam qui, ait, adversus deos agit, et sacrificia, vel jusjurandum parvi pendit, et propter haec alios deridet, plures sibi similes efficiet... Occisus impius extra Reipublicae fines projicitor, insepultusque relinquitor. Quod si eum quisquam e liberis civibus sepeliat, hunc qui volet, impietatis accusato: sin vero illum tumulet servus, is ob id ne interpellator. Hic jam te rogo: est ne tribunal Inquisitionis nostrae severius isto aut durius? Eant nunc liberiores Philosophi, et fidei quaesitores immites clament, clamantibus os obtundet Philosophorum maximus. Cur? quia recte norat nulla tam re Rempublicam perturbari, quam si religionis fundamenta subruantur. Ad Inquisitionem quoque pertinet, quod vetet Plato quicquam publice cani, nisi visum prius et approbatum sit a magistratu. Ecce hic tibi legitima examinatio librorum, qui plurimum bonis moribus vel obesse, vel prodesse possunt.

XXXIII. At objiciet aliquis, vel ipse tuus Plato carcere poenisque sacrorum quaesitorum dignus est, quippe qui Deos astruit: eosque colendos dicit. Audio: atque hac ego re vehementer illum vitupero, quod perverse usus sit vulgi consuetudine, veritus fortasse, nequis sibi (si scriberet aliter) malum pararet, quod paratum fuit immerenti magistro suo Socrati ab improbo Melito ob neglectos, ut ipse ajebat, Deos. Errasse autem animo Platonem vix puto, quandoquidem tam aperte, et toties pro vera divinitate stat, gravissimaque et solidissima demonstratione invicte ostendit existere DEUM OPTIMUM MAXIMUM, quem negare nemo, ait potest, nisi ultima laboret dementia.

31. Having first stated this, he goes on to say that, given that the impious are a diverse lot, the sort who have turned out like this not because of depraved habits but because of their senselessness, these the judge must detain in a coercive prison for no less than five years and during that entire time it must be forbidden for any of the citizens to approach them and speak with them. When the period of captivity has come to an end, one made more sane and more moderate by the punishment ought to then live among sane and moderate people. But if he is condemned of sacrilege again, he would be punished with death.

32. For such a severe punishment he gives the following cause: For he who acts, Plato says, against the gods and regards sacrifices or oath swearing of little value and derides others for [doing] these things, he will make many like himself. Once dead, the wicked must be cast outside the borders of the Republic and left unburied. And if one of the free citizens were to bury him, whoever wishes to may charge that man with impiety; but if a slave were to inter him, he should not be held accountable for it. Now I ask you, is our Inquisition tribunal more severe or more harsh than that? Let the libertine Philosophers and the merciless inquisitors of the faith go ahead and cry foul; the greatest of Philosophers will blunt the voices of those complaining. Why? Because he correctly recognized that the Republic is thrown into chaos by nothing so much as when the foundations of religion are undermined. Also relating to the Inquisition is the fact that Plato prohibits anything from being sung in public unless it has first been seen and approved by the authorities. Here you have the legitimate examination of books, which are exceptionally capable of either causing injury to good customs or benefiting them.

33. But someone will object: Does not your very own Plato actually deserve prison and the punishment of the holy inquisitors since he builds up the gods and says they ought to be worshiped. I take the point; and I vehemently reproach him for this because he perversely indulged in the customs of the common people, perhaps because he feared that (if he wrote otherwise) someone would cause him the harm that was caused for his innocent teacher Socrates by the wicked Melitus for neglecting, as he alleges, the gods. However, I scarcely think that Plato went wrong at heart, seeing that he so openly and so often stands on the side of true divinity and irrefutably declares by means of the most serious and most genuine demonstration that there exists a Best and Greatest God, which he says no one could deny unless suffering extreme dementia.

XXXIV. Fuisse is mos dicitur priscis philosophis, ut clam inter se, et in scholis, Deum unum esse docerent, publice autem et scripto, ob metum plebis, quae suos Deos Jovem, Bacchum, Venerem, ceteros tamquam criminum praesides atque exempla volebat, Polytheismon prae se ferrent, indigna prorsus et nefanda simulatione. Ceterum Plato cum deos nominat, heroas quosdam intelligi vult ab summo illo DEO creatos, ipsoque inferiores, quibus datum est, ut Soli, Lunae, stellis reliquisque naturae partibus praesint. Quae ille cum ait, haud scio equidem, an occulte et per ambages quiddam tradat de Angelis, eorumque ministerio, ex hausta doctrina ab Hebraeis, quorum mysteria in sua illa philosophica peregrinatione didicerat. In *Apologia* autem *Socratis* profitetur disertis verbis, *neque Solem, neque Lunam esse Deos credo, ut credit vulgus hominum.*

XXXV. Adde huc, quod de Dei bonitate, de divina providentia, de permissione mali, de officiis virtutum, de immortalitate animi, de praemio bonorum post mortem, de sontium suppliciis, ita disserit Plato, ut Christiana Philosophia institutus esse videatur. Quam graves illius adhortationes pro colenda justitia, et temperantia, et fortitudine? Quam recte praecipit de amore in parentes, de debita senibus reverentia, de observandis legibus, de contemnendis deliciis, de rebus omnibus sanctitati postponendis, de cohibendis imperio rationis pravis animi motibus, de retinenda patientia, et spe inter adversa, quandoquidem, ait, confidendum est piis viris, cum in graves labores inciderint, eos Dei ope leviores factum iri, et praesentibus malis meliorem divinitus sortem successuram. Quarum institutionum libenter ego specimen huc aliquod producerem, nisi excluderer angustiis propositae mihi brevitatis.

XXXVI. Rem unam, quam ille multo dignius et rectius, quam hujus temporis Philosophi, tractat, praeterire non possum. Agit de vehementi illa animi propensione, qua nos et nostra supra modum amamus. Et nimius, inquit, in semet hominum amor causa flagitiorum omnium est: obcaecat enim eum qui amat ardor amatae rei. Idcirco, qui se ipse pluris, quam veritatem pendit, is quid justum, et aequum sit male judicat. Qui autem vir magnus futurus sit, id agat, oportet, ut neque se ipsum, neque sua intemperanter diligat, et id sectetur, ac teneat, quod bonum est, sive hoc sibi ipsi insit, sive in alio videat. Sane ab illo sui amore nascitur, ut quis vel stultitiam suam esse sapientiam putet: quo fit, ut quamvis nihil sciamus, scire tamen nos omnia existimemus... Immoderatum igitur amorem sui ita debet quisque odisse, ut meliores sequi velit, rejecto pravo rubore, malaque spreta verecundia, qua nos quandoque pudet aliorum bona imitari. Sic Plato.

34. It was customary, it is said, for the ancient philosophers to teach that there was a single God privately among themselves and in schools, but publicly and in writing they embraced polytheism (shameful and abominable hypocrisy!) for fear of the populace, which wanted its own gods Zeus, Dionysos, Aphrodite, and others, as both protectors against and models of crime. Still, when Plato names the gods he wants them to be understood as what might be called heroes created by—and inferior to—that supreme GOD, who have been entrusted to preside over the Sun, the Moon, the stars, and the other parts of nature. And when he says these things, as far as I am concerned, perhaps he is covertly and enigmatically communicating something about Angels and their ministry, via a doctrine drawn from the Hebrews, with whose mysteries he had become acquainted during his own philosophical peregrinations. Moreover, in the *Apology of Socrates* he openly confesses in clear terms, "I believe that neither the Sun nor the Moon are Gods, as the common people believe" [26d].*

35. Add to this the fact that when it comes to the goodness of God, divine providence, tolerance of sin, the duties of virtue, the immortality of the soul, the reward for the good after death, and the punishment of criminals, Plato discusses these things just as if he had been trained in Christian Philosophy. How weighty are his exhortations to cultivate justice, temperance, and fortitude? How rightly does he give advice about love for one's parents, reverence owed to elders, obeying laws, disdaining delicacies, considering all things secondary to moral purity, hindering the improper impulses of the soul through the power of reason, retaining patience and hope in the face of adversity, seeing that, he says, when pious men meet with burdensome tasks, they have to trust that they are going to be made more bearable through God's aid and that through divine influence a better lot will take the place of the present ills. I would gladly produce further proof of these principles, were I not prevented by the constraints of brevity I set forth.

36. There is one thing, which he discusses much more suitably and accurately than the Philosophers of this time, which I cannot pass over. He deals with the soul's strong propensity for loving ourselves and our possessions immoderately. People's excessive self-love, he says, is the cause of all disgraceful acts: for passion for a thing loved blinds the one who loves it. For that reason, he who esteems himself above truth is a poor judge of what is just and equitable. By contrast, in order for someone to be a great man it is necessary for him to try to love neither himself nor his things intemperately, and both to pursue and hold onto what is good whether it exists in himself, or he should see it in another. To be sure, it is born out of that self-love that one considers even his stupidity to be wisdom; from which it comes about that although we know nothing, we still reckon that we know everything. Consequently, a person ought to hate immoderate self-love and instead desire to follow the example of better people, with improper modesty rejected and destructive shame spurned, on account of which imitating the good in others sometimes makes us feel ashamed. So says Plato.

* Here Peramàs misrepresents the ambiguity of Socrates' noncommital reaction to being accused of atheism.

XXXVII. Et philosophatur, dic, aliter hac in re post acceptum Evangelii lumen vel Theologus Thomas, vel puri amoris indagator Salesius, vel mystica Teresia, ceterique rerum spiritualium magistri? Contra vero hoc faecundum culpae saeculum philosophos (ita enim audire cupiunt) ab sedibus infernis excitavit, qui sui amorem, et perturbationes animi etiam maximas, tamquam labis omnis expertes, effectricesque optimarum rerum miris extollunt laudibus.[12] Non id quidem fecit Plato, qui philosophis istis minorum gentium multo sapientior fuit. (Lib. V. VII. X. de Legg.)

GUARANII.

XXXVIII. Guaranii, ceterique indi excepti sunt a privato sacrorum Inquisitorum tribunali: de gente enim indica (quod ad res fidei attinet) soli Episcopi judicant. Idcirco cum oppida Guaraniorum fit partim dioeceseos Paraguaycae, partim Bonaurensis, alterutrius Antistitis est cognoscere, si quid illi contra Religionem peccent. Verum ex quo Christiana sacra suscepere, ea semper (quae Dei bonitas est) coluerunt sancte casteque. Et quidem quaedam sunt graviora scelera, quibus nullus apud Guaranios locus est. Non ibi blasphemiae, non vana divini nominis usurpatio, non perjuria, non abusus rerum sacrarum, non ebrietas, non impudicae tabulae (quas Plato longe a Republica exterminari jubet) non magnarum fons culparum, aleae, pictaeque chartae ludus. Horum illic nihil. Quapropter Episcopi visis coram compositis gentis moribus, sacra functi lustratione neophytos illos magnopere laudabant. Jam vero Curiones Guaranici, et Religiosi alii viri, et Hispani cives subjecii sunt peculiari Inquisitionis tribunali, quod limae est pro America Meridiali.

XXXIX. Pavvius Philosophus *in disquisitionibus Americanis*[13] inter alias causas imminutae in Novo Orbe indigenarum sobolis hanc affert plane singularem: *Indos crematos ab Inquisitoribus Dominicanis.* Magnum malum! crimen inauditum? O Pavvi, o pie Pavvi? haereo hic, et nescio, an tui me misereat, an Indorum, quos dignate clementia miseraris. Miseret me tui potius, et taedet, qui adeo impudenter mentitus es, vel nesciens errasti turpissime calumniandi studio, ut tuus est mos, Cremati a Dominicanis Indi?

37. Tell me, after having received the light of the Gospel, does [St.] Thomas the Theologian have a different philosophy on this topic, or [St. Francis de] Sales the pursuer of pure love, or the mystic [St.] Teresa [de Jesús], or the other teachers of spiritual matters? On the contrary, this age abounding with fault has called forth "philosophers" (for that is what they like to be called) from the bowels of hell who exalt self-love and indeed the greatest disorders of the spirit with extraordinary praises,[12] as if these were free from of any defect and were accomplishers of the greatest things. Plato, who was much wiser than those lower order philosophers, certainly did not do that (*Laws* Books 5, 7, and 10).

THE GUARANÍ

38. The Guaraní and the other Indians are exempt from the private tribunal of the Holy Inquisition; regarding the Indian people (as far as matters of faith are concerned) only the Bishops pass judgment. Accordingly, since it happens that the towns of the Guaraní are partly in the Diocese of Paraguay and partly in the Diocese of Buenos Aires, it is up to each Bishop to find out if they commit any sins against Religion. But since the time they adopted the Christian faith, they have always practiced it scrupulously and piously (which is the goodness of God). And indeed, there are certain more serious crimes, for which there is no place among the Guaraní. There are no blasphemies there, no taking the name of God in vain, no perjury, no abuse of sacred things, no inebriation, no lewd paintings (which Plato orders be banished far from the Republic), no games of dice and playing cards, which are a font of great sins. None of these things are there. Thus, after witnessing the ordered customs of the people, the Bishops zealously praise those neophytes for performing the sacred rite of purification. Of course, the Guaraní priests, the other religious men, and the Spanish citizens were subject to a special tribunal of the Inquisition, which, for South America, was in Lima.

39. The Philosopher [Cornelis] de Pauw in his *Investigations on Americans*,[13] among other causes of the decline of the Indigenous population in the New World, alleges the following exceptionally peculiar cause: that the Indians were burned by the Dominican inquisitors! What an outrageous lie! Isn't that a bizarre slander? De Pauw, oh pious de Pauw? I am stuck on this, and I do not know whether I should pity you or the Indians whom you pity and deem worthy of sympathy. Should I pity you or rather be disgusted that you have lied with such impudence, or is it that out of your zeal for slander you have ignorantly and most shamefully erred, as is your habit? Indians burned by Dominicans!?

XL. Nusquam in Hispania Europaea, et nusquam in Americanis provinciis Patres Dominicani Inquisitores sunt, sed ubicumque in toto Catholici Regis imperio tribunal Inquisitionis est apud lectissimos Sacerdotes ex ordine Clericorum. Id primum, Pavvi. Deinde in Novo Orbe istud ipsum Inquisitorum Clericorum tribunal non agit in Indos, quorum causas de Religione solus decidit Episcopus; atque ita factum est ab initio usque detecti Novi Orbis, ut refert diligens, et accuratus rerum Americanarum scriptor Antonius Herera.[14] Episcopi autem lenissime cum Indis agunt, et Pavvium provoco, ut vel unum Indum proferat ab Antistite aliquo cremari jussum.

XLI. Ubi sunt ergo flammae illae Dominicanae Indorum voratrices? Haec volui de Pavvio dicere, ut vel hinc discas, quatenus tibi fidendum sit impiis philosophis, cum in religiosos viros, cum in censores sacros, cum in supremum Ecclesiae caput (neque enim huic parcit Pavvius) quaesitis consulto fabulis debacchantur, ac vel odio, vel malitia, vel rerum, quas tractant, inscitia, imperito imponunt vulgo. Quanto esset satius verae eos fidei, quae obscurari nequit dolis fallaciisque, sincera se se mente et animo submittere?

De Communione rerum.

PLATO

XLII. Post curam religionis nihil Platoni tam fuit cordi in statuenda Republica, quam rerum communio, sine qua eam recte consistere non posse existimabat; et fuit, cum rogatus ab Arcadibus, ut iret ad ordinandam ipsorum civitatem, id negarit, quod nosset detrectare illos aequabilitatem fortunarum. In opere *de Republica* nihil ille acrius urget, quam usum communem; idem facit in XII. libris de Legibus, quos pro colonia Magnesia a Cretensibus deducenda scripsit: hic tamen communionem bonorum temperat, et rem multo moderatius, et prudentius definit, quam *in Republica*, ubi provectus nimio studio omnia cum omnibus communicandi[15] graviter lapsus est, ut infra dicemus.

40. Nowhere in European Spain and nowhere in the American provinces are Dominican Fathers inquisitors, but everywhere under the dominion of the Catholic king the tribunal of the Inquisition is in the hands of the most select priests from the secular clergy.* This, de Pauw, is the first thing. Second, in the New World this tribunal of the Clerical Inquisitors does not itself deal with the Indians, whose cases in matters of Religion only the Bishop decides; and it has been done this way since the very beginning of the discovery of the New World, as the diligent and careful recorder of American matters, Antonio de Herrera, relates.[14] On the contrary, the Bishops are extremely lenient with the Indians, and I challenge de Pauw to produce even a single instance of an Indian who was ordered to be burned by some Bishop.

41. Where, then, are these Dominican flames of his—the devourers of the Indians? I wanted to cite this from de Pauw so that perhaps you might learn from it to what extent you can trust those impious philosophers when they fly into a Bacchic frenzy against religious men, against holy censors, against the supreme head of the church (for de Pauw does not spare him either), with deliberately contrived nonsense, and what's more whether out of hatred, malice, or ignorance of the subjects they treat, they deceive the uninformed populace. How much better would it be if with sincere heart and soul they submitted to the true faith, which cannot be obscured by either fraud or lies?

On Community Ownership

PLATO

42. After his concern for religion, nothing was so dear to Plato in the institution of the Republic as community ownership, without which, he judged, it would not properly take shape. There was even a time when he was asked by the Arcadians to come and organize their state, and he refused to do so because he knew that they would reject the equalization† of property. In his work *On the Republic*, he insists on nothing more ardently than on the common use of property; and he does the same in Book 12 of the *Laws*, which he wrote for the colony of Magnesia to be founded by the Cretans. Here, however, he qualifies the community of goods and defines the matter in a much more measured and prudent way than in the *Republic*, where, driven by an excessive zeal for sharing everything with everyone,[15] he fell into serious errors, as we will mention below.

* i.e., priests who were not members of religious orders.

† Cicero's coinage *aequabilitas* has a variety of meanings and here refers to a process of creating equity through rebalancing.

XLIII. Principio vult, ut ea, quae propria singulorum sunt, veluti oculi, aures, pedes, manus, brachia, fiant quodammodo communia ad publicum bonum ita promovendum, ut cives omnes idem cernere, idem audire, idem agere, eodemque collineare videantur. Jubet praeterea plebem patresque eadem laudare, et eadem vituperare, ac vicissim eisdem rebus laetari, eisdem contra dolere. Haec ille generatim. Exin species determinat; et cavendum, ait, est ne in civitate aliis inopia sit summa, aliis summae divitiae. Nihilo tamen minus (praeter magistratus, quorum plures ponit, et Principem unum, qui dignitate omnes, etiam optimates antecedat) quattuor civium classes distinguit, et primae, inquit, census esto quattuor minarum,[16] secundae trium, tertiae duarum, quartae denique unius.

XLIV. Regionem ex aequo metitur in partes quinque mille et quadraginta, quae totidem familiis attribuendae sunt, missa (nequis, si ei pars loco minus commodo contigerit, queri possit) sorte. Sortito etiam aedificatas in urbe domos dividi jubet patribusfamilias: ac danda est, ait, opera, ut aedes eodem semper numero constent, nec plures umquam sint, paucioresve: quam rerum aequabilitatem ne turbet avaritia, nemini, inquit, fas esto inhiare turpi lucro, quo mores generosi corrumpuntur. Nemo e contrario mendicare permittitor; nam qui bonus civis fuerit, et vixerit temperanter, usus recte ipsi publice concessis, numquam in paupertatem recidet, sin autem vitio egeat suo, ab urbe, totaque regione, expellendus est. (Lib. V. VI. XI. XII. de Legg.)

GUARANII.

XLV. Inter Guaranios quaedam erant communia, quaedam non item. Singulis attribuebatur certus agri modus, satis ille quidem amplus, ubi patresfamilias sibi suisque sererent frumentum Indicum (haec illorum annonae pars praecipua, nam triticum nostrum non valde curant) et varii generis legumina, edulesque radices, quarum alias vocant *Mandiò*, alias *Mandubì*, quae in ipso imi pedis stipite vaginas continent foetas nuce simili nostratibus amygdalis, terrestres item *batatas*, idest, tubera quaedam succosae medullae, saporisque gratissimi, appellant has illi *Yetì*. Colebant praeterea gossipium, et quas quisque optarat fruges indigenas. Haec omnia colonorum propria erant, dicebanturque *Abambae*, privata nimirum Indi uniuscujusque res. Boves e publico singulis patribusfamilias per vices commodabantur, ut suum illum agrum ararent. In oppido autem Candelariae (quoniam praedia trans flumen magnum Paranam sunt) lembi publici mane Indos in fundos suos mittebant gratis, et gratis vespere remittebant domum.

43. First, he wants those things which belong to individuals, such as eyes, ears, feet, hands, arms, to be essentially communal so as to promote the public good such that all citizens seem to see the same, hear the same, do the same, and have the same aim. Moreover, he commands that the masses and the elites praise the same things and condemn the same things, and in turn also rejoice about the same things, and by contrast lament the same things. He deals with these things categorically. Thereafter he focuses on particular examples; he says to guard against there being extreme poverty for some in the state while for others there is extreme wealth. Nonetheless, however, he distinguishes four classes of citizens (aside from the magistracies for which he establishes more categories, and one is the prince who surpasses all in rank, including the aristocrats): the property qualification for the first category will be four *minae*,[16] three *minae* for the second, two for the third, and finally one for the fourth.

44. He divides up the region equally into 5,040 parts, which are to be assigned to that same number of families by lot (so that no one can complain if the lot that falls to him is in a less favorable location). Once lots have been cast for houses built in the city, he commands them to be distributed to the heads of families; and care must be taken, he says, that the rooms in the houses be consistent in number, never greater nor less; so that greed does not throw the equitable apportionment of property into confusion, no one is allowed, he says, to long for shameful profit, through which the noble values are corrupted. On the other hand, no one is allowed to beg; for whoever is a good citizen and lives moderately, having correctly made use of the things publicly granted to him, will never fall into poverty; but if he is needy due to his own vices, he must be expelled from the city and from the entire region (*Laws* Books 5, 6, 11, and 12).

THE GUARANÍ

45. Among the Guaraní certain things were communal, others not. A certain quantity of land, large enough to be sure, was assigned to each; that is where the heads of families planted the grain of the Indies* for themselves and their family (this accounted for the majority of their annual yield, since they do not especially care for our wheat) and vegetables of various kinds, as well as edible roots, some of which they call "*mandi'o*" [yuca] and others "*manduvi*" [peanuts], which at the very base of the stalk contain pods filled with nuts similar to our almonds. There are also terrestrial "*batatas*," that is, knobs of juicy pulp with a most pleasant taste; they call these "*jety*" [sweet potato]. They also grew cotton and whatever indigenous fruits each one preferred. All this was the property of the farmers and was called "*avamba'é*," property that is indisputably private for each and every Indian. The communal oxen were lent by turns to individual heads of families so they could plow their own fields. In the city of Candelaria (given that its farms were located across the great Paraná River) in the early morning the public skiffs took the Indians to their plots free of charge and, again free of charge, returned them home in the evening.

* "Maize" or "corn."

XLVI. Ager privatus non erat idem semper, sed cum prior jam lassus vim amiserat, alius eligebatur, assignata singulis dynastis, eorumque clientibus portione sua. Cui modo dividundi agri simile quiddam Germanis olim fuit. "Agri (ait Cornelius Tacitus de mor. Germ.) pro numero cultorum ab universis per vices occupantur, quos mox inter se secundum dignationem partiuntur: facilitatem partiendi camporum spatia praestant. Arva per annos mutant, nec enim cum ubertate et amplitudine soli labore contendunt, ut pomaria conserant, et prata separent, et hortos rigent. Sola terrae seges imperatur."

XLVII. Praeter illa privata praedia erant alii agri communes minimum duo, alter, ubi frumentum cum legumine, alter, ubi gossipium colebatur: horum agrorum proventus, qui in horrea condebatur, erat publicus pro victu, et veste pupillorum, debiliumque, et puerorum, et puellarum, et viduarum, quibus alendis certa erat domus, domibus aliis amplior.[17] Aegris autem afferebatur quotidie ab aede Parochi caro elixa cum pulte, et pane triticeo.

XLVIII. Binis agris communibus ad certos anni dies oppidani publice operam dabant; omnes enim, etiam Praetor, et magistratus, Romanorum veterum more, rei rusticae studebant, id quod certe probasset magnus ille vir Thomas Morus, qui agricolas esse voluit, quotquot in suam illam Rempublicam *UTOPIAM* convenirent. Templum quoque, et privatas aedes, et ceteras oppidi substructiones communibus operis moliebantur reficiebantque Guaranii. Domus vero, non Platonis sorte, sed per magistratum, monito Curione, singulis assignabantur, easque retinebant patresfamilias sibi suisque, nisi, succrescente sobole, lar alius filiis uxorem ducentibus dandus esset.

XLIX. Quibus rebus fiebat, ut familiae omnes poene pares forent, et pari censa nisi quis forte agrum suum diligentius coleret, ac plura ex eo efferret; verum id et modicam inaequalitatem inducebat, et stimulo erat, aliunde, ut plenior ager vicini vicinum excitaret, ne se se otio desidiaeque traderet. De reliquo inter Guaranios mendicus erat nemo:[18] si enim aliquis laborare non poterat, publice alebatur; sin poterat, ad opus cogebatur. Jam vero Indorum alii, in id ipsum designati, armentum bovilli generis, quod singulis oppidis valde copiosum erat, tuebantur, alii equos publicos curabant, alii pascebant oves, alii aliis muniis praeficiebantur.

46. They did not always have the same plot of private land, rather when the first plot was exhausted and lost its fertility, another was chosen, with individual dynastic leaders and their followers being assigned their own portion. The Germans once had something similar to this way of dividing land. "The fields," says Cornelius Tacitus in *On the Customs of the Germans*, "are put to use by the whole community in turns according to the number of cultivators, among whom by and by the fields are apportioned according to rank. The expanse of open plains makes the partitioning easy. Their crops change annually, and due to the richness and amplitude of the soil they do not exert effort to plant orchards, separate meadows, or irrigate gardens. Grain is the only thing demanded of the land."

47. Beyond these private farms, there were at least two other communal fields: one where grain and vegetables were grown, the other had cotton: the produce from these fields, which was stored in granaries, was a public resource used to furnish food and clothing for orphans as well as disabled boys, girls, and widows, for whose care there was a special house, larger than the others.[17] As for the sick, meat cooked with porridge and wheat bread were brought to them daily from the parish priest's house.

48. On certain days of the year, the townspeople performed public service in the two communal fields; for all, even the Chief Executive and the magistrates, according to the custom of the ancient Romans, applied themselves to farming, which is something the great Thomas More certainly would have commended, given that he wanted all those who came to make up his republic, UTOPIA, to be farmers. The Guaraní also built and renovated the temple, the private houses, and all the other structures of the town with communal labor. The houses, however, were assigned to individuals not by Plato's lottery but by the authorities, with the advice of the priest. The heads of the family kept these houses for themselves and their families, unless, due to overflowing progeny, another household would have to be provided for sons who had taken a wife.

49. By these means, it happened that all the families were nearly equal and had equal assets, unless perhaps someone should cultivate his own field more diligently and so got more from it. Certainly, this introduced a bit of inequality, but on the other hand it served as a stimulus such that one neighbor's more abundant field would rouse another neighbor from giving himself over to leisure and idleness. As for the rest, no one was needy among the Guaraní;[18] because if someone was unable to work, he was supported publicly; but if he could work, he was compelled to work. On the other hand, some of the Indians, specially designated for this very task, looked after the herd of creole cattle, which were very abundant in each of the towns; others took care of the publicly available horses, others grazed the sheep, and others were given responsibility for other tasks.

L. Sepositis autem in horreum iis, quae supra diximus, quidquid e bonis publicis supererat, in onera publica impendebatur. Illinc prodibat annuum tributum in fiscum Bonaurensem. Erat illud unius aurei in capita: beneficio tamen Regis Catholici immunes erant plurimi, Caciquii nimirum, sive Dynastae, eorumque liberi majores natu, et foeminae omnes, et aeditui, et adolescentes minores annis duodeviginti, et viri majores annis quinquaginta. Illinc etiam impensae ad ornatum, cultumque templi, et quidquid denique pro publica re emendum erat. Quapropter hac agri communis, privatique vice diceres gentem Guaranicam esse similem apibus, quibus suum cuique mel est, et tectum, et victus, sed postquam communem finxerunt favum, et communiter ruri domique laborarunt.[19]

LI. Quod si Indis, quos in oppida coegeris, alimenta desint vel ipsorum negligentia, vel tua, exosi illi disciplinam in suas refugient silvas, et nota latibula, urgente fame, *venter* enim, ut optime ait Homerus, *magnum malum*. Mocovii feroces quondam, crudelesque Indi, qui Christiani dein optimi evasere, palam profitebantur inter alia, cur manus dederint, id fuisse, quod cum statorum imbrium tempore prohibiti a venando piscandoque aegre vitam sustentarent, sperarint fore, ut in opido S. Francisci Xaveri victus ipsis abbunde suppeteret: ac suppetiit quidem diligentia ac labore primi illorum cultoris Francisci Burgesii (quem diu novi) et sucessorum, qui parci in se ipsi, liberales erant in proselytos, quaesitis undique in eam rem provincialium civium subsidiis, uti olim diximus in vita Petri Joannis Andreu.

50. Moreover, after the items we mentioned above were set aside in the granary, whatever was left over from the public goods was spent on public obligations. From this source came the annual tribute to the Buenos Aires treasury. This was one gold piece per head. However, with the aid of the Catholic King, many were exempt: Caciques, or Dynastic Leaders, of course, and their adult children, all women, sacristans, adolescents under 18 years old, and men over fifty. From this source also came what was spent on the adornment and care of the temple, and whatever had to be bought for the public. For this reason, with this alternation of common fields and private fields, you might say that the Guaraní people are similar to bees, which all individually own their own honey, their home, their food, but only after they had built their communal honeycomb and worked communally in the fields and at home.[19]

51. Because if the Indians, whom you have gathered into towns, were to lack sustenance, either due to their own negligence or yours, they will hate what they have been taught and flee back to their forests and familiar refuges, with their hunger urging them on since "the belly," as Homer says very well, "is a great evil."* The Mocobí, formerly wild and fierce Indians who later turned out to be the best Christians, publicly confessed, among other things, why they had yielded; they said that it had been because during a period of persistent rains, they could barely keep themselves alive because they had been prevented from hunting and fishing, and they hoped perhaps that in the town of San Francisco Javier there would be an abundant store of food for them. And indeed, there was enough thanks to the diligence and labor of their first cultivator, Francisco Burgés (whom I knew for a long time) and his successors, who though frugal themselves were generous with the new converts, looking everywhere for aid in this matter for the citizens of the province, as I said in the biography of Pedro Juan Andréu [Orlandis].†

* This quotation actually comes from the comic poet Alexis as reported in Athenaeus's *Learned Banqueters* 10.19.

† In the 1791 volume of biographies.

LII. S. PIUS. V. Pontif. Max. Religioni tuendae, propagandaeque, diem noctemque intentus, cum omnia circumspiceret, in Occidentis quoque solis plagas paternum studium, et sacras curas extendit, scripsitque Regi Catholico: *oportere neophitos ali collectis eleemosynis more nascentis Ecclesiae, vel etiam pasci e regiis vectigalibus, ne fame compulsi ad pristinos mores, et vitia relabantur.*[20] Haec dignus ille Christi Vicarius, qui sancta prudentia, et animarum insigni zelo, vel osorum alioqui Romanae Cathedrae ita admirationem movit, ut eum magnopere laudet celebris ille Anglus Baco de Verulamio.[21] Paulus vero gentium Apostolus, quam sedulus fuit, et quanta egit, ne deessent necessaria recens conversis ad fidem? idque ex mandato Petri, et Jacobi, et Joannis, ut ipse testatur, qui omnia ejus, et Barnabae, acta probarunt, *tantum* (ait) *ut pauperum memores essemus, quod etiam solicitus fui hoc ipsum facere.*[22] Etenim ceu puerulus nec ali potest, nec vivere sine nutricis lacte, sic Indi, *sicut modo geniti* in Christo *infantes, ut crescant in salutem,*[23] paratis a cultore suo egent cibis; si hi desint, illi aures obstruunt: nam *venter praecepta non audit,* ut ait Seneca. (Epist. XXI.)

De nuptiis.

PLATO

LIII. Plato, vir ille ingenii maximi, deceptus trito Graecis proverbio Κοìνα φιλῶν, omnia amicorum communia, in libris de *Republica* plane desipuit, voluit enim uxores etiam, et liberos communes esse: atque id quidem, non quo ipse mulierosus esset, coelebs quippe et castus perpetuo vixit, sed quia commentus sibi est ex illa communione rerum omnium ingentia quaedam et praeclara bona: sic namque, ajebat, cives eximie inter se amabunt; puerique viros colent omnes tamquam patres suos; virique vicissim pueros omnes tamquam suos filios diligent.[24] Quin etiam desiderio illo malesano omnia cum omnibus communicandi progressus ultra, praecipit feminas militare cum viris, puellas cum matribus, atque utrasque bellica, quoad ejus aetas, et vires ferant, obire munia.

LIV. Tamen siquis *Reipublicae* libros attente legerit, sentiet mecum forsan, communionem illam foeminarum non omnibus promiscue concessam a Platone, sed tantum *legum custodibus,* quos civium optimos, decorique et aequi retinentissimos fore sibi finxit. Sed quidquid de istorum virtute, et moderatione praedicet, ac speret, dicendus est Plato, acerrimus ceteroquin veri indagator, non vidisse illud, quod ne vatem quidem Horatium fugit:

> Est modus in rebus, sunt certi denique fines,
> Quos ultra citraque nequit consistere rectum.

52. Pope Pius V was day and night intent on defending and propagating the faith and, since he paid attention to everything, he extended his paternal zeal and religious concerns even to western lands; and wrote to the Catholic King [Felipe II]: "that the neophytes ought to be fed with alms collected in the manner of the nascent church, or else be fed from royal tax revenues, so that they are not driven by hunger to slip back into their former habits and vices."[20] This was said by that honorable Vicar of Christ who with holy foresight and extraordinary zeal for souls so stirred the admiration of those who otherwise hated the Roman Throne that the renowned Englishman [Sir Francis] Bacon, Lord Verulam, praised him earnestly.[21] Indeed, how diligent was Paul, Apostle to the Gentiles, and how much did he do so that recent converts to the faith would not lack necessities!? And this by order of Peter, James, and John, as he himself attests. They approved of all of his and Barnabas's deeds "so long as," he says, "we remember the poor, which was the very thing I was concerned with doing."[22] For just as a small child can neither be nourished nor live without the wet nurse's milk, so the Indians, "as infants newly born" in Christ, need food provided by their cultivator "in order to grow toward salvation";[23] if this is lacking, they close their ears; for, as Seneca says, "the belly does not listen to commands" (*Epistle* 21).

On Marriage

PLATO

53. Plato, that man of supreme ingenuity, ensnared by the adage common among the Greeks, Κoὶνα φιλῶν, "everything is common among friends," was completely delirious in the books of the *Republic*, for he proposed that wives and children should be communal; and it was not because he was a womanizer, for in fact he was perpetually unmarried and chaste, but because he convinced himself that out of this community ownership of all things would arise certain prodigious and splendid goods: thus, he said, citizens will love each other exceptionally; young men will respect all men as if they were their own fathers; and in turn men will love all boys as if they were their own sons.[24] Indeed, driven further by that unhealthy desire to share everything with everyone, he bids women to do their military service with men, daughters with their mothers, and both to engage in wartime duties, as much as age allows.

54. However, if someone were to read the books of the *Republic* carefully, perhaps he would feel along with me that this sharing of women was not granted by Plato to all indiscriminately, but only to the "guardians of the laws," whom he conceived to be the best citizens and greatest defenders of what is proper and fair. But whatever he might predict and hope regarding the virtue and moderation of such men, Plato, an otherwise most shrewd seeker of the truth, has to be called out for not having seen what did not escape the notice of the inspired poet Horace:

> There is measure in things; and, moreover, there are certain limits,
> on either side of which right cannot exist.

LV. Non vidit ille mala infanda, quae ex ejusmodi communione oritura erant. Quo loco subit mihi cogitatio nostri saeculi philsophorum, qui omnia hominis officia, et bene ordinandae Reipublicae statuta e sola naturae lege definiri posse blaterant. Nam si sumus Philosophus, qui totus erat in speculandis naturae praeceptis, atque hac causa longas, laboriosasque peregrinationes obiit, ut sapientissimos quosque viros de recti aequique origine consuleret, turpiter nihilo minus erravit, quid fiet aliis? quid vano recentium sophistarum gregi, qui prae Platone caecus est? *Natura,* ait optime Seneca, *semina nobis scientiae dedit, scientiam non dedit.*[25]

LVI. Impotens sui amor, violentae corporis appetitiones, praesens mali occasio, visa aliorum vitia; virtutis arduum iter, *spatiosa, et lata via, quae ducit ad perditionem,* propensio in vetitum, prava educatio, mores incompositi, libido, ira ambitio, ceterae animi pestes, et ingenitae affectiones, difficultas denique veri reperiundi, ita rationis lumen obscurant, ut mens vix illud cernat, facileque caliget. Atque hinc discors hominum ingenium, et perversa indoles eorum, *qui dicunt malum, bonum; et bonum malum: ponentes tenebras lucem, et lucem tenebras: ponentes amarum in dulce, et dulce in amarum.*[26] Cujus generis quot nobis exempla suppeditat vel vetus, vel novus Orbis? Quot et fuerunt olim, et nunc sunt gentes, quarum apud alias una eademque res, unus idemque vitae modus, et mos, laudi est, apud alias vituperio. Ubi igitur, quae tam clara dicitur, rationis vis? ubi ejus lumen, quo se se minuti philosophi se se omnia et praecipienda, et vetanda, in rectam hominum institutionem perspicere posse confidunt?[27] *Sapientia* hic, *sapientia* necessaria est, quae *descendat a patre luminum.*

LVII. Plato in libris de legibus multo cautior prudentiorque est, quam in *Republica*: communionem faeminarum non ponit, sed singulis viris singulas uxores dat. De aetate autem sponsorum, et de conjugio sic statuit. Cavendum, ait, nequis hac in re hallucinetur, et erret. Norit probe paterfamilias cui filiam collocet, et quam, et a quibus, nurum domo excipiat. Quando aliquis, inquit, quinque et viginti jam natus annos videt quamdam e civibus puellis, quam existimat congruentem sibi sociam fore ad generis propagationem, eam (licet) honeste ducat, et caste amet.

55. He did not see the unspeakable evils that were going to arise from that sort of communalism. And on this point an idea comes to mind belonging to philosophers of our own age who babble that all the duties of mankind and the statutes of a well-ordered Republic can be determined based on natural law alone. For if the greatest Philosopher, who was completely devoted to examining the precepts of nature and to that end undertook extensive and wearisome pilgrimages in order to consult the very wisest men on the origin of what is right and fair, nevertheless made reproachful errors, what will happen with everyone else? What of the vain flock of modern-day sophists who are blind in comparison with Plato? "Nature," the great Seneca says, "gave us the seed of knowledge, but it did not give us knowledge."[25]

56. Uncontrolled self-love, violent appetites of the body, the occasion for wrong-doing that presents itself, seeing the vices of others, the arduous path of virtue, "the wide-open road that leads to perdition," the propensity for the forbidden, improper education, irregular habits, lust, anger, ambition, other plagues and inborn dispositions of the soul, and the difficulty, finally, of discovering the truth—these things so obscure the light of reason that the mind scarcely perceives it and is quickly enveloped in complete darkness. And hence the inconsistent character of humans and their perverse nature, "who call evil good and good evil; considering darkness to be light and light to be darkness; regarding the bitter as sweet and the sweet bitter."[26] How many examples of this kind does the world, whether old or new, have in store for us?! How many peoples were there before and are there now for whom one and the same matter, one and the same way of life and customs, are a source of praise for some but of censure for others? Where, then, is the force of reason, which is said to be so clear? Where is its light, by which petty philosophers are confident that they themselves are able to perceive everything that must be commanded and prohibited for the correct habituation of human beings?[27] In this circumstance it is "wisdom" that is necessary, "the wisdom that descends from the Father of lights" [St. Bonaventure, *Talks on the Six Days of Creation* II.1].

57. In the books of the *Laws* Plato is much more cautious and prudent than in the *Republic*. He does not propose sharing women but instead assigns individual wives to individual husbands. Regarding the age of betrothal and marriage, he establishes the following: Take care, he says, that no one goes astray and makes a mistake; the head of the family knows perfectly to whom he gives his daughter in marriage, and which daughter-in-law he receives in his household and from whom he receives her. When someone already twenty-five years old, he says, meets a particular young woman from the community and he considers that she would be suitable for him as a partner for making a family, he should marry her properly (no objections here!) and love her purely.

LVIII. Nuptias, pergit dicere, tales quisque contrahat, quales sibi optant viri prudentes, et pudici: atque ob hanc causam, qui animi ferocioris est, curet, ut quam quietissimorum parentum filiam (cujusvis illa sit classis,) petat; qui vero remissiorem naturam sortitus est, strenuam actuosamque sibi affinitatem asciscat. Una enim esse debet communis, et potior ratio connubii, ut quisque, non quod sibi jucundissimum sit, matrimonium sectetur, sed quod civitati utilissimum. Nuptiale autem tempus puellarum esto a sexto decimo ad vicesimum annum.

LIX. Dotes eae sunto, quae dantis accipientisque temperantiae conveniunt, non luxui; praeferendae enim res necessariae splendori sunt. Quocirca, qui pro dote dederint, aut acceperint, quod quinquaginta drachmas excedit, ita mulctentur, ut (pro conditione census) alius minam, alius sesquiminam, alius duas minas fisco pendat. Quidquid autem largitionis nomine vel sponsus prodigus det, vel avara accipiat sponsa, id totum templo consecretur judicum sententia.

LX. Ad convivium nuptiale non plures quam quinque amici, et totidem amicae e paterno genere vocantur: e cognatis autem, et propinquis par esto numerus. Qui ditissimus sit ad epulum expendet minam, non tam dives semiminam, ac sic deincepe proportione sic servata, ut quo quisque minor censu sit, minores huic fiant in apparando convivio impensae. Ceterum epulantes bibant citra ebrietatem, et hanc vitent maxime sponsus et sponsa, utpote qui gravis status gravem in primis conditionem ineunt: atque ita fere accidit, ut ab ebriis conjugibus non nisi monstrosa membris nascatur proles, futura dein moribus corruptis. (Lib. VI. de Legg.)

GUARANII.

LXI. Fiebant matrimonia inter Guaranios sine iis turbis, quae alibi aliquando cooriuntur. Curiones persuaserunt patribusfamilias, ut, cum filius jam natus erat XVII. annos, ei uxorem dignam quaererent, et virum vicissim designarent filiae quintum decimum annum agenti. Haec aetas optima visa est, ne, si conjugium diutius impediretur, e longiore mora succresceret adolescentibus occasio luxuriandi, et ne, contra, si immaturius properaretur, ab imbecilli mente, mobilique animo, novorum conjugum, perturbatio domestici ordinis, et casti convictus, nasceretur.[28]

58. He goes on saying that everyone should arrange marriages of the sort that prudent and modest men desire for themselves. And for this reason, a man who is headstrong should take care to seek out the daughter of very easygoing parents (whatever her social class may be); but a man dealt a more relaxed nature should join with an active and vivacious partner. For there should be a universal and preferred rationale for wedlock: namely that one should pursue the marriage that is most useful to the community, not the one that is most pleasing to himself. Marriageable age of young women should be between sixteen and twenty years.

59. Dowries should correspond to the giver's and the recipient's sense of moderation rather than be luxurious. For necessities are to be preferred to glamor. Wherefore, whoever gives or receives something whose value exceeds fifty drachmas as a dowry, should be fined such that they pay one, one and a half, or two *minae* (according to their economic situation). Whatever either a prodigal groom should give in the name of largess, or a greedy bride accept, is dedicated in its entirety to the temple according to the determination of the judges.

60. No more than five of the groom's friends and the same number of the bride's friends are invited to the wedding feast by the groom's father. Moreover for relatives and kin* the number should be the same. The very rich should spend one *mina* on the banquet, the not so rich, a half *mina* and so on with the proportion maintained such that the lower the income, the lower the spending should be on providing the banquet. Otherwise, diners should drink short of inebriation, and the bride and groom should avoid this most of all, since they are in a serious situation embarking on a particularly serious responsibility. And it commonly happens that offspring are not born from drunken spouses without deformed limbs, destined thereafter to corrupt habits (*Laws* Book 6).

THE GUARANÍ

61. Among the Guaraní, marriages happened without the tumult that sometimes arises elsewhere. The priests persuaded the heads of families to seek out a wife worthy for a son when he was seventeen years old and, in turn, indicate a husband for a daughter, when she was fifteen years old. This age seemed best so that an impulse for friskiness does not build up in adolescents as a result of a longer wait, in the event coupling is prevented any further, and so that, on the other hand, should one be too prematurely hasty, a disruption of the domestic order and pure intimacy would be born from the young couple's feeble minds and fickle wills.[28]

* Translating Plato's terms συγγενής and οἰκεῖος at *Laws* 6.775a.

LXII. Scriptor Regni Paraguayci Bernardus Ibanius (quicum diu vixi, dum piae mecum militiae secutus signa est) acerrime Curiones Guaranicos exagitat, quod tamdiu conjugia clientium protraherent, imminente interim periculo inuptis e desiderio naturae lasciviendi. Quid huic homini facies? Si Parochi illi Indis persuasissent, ut adolescentes quarto decimo anno, et puellae duodecimo (quod Canonicum tempus est) ad nuptias se se sisterent, traduxisset per ora hominum Ibanius ipse Guaranicos cultores tamquam stultos planeque rudes (hanc ipsis laudem liberaliter attribuit) declamassetque, non satis eos intelligere sacrarum legum vim, et Pontificum statuta: plusculum quippe morandum esse cum neophytis, quousque firmior illis animus, et maturius judicium sit ad sacramentum, cujus conditio, et nodus perpetuus est.

LXIII. Equidem sic reor vix ulla alia in re consideratius egisse et cautius Curiones Guaranicos, quam in dispiciendo quid opus factu esset de pristinis Indorum connubiis, ut inde statuerent, quid usu confirmandum esset. Tres initio sententiae fuerunt: prima probabat, tamquam legitimas, nuptias, quas Guaranii inierant cum uxore primaria, quam vocabant *Cherembicò*: altera sententia tam istius *Cherembicò* primariae, quam secundariarum (*Cheaguaza nomine*) uxorum an pellicum? conjugium reprobabat, ob levitatem, qua eas mutabant viri, e quo facile conjici posset, matrimonia illorum stabilia non esse, neque pacto vincta perpetuo, etiamsi quidam in amanda *Cherembicò* constantiores essent: sententia tertia Caciquiorum, sive dynastarum connubia censebat irrita ob facilitatem repudiandi faeminas, quas duxerant; clientium vero valida, quod hi firmius alerent domi uxorem suam. Disceptatio diu tenuit, eoque denique deducta est, ut, oratore Joanne de Lugo Cardinali (poterantne uti peritiore rei moralis interprete?) consulerent Urbanum VIII. Pontif. Max. quid ipsis in re admodum implexa agendum esset? an cogendi recens fide instructi ad retinendam faeminam, quam primo sibi adjunxerant, an vero sinendi aliam quamvis in facie Ecclesiae ducere.[29]

62. The author of the *Kingdom of Paraguay*, Bernardo Ibáñez [de Echavarri] (with whom I lived long ago, while he marched with me under the banner of the holy service) vehemently criticizes the Guaraní Priests because they delayed the marriages of their followers for so long despite the looming danger for the unwed of being overcome by lust in the meantime due to natural desires. What do you do with this person? If the parish priests had persuaded the Indians to have adolescent boys at fourteen and girls at twelve (which is the Canonical time) present themselves for marriage, Ibáñez himself would have made a spectacle of the Guaraní cultivators as stupid and completely backward (he liberally bestows this "praise" on these very men) and would have cried that they did not sufficiently comprehend the sense of the ecclesiastical laws and Papal statutes: naturally, it was necessary to wait a bit longer with the neophytes until their spirit would be more steadfast and judgment more ripe for a sacrament, the terms and obligations of which are perpetual.

63. For my part, I judge that there was scarcely any other matter in which the Guaraní priests acted with more consideration and caution than in reflecting on what it was necessary to do about the original Indian marriages since they would thereby establish what would become fixed in practice. At first there were three opinions. The first approved as legitimate the marriages that the Guaraní had entered upon with their first wife, whom they called *Che rembirekó*. The second opinion rejected the union with that first *Che rembirekó*, in favor of the second wives (or mistresses?) called *Che aguasá*, due to the fickleness with which the men abandoned those first wives. From this it could be easily conjectured that marriages between them were not stable nor bound by a perpetual agreement, although some were more steadfast in loving their *Che rembirekó*. The third opinion counted the marriages of Caciques, or Dynastic Leaders, to be void due to the ease of repudiating the women they had married; but it counted as valid the marriages of their followers, because they supported their wives at home more steadfastly. The dispute lasted for a long time and finally reached the point that, with Cardinal Juan de Lugo serving as embassy (could they have had a more skillful interpreter of moral matters?!), they consulted Pope Urban VIII about what should be done in such a complex matter. Whether those recently inducted into the faith should be compelled to retain the wife to whom they had first joined themselves or instead be allowed to marry anyone they please in the eyes of the Church?[29]

LXIV. Atque hinc velim arguas, quam circumspecti fuerint Curiones Guaranici super neophytorum matrimonio. Et tamen eos bonus ille scriptor Regni Paraguayci stupidos et indoctos praedicat. Sed ommittamus hominem iracundum, qui fervens odio, et felle, in res Guaranicas invectus est, et Reges fecit, quos vix viros ducit . . . Postquam parentibus filiisque convenerat inter se de optanda affinitate, monitus Curio sponsum et sponsam examinabat seorsum de libero consensu, praelegebatque dein in templo impedimenta, quae inofficiosas, atque irritas reddunt nuptias. Quod ad dotem attinet, cum fortunarum parfere modus esset, nihil illic negotii. Patellae aliquot, ollae, amphorae, vestesque gossipinae, et pensilis hamaca, atque alia, id genus, satis erant sponso, qui sponsae haud multo pretiosiora reddebat in usum familiae. His Guaranicis dotibus Germanorum veterum dotes fuerunt similes: *munera non ad delicias quaesita,* ait C. Tacitus, *nec quibus nova nupta comatur, sed boves, frenatus equus, et scutum.*[30] Atque haec quidem non sponsa sponso, sed sponsus dabat sponsae, ob causas, quas idem Tacitus affert.

LXV. Convivium nuptiale fiebat more Platonico; intererant consanguinei affinesque: et quoniam uno die multi saepe initiabant se se Sacramento, dabantur e re communi ad epulum obsonia quaedam, praeter illa, quae singuli habebant domi. Omnia autem ibi et temperata, et honesta. Josephus Cardiel, qui in oppido S. Francisci Borgiae uno olim die nonaginta paribus sponsorum bene precatus fuerat jusso ritu, voluit deinde visere eorum convivia, et continere vix potuit (ut ipse narrat) lacrimas ob modestiam, ac moderationem, qua convivae omnes intra justae laetitiae fines publice vescebantur.

De educatione.

PLATO

LXVI. Animus, ait, vel praestantissimus natura, si male fuerit educatus, evadit pessimus, idque argumentis, exemplisque confirmat. Res fere omnis pendet, inquit, a parentibus, atque hac causa cavendum ipsis maxime est, ne filii filiaeque quiddam videant, quod inficere eorum mores possit, et mentem et oculos adhuc mali nescios in malum trahat. Ob id ipsum praecipit, nequis artificum fingat simulacrum aliquod, pingatve effigiem, e qua civium quispiam vitium tuendo discat. Optime in hanc rem poeta Juvenalis cavens puerorum institutioni cecinit.

64. At this point I should like to make clear how circumspect the Guaraní priests were with respect to the marriage of neophytes. And yet that good man, the author of the *Kingdom of Paraguay*, proclaims that they are stupid and ignorant. But let us say nothing of the irritable man who, seething with hatred and venom, inveighed against Guaraní matters and turned those he hardly considered men into kings.* After an agreement had been reached between parents and children on the preferred marital alliance, the priest would be notified and would question the groom and the bride separately about whether they were freely consenting; then in the church he would read out the impediments that would render the marriage invalid and void. As concerns the dowry, since the extent of everyone's fortunes was just about equal, there was nothing to negotiate there. Some dishes, pots, jugs, along with cotton clothing, a hanging hammock, and other things of that sort were enough for the groom, who gave to his bride things for household use that were not much more costly. The dowries of the ancient Germans were similar to Guaraní dowries. "The gifts were not sought for delight," says Tacitus, "nor were they things with which the new bride would be adorned, but rather oxen, a horse with its bridle, and a shield."[30] And the bride would not give these things to the groom, but the groom to the bride, for the reasons Tacitus himself reports.

65. The wedding banquet would happen according to the Platonic custom. Blood relatives and in-laws would take part; and since it would often happen that many would be initiating themselves into the Sacrament on a single day, certain foods would be contributed to the feast from the common store in addition to the things that individuals had at home. But everything there was modest and proper. José Cardiel, who once in a single day had blessed ninety couples in the town of San Francisco de Borja in the prescribed ceremony, later wanted to visit their banquets and he could scarcely contain his tears (as he himself recounts) at the modesty and moderation with which all the guests were feasting all together within the bounds of righteous joyfulness.

On Education

PLATO

66. The spirit, he says, even the most outstanding in nature, should it be badly educated, turns out exceptionally bad; and he confirms this with arguments and examples. Almost the whole matter, he adds, depends on the parents and that is why they must be especially on guard that their sons and daughters do not see anything that could infect their habits and drag toward evil those minds and eyes thus far ignorant of it. For this very reason he directs that none of the artists should sculpt any likeness or paint any image from which any citizen might become acquainted with vice by beholding it. On this matter the poet Juvenal concerned about the education of children sang best:

* A reference to Ibáñez's characterization of Paraguay as a kingdom.

Velocius, et citius nos
Corrumpunt vitiorum exempla domestica magnis
Cum subeant animos auctoribus.

... Quoniam dociles imitandis
Turpibus ac pravis omnes sumus ...

Nil dictu foedum, risuque haec limina tangat,
Intra quae puer est. Procul hinc, procul inde puellae
Lenonum, et cantus pernoctantis parasiti.
Maxima debetur puero reverentia, siquid
Turpe paras, nec tu pueri contempseris annos,
Sed peccaturo obsistat tibi filius infans ...

Gratum est, quod patriae civem populoque dedisti,
Si facis, ut patriae sit idoneus, utilis agris.
Utilis et bellorum, et pacis rebus agendis.
Plurimum enim intererit, quibus artibus, et quibus hunc tu
Moribus instituas.[31]

Et sigillatim matres monet:

Scilicet expectas, ut tradat mater honestos
Aut alios mores, quam quos habet?[32]

Haec Juvenalis consona Platoni, cujus e libris, ac doctrina, vates et Philosophi Romani creverunt.[33]

LXVII. Quemadmodum sine pastore vagari agni non debent, ne forte errent, incidantque in lupum, sic nec decet, ait Plato, pueros seorsum agere sine probo paedagogo, qui eos puniat, siquid peccent. Itaque optimus eligatur vir, qui pueris educandis praesit. Adducendi autem sunt omnes a triennio quotidie ad sacrificium, et praeterea ad sollemnitatem menstruam, quae a propria illorum tribu per vices celebrabitur; et tum quidem nutrices, magistraeque modestiam, immodestiamve singulorum observanto, et corrigunto quidquid ab alumnis suis male fiat. Post sex vero aetatis annos foeminae a maribus separantor; et deinceps pueri cum pueris, puellae cum puellis versantor separatim, ac navanto operam artibus honestis.

> More speedily and sooner
> do domestic examples of vice corrupt us
> since they enter our souls with great authority.
>
> Since we are all easily taught
> to imitate foul and depraved examples
>
> Let nothing disgusting to say or laugh at touch this threshold,
> within which there is a child. Far away, far from there the pimps'
> girls should stay along with the night-long freeloader's song.
> The greatest reverence is owed to your boy, if you are planning
> anything foul, you should not disregard the years of your son,
> but let your speechless son be an obstacle to you who are about to sin.
>
> Thanks are due because you gave a citizen to the fatherland and the people,
> If you make him suitable for the fatherland, he will be useful in the fields,
> useful for the things that need doing in war and in peace.
> For it will make the greatest difference with which skills and habits
> you train him up.[31]

And he advises mothers separately:

> Of course, do you expect a mother to instill respectable habits
> if those are different from the ones she has?[32]

On these things Juvenal is in harmony with Plato, on whose books and doctrine the Roman poets and Philosophers grew up.[33]

67. Just as lambs should not wander without a shepherd so that they do not go astray by chance and encounter a wolf, it is also not appropriate, says Plato, for children to go off separately without an upright pedagogue, who can correct them if they go astray. Thus, an exceptional man is selected to oversee the children being educated. From the age of three, everyone must be brought every day to the rite of sacrifice and additionally to the monthly festival which is celebrated in turns by each of their individual tribes. And then let the nurses and teachers observe the modesty or immodesty of individuals and correct whatever was done wrongly by their pupils. After six years of age the females will be separated from the males and thereafter boys will go about with boys and, separately, girls with girls; and then they can fully apply themselves to the liberal arts.

LXVIII. Matres porro nutricesque curent, ut pueri puellaeque utraque aeque utantur manu: nam dexterae potiorem usum dare, quam sinistrae, officit rectae institutioni, abususque est quodammodo contra naturam, quae nos docet sine ullo discrimine ingredi pede pariter dextro laevoque. In libris de *Republica* vult pueros communi in domo ali, educarique separatos a parentibus; id vero non praecipit in Legum opere, sed tantum gymnasia ponit publica, ubi communiter doceatur puerorum grex legere, et scribere, et numerare: vetat exin, ne puellae domi otio corrumpantur, et deliciis affluant, sed se se labore exerceant utili. (De Repub. lib. V. de Legg. lib. II. III. etc.)

GUARANII.

LXIX. Educatio et disciplina Guaraniorum erat haec. Pueri partim domi (ne parentes privarentur voluptate illa et gaudio, quod illis affert praesentia liberorum) partim publice educabantur. Habitabant per noctabantque apud suos. Sub auroram excitati tympanorum pulsu ibant ad templum, recitatisque sacris precibus cum Catechesi (binis eorum voce praeeuntibus) intererant sacro Missae. Egressis sancta ex aede apponebatur in atrio Curionis jentaculum de re communi, eoque refecti, si quidem erat profestus dies, ducebantur a sene duce, et censore morum ad opus aetati conveniens, ad purgandum (exempli causa) noxiis herbis agrum publicum, vel ad vias impeditas saxis, arborumve lapsis frondibus, aut luto caecas, aperiendas. Quo autem is labor gratior eis accideret, ferebant secum inter laetos tibiarum sonitus statunculam S. Isidori Agricolae, innitentem basi, quam bini excipiebant vectes ad gestandum. Ubi ad locum designati laboris pervenerant Divi simulacrum propatula in parte, unde conspici posset, locabant; et ipsi jussum urgebant opus.

LXX. Vespere ad signum aeris e turri sacra conveniebant rursus in templum pro obeunda Catechesi, qua illos exercebat Curio, vel ejus collega. Catechesin excipiebant Virginei Rosarii preces, quibus omnes intererant cum binis iis Sacerdotibus (quos modo diximus) qui ante aram maximam nixi genibus orabant simul cum populo, illorumque alteruter, recitatis jam Litaniis, pium officium extrema precatione concludebat. Post id pueri, accepta merenda ex atrio Curionis, revertebantur domum parte aliqua laboris matrem quisque suam levaturi.

68. In turn mothers and wet nurses take care that boys and girls use both hands equally, for giving the right hand more use than the left obstructs proper training and, in a certain way, is an abuse against nature which teaches us to walk with the right and the left foot equally without any distinction. In the *Republic*, Plato wants children to be raised in a communal home and to be educated apart from their parents, but he does not prescribe this in the *Laws*. He just proposes public gyms where the flock of children communally learn to read, write, and count. Beyond that, he prohibits girls from being corrupted by leisure time at home and abounding in delicacies but rather they should busy themselves with useful work (*Republic* Book 5; *Laws* Books 2, 3, etc.).

THE GUARANÍ

69. The education and teaching of the Guaraní was as follows: The children were educated partly at home (so that the parents would not be deprived of that delight and joy that the presence of their children brings to them) and partly in the community. They would reside and spend the entire night at their parents' homes. Awoken by the ringing of the bells at dawn, they would go to church and participate in holy Mass by reciting holy prayers along with the catechism (with two of them leading the recitation). Breakfast was served to them at public expense in the priest's atrium as they left the sanctuary. After being reinvigorated by this, if it was a non-holiday, they would be led by an elderly leader and the supervisor of conduct to do work appropriate for their age; for example, clearing the community field of harmful weeds, or opening up roads blocked by stones or fallen tree branches or washed out by mud. And so that this work would strike them as more agreeable, amid the happy sound of flutes they would bring with them a statuette of San Isidro the Laborer, resting on a base supported by two poles so that it could be carried. When they had reached the location of their designated task, they placed the image of the saint in an open space where it could be seen and they pressed on with the prescribed work.

70. In the afternoon, at the sound of the bell in the holy tower, they would come back to the church for Catechesis, in which the priest or his companion would drill them. Following the Catechesis was the prayers of the Virgin's rosary, in which everyone took part together with the two priests (whom we just mentioned), who would kneel before the main altar and pray together with the people; one of the two, once the litanies had been recited, would conclude the holy service with a final prayer. After this, the children took a snack in the priest's atrium and returned home, each one trying to relieve his mother from some part of her work.

LXXI. Puellarum, quibus item praeerat gravis et vigil custos, seorsum a pueris eadem erat institutio, nisi quod levior illis committebatur labor, qualis erat vel decerpere e gossipii arbusculis hiantes calices, quibus molle vellus includitur, vel abigere oris murmure, manumque percussione, e praedio publico voraces psittacos, avesque alias, quarum illac ingentia examina. Et quoniam nec puellis, nec faeminarum ulli patebat aditus in atrium Curionis, illis matutina et vespertina corporis refectio foris curabatur.

LXXII. Pueri, et puellae separatim agebant semper (non solum ab anno aetatis sexto, ut vult Plato) etiam in templo, cujus quattuor descriptae erant partes, una pro viris, altera pro adultis faeminis, tertia pro pueris, quarta pro puellis, neminique harum classium licebat alieno in loco consistere:[34] quin et in aedem sacram alia intrabant porta viri puerique, alia matres puellaeque, idque valebat ad morum honestatem, modestiamque et silentium, quod erat summum in rebus divinis. Narramus, quae vidimus.

LXXIII. Legere, et scribere, cum calculorum ratione non omnes pueri docebantur, sed tot dumtaxat, quot oppidi bonum poscebat, ut ex eo dein numero eligerentur Praetor, et senatores, et magistratus, et scribae, et procuratores publici, et aeditui, et medici. Erant autem elementarii pueri isti e familiis praecipue Caciquiorum, primorumque Indorum, quibus is honor prae ceteris habebatur. Legebant autem optime seu Guaranice, seu Hispane, seu Latine, eorumque multi scribebant elegantissime, ut nihil cederent vel pulcherrimis typographorum formis.

LXXIV. Guaranii olim in numerandi ordine vix quicquam promoverant, Quaternae illis tantum erant voces in numeros, *Petei* videlicet, unus; *Mocoi,* duo; *Mohapì,* tres; *Jrundì* quattuor. Quinque *peteipo*: id est, manus una propter quinos dignitos: decem erant *mocoipo*: Viginti autem ambae simul manus, et ambi pedes. Quod si magna esset rerum multitudo dicebant generatim *Hetà,* multa; sin vero plurima *Hetahetà,* geminata vocula, qui modus apud eos vim superlationis habet, iterant enim nomen, ut id, quod eo exprimunt, optimum indicent. Alias simplici voci addunt *etè,* ut *Heta etè,* valde multi, *Etè* enim idem est ac valde. Quod si rei numerus iniri non possit, sic istud enunciant *Ndipapahàbi,* innumerabilis.

LXXV. Mensem ab Lunae crescentis ortu inchoabant, ut Hebraei, et, ut Graeci, ab eadem luna, nomen dabant mensi. dicunt enim illi τετράμηνον (quod exemplo sit) quattuor Lunas, sive menses. Ceterum Guaranica illa numerandi ratio impedita admodum est, si qua rei summa magis magisque crescat[35] Idcirco visum est Curionibus Jesuitis oportere disci a neophytis numeros Hispanos. Res facili negotio successit.

71. The education of the girls, over whom a serious and vigilant guardian would also preside, although separate from the boys was the same except that the labor that would be entrusted to them was lighter, such as plucking the open bolls, in which the soft fleece is enclosed, from the cotton plants, or by shouting or clapping their hands driving off the voracious parrots and other birds from the public farm, since there are enormous flocks of them there. And since entry to the priest's atrium is not allowed for girls nor any females, morning and afternoon refreshment of the body would be provided for them outside.

72. Boys and girls would always (not only from the age of six, as Plato wants) do things separately, even in the church whose four parts had been divided up: one for the men, another for the adult women, the third for the boys, and the fourth for girls; no one from these groups was permitted to be in the others' space.[34] Indeed, men and boys would even enter the holy church through one door, and mothers and girls through another. This was beneficial for their modesty and the integrity of their character as well as for maintaining silence, which was extremely important in divine matters. I describe what I have seen.

73. Not all children were taught reading, writing, and basic mathematics, but only so many as the good of the city demanded so that from this number the Chief Executive, councilors, magistrates, clerks, public treasurers, sacristans, and doctors were chosen. These elementary-school children were mainly from the families of Caciques and leading Indians for whom this honor was reserved over others. They read perfectly in Guaraní, Spanish, and Latin, and many of them wrote with such elegant handwriting that it was in no way inferior to the most beautiful of the printers' characters.

74. In times past, the Guaraní had made hardly any progress on their system of counting. They only had four words for numbers, namely: *peteî* is "one"; *mokôi* is "two"; *mbohapy* is "three"; *irundy* is "four." "Five" is *peteî po*; which means "one hand" on account of its five fingers: "ten" was *mokôi po*; "twenty" was both hands and both feet all together. But if there was a great multitude of items, they would generally say: *hetá* meaning "many"; if they were even more: *Hetahetá*, doubling the words; this form has the sense of superlative for them; for they repeat the word to indicate that what they describe with it is the best. At other times they add *eté* to simple words, as in *hetá eté* meaning "very many." For *eté* is the same as "very." But if the number of a thing cannot be calculated, they declare that it is *ndipapahabi* meaning "uncountable."

75. The Guaraní began the month from the rise of the crescent moon and from that same moon they give the month its name, just like the Hebrews and the Greeks. For the Greeks say τετράμηνον [*tetramēnon*], for example, to mean "four Moons" or "four months." For the rest, this Guaraní way of counting is extremely cumbersome, if the total number of items grows greater and greater.[35] For this reason, it seemed appropriate to the Jesuit Priests for the neophytes to learn the Spanish numbers. This turned out to be an easy task.

LXXVI. Singulis quibusque diebus Dominicis post recitatas Catechismi formulas, et decantata ab omnibus Religionis mysteria, bini, qui voce aliis praeibant in medio stantes templo, en vobis, ajebant, ordinem et nomina numerorum: *UNO*; respondebat populus *UNO*. Illi dein: *DOS*; universi vicissim *DOS*. postea *TRES, QUATRO*, et sic deinceps ad *CIENTO*, et *MIL*. Sub haec, iidem turbae duces en vobis nomina dierum Hebdomadae: *DOMINGO* iterabant cuncti *DOMINGO*. Illi post, *LUNES*. hi *LUNES*. atque ita usque ad Sabbatum. Inde ad menses procedebant. En vobis mensium nomina ab initio anni. *ENERO*; repetebant universi *ENERO*. Deinde *FEBRERO, MARZO* etc. ad *DICIEMBRE* ut dicunt Hispani. Ita fiebat, ut Indi a teneris haec sibi nomina familiaria redderent, atque expedite eo numerandi modo et ad rem sacram, et ad rem civilem uterentur.

LXXVII. Quid? (dicet hic forsan aliquis) docebantur ne Guaranii linguam Hispanam perinde ac Hispanos numeros? Atqui fama est Curiones illos severe vetuisse, ne clientes sui Hispanice loqui discerent, quominus a quoquam peregrino mysteria Guaranica, vel intelligi, vel introspici possent. Nugae et mera somnia hominum delirantium! Quippe Guaranicae linguae usus communis est civibus Hispanis urbis Fluentinae, et municipibus Hispanarum item Coloniarum Villaricianae, et Curuguatiensis. Immo vero in ipsa Assumptionis urbe (quae praetoria est, et totius provinciae princeps) P. Rochus de Rivas (obiit is Faventiae an. MDCCXC.) mysteria Religionis, et morum officia e loco superiore Guaranice explicabat magno plausu, fructuque civium, qui tametsi loqui Hispane sciunt, malunt sibi verba fieri lingua Guaranica, cui a pueris assuescunt, et qua inter se ruri agunt domique.

LXXVIII. Quorsum igitur secretum linguae innumerabilibus notae Hispanis, quibus (ut postea docebimus) liber erat aditus ad oppida Guaraniorum? Ad celandum scilicet arcana politica. Quae arcana? Nihil erat rerum Guaranicarum, quod non saepe introspexerint Sacri Antistites, Regiique Praetores, qui oppida illa pro munere lustrarunt. Rex ipse Catholicus Philippus V., omnia ibi fieri solita publice explicavit, approbavitque. De ejus decreto erit infra nobis dicendi locus. At quid multis opus est in re clara? VV. Sacerdotes e Clero, et RR. PP. Franciscani, qui aliquot oppida gentis Guaranicae in praetura Paraguayca curant, oppidanos Guaranice instituunt, nequedum quisquam id illis vitio vertit. In oppidis item Peruvicis Hispani Parochi Indos suos erudiunt lingua Peruvica, id est, Quichua: cur non ergo Guaranici Curiones Guaranica uterentur?

76. Each and every Sunday, after the formulas of the Catechism had been recited and the mysteries of faith had been sung by all, two of them, who were better than others with respect to their voices, would stand in the middle of the church and say: "Hear ye the names and the sequence of the numbers: ONE," and the people answered: "ONE"; then "TWO," and all in turn, "TWO." Afterward, "THREE," "FOUR," and so on to "ONE HUNDRED" and "ONE THOUSAND." After this, the same leaders of the crowd: "Hear ye the names of the days of the week: SUNDAY" and altogether they would repeat, "SUNDAY." Afterward, "MONDAY" and the crowd repeats "MONDAY" and so on until the Sabbath. From there they would proceed to the months: "Hear ye the names of the months from the beginning of the year: JANUARY," and they would all repeat, "JANUARY." Then "FEBRUARY," "MARCH," etc., until "DECEMBER" as the Spanish say. Thus, it happened that from a tender age the Indians made these names familiar for themselves and used this way of counting for sacred and civil matters without impediment.

77. Why? (Perhaps someone will ask at this point.) Why were the Guaraní not educated in the Spanish language just as in Spanish numbers? Somehow there is a rumor that the Priests had severely forbidden their followers from learning to speak Spanish so that the Guaraní mysteries could not be understood or examined by any outsider. Nonsense! Nothing but dreams of delusional men! Naturally, the Guaraní language is in common use among the Spanish citizens of the city of Corrientes and the inhabitants of the Spanish colonies of Villarrica [del Espíritu Santo] and Curuguaty. What's more, in the city of Asunción itself (which is the seat of the Governor and the principal city of the entire Province), Father Roque Ribas (who died in Faenza in 1790) explained the mysteries of religion and moral duties from the pulpit in Guaraní to great delight and applause of the citizens, who although they know how to speak Spanish prefer that the language used around them be their Guaraní language, to which they are accustomed from childhood and in which they converse among themselves in the fields and at home.

78. To what end, then, is the secrecy of a language known to countless Spaniards, for whom (as we will say below) there was free access to the Guaraní towns? To conceal political secrets, right? What secrets? There was nothing about the Guaraní that the Holy Bishops and the Royal Governors did not inspect when they examined these towns in their official capacity. The Catholic King himself, Felipe V, publicly stated that everything done there was normal, and approved it. We will have the opportunity to speak about his decree later. But what need is there for more discussion in such a clear matter? The Most Venerable Priests of the secular Clergy and the Most Reverend Franciscan fathers, who look after several towns of Guaraní people in the Paraguayan governate, instruct the townspeople in Guaraní, and no one has yet interpreted it as a blemish on them. Likewise, in the Peruvian towns the Spanish parish priests instruct their Indians in the Peruvian language; that is, in Quechua. Why shouldn't the Guaraní Priests use the Guaraní language?

LXXIX. Illud hic certum est Guaranios numquam coactos fuisse a Jesuitis ad addiscendam linguam Hispanam, quem admodum ne in media quidem Hispania, et sub Regis oculos, Baleares, Valentini, Cantabri, Callaici,[36] et Catalauni coguntur loqui Castellanice, quae Aulae lingua est. Data opera Catalaunos extremo posui loco, ut indicarem paucis piam severitatem Il. D. Josephi de Mezquia, ex ordine Redemptorum, Episcopi Solsonensis, qui nemini umquam potestatem fecit concionandi nisi lingua Catalaunica, rogatusque quondam, ut Sacerdoti Caesaraugustano (cum hoc vixi diu, et superstes est) magni in Academia Cervariensi nominis veniam daret habendi Castellanice Divorum laudationes, negavit Antistes, velle se ajens oves suas pasci ea lingua, quam a matribus didicerunt, meliusque omni alia intelligunt. Et quidem Il. Mezquìa non Catalaunus, sed Castellanus erat: tamen prudens Pastor (quem novi) majorem sui gregis fructum nativae antetulit linguae. Ut videas autem superiori suo sancte obtemperantibus rem semper bene cedere, idem ille Sacerdos majorem usum nactus Catalaunici sermonis, sermone dein hoc optime superos laudabat, et cives Christiani hominis officia docebat: illum audivi, et potui, quippe Catalaunus, de vi, et ornatu elocutionis nonnihil cognoscere.

LXXX. Lex Indica summo consilio, de re quam agimus, sic praecipit: *doceantur Hispanam linguam Indi, qui eam sponte sua velint discere,*[37] *los que voluntariamente la quisieren aprehender.* Audin? *voluntariamente, sua sponte.* Vidit Rex, quam sit difficile nolentes cogi ad novam loquendi formam. Suppetunt domestica exempla. Victi a Punicis quondam Hispani, victorum linguam recipere constanter renuerunt: Punice regi sustinuere, loqui non sustinuere. Ad hanc rem propius pertinet, quod gravis Virgilius, probe noscens vix flecti homines posse ut externo sermoni accommodent ora, de conditionibus jungendae societatis urbisque inter Troas latinosque sic consulto cecinit:

> Ne vetus indigenas nomen mutare latinos,
> Neu Troas fieri jubeas, teucrosque vocari,
> Aut vocem mutare viros, aut vertere vestes.
> . . .
> Do quod vis, et me victusque volensque remitto.
> Sermonem Ausonii patrium, moresque tenebunt:
> Utque est, nomen erit.[38]

79. What is certain here is that the Guaraní were never forced by the Jesuits to learn the Spanish language, just as in the heart of Spain itself, right under the King's eyes, the Balearics, the Valencians, the Cantabrians, Galicians, and the Catalans[36] are not obliged to speak Spanish, which is the language of the Court. I intentionally put the Catalans last, so that I might briefly point out the pious severity of the most illustrious José Mezquía, of the Mercedarians, Bishop of Solsona, who never gave anyone permission to preach unless it was in Catalan. He was once asked to give permission for a Priest from Zaragoza of great renown at the University of Cervera (I lived with this man long ago and he is still alive), to conduct the praises of the Saints in Spanish; the Bishop refused, saying that he wanted his sheep to be nourished by the language that they learned from their mothers and that they understand better than any other. And indeed, the most illustrious Mezquía was not Catalan, but Castilian. However, as a prudent shepherd (whom I knew) he put the greater enjoyment of his flock before his native tongue. And so that you can see that things always turn out well for those who scrupulously obey their superior: that same priest, after having achieved greater skill in the Catalan language, would later praise those on high and teach the citizens the duties of being Christian very well in that language. I listened to him and was able, as a Catalan myself, to recognize no lack of force or elegance in his expression.

80. A Law of the Indies on the matter under discussion very prudently orders as follows: "Those Indians who want to learn Spanish of their own volition should be taught it."[37] Are you listening? "Of their own volition." The King saw how difficult it would be for the unwilling to be compelled to speak a new language. Domestic examples are abundant. In the past, after the Spaniards were defeated by the Carthaginians, they repeatedly refused to accept the language of the victors. They put up with a Carthaginian king but not speaking Carthaginian. Quite pertinent to this is what the venerable Vergil sang, knowing perfectly that men can scarcely be bent to adapt their mouths to a foreign language. So, he sang deliberately about the circumstances of uniting a society and a city between Trojans and Latins:

> Let not the native Latins change their ancient name,
> nor bid the men to become Trojans and be called Teucri,
> or change their language or alter their dress.
> . . .
> I grant what you wish; I am won over and I willingly yield.
> The Ausonians will hold onto the language and the customs of their forefathers:
> And their name will be just as it is now.[38]

LXXXI. Voluit ad extremum Plato (uti diximus) pueros puellasque utraque uti manu sine dexterae prerogavita; atque id quidem recte: praejudicium enim haud laudabile parentum est, liberis vetare aequum sinistrae manus ac dextrae usum, quo fit, ut laeva paene inutilis reddatur. Sacer liber[39] vocat *fortissimos* Gabaaitas *ita sinistra, ut dextra proeliantes.* Ac de Aod Israelitarum supremo duce, et judice dicitur: *qui utraque manu pro dextera utebatur.*[40] Guaranii (si bene memini) non interdicebant filiis promiscuo utriusque manus usu. Ceterum non id dicimus, quod improbemus urbanam consuetudinem quaedam vel accipiendi, vel porrigendi dextera potius manu, quam sinistra (valeat civilis mos) sed ut indicemus oportere laevam assuefieri ad quaevis agenda, et habilem esse perinde ac dextram: saepe enim accidit, ut habilitas haec magno adjumento sit rei bene gerendae domi militiaeque, Miles, civis, artifex sit, oportet, *aequimanus*, ut Ausonii utar verbo.

De Musica.

PLATO

LXXXII. Incredibile dictu est, quantum pro educatione puerili ponat Plato in Musica, ut vel hinc intelligas data eum opera Pytagoram musicis numeris omnia explicantem audisse. Nec minus ille choreas laudat in rectam urbis institutionem. Quippe utraque hac re, ait, aequabilis et proba animi habitudo sit: Musica enim delinit, et temperat id, quod ab atra bili inest nobis asperi, et duri: choreae autem graves, et laboriosae, mollem illam minuunt appetionem, et humorem pigrum, quo ad voluptatem et otium trahimur: ubi autem utriusque vitii extrema vitaveris, medium virtutis teneas, necesse est. Aristoteles, qui certe non jurarat in magistri verba Platonis, quo aequa, et bona puerorum eruditione etiam Musicam commendat.

81. Finally, Plato wanted (as we said) boys and girls to use both hands without preference for the right. Indeed, this is correct, since it is a hardly laudable prejudice of parents to forbid children from using their left and right hands equally, and thereby rendering the left essentially useless. The Holy Bible[39] calls the men of Gibeah "most valiant because they fought with the left just as with the right." And of Ehud, judge and supreme leader of the Israelites, it is said "that he used either hand as if it were his right."[40] The Guaraní, if I remember correctly, would not prohibit their children from using both hands indiscriminately. Notwithstanding, we do not mean that we disapprove of that courteous custom of receiving or giving something with the right hand rather than with the left (long live the polite custom!) but rather that we indicate that it is reasonable for the left hand to be habituated to doing anything whatsoever and to be skillful just like the right. For it often happens that this ability is a great help for doing things well, both at home and in war. It is useful for the soldier, the citizen, the artisan to be "equal handed," if I may use Ausonius's word [*Technopaegnion* 12.3].

On Music

PLATO

82. It is unbelievable how much importance Plato attaches to Music for the education of children; so much so that you might feel as if he took his cue from Pythagoras who explains everything using musical figures. And no less does he praise choruses for the correct habituation of the city. Since with either of these, he says, the condition of the soul would be balanced and upright. For Music soothes and tempers what is rough and hard in us due to melancholy.* On the other hand, serious and physically challenging choruses diminish that soft desire and lazy humor by which we are drawn to pleasure and leisure. But should you succeed in avoiding the extremes of both vices, it is then necessary to master the virtue's mean. Aristotle, who certainly had not sworn allegiance to the words of his teacher Plato, also commends Music insofar as it is balanced and good for educating children.

* Lit. "black bile."

LXXXIII. Hebraeus Philo Graece sciens, et Graecorum scriptorum justus aestimator, secundum praecepta Platonis: Musica, ait, est velut lac quoddam puerilium animorum:[41] videmus enim nutricum cantilenis illorum lacrimas sisti, et vigilantibus somnum conciliari: ipsi pueri, ubi firmo pede premere caepere solum, fistulis, tibiisque e nodo arundinum factis, cum aequalibus oblectant se se. Quippe est hic naturae certus instinctus, quem ubique gentium licet cernere; dum nulla sit natio tam barbara, atque inculta, quae in nuptiis, conviviisque, et ludis Musica non utatur, eamdemque adhibent vel in ipsis funeribus, ut quodammodo lenior fiat fletus, et acerbitas doloris mitigetur. Et quidem in quibusdam civitatibus bene moratis Musicae usus lege sancitus est: ac summus ille Orator Tullius ad efformandum Oratorem valere plurimum Musicam existimat (Cic. de Orat.) ut doctus ille vocum inflexiones, flectat dein quo velit auditorum animos.

LXXXIV. Marcus autem Fabius Quintilianus, eximium Hispaniae decus, in Institutionibus, quas sapientissime scripsit, praecipit, ut Orator ille, quem sensim fingit, discat a puero Musicam, praeceptique reddens causam, "Claros, inquit, nomine sapientiae viros nemo dubitaverit studiosos musices fuisse, cum Pythagoras, atque eum secuti, acceptam sine dubio antiquitus opinionem vulgaverint, mundum ipsum ea ratione esse compositum, quam postea sit lyra imitata . . . Nam Plato cum in aliis quibusdam, tum praecipue in Timaeo, ne intelligi quidem nisi ab iis, qui hanc quoque partem disciplinae diligenter perceperint, potest. Quid de Philosophis loquar, quorum fons ipse Socrates jam senex institui lyra non erubescebat? Non igitur frustra Plato civili viro, quem Πολιτικὸν vocant, necessariam musicen credidit . . . Atque eam natura ipsa videtur ad tollerandos facilius labores velut muneri nobis dedisse. Siquidem et remiges cantus hortatur: nec solum in iis operibus, in quibus plurium conatus praeeunte aliqua jucunda voce conspirat; sed etiam singulorum fatigatio quamlibet se rudi modulatione solatur."[42]

LXXXV. Ac, ne in re aperta sim fusior, Tullius, praestantissimus inter Philosophos Orator, et inter Oratores Philosophus, de Musica sic disserit: "civitatum hoc multarum in Graecia interfuit, antiquum vocum servare modum: quarum mores lapsi ad mollitiem pariter sunt immutati in cantibus, aut hac dulcedine corruptelaque depravati, ut quidam putant, aut cum severitas morum ob alia vitia cecidisset, tum fuit in auribus animisque mutatis etiam huic mutationi locus."[43]

83. The Hebrew Philo [of Alexandria], skilled in Greek and a fair critic of Greek authors, follows the precepts of Plato and says that Music is like a sort of milk for infants' souls.[41] For we see that by the nurses' ditties their tears are stopped and the restless are brought over to sleep. These same children, when they are just grasping the ability to stand with a firm footing, amuse themselves along with their peers with pipes and flutes made from hard reeds. Certainly, this is a fixed impulse of nature, which it is possible to observe anywhere in the world, so long as there is no nation so barbarous and uncivilized that it does not use music at weddings, banquets, and games. They employ Music even at funerals to make the crying somehow gentler and to mitigate the bitterness of the pain. Indeed, the use of Music is legally sanctioned in certain well-mannered states; and what is more, the greatest Orator, Cicero (in *On the Orator*), judges Music to be a most powerful resource for the formation of the Orator since, for example, a man trained in the inflections of voice can then bend the minds of his listeners in the direction he wishes.

84. Marcus Fabius Quintilian, the pride of Spain, in his work *On Oratorical Education*, which he wrote most wisely, advises that the Orator, whom he shapes bit by bit, learn Music from childhood, giving the following reason for this precept: "No one," he says, "could have doubted that men famous because of their reputation for wisdom had been devoted to music, since Pythagoras and those who followed him popularized the opinion, doubtlessly accepted since ancient times, that the universe itself has been composed with the same harmony which the lyre later imitated. . . . For Plato, in various other works but especially in the *Timaeus*, cannot be understood except by those who have fully and diligently grasped this aspect of his teaching as well. What should I say about the Philosophers, whose source is Socrates himself, who felt no shame at learning to play the lyre though he was already an old man? . . . Not in vain did Plato believe music to be necessary for 'a man of the city,' whom they call Πολιτικός [*Politikos*]. . . . And nature itself seems to have given it to us as a gift to make it easier to tolerate hardships. Since indeed singing encourages even rowers. And not only in those tasks where the endeavors of a great many harmonize with some pleasant voice leading the way; but also, the fatigue of individuals is assuaged with a melody however clumsy it may be."[42]

85. And, so as not to expand further on something so clear, Cicero, the most outstanding Orator among Philosophers and a Philosopher among Orators, discusses Music as follows: "It was important to many states in Greece, to preserve the ancient way of singing. The habits of these states having declined toward laziness, they were equally altered in their songs, either because they were perverted by this sweetness and seduction, as some think, or because when the strictness of customs had yielded to other vices, there was then room for this change in the changed ears and souls."[43]

LXXXVI. Quae ego doctissimorum virorum testimonia de vi, et virtute Musicae in disciplinam publicam cum lego, quid hoc rei est? ajo apud me. An veteres illi alio, eoque meliore, quam nos modulandi genere utebantur? Ubinam enim dulcis, et efficax modus, qui adeo in probos civium mores influebat? Si fateri verum volumus, dicendum prorsus est, musicam, cui nunc operam damus, plerumque obesse potius adolescentium rectae institutioni, quam prodesse. Cur id autem? quia mollem, et adulterinum cantum sequimur, non graves et viriles modos, ac generosos fidium sonos, qui inordinatae mentis habitum temperent, componantque, atque exleges sensus rationi subjiciant. Ferunt morsos ab Apula aspide curari musica. Esto, curantur corpora, sed animi corrumpuntur musicis nostris; corrumpentique aures, et cor, cantori, cantatricique, datur saepe in triduum merces, quae satis foret alendo in annum toti gregi honestae familiae, quae prae fame balat. (Lib. III. V. de Repub. de Leg. II. III. etc.)

GUARANII.

LXXXVII. Musica apud Guaranios optima erat electis e toto puerorum grege, et adolescentium turba pluribus qui musicas docti notas, ore canerent, et pulsarent plectra, et Organa aerisona, et citharas, et tetrachorda; tibiisque et lituis, et tubis rite uterentur. Illos instituit hac arte omnium primus Joanes Vasseus, qui fuisse dicitur Musicus Caroli V. Imperatoris et paratis jam sibi opibus ultro renunciavit, ut transmisso Oceano silvestres homines Orphei instar lyra mansuefaceret: atque is quidem ex immani labore ministrandi neophytis, quos pestilentia afflarat, occubuit in oppido Laureti an. MDCXXIII.[44]

86. As I read the testimonies of the most learned men about the power and excellence of Music for state education, I ask myself, "What does this mean?" Did the ancients use another, somehow better, type of melody making than we do? For where is that sweet and effective rhythm that would insinuate itself into habits of citizens far enough to make them upright? If we want to acknowledge the truth, it must be said straightforwardly that the music we pay attention to today mostly hinders the correct education of adolescents rather than profiting it. Why is this? Because we pursue the soft and counterfeit song, not the noble and virile rhythms or the noble sounds of instruments that would temper and unite the condition of a disordered mind and subject the lawless senses to reason. They say that bites from an Apulian snake were cured by music. So be it. The bodies are healed, but the souls are corrupted by our music. The singer, male or female, who corrupts the ears and the heart is given a salary for three days work that would be sufficient for a year's sustenance for the entire flock of a respectable family bleating from hunger (*Republic*, Books 3 and 5; *Laws* 2, 3, etc.).

THE GUARANÍ

87. The music among the Guaraní was excellent. Out of the entire flock of children and the throng of adolescents many were chosen who, once they had been taught the musical notes, would sing and play harpsichords,* pipe organs,† guitars,‡ and violins,§ as well as employ flutes, shawms, and trumpets¶ in religious ceremonies. The first to instruct them in this art was Jean Vaisseau, who is said to have been musician to [Holy Roman] Emperor Charles V, and who, once he had enough wealth set aside for himself, later resigned so that he might cross the ocean and after the fashion of Orpheus tame the forest dwellers with his lyre. Indeed, due to the immense toll of ministering to the neophytes afflicted by the plague, he died in [Nuestra Señora de] Loreto in 1623.[44]

* Or "clavichords."

† Or "wind instruments," more generally.

‡ Or "lutes."

§ Tetrachorda may imply both violins and string bases.

¶ *Lituus* and *tuba* could refer to a variety of instruments in use in Paraguay including the trumpet, cornett, and French horn.

LXXXVIII. Jam vero cum indi propensissimi ad Musicam sint (diceres eos donatos ingenio avium quibus natura ipsa cantum inspirat) ita illam belle arripuerunt, ut Europaeis admirationi fuerint, et esse nunc etiam pergant. Cajetanus Cattaneus, qui ex Italia illuc navigavit an. MDCCXXIX. scripsit Mutinam ad suos, visum sibi Guaranicum puerum duodennem difficillimas quasque Bononiensium Compositorum notas nusquam errantem fidibus reddere.[45] Quotidie autem ad Sacrum Missae canebant Guaranii voce, et Organo pneumatico, et cetero symphoniae instrumento. Vespere dein sub Rosarii preces brevior erat cantus in laudem Eucharistiae, et Dei Matris MARIAE, cui cantui respondebat populus, addita postremo formula Actus Contritionis. Id generatim de Musica Guarraniorum dici potest, eam et castam omnino et seriam fuisse in templo, numquam temerato modis et sonis theatralibus (quos, pudor! inepti quidam profanique Musici vel in odaea sacra ausi sunt transferre) et honestam ac pudicam domi rurique, ut nihil uspiam audires quod posset mores corrumpere.[46]

De Choreis.

PLATO

LXXXIX. Erudiantur, inquit, pueri, puellaeque gymnicis choreis, quae ad membrorum exercitationem, agilitatemque pertinent, et sunt quodammodo bellica quaedam praeludia: nam armorum usum ignorare non debent foeminae, erit enim forsan aliquando opus, ut, absentibus maritis, stantes ipsae pro vallo urbem patriamque defendant. Sunto itaque choreae graves, laboriosaeque, et symbolicae, per quas morum variorum, diversarumque actionum imitationes fiant honestae, et usu probatae. Quae autem his contraria sunt, ut saltationes molles, et lascivae, Baccharumque tripudia (id est Bacchanalia) permitti in Republica non debent.

XC. Publicae puerorum educationi a Musica, et Choreis adjicit Plato privatum, et domesticum praeceptum ad matres nutricesque pro rite curandis infantibus, qui instar mollis cerae diligenter fingendi sunt, nequod eorum membra vitium contrahant; vultque illos biennio adstringi fasciis, ratus id prodesse bonae corporum conformationi. Quo siqui parentibus orbi sint, iis jubet optimos, et vigiles tutores curatoresque praefici. (De Repub. et Legg. loc. citt.)

88. Thus, since the Indians were already very well-disposed toward music (you might say that they were endowed with the ingenuity of the birds whom nature itself inspires to sing) they took to it so beautifully that they were the object of admiration for Europeans and continue to be so even now. Gaetano Cattaneo, who sailed to these lands from Italy in 1729, wrote to his family in Modena that he had seen a twelve-year-old Guaraní boy render on the cello* the most difficult scores of Bolognese composers, never making a mistake.[45] The Guaraní sang every day at Mass with the pneumatic organ and other musical instruments. In the afternoon, after the recitation of the rosary, there was a shorter song in praise of the Eucharist and of MARY, Mother of God, to which the people responded, adding, at the end, the formula of the Act of Contrition. It can be said generally of the Music of the Guaraní, that it was completely pure and earnest in the temple, which was never desecrated with rhythms and theatrical sounds (which, for shame!, some inept and profane musicians have dared to introduce even into the holy chamber), and it was upright and modest both at home and in the countryside so that you would not ever hear anything capable of corrupting morals anywhere.[46]

On Choral Dancing

PLATO

89. Boys and girls, Plato says, should be instructed in gymnastic choral dances, which pertain to the exercise and agility of the limbs. In a sense, they are a means of preparing for war! For females should not be ignorant of the use of weapons; indeed, there will perhaps be a need at some point for them to stand up, in the absence of their husbands, like a bulwark and defend their city and their country themselves. And so, the choral dances must be serious, labor-intensive, and full of symbolism. Through these, imitations of various customs and diverse actions become respectable and accepted through practice. Those opposite to these, such as emasculating and lascivious cavorting and the gyrations of the Bacchae (that is, Bacchanalia), should not be permitted in the Republic.

90. In addition to public education of children through Music and Dance, Plato adds another precept of a private and domestic nature for mothers and wet nurses on correctly caring for infants, who, like soft wax, must be molded diligently, so that their limbs do not contract any defect. He wants them to be swaddled for two years, having calculated that this is beneficial for the healthy constitution of the body. If there are any children who lack parents, he orders that excellent and vigilant minders and caretakers be put in charge of them (*Republic* and *Laws*, books cited).

* Lit. "strings."

XCI. Quod ad choreas attinet, hae laetissimis tantum diebus per annum habebantur in foro, toto inspectante populo, et coram Curione, ejusque collega sedentibus pro templi porticu. Saltabant autem soli pueri adolescentesque: ac seorsum viri, seorsum foeminae publico huic ludo intererant. Choreae erant graves, et hieroglyphicae, sive symbolicae. Quippe alias repraesentabant pugnam Archangeli Michaelis (cujus in scuto scriptum erat *QUIS UT DEUS*) cum rebelli dracone, et asseclis ejus, victis tandem iis, detrusisque in tartarum; illo victore, et triumphante. Alias referebant quattuor augustos Reges, e sua quemque terrarum Orbis parte, venientes stellae indicio, ut adorarent *Regem Regum*, et *Dominum dominantium*; eique jam invento, recumbentique ad pulchrae puerperae sinum, sceptra sua, et coronas venerabundi submitterent.

XCII. Alias sistebant in medium insignia, et tesseram Virginis MARIAE, cujus nominis litteras singulas, singulis descriptas in scutulis, per varios cursus recursusque miscebant, atque ita paulatim eas in ordinem redigebant, objiciebantque spectantium oculis, ut dulce Reginae Coeli nomen conjunctim legi posset: ipsi autem auctores ludi, submissis ad numerum genibus, et prono capite, ac pectore procumbebant ad sacrum simulacrum ejusdem Magnae Matris, quod in idipsum antea parabatur. Alias velitationem, et praelia simulabant Christianas acies inter et Mauricas, ita tamen, ut Dei illae praesidio vicerent, hae fusae fugataeque terga turpiter verterent; servato inter certandum justo semper ad symphoniam motu coporis membrorumque. Alias saltabant simul, et ludebant musice. Bini (puta) canebant binis lyris; bini binis citharis; bini binis plectris, bini binis tetrachordis; bini binis lituis! numquam interim cessante numerosa pedum vibratione.

XCIII. Accipe hujus rei illustre documentum. Habebat stativa in oppido S. Francisci Borgiae clarissimus Imperator Petrus Cevallius cum exercitu, qui eo venerat ob exortas turbas Cisuruguaycorum, detrectantium famosum illud foedus Lusitanicum, quo foedere jussi illi fuerant finibus e suis migrare, ut supra docuimus. Interea acceptis ab Europa laureatis litteris de adito Hispaniarum solio a Carolo III. demortui Ferdinandi VI. fratre, voluit Cevallius (qua erat in Regem fide) quam posset magnifice ejus auspicia ad regnum celebrare. Festivi ludi tenuerunt complures dies; excitique sunt ex aliis oppidis Guaranii cantores saltatoresque plurimi.

91. As regards choral dances, they were only held on the most joyous days of the year, in the town square, with the whole community watching, in the presence of the Priest and his companion who were seated on the church portico. Only children and adolescents danced about; and the men and women separately attended this public spectacle. The dances were serious and hieroglyphic, or symbolic. You see, sometimes they represented the fight of the Archangel Michael (on whose shield had been written "WHO IS LIKE GOD")* against the rebellious dragon and his henchmen who were finally defeated and cast into hell, with the Archangel victorious and triumphant. At other times they represented four majestic Kings, each from his own part of the world, coming in response to a star, in order to worship the King of Kings and Lord of Lords. Once he was found, reclining in the lap of the beautiful new mother, they lowered their scepters and crowns for him as a sign of veneration.

92. Other times, they would set up the insignia and token of the Virgin Mary in the center, and the individual letters of her name were written on individual little shields, which they would mix up and then one at a time put back in order again. They were thus presented before the eyes of the onlookers so that the sweet name of the Queen of Heaven could be read all together. And the actors in the performance, with knees bent and head and chest bowed to the rhythm, would prostrate themselves before the sacred image of the same Great Mother, which was prepared in advance for that very purpose. Other times they simulated skirmishing and battles between Christian and Moorish armies, in such a way that the former conquered with God's aid and the latter, having been scattered and put to flight, shamefully turned their backs. Throughout the fight they always kept the movement of their body and limbs perfectly in harmony with the music. Other times they danced and at the same time performed music. Just picture it—a pair would be playing a pair of harps, another pair on guitars, another with lutes,† another with violins, and yet another pair with cornetts! Meanwhile the rhythmic fluttering of their feet never ceased.

93. Take the following as manifest proof of this fact. The very famous General Pedro Antonio de Cevallos was stationed with his army in the town of S. Francisco de Borja. He had come because of the popular uprising of the East Bank Uruguayans who rejected that famous Portuguese treaty by which they had been ordered to leave their own lands, as we explained above.‡ Meanwhile, a laureate letter was received from Europe about the accession to the throne of Carlos III, due to the death of his brother Fernando VI, and Cevallos wanted, out of his loyalty to the King, to celebrate the beginning of his reign as magnificently as he could. The festive spectacles lasted for several days, and many Guaraní singers and dancers were summoned from other towns.

* The meaning of "Michael" in Hebrew.

† *Plectrum* mainly refers to the harpsichord or clavichord, but here refers generically to a handheld stringed instrument.

‡ The 1750 Treaty of Madrid; see *DAG* 18n7.

XCIV. Cantoribus commissa est templi Musica, quam illi dexterrime exercuerunt ad divina mysteria pro novi Regis felici faustoque imperio. Saltatores autem arte sua usi sunt in foro coram Imperatore, et ducibus, et militibus, et populo innumerabili. Tanta vero fuit chorearum Varietas, ut semper illi nova afferrent genera, mutaruntque formas sexies quotidie: quippe didicisse dicuntur a Josepho Cardiele septuaginta saltationum modos diversos; et, quod magis laudes, in tanto chorearum numero nihil petulans erat, nihil lascivum (id ut caverent, ludis aderant publicis Curio, ejusque collega) et cui conveniret illud a Gersone graviter dictum: *omnia peccata chorizant in chorea.*[47] Vivunt etiam num, opinor, aliquot Centurionum, et quam multi militum (Imperator jampridem obiit) qui testari possint, quid tum et viderint, et videntes mirati sunt.

XCV. In Divi Praesidis festo die, quem singula oppida agitabant cultu maximo, solebat dari spectaculum seriae alicujus actionis, ut properantium pastorum ad antrum Bethleemicum post legatum ad ipsos e superis sedibus nuncium, auditosque choros coelestis militiae canentes: *GLORIA IN EXCELSIS DEO.* Exhibebant scilicet Indi pia pastorum obsequia, quibus Deum recens natum, Deique Matrem, mira simplicitate, et candida innocentia prosecuti sunt. Ad haec autem dramata (quae pueri rite instituti reddebant, nulla ad agendum admissa faemina) et ad statas anni choreas, fiebant e publico vestes singulis personis, scaenisque accomodatae; quae vestes (dum rediret iterum earum usus) asservabantur in armariis apud Curionem, cujus in atrio erant gymnasia ad puerilem eruditionem, ut ipse facile observare posset, an magistri (Indi delecti erant) suo munere recte fungerentur.

XCVI. Atque haec quidem de Musica, et choreis Guaranicis. Restat dicere de curandis infantibus. Hos non biennio (quod vult Plato) stringebant fasciis Guaranicae matres, sed laxo sinu ita induebant, ut teneris membris liber esset usus, et motus. Sane modus ille pueros obvolvendi (ut ut fieret, neque enim satis eum memoria teneo) optimus est. Equidem multa Guaraniorum vidi oppida, et nusquam Indum claudum, vel mancum, vel gibbum, vel alio corporis vitio affectum vidi:[48] omnes perfectis erant artubus: tantum unius recordor, qui mutus erat: at id mali (ut omnes sat norunt) vitio curantium matrum non sit.

94. The music of the temple was entrusted to the singers, and they performed it most skillfully for the divine mysteries on behalf of the new King's prosperous and auspicious government. The dancers performed their craft in the town square, in front of the General, the leaders, the soldiers, and a crowd too large to count. The variety of dances was such that they were always presenting new types; indeed, they changed the type of dance six times each day. Furthermore, they are said to have learned seventy different forms of dance from Father José Cardiel; and, what you would praise even more is that, in such a great number of dances, there was nothing lewd, nothing obscene (to guard against that, the Priest and his companion attended the public performances) to which might apply Jean Gerson's severe saying: "Every sin joins in on the dance."[47] Even to this day some of the Captains and quite a few of the soldiers are, I think, still alive (the General passed away a long time ago) and they could testify to what they saw then and how they were amazed at the sight.

95. On the Patron Saint's feast day, which each town celebrated with the maximum reverence, it was customary for a performance of some serious saga to be offered, such as the shepherds hastening to the cave in Bethlehem after the messenger had been dispatched to them from heaven and the choirs of the heavenly militia were heard singing "Glory to God in the Highest." So, of course, the Indians exhibited the pious deference of the shepherds, with which they honored the newborn God and the Mother of God, with admirable simplicity and unblemished innocence. For these dramatic performances (which religiously trained boys put on, since no female was allowed to take part) and for the dances established during the year, the clothes appropriate for each character and each scene were fashioned from community resources. These clothes (until it was time to use them again) were kept safe in cabinets at the priest's house, in whose courtyard there were also schools for the education of children, so that the priest himself could easily observe whether the teachers (Indians selected for the task) properly executed their duties.

96. Indeed, these are the things that concern Guaraní music and choral dancing. It remains to discuss how infants should be cared for. Guaraní mothers did not swaddle them for two years (as Plato wanted) but instead dressed them in loose garments so that their tender limbs would have free use and mobility. To be sure, that way of wrapping up children (however it was done, I don't have a clear memory of it) is excellent. I have seen many Guaraní towns and never have I seen an Indian who was lame, disabled, humpbacked, or afflicted by some other bodily defect;[48] they all had perfect limbs, and I only recall one who was mute, but this sort of evil (as all know well enough) does not come from a lack of caring mothers.

XCVII. Ad haec: sua quemque parens ubere alebat, nec ancillis (quae nullae illic) nec nutricibus (nisi vel mortua matre, vel aegra, utendum foret alienae mulieris ope) teneri partus delegabantur: qua in re gens illa sequitur ductum naturae, quae matri in idipsum munus alendae prolis providet statim lac.[49] De tutoribus, et curatoribus, quos orphanis praeficit Plato, nihil nobis negotii est. Orbos parentibus educabant consanguinei domi suae; illorum autem cibo, et vestibus e publico consulebatur. Hactenus de educatione, quae schola quaedam est, ubi finguntur animorum habitus, *altera* nimirum (ut recte a Philosophis dicitur) *natura*, quam cum semel indueris, vix umquam exues.

De opere diurno.

PLATO

XCVIII. De diurnis actionibus sic ille generatim praecipit. Turpe est, ait, siquis civium nimio indulgens somno totam dormiat noctem; prorsusque indignum bono hero, nisi ipse domesticis suis surgat prior. Dominam autem ab ancillis, non ancillas ab domina excitari, ingens dedecus. Expergiscantur itaque bene mane cives, et vigil Magistratus ante lucem publica tractet commoda, patresque et matresfamilias privatem rem mature domi curent: sopor enim, neu animo, neu corpori utilis, officit plurimum negotiis gerendis.

XCIX. Nemo certe cum dormit, pluris faciendus est, quam si non viveret: ob idque ipsum, qui vivere, et sapere optat maxime, quam maximo vigilet tempore; dummodo habeatur ratio sanitatis, ad quam quidem haud opus est longo somno, si bene assueveris. Adde, quod Praefecti civitati, si sollerter excubent, malis civibus terrori sunt, impediuntque nequis hostili animo, et nocturnis armis, in urbem irrumpat. Haec Plato graviter, ut solet.

C. In exercitationibus civium, praeter agri culturam, urbanasque artes, venationem ponit. Venatio autem alia est inquit, aquatilium, alia ferarum, alia volatilium, alia hominum, quae sit, cum quis libero capiti insidiatur, ut abducat in servitutem. Hoc posito discrimine, pergit dicere: quibus fortitudo, et membrorum robur curae est, eos in primis fatigare cursu feras, et telo persequi, oportet. Auceps, et venator per inculta tantum loca, montesque vagari sinitor, ne satis agris, et natae segeti noceat circumcursando.

97. Moreover, a mother would feed her child from her own breast, and the newborns were not entrusted to servants (since none existed there) or to wet nurses (unless there was a need for another woman's help due to the mother dying or being ill). Under such circumstances those people follow the lead of nature, which straightaway provides milk to the mother for the very task of nourishing the offspring.[49] As for the minders and caretakers that Plato assigned to the orphans, this is no problem for us. Relatives would raise orphans at home, but responsibility for their food and clothing belonged to the community. That's it, then, for education, which is a sort of school where the habits of our souls are molded, indisputably a "second nature" (as the Philosophers rightly say) that once you put on, you hardly ever take off.*

On Daily Labor

PLATO

98. Regarding daily activities, Plato generally prescribes the following: It is shameful, he says, if one of the citizens, who is overly indulgent in sleep, should slumber the whole night through; it is absolutely unworthy of a head of the house not to rise before the members of his own household. Likewise, it is an enormous disgrace for the lady of the house to be roused by the maids instead of the maids roused by the lady. Citizens ought to wake in the very early morning, the vigilant magistrate ought to be managing the public interest before dawn, men and women who are heads of their household ought to tend to the private affairs of the home early; for drowsiness is not useful either to the spirit or the body, and it most stands in the way of getting work done.

99. Certainly no one can be more useful when asleep than if he were not alive. For this very reason, he who wants to live and be most sensible, should be awake as much as possible—so long as you take account of your health, for which there is scarcely need of much sleep if you habituate yourself to it well. Additionally, if the state's officials shrewdly keep vigil, they serve as a source of terror for bad citizens and they prevent anyone with hostile intent from invading the city under the shield of darkness. Plato says these things seriously, as usual.

100. In the citizens' training, he places hunting alongside agriculture and the urbane arts. One type of hunting is for aquatic animals, he says, another is for game, another for birds, and another for men, which would be when one ambushes a free person in order to enslave him. Having made this distinction, he goes on to say that those who are concerned about the strength and the robustness of their limbs ought to first get the beasts to weary of running and then pursue them with a spear. Permit the hunters of birds and beasts to wander only through the mountains and uncultivated places, so as not to harm the fields and growing crops by running about.

* The figurative language here of putting on and taking off clothing plays on the double meaning of *habitus* as both "attire" and "disposition."

CI. Piscationem Plato non probat, nescio cur: an quod remissior in piscando opera sit, et ipse nihil in civibus molle et languidum vult? Sed sunt piscationes quaedam admodum operosae, magnoque egentes nisu Corporis: et certe in remigando, trahendoque reti levis labor non est. Piraticum latrocinium, et plagiarios, tamquam immania monstra, ac nefarias hominum pestes, merito detestatur.

CII. Jubet praeterea amplum in urbe locum designari (campum Martium dixeris) ubi juvenes torquendis arcubus, mittendisque sagittis se se crebro exerceant. Etenim jaculorum usus, ait, hastarumque vibratio, atque alia hujus generis, ad corporis motum agilitatemque, et vires alendas juvant plurimum: ipsaque alioquin armorum tractatio est quodammodo militiae quoddam specimen, et belli prolusio. Foeminas quoque (ut supra demonstravimus) bellicosas optat Plato, neque eas a palaestra publica arcet, et cavet maxime, ne otio corrumpantur, et torpeant.

CIII. Itaque et laborem ille utilem gravibus oblectamentis miscet, et oblectamenta vicissim gravia utili labori; idque digno legum latoris consilio; nisi enim civibus recreatio animi publica et licita idemtidem procuretur, quaerent illi sibi clandestinam, et illicitam, magno civitatis malo, et luctuosa familiarum perturbatione. In puerorum denique opere diurno id servetur, inquit, ut oriente Sole ad gymnasia ire compellantur, nisi forte ipsi sponte eant. (Lib. VII. de Legg.)

GUARANII.

CIV. Profestis diebus in artes quisque suas incumbebant. Cum otium erat, vacabant aucupio per silvas, saltusque devios; tanta enim illac volucrum copia est, et tam illae sunt pulcrae visu ob plumas versicolores, ut elegantius nihil, et venustius usquam videris, Venabantur etiam, et piscabantur, feris nam cibo bonis abundat regio, et plurimi sunt amnes piscosissimi. Michael Marimon, Guaraniorum olim cultor, et studiosus historiae naturalis, reperiri ait ibi avium CIII. genera, quadrupedum XLV., piscium XL.; quorum omnium animantium nomina Guaranica sigillatim reddit.

101. Plato does not approve of fishing, and I do not know why. Perhaps it is because the work involved in fishing is very relaxed and he does not want anything delicate or lethargic in his citizens? However, there are certain types of fishing that are very labor-intensive and that require great bodily exertion; and certainly, the labor involved in rowing and pulling in the net is no trifle. He justly detests bands of pirates and plunderers as inhuman monsters and abominable pests to mankind.

102. Moreover, he commands that a large space be designated in the city (you might say a Campus Martius),* where youths can regularly practice handling bows and shooting arrows. The use of projectiles, he says, and the brandishing of spears, as well as other things of this kind, are most beneficial for the movement and agility of the body and for developing strength; in itself, the handling of weapons is, to a degree, something of an example of soldiering and a precursor to war. As we pointed out above, Plato prefers females to be militaristic as well. He does not keep them from the public wrestling grounds, and he takes great care that they are not corrupted by leisure and so become listless.

103. Thus in this way he blends useful labor with serious amusements and in turn serious amusements with useful labor. And it is a source of worthy counsel from a legislator: for, if honest, public means of restoring of one's spirits are not regularly provided for citizens, they will seek out clandestine and illicit means of doing so for themselves, becoming a great calamity to the state and a deplorable disruption for families. In the daily work of the children, it should be observed, he says, that when the sun rises, they are compelled to go to the gymnasium, unless they happened to go there on their own accord (*Laws* Book 7).

THE GUARANÍ

104. On working days they would devote themselves to their occupations. When they had leisure time, they were free to hunt birds throughout the forests and remote wilderness; there is such an abundance of birds there and they are so beautiful to behold on account of their variegated plumage, that you will never see anything more elegant and more delightful. They also hunted and fished, for the region abounds in wild animals that are good for food and there are a great many rivers absolutely teeming with fish. Miguel Marimón, a former cultivator of the Guaraní and student of natural history, says that he found there 103 species of birds, 45 species of quadrupeds, and 40 species of fish, all of whose names he recorded, one by one, in Guaraní.

* Lit. "Field of Mars"; during the Roman Republic, it was a public space where military exercises and assemblies took place.

CV. Diebus festis post vespertinum Officium simulacra belli quaedam obibant viri in foro, vibratis ad scopum sagittis, quarum mittendarum ita sunt periti, ut sive fugientem feram, sive praetervolantem avem petant, vix umquam errent. Ludebant item pila compacta e gummi sic saltitanti, et tremulo, ut concepto simul impetu pergat diutissime subsilire, omnis morae, et quietis impatiens, repetitisque e casu ipso altis plagis. Pilam autem Guaranii non (ut nos) manu, sed superiore parte nudi pedis mittunt remittuntque, idque expeditissime, ac dexterrime.

CVI. Piraticam artem adeo exosam Platoni numquam illi exercuerunt; immo infausta fuerunt praeda immanium Mammalucorum, qui innumerabiles miserae nationis turmas in vincula abductas, et infami venditas pretio, exauserunt. Sed quorsum haec, quae meminisse horret animus? Maximus Americae Meridialis tractus frequentissimis habitabatur Guaraniorum pagis. Ubi nunc illi sunt? Quo gentis ceteroqui faecundae soboles paene omnis recidit? Vastae solitudines, deserti saltus, silvae densae, et horrida ferarum lustra priscas indigenarum sedes tenent. Neque tamen piratica Mammalucorum colonia captivis Indis crevit: sit quippe justo Dei Judicio, ut male parta male dilabantur.

CVII. Contra grassatores istos concessus fuit Guaranicis populis a Rege Catholico usus martiorum ignium, quibus praedatrix gens illa tandem aliquando repressa fuit, ne in neophitos, tamquam lupi in agnos, irruerent. Poscit hic locus, ut nonnihil dicamus de Guraniorum militia. Inter eos, qui professione miles tantum esset, erat nemo, et tamen nemo non miles, si res exigeret; idque secundum instituta Platonis, qui ad necessarium bellum cives omnes exercitatos pugna vult, etiam foeminas, ut supra diximus. Quod autem Guaranii saepe evocarentur in subsidium a Regio Praetore, ut ad hujus imperium parati essent, in quasdam divisi erant cohortes certis sub decurionibus, tribunisque.

CVIII. Milites hi nihil ab aliis Indis vel domicilio, vel veste differebant, neque militiae nomine quicquam e re communi accipiebant, ibantque ab armis ad aratrum, ab aratro vicissim ad arma. Adsciti in auxilium Hispanorum (ut iterum atque iterum factum est pro oppugnanda celebri illa Lusitanorum colonia) e singulis oppidis tot distincti in turmas egrediebantur, quot opus erat ad numerum trium, quattuor, vel sex millium, quem Regius minister poposcerat: militabant autem suis stipendiis, id est, impentis sui quisque pagi; nec tamen sine remuneratione, ob hanc enim operam publice praestitam Philippus V. Rex, plurima Guaraniis, collaudato eorum in bonum regni studio, benigne ac liberaliter indulsit.

105. On feast days, after the evening service, the men would engage in a sort of war games in the town square, with arrows whistling toward a target. They are so expert at shooting these that they almost never miss, whether they are aiming at a fleeing beast or a bird in flight. The Guaraní would also play with a ball made of rubber so bouncy and restless, that once rapid motion is introduced, it continues to bounce for the longest time without pause or rest, with great blows being delivered again and again from its own falling. The Guaraní do not play ball with their hand (like us), but they send it and return it with the top of their bare foot, and they do it very swiftly and with great dexterity.

106. The Guaraní never practiced the craft of piracy, so hated by Plato. On the contrary, they were the unfortunate prey of the inhuman Mamelukes,* who siphoned off incalculable multitudes from this unfortunate nation—people led off in chains and sold vilely at a price. But what was the outcome of these things that the soul shudders to recall? Most of the territory in South America was taken up by Guaraní districts that were extremely crowded. Where are they now? Where did almost all the descendants of this otherwise prolific people end up? Vast wastelands, deserted wilderness, dense forests, and wild dens of beasts occupy the former dwellings of the Indigenous peoples. Yet even the pirate colony of the Mamelukes did not prosper from the captured Indians. Aha! God's judgment is fulfilled: what's acquired evilly, evilly slips away.

107. The Catholic King [Felipe IV] made a concession for the Guaraní people to use firearms against these marauders in order to keep them from falling on the neophytes like wolves on lambs. That predatory band was finally held in check by these means. This issue demands that we say something about the Guaraní militia. Among the Guaraní, there was no one who was just a soldier as his profession and, at the same time, there was no one who, if the situation required, was not a soldier. This is according to Plato's instructions, since he wants all citizens, even females, to be trained for combat in case war is unavoidable, as we said above. Moreover, because the Guaraní were frequently called up by the Royal Governor for the reserves, they had been divided into cohorts under particular commanders and tribunes so that they would be prepared for his command.

108. These soldiers differed in no way from the other Indians, neither in residence nor in attire, and they didn't receive any community funds for being in the militia. They would go from their weapons to the plow, and from the plow back to their weapons. Enrolled in the auxiliaries of the Spaniards (as was done again and again to attack that famous colony of the Portuguese) as many men from each town were divided into squadrons and marched forth as were needed to make up the three, four, or six thousand that the King's minister had requested. They served as soldiers at their own expense, that is, each one at the expense of his own district; however, not without remuneration, for in consideration of the public service they had performed, King Felipe V generously and liberally granted a great many concessions to the Guaraní, in honor of their zeal for the good of the kingdom.

* i.e., slave raiders.

CIX. Foeminae, tametsi nullam belli partem attingerent (neque enim tanti est praeceptum illud Platonis de Martiis matronis, quas vel ipsa natura virium debilitare, et corporis habitudine, et ignavia timidi ingenii, ab usu tractandorum armorum sat eximit) nequaquam otiabantur. Cura domus in eas recumbebat: ipsae lignatum ibant in silvam oppido vicinam, ipsae aquatum in propinquos fontes, seu flumen, ipsae viris aderant in privatis praediis, si metendae, si colligendae erant fruges, si portandae in aedem, ipsae cibum parabant, ipsae cantharos, et ollas, catinosque, et pateras in domesticos usus e subacta creta fingebant.

CX. Singulae insuper matres familias in singulas hebdomadas certum gossipii pondus e publico nebant, netumque referebant ad oppidi Aeconomos, qui e toto glomerum acervo texi curabant telas in vestem oppidanis dividendam: quidquid autem inde supererat, venumibat, ut e pretio emerentur necessaria artium instrumenta, et ferrum, et alia, de quibus postea dicemus. Haec de foeminis. De puerorum vero exercitationibus, satis, arbitror, supra memoravimus.

CXI. Ceterum, quo diurna opera pie casteque (ut Christianos decet) viri foeminaeque, et pueri, et puellae exercerent, P. Ignatius Insaurralde, Guaranicae linguae peritissimus, duo scripsit volumina (edita typis Matriti sunt) opera P.J. Escandon quae inscripsit ipsorum lingua *ARAPORUAGUIYEYHABA*, de recto usu diei, sive temporis, utrumque enim significat Guaranica vox *Ara*; *poru* est utor, *aguiyey*, recte, bene, *haba* verbalis nota, ut vocant Grammatici: atque ecce tibi compositum nomen e quattuor vocabulis.

CXII. Jam vero his ille libris docet Indos sigillatim, qua ratione sancte et digne totum diem transigant sive laborent domi, sive agrum colant, sive sumant cibum, sive in templum eant, sive intersint Sacro Missae, sive Rosarii preces fundant, sive quid aliud agant: sed praesertim modum explicat, quo Sacramenta Ecclesiae rite obeant, et pro re quaque officio virtutis, rei illi conveniente, fungantur. Quae quidem Insaurraldii institutio pro neophytis similis ei est, quam clemens Alexandrinus titulo ΠΑΙΔΑΓΩΓΟΣ (*Paedagogus*) pro veterum Christianorum disciplina et cultu composuit. At hoc differunt, quod Guaranicus scriptor presse rem tractat, Graecus autem auctor variae eruditionis, qua cives suos delectari norat, plurimum admiscet.

109. Women were in no way living a life of leisure even if they took no part in warfare (since Plato's precept about warrior matrons is of no consequence, because nature herself deprived them of physical strength and essentially exempted them from handling weapons due both to their bodily constitution and the inaction caused by their cautious temperaments). The care of the house fell to them: they would go to the forest near town for firewood and to nearby springs or to the river for water. They would assist the men on the private farms, if there were crops to be harvested, gathered, or brought back to the house. They prepared the food, they fashioned the jugs, pots, plates, and bowls for domestic use from kneaded clay.

110. In addition, every week, every female head of household spun a certain amount of cotton from the public store and then gave the yarn to the town's Administrators. They took care that the fabric was woven from the great heap of yarn balls for clothing that would be distributed to the townspeople. Whatever was left over was put up for sale so that with the proceeds necessities could be purchased such as trade-specific tools, iron, and other things that we will talk about later. These are the details regarding women. As for the activities of the children, I think we have recounted enough above.

111. Otherwise, so that men and women, boys and girls could carry out their daily labors piously and virtuously (as befits Christians) Father Ignacio [*corr.* José] Insaurralde, a man extremely skilled in the Guaraní language, wrote a work in two volumes (published in Madrid [in 1759–1760]) with the help of Father Juan de Escandón, which he titled in their own language ARA PORU AGUĬYEY HABA, that is, "On the proper use of the day," or "of time," since the word *ara* has both meanings; *porú* means "I use" and *aguyjé* is "properly" or "well." *Hába* is what the Grammarians call a nominalizer. And so here you have a name made up of four words.

112. And so, with these books, the author teaches the Indians one by one how to spend the whole day in a holy and dignified way, either working at home, cultivating the fields, consuming food, going to the temple, attending the sacrifice of Mass, uttering the prayers of the Rosary, or doing anything else. But chiefly, he explains how they should ritually observe the Sacraments of the Church and how they should carry out the obligations of virtue in whatever way corresponds to their circumstances. Father Insaurralde's program of instruction for the neophytes is similar to the one Clement of Alexandria composed entitled *The Tutor* for the training and cultivation of ancient Christians. But they differ in the fact that the Guaraní writer treats the matter concisely, while the Greek author, a man with a breadth of learning, mixes in a great many things that he knew would be pleasing to his fellow citizens.

De conviviis publicis.

PLATO

CXIII. Mirum est, Platonem cives suos vesci publice voluisse. Illum audi: servi in urbem ex agris tantum ferant annonae, pomorumque, quantum satis sit homini temperate viventi. Prandia fiant palam: his primus locus virorum esto, alter propinquorum et affinium, tertius matrum, et puerorum puellarumque. Praeficiuntor autem vescentibus viri quidam primores, et matronae, qui omnia quotidie observent. Postquam ad cibi finem ventum erit, magistri illi mensarum dimittant pransos jam cives, atque hi, ubi diis, quibus praesens dies, seu nox dicata sit; rite libarint, domum suam modeste redeant.

CXIV. Quid? Prandiane haec frequentia? Quidni? quotidiana erant, idque diserte explicat Plato ipse. Cur autem id praecipiat, hanc redit causam. Cum animantibus, inquit, omnibus innatum sit desiderium cibi potusque, quibus, si recte utimur, ad virtutem alimur, sin contra, trahimur in vitium victi ingluvie, ob id curandum est, ne appetitio ista, quae homini communis est et belluis, frenum mordeat, sed dometur metu legis, et rationis ductu. Id autem fiet, si fuerint probi quidam censores publicarum commessationum, eorum enim oculos fugiet nemo.

CXV. Laudo hoc tuum, Plato, temperantiae studium, illamque etiam probo legem, qua jubes, adolescentes usque ad annos duodeviginti abstinere prorsus vino: neque enim, ut recte mones, ferventi aetatis igni addendus est extrinsecus ignis alius, qui corpus et animum inflammet. Atque id quidem pro juvenum bono, ne lasciviant. De viris porro sic cavet: ubi quis gravem subire laborem caeperit, huic fas esto uti moderato vino, quod medicina quaedam est tuendae apta sanitati, reficiendisque membrorum fessis viribus: quae ratio magis pro senibus valet.

CXVI. Haec recte se habent, Plato; sed non item illud, quod progressus plus justo, indulgentia non ferenda, posuisti. Bibere ad ebrietatem, ais, numquam decet, praeterquam in solemnitatibus ejus Dei (Bacchi) qui auctor inventorque vini fuit. Itane vero, obrui tum vino decet? Permissio haec indigna est te Philosopho, qui sancte, casteque, et secundum naturae modum, homini vivendum, esse, toties, et tam graviter praedicas. Nam si temulentiae inter sacra illa Lyei assueverint viri, senesque, quis ab illa, quaeso, eos deinde retrahet? Quid si idem sibi arrogent in festis diebus Veneris, quandoquidem amica Baccho venus est? Nullum certe vitium postquam semel hominem occupavit, curatu difficilius est; citiusque tigris varia maculosam exuet pellem, quam ebriosus dirum vini hydropem (ut ita dicam) expellet victor abs se. Quocirca sapientior te et prudentior hac in re fuit Rex ille Thraciae Lycurgus, qui ne cives ebrii evaderent, causam e medio sustulit, jussis tota regione vitibus exscindi. (Lib, II, VI. VII. de Legg.)[50]

On Public Banquets

PLATO

113. It is a wonder that Plato wanted his citizens to eat communally. Hear what he says: slaves bring into the city from the field only as much grain and fruits as is sufficient for a person living in moderation. Meals should take place out in the open. In them, the first place is for men, the second for paternal and maternal relatives, and the third place for mothers, boys, and girls. In charge of the meals there are certain leading men and married women who oversee everything daily. After the end of the meal has come, the heads of the tables dismiss the citizens who have already eaten. These, after they pour ritual libations to the gods for whom that particular day or night has been consecrated, return modestly to their homes.

114. What? Were these meals frequent? Why wouldn't they be? They were daily and Plato himself explains it clearly. Indeed, he gives the following cause for why he advises doing this. Since innate in all living beings, he says, is a desire for food and drink, and if we indulge in these correctly, we nourish ourselves toward virtue; otherwise, we are conquered by gluttony and drawn into vice. For this reason, care must be taken that this appetite common to men and beasts, bites down on the bit and is tamed by fear of the law and the guidance of reason. This will happen if those supervising public feasting are upright people, for no one will escape their notice.

115. Oh Plato, I praise this zeal of yours for temperance and I also approve of that law by which you order adolescents, up to the age of eighteen, to abstain from wine completely; for, as you rightly warn, to the raging fire of youth, must not be added yet another external fire that inflames body and mind. This is certainly for the good of the youths so that they do not behave immorally. As for men, he warns as follows: whenever anyone has undertaken a difficult task, it is permissible for such a man to drink a moderate amount of wine, which is a sort of medicine suitable for preserving one's health and restoring the strength drained from his limbs. This reasoning is even more sound for old men.

116. Oh Plato, this is all well and good. But that is not the case with one thing you proposed when you went too far with unbearable indulgence. Drinking to the point of inebriation, you say, is never appropriate, except during celebrations for the God (Dionysus) who was the creator and inventor of wine. So then, is it appropriate to be drowned with wine then? This permissiveness is unworthy of you, the Philosopher who proclaims so seriously and so frequently that people must live scrupulously, virtuously, and according to the ways of nature. For if men and old men grow accustomed to drunkenness during the "Loosener's" religious events, who, I ask, will recall them from there? What if they claim the same for themselves on the feast days of Aphrodite, since Aphrodite is Dionysus' (Dionysus's) friend? There is surely no vice that is more difficult to cure after it has taken hold of a person. The dappled tiger will sooner shed his spotted pelt than a drunkard turn champion and expel the dreadful swelling (so to speak) of wine. On account of which that Thracian king, Lycurgus, was wiser and more prudent than you. So that the citizens would not wind up drunk, he removed the source from their midst, ordering the vines in the entire region to be destroyed (*Laws* Books 2, 6, and 7).[50]

GUARANII.

CXVII. Guaranii patres matresque familias cum liberis domi vescebantur parce, et sobrie, contenti agri frugibus, et bubula, quae singulis publice dividebatur. *Cibi simplices,* ait de priscis Germanis Tacitus, *agrestia poma, recens fera, aut lac concretum. Sine apparatu, sine blandimentis expellunt famem.* Atque is quidem alendi corporis modus naturam paucis contentam decet. Neque tamen Guaranii, si vel ferinam e venatione, vel pisces ex amnibus, vel, quos domi alebant, pullos gallinamve mensae aliquando adderent, ob id deliciis indulsisse dicendi sunt: temperantiae quippe virtus hispida non est, neu adeo severa, ut vetet corpus nonnumquam justa e causa benignius curari.

CXVIII. Convivia illic publica non fiebant nisi in quibusdam sollemnioribus per annum diebus. Tum in foro mensae locabantur instructae iis, quae patresfamilias e domo quisque sua in symbolam conferebant. E publico autem, quo lautius epulum esset, obsonia quaedam liberaliter in singulas tribus praebebantur. Paratis jam ordine cibis varii generis beneprecabatur Curio, cui praeeunti sacra verba respondebat chorus Musicorum, qui deinde inter prandium instrumenta sua pergebant festive pulsare.

CXIX. Post captos hilare et modeste cibos, convivae illi bene Deo dicebant pro data ipsis dapum copia. Omnia ibi intra modum, cui procurando aderat singulis mensis unus ex Indis primoribus. Agapas diceres veterum Christianorum: et quidem sanctiora erant haec prandia iis, in quibus nec inter initia, nec sub medium, nec ad finem, largitoris omnium Dei mentio sit ulla, nullaeque eidem redduntur grates, quas vel Plato referendas diis post mensam posuit. Proh inversi majorum nostrorum pii mores!

CXX. Prandebant publice soli viri, neque ideo foeminae expertes erant sollemnis laetitiae: cum enim cuncta abundarent, ad eas domum bona pars ferculorum perveniebat. Inter Guaranios autem nec vinum nec vites erant, has regio non patitur; illud si ex urbibus Hispanis importaretur, magno constaret pretio, nec vero ibi vendebatur. Nihil magis Guaraniorum cultores curarunt, quam ut longe abesset ab oppidis, quidquid ebrietatem ciet, norant enim hoc esse princeps Indorum vitium, quod optime describit Lusitanus vates eximius Josephus Rodriguez de Mello.[51]

117. Male and female Guaraní heads of households ate at home with their children, sparingly and soberly, content with the fruits of the field and the meat that was publicly distributed to each of them. Of the ancient Germans, Tacitus says: "their food is simple: such as wild fruits, fresh game, or quark.* They drive out their hunger without elaborate preparation and without condiments." And indeed, this way of nourishing the body is suited to a nature content with little. Yet if from time to time the Guaraní added game to their table from hunting, fish from the rivers, a hen or chickens they raised at home, they should not be said to have indulged in delicacies on account of it; for indeed, the virtue of temperance is not prickly nor so severe that it forbids the body from sometimes being nourished more generously when there is good reason.

118. Public banquets did not take place there except on certain especially sacred days of the year. On those occasions, tables were placed in the town square and set up with the things that each head of household brought from his own home as a contribution. And certain provisions from the public store were provided generously for each tribe so that the feast would be more splendid. Once the foods of various kinds were properly arranged, the parish priest would say a prayer and a chorus of musicians responded to him as he led them in the blessings. Afterward these musicians carried on playing their instruments festively throughout the meal.

119. After the food was cheerfully and modestly taken up, the guests would thank God for the abundance of food given to them. Everything there was within moderation and one of the foremost Indians was present at each table to see to this. You might even call it one of the early Christians' love feasts!† And certainly, these meals were holier than those in which neither at the beginning, nor in the middle, nor at the end is there any mention of God, the giver of all things, nor is any thanks given to him, which is something even Plato maintained had to be given to the gods after the meal. Alas! How changed are the pious customs of our ancestors!

120. Only the men ate in public, but it should not be concluded from this that the women were deprived of sacred delights. For since everything was abundant, a good part of the dishes reached them at home. Among the Guaraní there was neither wine nor grapevines, which the region does not support. If it were imported from Spanish cities, it would be at a great price, and it was not sold there anyway. The cultivators of the Guaraní had no greater concern than keeping whatever encourages drunkenness far away from the towns, since they knew that this is the principal vice of the Indians, a fact that the distinguished Portuguese poet José Rodrigues de Melo describes best.[51]

* Lit. "solidified milk."

† The *agape* feast was a term used for a variety of communal meals shared by early Christians as described in Jude 1:12.

CXXI. Operariorum sacrorum diligentiae, et studio respondit optatus fructus. Nulli apud neophytos illos ebrii: neque ego, dum ibi fui, ullo in oppido ullum vidi victum crapula. Sua illis potio ex herba Paraguayca, quam vehementer amant, satis erat: atque hunc quidem liquorem vel si millies ad horae, vel semihorae spatium biberis, impune biberis. Rem, quam vidi expertusque sum refero: qui autem scripsit, potu illo, si large bibatur, ebrietatem pari, nec biberat ipse, nec bibentes viderat. Americanae vero massae e fuscis baccis, et saccaro temperatae, nullus ibi usus, quod pace dixerim Pavvii Philosophi, qui delicias has liberaliter tribuit cultoribus Guaranicis, ut hac etiam eos parte castiget.

CXXII. Clemens Alexandrinus, qui plurimum Platoni defert, qualia esse debeant bonorum convivia erudite et sapienter explicat in Paedagogo, vetatque illis interesse foeminas, maxime innuptas. Tum temperantiae Christianae leges tradit, nequid a prandentibus inverecunde vel clamose fiat: praeclare autem monet, tam esse fugiendam vinolentiam, quam cicutae haustum, quoniam utriusque usus ad certam mortem raptat. At sanctus hic scriptor in epulis publicis Guaraniorum, nihil, opinor, reprehendisset.

De Artibus.

PLATO

CXXIII. Artifices, ait, singuli singularum dumtaxat artium opus factitanto. Unusquisque autem id opificii aggreditor, ad quod ejus ingenium apprime aptum est. Binas artes, vel duo simul rei gerendae gravia negotia, recte tractare mens humana non valet. Hoc igitur stet, ut nemo aerarius sit, et lignarius faber, sculptorve et pictor; sed suam quisque artem obeat, ab eaque sibi victum paret. Quod si aliunde, inquit, ad nos peregrinus aliquis advenerit, qui duabus artibus vacare pariter velit, is minis, et vi cogatur uni tantum insistere; ac si id recuset, in urbem aliam male mulctatus amandetur. De operum aestimatione, et mercede opificum, deque injuria quam artifices forsan patiuntur, aut ipsi contra aliis inferunt; aediles (si quidem intra drachmas quinquaginta damnum verterit) cognoscant: sin vero fraus et noxa major sit, res ad publicum consilium delata secundum leges judicetur.

121. The desired fruit corresponds to the diligence and zeal of the devoted laborers. Among the neophytes there are no drunks; and while I was there, I never saw anyone overcome with intoxication in any town. Their beverage made from Paraguayan yerba, which they love a great deal, was enough for them. And that liquid, even if you drink it a thousand times in the space of an hour or even half an hour, you will drink safely. I relate a fact that I myself have seen and experienced. He who wrote that drunkenness is brought about by this drink, if consumed liberally, has neither drunk it himself, nor seen others drinking it. There is no use there of the American paste made from dark berries tempered with sugar, which I hope I can say without offending the Philosopher de Pauw, who liberally ascribes these delicacies to the Guaraní cultivators in order to scold them on this score.

122. Clement of Alexandria, who esteemed Plato most of all, explains in *The Tutor* with skill and wisdom what sort of banquets good people ought to have, and forbids women from taking part in them, especially the unmarried. Then he recounts the laws of Christian temperance so that nothing immodest or raucous is done by those dining. He warns very clearly that intoxication from wine should be avoided as much as drinking hemlock, because the use of either leads quickly to certain death. This holy writer would have found nothing reprehensible, in my opinion, at the public feasts of the Guaraní.

On the Arts*

PLATO

123. Individual craftsmen, he says, will dedicate themselves exclusively to the practice of a single art. Each one, then, will undertake that work for which his talents are especially suited. The human mind does not have the ability to practice two trades properly or to conduct two important matters of public business at the same time. Thus, let it be enacted that no one be at the same time a coppersmith and a carpenter nor a sculptor and a painter; instead, let each person engage in his own trade and from it obtain nourishment for himself. Because if some stranger from elsewhere, he says, should come to us and want to devote himself equally to two trades, he should be compelled by threats and by force to pursue only one. And if he refuses, let him be fined severely and banished to another city. Regarding the value of the jobs, the wages of workers, and instances of craftsmen suffering an injury or, alternately, inflicting injury upon others, the city magistrates should handle the case (so long as the damage does not exceed fifty drachmas). But, if the fraud and damage are greater, the case is brought before the public council and judged according to the laws.

* *Ars*, translating Greek τέχνη, encompasses a variety of areas of expertise, including what we might call arts, crafts, and skilled trades. The translation of this and related terms (e.g., *artifex*, *artificium*) follows English usage and demonstrates the breadth of the category described in Latin.

CXXIV. Qui animorum disciplinae praesunt, ii gymnasiorum cultum et ornatum curent, edicantque, qui ordo a magistris tenendus sit, dentque iidem operam, ut pueri puellaeque seorsum ad scholas honeste ventitent, modesteque ibi agant custodes autem legum eo incumbant, ut optimus suae quisque artis opifex sit, et caveant, ne divitiae, aut paupertas artifices corrumpant: quia si (exempli causa) figulus admodum dives sit, is pigrior, negligentiorque ad artem suam fiet, parum jam sollicitus ob partas opes de fingendo luto. E contrario, siquis figulinam exercens ob inopiam careat necessario instrumento, et rebus ceteris, quibus ad laborem indiget, opera deteriora faciet, ac filios, aliosque, quos artem docendos excipiet, male prorsus instituet. Ex opulentia igitur, vel egestate accidit, ut mali in urbe sint artifices, et vilia artificia. (Lib. III. et IV. de Rep. VI. et VIII. de Legg.)

CXXV. Artem Dramaticam eliminat e Republica, cui scaenica licentia plurimum nocet, cum videant cives, et audiant, quae nec videre, nec audire oportet. Atque hac fortasse causa D. Thomas diserte docuit: *si operibus alicujus artis plures aliqui male uterentur, quamvis de se non sint illicitae, sunt tamen per officium Principis a civitate exterminanda secundum documenta Platonis.*[52] Et vero qui dicunt theatra scholam esse virtutis, nae illi virtutem nimis sibi blandam, et mollem fingunt, nec reputant, quam multi e bona illa schola, visu audituque corrupti, tandem ingemuerint:

> Ut vidi, ut perii, ut me malus abstulit error.[53]
>
> Seneca autem graviter, *nihil est,* ait, *tam damnosum bonis moribus, quam in aliquo spectaculo desidere.*[54]

GUARANII.

CXXVI. E Guaraniis, qui omnium aptissimi visi erant, ad artes rei publicae necessarias deligebantur. Exemplo sit Musica, quae triginta circiter cantoribus, et fidicinibus constabat in singulis oppidis. Cum pueri quotidie Catechismum alte recitarent, et preces aliquot mane canerent et vesperi; facile observatu erat, qui liquidiore, et gratiore voce essent: iique edocti prius a ludimagistro legere, et scribere, Musicorum choro aggregabantur, id quod eorum parentes magno sibi honori ducebant, quod *Tuparogmbaeupe,* id est domus Dei obsequio liberi sui addicerentur.

124. Those who have charge over the training of souls should look after the maintenance and furnishing of the gymnasiums and determine what order must be preserved by the teachers. These same ones should take care that boys and girls, separately, regularly attend school as they should and behave modestly there. The law guardians take pains that each one is the best artisan in his craft and are on guard so that neither wealth nor poverty corrupts the craftsmen. Because if the potter, for example, becomes quite rich, he will become lazier and more negligent in his craft, having little excitement for shaping the clay due to the wealth he has acquired. On the other hand, if someone who works clay lacks instruments and other things necessary for the work due to his poverty, he will produce work of poorer quality, and he will certainly provide a poor education to the children and those he takes on for the purpose of teaching them his craft. Thus, it turns out that the craftsmen in the city may be bad and their trades worthless due to either opulence or impoverishment (*Republic* Books 3 and 4; *Laws* Books 6 and 8).

125. He eliminates the dramatic arts from the Republic because the licentiousness on stage harms the state tremendously, since citizens see and hear what is not appropriate to see or hear. And perhaps it was for this reason that Saint Thomas expressly taught: "If there are many who misuse the works of some craft, even if they are not themselves forbidden, they must, nevertheless, be banished from the state by the authority of the Prince according to Plato's writings."[52] Those who say that the theater is a school of virtue surely imagine a virtue that is too pliant and alluring to themselves, and they do not calculate how many from that good school were corrupted by what they heard and saw and in the end groan:

> "As soon as I saw you, I was done for! Oh how my wicked mistake swept me away!"[53]
>
> Seneca authoritatively says: "There is nothing," he says, "so damaging to good habits as sitting down in some theater."[54]

THE GUARANÍ

126. Among the Guaraní, those who seemed most capable were selected for the professions necessary for the Republic. Take Music as an example, a profession which consisted of thirty singers and stringplayers in each town. The children recited the catechism aloud every day and sang a few prayers in the morning and in the evening. It was easy to observe who had the clearer and more charming voices; and these, once they had first been taught by the schoolteacher to read and write, were added into the choir of musicians. Their parents considered it to be a great honor for them that their children would be *Tupa ro mbaekuépe*, that is, "devoted to the service of the house of God."

CXXVII. Erant illic utiles artes fere omnes. Erant fabri lignarii, et ferrarii, et aerarii ad conflanda aera campana; erant caementarii, pictoresque et sculptores, quique altaria, et templi columnas, et Divorum statuas partim vario colore, partim auro argentove obducebant; erant, qui ligna torno figurabant; erant curatores aegrorum, et medici. Hi, reliquique artifices artem quisque suam tractabant, neque se se immiscebant alienis opificiis. Serviebant autem rei communi, atque e publico praemium illis rependebatur. Magistris autem (ut futuro provideretur) adjungebantur idonei tirones, qui paulatim artem discerent, illisque deinceps succederent.

CXXVIII. Nolim vero, quod Indi essent artifices, rudes quosdam artium homines, abnormesque putes: tam enim dextre opificiis illi suis utebantur, quam egregii quique Europaeorum sellularii. Mirareris profecto, si adesses coram, eximii artificii Organa pneumatica, et fabrefacta omnis generis instrumenta musica, tornatosque pulchre scyphos, textilesque labores, atque alia doctae manus opera. Habuerunt nimirum e laicis Jesuitis magistros optimos, ut pro arte sculptoria Josephum Brasanelium, et pro architectonice Joannem Baptistam Primoli, et pro fabrili Carolum Franckium, qui omnes mortui sunt apud Guaranios. Gens autem Indica cum retinentissima sit rei sibi traditae, doctrinam, quam ab iis, ceterisque acceperunt, sedulo tuebantur, atque alii aliis per manus tradebant.

De artium progressu.

PLATO

CXXIX. Ignorarunt quondam Novi Orbis incolae culturam artium, quas ne colere quidem poterant, si Platoni vera dicenti credimus. Patere me, quaeso, hic paulo longius digredi, agimus enim de argumento maximi momenti pro scriptore rei Americanae. Profundi ille ingenii Philosophus, eventorumque latentium acer indagator, tempus ait fuisse, cum vel terrae insolens motus quidam, vel maxima imbrium vis, vel immane incendium, totum paene hominum genus extinxerit. Pastores autem (nam ii soli ferme superfuere excelso montium culmine servati) post stragem ceterorum non modo caruerunt corporis ornatu, luxuque, sed etiam artes propemodum omnes amiserunt.

CXXX. Audi hujus rei rationem dignam Philosopho. Aes, inquit, et ferrum, et reliqua metalla, ingenti illa alluvione, vel voraci incendio, vel horrendo terrae motu, depressa, et confusa ita alte delituerunt, ut reperiri, atque in lucem proferri diutissime nequiverint. Sine ferramentis autem nec fabri erant, nec esse poterant. Siquod vero artis instrumentum supra montes forsan restitit (ut securis, ut serra, ut culter) usu ipso deteri, et brevi inter pastorum opera absumi necesse fuit.

127. Nearly all the useful arts were present there: there were carpenters, blacksmiths, coppersmiths to cast bronze bells. There were stonemasons, painters, and sculptors, who covered the altars, the temple columns, and the statues of the saints—some in various colors and others in gold or silver. There were those who shaped wood on the lathe, caretakers for the sick, and doctors. These and the other craftsmen each practiced his own craft, and no one meddled in other people's trades. They served a common purpose and in return a reward was paid to them from the public store. To prepare for the future, they assign suitable apprentices to the teachers, so that gradually they would learn the craft and eventually succeed them.

128. I would not want you to think that as craftsmen the Indians were unsophisticated and irregular with respect to certain crafts. For they practiced their trades as dexterously as the standout specialists in Europe. You would be amazed if you saw personally the pneumatic organs made by exceptional craftsmen, the musical instruments of all types fabricated by them, the beautifully turned goblets, the textile products, and other works produced by skilled hands. To be sure, they had excellent teachers in the Jesuit laity like José Brassanelli for sculpture, Juan Bautista Prímoli for architecture, and Karl Franck for fabrication. All of these men died while among the Guaraní. The Indian people, since they were most tenacious in handing things down among themselves, diligently preserved and energetically transmitted to one another the teachings they had received from these and other men.

On the Development of the Arts
PLATO

129. There was a time when the inhabitants of the New World were unaware of the cultivation of the arts, which, if we believe that Plato speaks the truth, they were not even able to practice. Allow me, I beg, to digress a little longer here, for we are dealing with a matter of the greatest importance to anyone who writes about American matters. That Philosopher of profound genius, a shrewd investigator of obscure events, says that there was a time when a certain extraordinary earthquake, a most violent rainstorm, or an immense fire almost extinguished the entire human race. However, the shepherds (for they were almost the only ones who survived, sheltered in the high mountaintops), after the destruction of the others, not only lacked luxuries and apparel for the body but they also lost nearly all of the arts.

130. Listen to the reason for this, worthy of that Philosopher: After having been buried and jumbled up in that enormous flood, voracious fire, or horrendous earthquake, he says, copper, iron, and the other metals lay hidden so deeply that for a long time, they could neither be found again nor be brought forth into the light. Without metal tools, there were no artisans, nor could there be. And if by chance some tool was left up in the mountains (such as an axe, a saw, or a knife) it was unavoidable for it to wear away from simple use and in a short time be ruined in the course of the shepherds' work.

CXXXI. Arma porro alia ad fabricandum nusquam erant, defueruntque penitus quoad iterum aes, et ferrum (vel pluvia, vel fluminum lapsu superinjectam humum eradente) paulatim emersere, artique ferrariae materiam suppeditarunt, idque factum non est, nisi post plurimas hominum aetates: mille certe anni, vel etiam bis mille praeterierunt ante tempus illud; quo quaedam artificia in usus humanos invexisse dicuntur Daedalus, et Orphaeus, et Palamedes. Quin etiam multa pro communi utilitate heri (ut ita dicam) et nudius tertius primo nobis palam apparuerunt.

CXXXII. Igitur artes omnes (pergit Plato dicere) quae ferro et aere utuntur, jacuere tenebris sepultae, abolitaeque penitus, donec sensim tellus sinum rursus aperuit, et obruta metalla mortalibus patefecit. Illud tamen interea fuit boni, quod nec bella, nec seditiones, tumultusve sollicitarent eas humanae gentis reliquias: cum enim pauci essent numero, inter se sancte amabant, neque ulla alioquin erat discordiarum causa vel ob pabulum, vel ob tectum, vel ob alia vitae frugalis commoda; quandoquidem agrorum segetes, silvarumque baccae et poma, omnibus abunde suppetebant, praeter lacuum fluminumque pisces, et largam lactis copiam, et feras multiplicis foeturae, et faciles captu.

CXXXIII. Rudes autem vestes, et stragula, et casas, et larem, et ollas, et cetera domi vasa, exiguo sibi illi labore comparabant. Namque opus fingendae cretae, et nendi, texendique ars ferro non egent:[55] quo fit, ut siquando homines in summam generis paucitatem ob commune aliquod malum redacti fuerint, resurgere, et propagari iterum queant eo, quod Dei, ait, providentia res usu magis necessariae praesto sint superstiti prosapiae.

CXXXIV. Ceterum gens illa, quae publicam mundi calamitatem evasit, ut valde inops non fuit, sic nec fieri valde dives potuit, cum neque aurum, neque argentum, neque gemmas haberent. In hominum autem coetu, qui nec opes possidet, nec premitur inopia, justissimi sint mores necesse est. Nullus quippe ibi e malesani spe lucri contumeliae locus, nullus injuriae, aemultationive aut invidiae. Quocirca residui illi mortalium boni probique erant, idque maxime ob agendi simplicitatem, qua fiebat, ut neque rixae essent inter eos, neque lites, quibus plerumque urbem sus deque vertit, et turbat civis aliquis injustus avarusque, qui aliorum paci, et bonis insidiatur: parvus vero ille priscae gentis grex sedatior erat, et aequior, quietisque amantior, idemque modestior, et justior.

131. Moreover, there were no implements anywhere for use in fabrication. In fact, they were completely absent until once again copper and iron gradually emerged (with the rain or the rivers' flow eroding the accumulated soil) and supplied raw materials for blacksmiths. But this did not happen except after a great many generations; certainly, a thousand years, or even two thousand, had passed before that time when Daedalus and Orpheus and Palamedes are said to have reintroduced certain trades into human use. Thus, many things useful to the community first became apparent to us yesterday (so to speak) or the day before.

132. Thus, all the crafts, Plato goes on to say, which make use of iron and bronze, lay in darkness—buried and obliterated—until little by little the earth once again revealed its hiding place and exposed the buried metals to the view of mortals. However, in the meantime it was good because neither wars, insurrections, nor riots agitated what remained of the human race. Since they were few in number, they loved each other religiously and, besides, there was no cause for discord on account of food, lodging, or any other convenience of that frugal life since the crops of the fields and the berries and fruits of the forests were abundantly available for everyone, not to mention the fish from the lakes and rivers, the great profusion of milk, and the easy to hunt wild animals with their profusion of offspring.

133. With minimal work they provided themselves with simple clothes, blankets, huts, a hearth, pots, and the rest of the household equipment. For the work of molding clay, spinning, and weaving do not require iron.[55] Thus, if ever humans were reduced to the race's absolute minimum as the result of some common evil, they could rise again and be made plentiful once more because of the fact that, by God's providence, Plato says, the things they truly needed to use would be at hand for the surviving stock.

134. On the other hand, that group that escaped the universal destruction of the planet, just as it was not truly destitute, could not become truly rich either, since they did not have gold, silver, or jewels. In fact, in a human society, which does not possess wealth, but is not oppressed by scarcity, their customs are necessarily the most righteous. Naturally, there is no place there for the affronts born out of a hope of maddening profit, nor for injury, rivalry, or envy. That is why these remaining mortals were good and upright, and it was mostly due to the simplicity with which they did things. That meant that there were no quarrels or disputes between them. Very often these are the means by which an unjust and greedy citizen conspires against the peace and property of others, turns the city upside down, and throws it into chaos. To be sure, that small flock of ancient people was more composed and more equitable, more loving of calm, and therefore more modest and more just.

CXXXV. Ad haec, familiis illis, agri silvaeque cultricibus, nec libri erant, nec litterae, contentionum non raro fomes. Vivebant (sine scripti juris tabulis) tradito sibi a senioribus more: nec tamen ob id parvo eidem populo deerat probabilis quidam et aequus rectae disciplinae modus. Etenim quicumque seorsum degunt, privatimque sibi consulunt propter egestatem ortam ab strage regionis, iis semper aliquis aetate provectior praeest, moderaturque domi sine cujusquam offensione, querelisque; propterea quod fons et principium generis idem omnibus est, utpote ab eodem patre et avo genitis, eademque avia et matre. Liberi autem (instar avium cognatarum, quae una volitant, et una cibum legunt) ducem illum domesticum ultro sequuntur, ejusque voluntate usi pro lege, reverentur sancte casteque paternum imperium, quod omnium imperiorum justissimum est. (Lib. III. de Legg.)

GUARANII.

CXXXVI. Guaraniis olim non aes fuit, non ferrum; non plumbi quicquam, non stanni. Sacri cultores cum sine metallis his nihil fere fieri posset domi, rurive, illuc secum ea metalla cum artium instrumentis importaverunt, curaruntque deinceps, ut adveheretur quotannis ex urbe Bonaurensi infecti ferri magnum pondus, idque impendiis magnis: nam nostra memoria centum librae (*quintal* vocant Hispani) valebant sedecim circiter aureos, ex quo fieri conjectura potest, quanta ibi esset aestimatio mercium allatarum ab Europa. Nunc fortasse minoris aes ferrumque veneunt beneficio Caroli III. Regis, qui commercium in flumen Argenteum, atque adeo Bonasauras liberaliter aperuit, tanta frequentia, ut prius vix centesima pars navium illuc iret prae numero euntium in praesentia.

CXXXVII. De opificiis autem, quae ferri et aeris ope fiebant apud Guaranios, dixi supra, sed consulto illic reticui de textoribus, qui singulari mentione digni sunt. Horum habebant plurimos singula oppida pro texendis telis, quae in vestem publice dividebantur. Erant etiam seni quaternive, qui pro privatis Indis texebant. Quippe nuptae foeminae e gossipio, quod patresfamilias suo in praedio colebant, globos nebant domi, atque ubi bonam illorum vim agglomerarant, afferebant ad oppidi Aeconomum, qui allatorum pondus, et nomen afferentis in commentarium referebat.

135. In addition, those families who were cultivators of the countryside and the forest had neither books nor writing, which not infrequently are tinder for controversy. Without records of written law, they lived according to the customs handed down to them from their elders and for that reason this same small population did not lack a commendable and fair means of proper discipline. For, whatever people live in isolation and look after their own affairs apart from any government due to the impoverishment that arose from the destruction of their region, they are always governed by someone rather advanced in age, who manages the home without offense to anyone or complaints. This is because the same is true for everyone, that this person is the origin and beginning of the clan, inasmuch as they have all proceeded from the same father and grandfather, and from the same grandmother and mother. After the fashion of kindred birds who fly as one and eat as one, the children voluntarily follow their domestic leader, adopting his or her will in place of law, they religiously and virtuously revere ancestral authority, which is the most just of all authorities (*Laws* Book 3).

THE GUARANÍ

136. Formerly, the Guaraní had no copper, iron, lead, or tin. Since almost nothing could be done either at home or in the field without these metals, the Holy cultivators brought these metals there with them, along with trade-specific tools; and thereafter they had a large quantity of raw iron brought from the city of Buenos Aires each year and they did so at great cost. For in my memory, one hundred pounds, which the Spanish call a "quintal," was worth about sixteen gold pieces. From there conjecture can be made regarding how much merchandise imported from Europe would be worth there. Now, perhaps, copper and iron cost less, by the grace of King Carlos III, who opened up commerce on the Río de la Plata and therefore also Buenos Aires so liberally and on such a scale that beforehand scarcely one hundredth of the ships would go there compared with the number going at present.

137. I have spoken above about the craftwork done among the Guaraní with the aid of iron and copper, but I intentionally remained silent about the weavers, who certainly deserve special mention. Individual towns had a great number of these to weave the fabrics, which were distributed throughout the community for clothing. There were also four or six who wove for the Indians' private use. Naturally, the married women at home spun balls from the cotton that the head of their household grew on their farm. Once they had amassed a good quantity, they took them to the town Administrator who would record in the register the weight of what was brought and the name of the person who brought it.

CXXXVIII. Tum uni e quaternis illis senisve textoribus, quorum modo meminimus, ea tradebat, ut telam texeret: tela dein (pondere ad trutinam rursus revocato, nequid cui de suo periret) Indae, quae attulerat glomera, reddebatur ab Aeconomo gratis, nam textori praemium laboris e re communi pendebatur. Nempe matres familias praeter amictum illum, quo donabantur publice earum liberi, his, et maritis, et sibi vestes alias conficiebant e proventa agri a viris culti proprios in usus.

De populorum origine.

PLATO

CXXXIX. Ut respiravit tandem a malis vel motae, vel exustae, vel demersae terrae, superstes hominum stirps, convenere in locum unum alii atque alii, majorque sensim coetus factus est. Hinc ex studiorum operumque similitudine, et desiderio mutuae opis, communisque auxilii, conjunctis invicem animis, coaluit nova societas.[56] Huic ante omnia pro cunctorum securitate et bono, ea fuit cura, ut ad montium radices, vicinosque fontes, sepem inducerent, tamquam parvae urbis muros, contra ferarum repentinos incursus. Verum prima illa advenarum collectio cum e multis alibi, alibique natis educatisque, consisterit, id oriri necesse fuit, ut singulae tribus colere pergerent, et revereri senem eum patrem, et ducem, quem antea secutae fuerant. Habebant praeterea suos quisque mores, ritusque, quibus olim assueverant. Ut vero nos nostra, magis quam aliena, delectant, priorem illam vivendi formam, cui seorsim familiae singulae institerant, unaquaeque tribus volebat ceteris anteferri.

CXL. Ejusmodi intestina contentio nascenti illi oppidulo obesse plurimum poterat, exorta discordia, ruptoque faedere, recens inito. Malo huic ita obviam itum est. Habito inter se consilio, designarunt quosdam arbitros, qui singularum tribuum consuetudines examinarent, et aptiores publico bono seligerent. Exin unum ex iis, qui mente, et animi altitudine, et prudentia, reliquis anteibant, sibi communiter praefecerunt, ut expensos jam mores, et probatos judicum illorum consensu, deduci in usus, et pro lege haberi juberet, ac plebem, et plebis item priscos duces, justo imperio regeret, adjectis, si opus esset, novis repagulis boni publici. Ecce tibi incunabula, atque exordia latarum legum, et principia inducti regni, jurisque communis fontem, et originem; idque vel Deo ipso auctore, qui humanae providens naturae alios hominum gubernari vult ab aliis, quorum persona et auctoritas divino humanoque jure sacra et inviolabilis est.[57]

138. Then he would give them to one of those four or six weavers, whom we just mentioned, to weave the fabric. Later, the fabric (after its weight was checked again on the scales so that no one would lose anything that was theirs) was returned by the Administrator to the Indian woman who had brought the yarn balls. This was done at no charge; for the recompense for the weaver's labor was paid out from the community resources. Of course, aside from the amice that their children were presented with by the community, matriarchs made clothing for their children, their husbands, and for themselves out of the produce of the land cultivated by the men for private use.

On the Origin of Peoples
PLATO

139. As soon as the surviving stock of humans finally recovered from the evils caused by the earth's shaking, scorching, or flooding, they variously came together in one place and, little by little, a larger group was formed. Thus, out of the similarity of their inclinations and needs, their desire for mutual support and common aid, as well as their souls, which had formed mutual bonds, a new society coalesced.[56] First of all, for the security and well-being of the whole, they made sure to extend a barrier against repeated incursions of wild beasts, like the walls of a small city, stretching to the slopes of the mountains and the nearby springs. Even so, since that first collection of strangers consisted of many people born and raised in many different places, it necessarily arose that the individual tribes continued to honor and revere as father and chief that old man whom they had previously followed. Moreover, they each had their own customs and rites to which they had long ago grown accustomed. Given that our own ways please us more than what is foreign, each and every tribe wanted that prior way of life, upon which individual families separately insisted, to be preferred over the others.

140. Internal struggle of this sort could have been a great obstacle for that nascent village, if discord had arisen and the freshly formed alliance had been broken. This evil was prevented as follows: After deliberating amongst themselves, they appointed certain arbitrators to study the customs of the individual tribes and single out the ones more conducive to the common good. Next, those who surpassed the others in intelligence, greatness of soul, and prudence appointed one of their number by common agreement as leader. He would then put into practice and make legally binding the customs that had already been evaluated and approved by the consensus of those judges. And he would rule with righteous authority over the whole nation, including its former leaders, with new restraints being added if necessary for the public good. Here you have the cradle and, indeed, the beginning of widespread laws, the foundations of the introduced regime, the source and origin of common law. And the instigator of this was certainly God himself, who, with foresight regarding human nature, wants some people to be governed by others, whose person and authority are, by divine and human law, sacred and inviolable.[57]

CXLI. Plato igitur, de populorum origine et societate sapienter disserens, mihi quidem videtur paene oculis ipsis hausisse, quae acciderunt post diluvium genti pristinae e veteri orbe in Americam migranti. Sane Novum ille Orbem melius propiusque describit hoc loco, quam ibi, ubi acceptam a Sacerdotibus Aegyptiis narrationem de magna ATLANTIDE ultra fretum Herculeum reddit explicatis sigillatim rebus et moribus hominum transmarinorum.

CXLII. Lege Timaeum illius et Critiam. Hi libri tales sunt, ut (sive prisca historia, sive prudenti conjectura usus sit ibi Plato) in eis eruditi viri expressa quaedam Americae vestigia deprehenderint; adeo narratae res rebus inventis respondent. Verum, ut ut pulchra haec sint, nihil ad pulcherrimum judicium istud, quod modo retulimus de perditis casu artibus, eisdemque paulatim instauratis, et de coeuntibus sensim in vitae societatem post generale terrarum excidium dispersis hominum tribubus. (De Legg. lib. III.)

CXLIII. Equidem, qui fuerint mores, et qui vitae modus, primis illis Novi Orbis incolis e Platonis ista sive divinatione, sive descriptione, videre mihi apertissime videor. Video turmas hominum vagas, errantesque, quales etiam num multae ibi sunt: video latentes sub patrum moderamine teneros liberorum greges: video terrae opibus, silvarumque baccis vitam eos tolerare, et venari, et piscari: video rudes artium vilibus in tuguriis degere, et coeli intemperiem, ac imbres, ventosque, tectis e caespite structis, et tomento arcere.

CXLIV. Video illos uti pro veste consutis tigrium pellibus, et pro lecto stratis arborum frondibus, proque domestica supellectili, vasis fictilibus: video numerum indigenarum subinde crescere, auctis sensim familiis, deligique unum e primoribus communi consilio, qui toti tribui praesit Caciquii titulo: video pollentem viribus jam populum sibi privatim consulere, et seorsum agere, ut nunc sunt in Paraguaya Pampae, et Guaycurui, et Tobae, et Mocovii, et Abipones, et Mbayaeae, aliique plures in suas quisque distincti turmas, divisique in contubernia se se tuendi causa. Haec video, et intelligo placita Platonis optime convenire Americanis gentibus.

141. As Plato wisely discusses the origin and association of peoples, he almost seems, at least to me, to have drunk in with his very own eyes what happened after the flood to the ancient tribe that migrated from the old world to America. To be sure, in that passage he describes the New World better and more accurately than when he reports the narrative, which he got from the Egyptian priests, about the great ATLANTIS beyond the Strait of Hercules* with the details and customs of the people from across the sea explained one by one.

142. Read his *Timaeus* and *Critias*. These books are so extraordinary that scholars have detected certain traces of America expressed in them, where Plato either made use of an ancient history or prudent conjecture. So much so that what's described corresponds to what was found. But, as beautiful as these things may be, nothing compares to that most glorious concept which we just related: how the arts were lost by chance and then the same ones were restored little by little and how the tribes of humankind came together to form a social partnership after having been dispersed following the overall destruction of the earth (*Laws* Book 3).

143. Indeed, from Plato's either divination or description I seem to see most clearly what the customs and way of life were for the first inhabitants of the New World. I see throngs of people roving and wandering about, for there are many of this sort there even now. I see tender flocks of children, safely under their parents' guidance. I see them hunting, fishing, and sustaining life with the riches of the earth and the fruits of the forests. I see them living in ordinary shelters, unacquainted with the arts and keeping off the intemperance of the sky, the rain and the wind, by means of roofs made from sod and stuffing.

144. I see them use tiger skins sewn together for clothing, foliage from the trees spread out for bedding, and clay vessels for kitchenware. I see the number of Indigenous people continually growing, as families are enlarged gradually, and one of the primary men being selected by the consent of the community to govern the entire tribe with the title of Cacique. I see a people already rich in strength that takes care of itself apart from the State and acts independently, such as those currently in Paraguay: the Pampas, the Guaycurús, the Tobas, the Mocobíes, the Abipones, the Mbayás, and many others, all separated into their own groups and divided into cohorts for the purpose of looking after one another. I see these things and I understand how Plato's principles are perfectly in harmony with the peoples of America.

* i.e., Strait of Gibraltar.

CXLV. Neque id tantum, (quod multo est gravius) video, et miror Philosophorum maximi sensa quammaxime consentanea esse iis, quae divini nos docent libri de Sem, Cham, et Japhet, Noemi liberis, qui post diluvium sub paterno imperio egerunt diu cum sucrescente prole, donec hac jam nimis aucta, ex eisdem propagati generis stirpibus *divisae sunt insulae gentium in regionibus suis, unusquisque secundum linguam suam, et familias suas in nationibus suis.* Ad extremum video ab iis ipsis tribubus Noemicis processu temporis instauratas artes, quae maximum ab obruta imbribus terra detrimentum passae fuerant; et demum aedificatas (cum jam ad fabricandum instrumenta suppeterent) urbes, alias ab aliis, ut Babylonem, et Niniven, et Chalem, et Resem.[58]

CXLVI. Redeo ad indos: caruerunt hi, et plures eorum adhuc carent, aere, et ferro, et plumbo, quorum penuriam student utcumque supplere. Nam loco securis, et serrae, et dolabrae, utuntur igne ad sternendas arbores, quarum rectos ramos circum exurendo deducunt sensim in gracilitatem hastae vel jaculi: scabros autem sinus, a foco relictos, acuta perpoliunt silice. Iidem quod desint ipsis hami, subsilientes pisces sagittae jactu transfigunt, transfixosque nando capiunt. Ad suendas autem belluarum pelles legunt duras dumorum spinas pro acu, proque textorio praelo crassas implicant inter se cannas, quibus sibi telas texunt in vestes, et retia conficiunt e cujusdam cardui fibris ad servandas domi agri fruges, et silvae baccas.

CXLVII. Acuit videlicet Indorum industriam ferri inopia, quae causa est, cur illic artium cultura tamdiu jacuerit. Quippe vis ingenii per se sine idoneis ad agendum armis parum valet. Vel in ipsa Europa ante reperta quaedam praestantiora instrumenta minor artificum et elegantia, et nitor fuit: ac Nautica ars, et Astronomica, priusquam index magneticus, et telescopia in usus deducerentur, exiguos fecere progressus; dein vero illorum ope patuerunt nobis novum mare, novi coeli, nova terra.

CXLVIII. Mexicanae quidem Peruvicaeque gentes, quod venas aeris, et argenti, et auri, jampridem reperissent, atque inde ad fabricandum instrumenta sibi comparassent, ante Europaeorum illuc ad ventum exercebant plures artes, quarum exquisitus labor admirationi fuit non Hispanis tantum conquisitoribus, sed illis etiam litteratis viris e Gallia Bouguersio, et Lacondemine, ceterisque, quamvis hi reliquias dumtaxat viderint operum priscorum.

145. And that's not all. I also see (and this is much more serious) and am astonished that the ideas of the greatest of the Philosophers are as consistent as they could be with what the sacred books teach us about Shem, Ham, and Japheth, sons of Noah. After the flood, they lived for a long time under paternal authority, with descendants springing up until the point that they were too numerous, and from these same lineages of the extended clan "the islands of the peoples were divided into their own territories, each according to their own language, and into own nations, each according to their own families." In the end, I see that with the passage of time the arts, which had suffered the most damage when the earth was covered with rain, were reestablished by these very Noahtic tribes, and finally, when there were instruments available for construction, the various cities, such as Babylon, Nineveh, Calah, and Resen, were erected by various tribes.[58]

146. I return to the Indians. They also lacked, and many of them still lack, copper, iron, and lead, the scarcity of which they try to supplement however they can. Thus, instead of axe, saw, and mattock, they use fire to clear out the trees, whose straight branches they refine little by little into the slender shape of a spear or javelin by burning around their circumference. And then they smooth out rough ridges left behind by the fire with a sharp stone. Also, because they lack hooks, they pierce fish by launching an arrow at them as they leap, and by swimming after them they capture the pierced fish. To sew the beasts' pelts, they select hard thorns from brambles for needles, and for the weaver's press they enmesh thick reeds on which they weave cloth into clothes for themselves. From the fibers of a certain thistle, they also make nets to store the fruits of the field and the berries of the forest at home.

147. The lack of iron clearly stimulated the Indians' industriousness, which is the reason why the cultivation of the arts lay dormant for so long there. Because without the tools appropriate for a given task the power of ingenuity is in itself not enough. Even in Europe itself, before certain rather remarkable instruments were devised, the craftsmen had less elegance and splendor. Even the nautical and astronomical arts, before the compass and the telescope came into use, made minimal progress. Later, however, with the help of these tools, a new sea, new skies, and new lands lay open to us.

148. Since they had found veins of copper, silver, and gold long ago and had secured them for fabricating tools for themselves, the Mexican and Peruvian peoples practiced many arts before the arrival of Europeans there. And their exquisite work served as a source of admiration not only for the Spanish conquistadors, but also for those men of letters from France, like Bouguer, La Condamine, and others, although they only saw remnants of the earlier works.

CXLIX. Quod si PAUVIUS Philosophus in suis illis disquisitionibus de America, exemplo, et norma Platonis philosophatus fuisset, haud ita longe abreptus esset, neque tot a vero aborrentia scripsisset de Novo orbe, ejusque incolis, et brutis animantibus, ut cum posuit de cane ibi non latrare, adeo inertem tellus pigra, et deses (ut vult ipse) illum reddidit: et tamen ego Americanorum canum latratu paene obsurdui olim.

CL. Addo denique non satis esse copiam ferri ad cultum gentis, et artium, si fabri desint. Hebraeis quondam, Saule Rege, non ferrum deerat, non aes, et tamen, cum a victoribus Philistaeis eo angustiarum redacti fuissent, ut *faber ferrarius non inveniretur in omni terra Israel,* carebant apto instrumento agri, *retusae* enim *erant acies vomerum, et ligonum, et tridentum, et securium.* Et quod ad belli usum attinet, ita erant imparati, ut de eisdem dicatur: *non est inventus ensis, et lancea in manu totius populi.*[59] Confer tu calamitosum hoc tempus cum fausto illo tempore Regis Salomonis, quo regnante, quidquid eximii, et magnifici efficere artes possunt, id totum in templi fabricam collatum est. Adeo et sapiens Rex, et parata ferri et aeris copia, et fabri industrii bono prosunt publico.

GUARANII.

CLI. Poscit hic locus, ut de instituta apud Guaranios populos civili, et Christiana societate agamus. Gens illa longe lateque per Americam Meridialem diffusa linguae communione vetus inter capita familiarum commercium retinere facile potuisset. Sed cum infinita propemodum multitudo succrevisset, vel necessarii, vel largioris victus causa insederunt seorsum silvas camposque, ut singulis libitum fuit tribubus. Ob id ipsum vicinitatem amnium, qui plurimi illac sunt, et piscosissimi, ac felicibus umbrosi arboribus, incolere coeperunt. Pars autem ingens secuta littus est Brasilici Oceani, qua is ad Austum, et ad solem orientem spectat.

CLII. Rex apud illos nullus: et sunt, qui in hanc rem trahant tria eis ex Alphabeto elementa *F. L. R.* defuisse, haud omnino, ajunt, absurde, quod *Fide,* et *Lege,* et *Rege* carerent. Verum nihil hic est praeter ludum, et quidem falsum, ne dicam puerilem. Quippe *R.* linguae illi frequentissima est. Paraguay, Parana, Uruguay, tria sunt nobilissima flumina, et nomina Guaranica, habentia *R.* quam illi litteram ita passim in loquendo adhibent, ut equidem dubitem, numcui Europaearum linguae major ejus sit usus.[60]

149. But if the Philosopher de PAUW, in his investigations on America, had philosophized according to the example and pattern of Plato, he would hardly have gotten so carried away, nor would he have written things so inconsistent with the truth about the New World, its inhabitants, and its brute creatures, such as when he asserted that the dogs there do not bark, because that land is so backward and idle that it rendered them unproductive (or so he claims). And yet, I almost went deaf back then from the barking of those American dogs.

150. Finally, I add that an abundance of iron is not sufficient for the cultivation of people and plants if craftsmen are in short supply. Once, the Hebrews, when Saul was King, lacked neither iron nor copper, and yet, when they had been reduced by the victorious Philistines to such dire straits that "not a blacksmith could be found in all the land of Israel," they had no tool suitable for the field, for "the edges of the plowshares, hoes, harpoons, and axes were blunt." And as for things war requires, they were so ill-equipped that it was said of them: "not a sword nor a lance was found in the hands of the entire population."[59] Compare this calamitous time with that auspicious time of King Solomon, in whose reign whatever the exceptional and magnificent arts could produce, all of it was brought together in the building of the temple. So very much do a wise king, a ready supply of iron and copper, and industrious craftsmen serve the public good.

THE GUARANÍ

151. This is the place to ask how we handle the civic and Christian community established in the Guaraní populations. This group of people, spread throughout the length and breadth of South America, could easily have kept up the old system of communication between the heads of families due to their common language. But when the mass of people grew to almost incalculable size, either because food was needed or because it was more abundant elsewhere, they settled separately throughout the forests and plains according to each tribe's preference. For this reason, they began to inhabit the areas near the rivers, which are plentiful there, teeming with fish, and shaded by fruiting trees. However, a sizable portion of them followed the very wide coastline of the Brazilian ocean, where it looks to the south and to the rising sun.

152. They have no Regent. And there are those who attribute this to the fact that the three letters "F," "L," and "R" are missing from their alphabet, and say, altogether absurdly, it is because they lacked "Faith," "Law," and a "Regent." But that's nothing more than a play on words, and a false—dare I say puerile—one at that. Obviously, the letter "R" is quite common in that language. Paraguay, Paraná, and Uruguay are three extremely well-known rivers and their names in Guaraní have the letter "R," a letter they use so frequently when speaking that I really doubt it is used more frequently in any of the European languages.[60]

CLIII. *L.* et *F.* vere illi carent, ac siquando peregrinum aliquod nomen his affectum litteris occurerit, *L* per *R*, *F* autem per *P* efferunt, quocirca *Alferez Real* (id est Vexillifer Regius) Hispanum nomen, pronunciant ipsi *Arperez Real.* Tamen pueri in ludo edocti, geminum elementum *L* et *F* in legendis Hispanis, et Latinis libris expeditissime reddunt. Qui vero sit factum, ut in linguam ceteroqui numerosissimam utriusque istius elementi admissus usus non fuerit, haud facile dictu est. De re constat, de causa rei non constat.

CLIV. De Guaraniis Brasilicis Joannes Petrus Maffejus ex monumentis, ipsi ad scribendum datis refert haec: "Fide, Lege, Rege carent . . . Nudi aeque viri ac foeminae prorsus incedunt . . . gregatim peregrinantur ordine simplici, silentio miro: virum uxor anteit . . . numerandi rationem, ac litteras ignorant omnes, tantum tenui quadam traditione nonnulla de Noe, deque diluvio a patribus accepisse dicuntur: ut probabile sit, post dissipatos quondam divino jussu mortales, nullum huic genti cum nostri orbis hominibus fuisse commercium . . . Sub eodem tecto, ad inversae modum carinae praelongo, multae simul familiae degunt, noctu ad noxia vitanda animalia cubantes in retibus a terra suspensis: vivuntque in diem; et quidquid habent in commune facillime conferunt, nihil in posterum soliciti . . . Sparsis domiciliis habitant, nullo magistratu legibusve constricti."[61]

CLV. Haec ille, quae mihi e visis Guaraniis Paraguaycis partim quidem probantur, partim non item. Et quoniam singula persequi non est animus, unum ajo, Guaranios tam viros quam foeminas, uti olim veste consuevisse. Nam si veste prorsus caruerunt, quorsum apud eos prisca vestium nomina? Vestes generatim dicunt *Aò*; vestem autem viri *Aobacì*: *Aocaracarà*: vestem vero foeminae *Tupoì, Carazà, Tupaì*: se se porro veste induere explicant verbo, *Ayeaomonde.* Si vestis igitur illis non fuit, cur haec, dic, fuerunt nomina? Quaere Guaranicum nomen calcei, aut tibialis; nusquam reperies: quippe ut re caruerunt, carent etiam rei nomine: et calceos mutuata aliunde voce *zapatù* (zapato Hispanis) vocant. Quid multa? Chiriguani stirpis Guaranicae sunt, et virum penitus nudum (quamvis ethnici adhuc sint) nudam apud eos foeminam non videris. Numerandi vero rationem, quam habuerint (ne dicantur eam ignorasse) supra docuimus.

153. They actually do lack "L" and "F," and whenever they come across some foreign word that has these letters, they change the "L" to "R" and the "F" to "P," so that they pronounce the Spanish title ALFÉREZ REAL (that is, the royal standard-bearer) as "Arperez Real." Children, however, educated in schools, effortlessly render the letter pair "L" and "F" when reading books in Spanish and in Latin. How it could be that in an otherwise extremely rich language use of neither letter has been adopted, is not easy to explain. There is agreement as to the fact, but not as to its cause.

154. Regarding the Brazilian Guaraní, Giovanni Pietro Maffei relates the following from the records provided to him for his writing: "They lack Faith, Law, and a Regent . . . Men and women alike strut about naked . . . They travel in groups, single file, in astonishing silence; the wife walks before her husband . . . they are all ignorant of numbers and letters. They are said to have received just some sort of basic tradition about Noah and the flood from their elders, namely that it is likely that, after mortals had been scattered long ago by divine decree, their nation had had no interaction with the people of our world . . . Under one, very long roof that looks like the inverted keel of a ship, many families live together, and at night, to avoid harmful animals, they sleep in nets suspended off the ground. They live day by day and whatever they have they readily contribute to the community, not at all concerned for tomorrow . . . They live in houses that are scattered about and are not bound by any magistrate or laws."[61]

155. The things Maffei says are confirmed partly by the Paraguayan Guaraní I have seen, but at the same time partly not. Since I do not intend to follow up on each of these matters, I'll address one of them: namely, that the Guaraní, men as much as the women, have been habituated to wearing clothes since ancient times. For, if they truly lacked clothing, what is the purpose of the ancient words they have for clothes? Clothes in general they call *Ao* while *Aovasy* and *Aokarakará* are men's clothing and *Tupói*, *Karasá*, and *Tupái* are women's clothing. They moreover describe putting on clothing with the verb *Añeaomondé*. So, if they did not have clothes, tell me, why did they have these words? Search for a Guaraní word for shoe or sock; you will never find one. Naturally, when they lacked something, they also lack a word for that thing. Borrowing a word from elsewhere they call shoes *zapatú* ("zapato" in Spanish). What more can I say? The Chiriguanos are of Guaraní origin, and you will not see a man completely naked nor a naked woman among them (despite the fact that they are still pagan). Moreover, we explained above the numbering system that they had (so they cannot be said to be ignorant of counting).

CLVI. Negato Rege, non dat Maffejus saltem dynastas illis et duces, quos caciquios dicimus. Atqui Guaraniis et olim fuerunt, et etiamnum sunt capita sua, et tribuum principes, idque vel ipso naturae instinctu, vel exemplo accepto a Noemi liberis, quibuscum eorum majores ante dispersum genus humanum versati sunt, et quorum deinceps (ut Maffejus ait) nonnullam memoriam retinuerunt. Itaque Guaranii populi indum aliquem e primoribus sibi praeficiebant, eumque in bellum sequebantur, domique colebant aliquot obsequiis. Procedente post tempore Caciquiorum munus et jus haesit haereditaria successione quibusdam familiis atque id adhuc durat. Erant autem in XXX. oppidis Caciquii quingenti, quorum omnium avitam nobilitatem Philippus V. Rex, qui singulari amore Guaranicum nomen prosequebatur, dicitur condecorare voluisse insignibus, et stemmate Equestris Ordinis S. Jacobi: sed facta res haec non fuit, quod dictum sit Regi, Caciquios illos assuetos simplici et naturali vitae generi haud curaturos pro merito ejusmodi laudem, et decus. Ceterum priscis Guaraniis perfecta societatis urbanae, et civilis formae, consuetudo non fuit. Haec qua ratione illuc inducta sit paucis expediam.

CLVII. Regii Praetoris auspiciis, et Sacrorum Antistite bene precante, egressi sunt ex urbe Assumptionis Paraguayae, inermes, solaque innixi Cruce, quam pro baculo gestabant, Jesuitae quidam. Hi longissimo, et deterrimo itinere penetrarunt in loca, ubi erat maxima Guaraniorum vis. Nacti linguae usum, id primo egerunt, ut sibi Caciquiorum, plebisque animos conciliarent. In hanc rem ipsis quam poterant cumque opem conferebant ultro: salutabant blande et comiter obvios quosque, tuguria circumibant, moerentes consolabantur, aegros invisebant, et morbi remedia monstrabant. Iidem valentibus aderant consilio, et siquid laboris erat ruri domive, manum admovebant, facti omnia omnibus, nec refugiebant ipsa mortis pericula, adeo, ut e nimia corporis defatigatione, et gravi rerum inopia occubuerint insignes virtute viri Joannes Vasseus Belga, et Martinus Xavier Urtasun, qui D. Francisco Xaverio Indiarum Apostolo propinquitate conjunctus erat.

CLVIII. Benignis humanitatis officiis addebant illi data tempore quaedam munuscula, quae, ut ipsas feras mulcent, flexere barbaras Guaraniorum mentes. Crevit paulatim gentis amor in novos hospites, a quibus boni plurimum, mali nihil accipiebat. Ipsa illa alta confidentia, et animi securitas, qua inter armatos soli inermesque sine ullo metus, aut laevae suspicionis indicio versabantur, atque apertis in locis vel humi cubabant, vel strati ad arborum truncos somnum capiebant, excitabat omnium admirationem, et cum admiratione quamdam in advenas Sacerdotes reverentiam.

156. Having denied that there was a King, Maffei does not even grant that they had dynastic rulers or leaders, whom we call "Caciques." However, the Guaraní of old had, as indeed they do now, their tribal heads and chiefs. And this comes either from nature's own impulse or from the example received from Noah's sons with whom their ancestors lived before the dispersal of the human race and of whom they retained some memory across the generations, as Maffei says. Thus, then, the Guaraní peoples would choose a particular Indian from among the leading men to preside over them, and they would follow him into war and honor him with various indulgences at home. Later, as time went on, the office and the right of the Caciques stayed with certain families by hereditary succession, and this endures to the present day. There were five hundred Caciques in the thirty towns and King Felipe V, who had a singular affection for the Guaraní, is said to have wanted to enhance their ancestral nobility further with the insignia and distinction of the Order of Chivalry of Santiago; but it did not happen, because the King was told that since they were accustomed to a simple and natural way of life those Caciques would care little for a meritorious commendation and honor of this sort. In other respects, the ancient Guaraní were not thoroughly habituated to urban society and civic structure. I will relate briefly why these customs were established there.

157. Under the auspices of the Royal Governor and with the Bishop's blessing, some Jesuits left the Paraguayan city of Asunción, unarmed, relying only on a cross which they carried in place of a staff. After a very long and most terrible journey, they reached the places where the Guaraní numbers were greatest. Once they acquired skill with the language, the first thing they tried was to win the hearts and minds of the Caciques and the people. To this end, they brought to bear whatever means they could without being prompted: they pleasantly and affably greeted whomever they encountered along the way, they made the rounds of their shelters, they comforted those who were grieving, they visited the sick and demonstrated cures for disease. The same Jesuits aided the healthy with advice and if there was any work to be done in the fields or at home, they would lend a hand, and they "became all things to all people" without ever shrinking from the risk of death: so much so that due to excessive bodily fatigue and serious lack of supplies men distinguished for their virtue died, including the Belgian Jean Vaisseau and Martín Javier de Urtasún, who was related to Saint Francisco Javier, the Apostle of the Indies.

158. To these kindly human courtesies, they added, when the opportunity arose, some little gifts that, just as they soothe wild animals, also prevailed upon the barbaric minds of the Guaraní. Gradually, there developed a love among the people for their new guests, from whom they received a great deal of good and nothing bad. That same high confidence and security of spirit, with which they lived alone and defenseless among armed people, without any indication of fear or unfavorable suspicion, sleeping in the open or on the ground, or catching a nap sprawled out on tree trunks, excited everyone's admiration and along with that admiration, a certain reverence for the foreign priests.

CLIX. Ubi jam advenisse visum tempus opportunum, injectus sermo est de eximiis commodis, quae consecutura eos essent, si e temere sparsis casis plures pluresque Caciquii cum clientum grege in sedem unam migrarent, et oppidum conderent, se seque collatis invicem operis consiliisque foverent: esse multa, quae de artibus vitae utilibus, et de colendo fructuosius agro, et de struendis melius tuguriis suis discerent: esse item quaedam altioris cujusdam ordinis, quae ubi compositis rebus quiete ac tranquille caepissent agere, docerentur, de praemiis nimirum, vel paenis, hominem bonum malumve post mortem corporis, animo superstite manentibus, et de cultu item, qui debetur Deo optimo, maximo, cujus nomen norant, infinitam vero majestatem, et sapientiam, et justitiam ejus non norant: quod si paci studere cuperent, et hostibus suis superiores esse, id conjunctis in commune viribus factu facilius fore, utique si in potentissimi Regis Catholici fidem, et clientelam concederent.

CLX. Quid multis opus est? Ut Dei immensa est bonitas, divinus imber sparsus in terram bonam a sacris operariis e coelo incrementum dedit, et persuasum est caciquiis, et horum clientibus, ut in locum consensu delectum undique convenirent, et domos aedificarent, et templum ponerent, et mysteria Relgionis sanctae susciperent. Primo oppido factum nomen Laureto. Hujus rectus ordo, et visa oppidanorum felicitas, alios aliosque in idem vitae genus pertraxere; ac ponenda deinceps complura fuerunt oppida, crescente plurimum neophytorum numero. Ecce tibi initia Reipublicae Guaranicae ab Hispanis Jesuitis institutae.

159. When it seemed that the opportune moment had arrived, mention would be made of the extraordinary advantages that would come to them if more and more Caciques along with their flock of followers were to migrate from their haphazardly scattered homes into a single settlement, establish a town, and, moreover, help one another through their labor and judgment united in common cause. Mention would also be made that there are many things they could learn about the skills useful for life, about cultivating fields to be more fruitful, and building their shelters better; likewise, that there are certain things of a higher order that they would learn once they had resolved to live with their affairs peacefully and calmly arranged. Namely, they would learn about rewards, or, of course, punishments that await a good or bad person after the death of the body when the soul lives on, and also about the worship which is owed to almighty God whose name they knew but whose infinite majesty and wisdom and justice they did not. Mention was also made that if they desired to pursue peace and to be superior to their enemies, this would come to pass more easily with their forces joined in common, especially if they put themselves in the protection and patronage of the all-powerful Catholic King.

160. What more is needed? Since God's goodness is immense, the divine rain sprinkled from heaven upon the good earth by devoted laborers yielded growth. The Caciques and their followers were persuaded to come together from various places into a site chosen by consensus, to build houses, to erect a temple, and to receive the mysteries of the holy religion. The name given to the first town was [Nuestra Señora de] Loreto.* Its right order and the manifest happiness of the townsfolk enticed more and more to the same way of life; and so, several towns had to be founded in succession given the growing number of neophytes. Here you have it—the beginnings of the Guaraní Republic, founded by the Spanish Jesuits.

* Founded in the summer of 1610 near the Paraná River, the first settlement quickly became overpopulated and a second, San Ignacio Miní, was founded the following month just a few miles away.

CLXI. Maffeus haud aliter factum esse narrat Brasilicae genti ab Emmanuele Nobrega Lusitano, ejusque sociis, quorum unus fuit V. P. Josephus Anchaeta tot editis illic clarus miraculis. "Ad Brasilicam, inquit, linguam (*Guaranica est excepto in vocabulis quibusdam pronunciandi modo*) addiscendam cuncti pariter animum adjiciunt: acrique studio, ac pia aemulatione perfectum haud magno temporis intervallo, uti essent ad confessiones audiendas, et habendas conciones idonei... Sub ejusmodi rerum initia subito factum, uti neophyti paene omnes in morbum alvi, oculorumque, ac varios abcessus inciderent. haec magi videlicet ad baptisma invidiose referre; Lavatione illa tentari valetudinem; doctrina ac praedicatione pestem ac perniciem populis importari calumniabantur. Sed ipsorum mendacia et improbitatem, Dei beneficio redita mox Brasiliis firmitas aperte redarguit. Ea recepta, instituere cum aliis monitu patrum, oratoria sacrasquae aedes publice extruere, quo ad conciones et cathechismum undique convenirent: duae duobus locis magno Christianae rei bono excitatae. Agitatum etiam a patribus (idque dein tempore procedente perfectum est) uti quod de Theseo jactat Graecia, sparsos per tuguria indigenas, in pagos et oppida cogerent; agris colendis adsuefacerent; eorumque coetus legibus ac magistratibus temperarent."[62]

CLXII. Hic ego non tam miror pulcherrimi scriptoris venustum dicendi genus, quam moveor, et gaudeo visis ubique gentium humanae culturae vestigiis, quae vera impressit (quoquo pedem intulit) Religio. Sic profecto est. Post extinctum paene ab inducta Idolatria rationis lumen, populi in caecam caliginem relapsi sunt, quousque Evangelii lux obductas Orbi terrarum tenebras in Asia, in Europa, in Africa, in America dissipavit. Circumfer quoquoversus oculos, et passim cernes hujus rei exempla. Vin horum unum e regione, quae proxima Italiae est, ubi haec scribimus? Quidcultius nunc Germania? Et quid eadem incultius ante acceptam legem Christi et doctrinam?

161. Maffei recounts that what Manuel da Nóbrega of Portugal and his companions did with the people of Brazil was hardly any different. One of these companions was the venerable Father José de Anchieta, famous for the many miracles he produced there. "All in equal measure," he says, "they set their minds to learning the Brazilian language" (which is Guaraní aside from the pronunciation of certain words); "and it was accomplished with zealous dedication and pious competition after no great interval of time such that they were fluent enough to hear confessions and deliver sermons. . . . Right at the beginning of these endeavors, it suddenly happened that almost all the neophytes experienced maladies of the stomach and eyes as well as various abscesses; of course, the sorcerers* invidiously related these things to baptism. They falsely claimed that health was disturbed by that 'washing'† and that plague and calamity were introduced to the people through the priests' doctrine and preaching. But through God's kindness vigor was soon restored to the Brazilians and this refuted the lies and wickedness of the sorcerers. Once their strength had been recovered, they and others, on the advice of the Fathers, set about to build places for prayer and holy sanctuaries for public use, where they gathered from all over for sermons and catechism. Two were erected in two places with great benefit for Christianity. There was even a movement among the Fathers (and it was accomplished as time went on) to gather together into districts and towns the Indigenous people who were spread out in their shelters, so that they would become accustomed to cultivating the fields and would govern this collection of people with laws and magistrates. This is something Greece boasts about Theseus doing."[62]

162. Here I am not so much in awe of the elegant style of the excellent author as I am moved and overjoyed at seeing everywhere the traces of human culture that true Religion imprinted (wherever it set foot). It is assuredly so. After the light of reason was nearly extinguished by widespread idolatry, the peoples sunk down into a blinding fog until the light of the Gospel dissipated the darkness that had enveloped the earth—in Asia, in Europe, in Africa, in America. Cast your eyes in any direction and you will discern examples of this fact nearly everywhere. Do you want an example taken from a region near Italy, where we write this? What country is more sophisticated now than Germany? And likewise what country was more unsophisticated before receiving the law and doctrine of Christ?

* The Tupí-Guaraní terms *pai* and *paye* are often translated as "shaman," from the Manchu-Tungus word *šaman*.

† i.e., baptism, which was initially performed only on Guaraní on their deathbeds.

CLXIII. "Nullas Germanorum populis urbes habitari, ait Tacitus,[63] satis notum est, ne pati quidem inter se junctas sedes. Colunt discreti ac diversi, ut fons, ut campus, ut nemus placuit. Vicos locant non in nostrum morem connexis et cohaerentibus aedificiis. Suam quisque domum spatio circumdat, sive adversus casus ignis remedium, sive inscitia aedificandi. Ne caementorum quidem apud eos aut tegularum usus: materia ad omnia utuntur informi, et citra speciem aut delectationem... tegumen omnibus sagum, sibula, aut si desit, spina consertum. Cetera intecti, totos dies juxta focum atque ignem agunt... Gerunt et ferarum pelles etc."

CLXIV. Hujusmodi erat, Trajano Imperatore, Germaniae status, quam culturae, quam artium indigens? Artes autem et culturam eo demum intulit Christiana Religio, cui debent Germani, ut felices, et beati sint, ut vivant secundum naturae perfectius genus, ut tot habitent pulchris urbibus, ut tanto praestent reipublicae splendore, tanta opificum sollertia, tantis ingeniorum studiis disciplinisque, ut nihil supra. Vecors vero et amens sit, qui haec Germaniae bona non referat accepta Christianis institutis, quae ut mores, ita mentes insigni rerum conversione mutarunt.

CLXV. Plurimum ergo communi rei, publicaeque felicitati contulit Evangelium, quo cuncta naturae bona multo melius, multoque stabilius hominum societati proveniunt. Et tamen liberiores Philosophi (si nomine philosophorum digni sunt) legis naturalis, quam ne intelligunt quidem, decus unice et laudem praedicantes, Christianam legem, ac inspiratam divinitus Religionem, e medio tollere conjurarunt, qua sublata, in vetus chaos provinciae omnes (quae et olim misera malorum sorte similes Germaniae fuerunt, et larga nunc bonorum copia abundant) relabantur necesse prorsus est: cujus rei recens, et coram est exemplum florentissimi paucis abhinc annis regni, et hoc infausto tempore horride silvescentis, et barbare efferati. Sed redeo ad Platonem, et Guaranios, qui nobis, originem populorum indagantibus, causa fuerunt de hoc argumento fusius differendi.

De commerciis.

PLATO

CLXVI. Merces ait, peregrinas, praeterquam necessarias, in urbem nemo invehito, neque contra evehito ea, quae opus civibus sunt. Thuris, et purpurae, aliusve rei pretiosioris non plus aliunde importetur, quam quantum templorum usus postulat. Augendae pecuniae causa neu in urbe, neu foris fiant nundinae. Tritici, hordei, et ceterarum frugum, brutorumque animantium partes duae pro incolarum annona, et victu reservantor; tertia dumtaxat pars venum exponitor advenis, siqui propter publicam, privatamque alicujus incolae utilitatem inter cives commorentur.

163. “It is well-known,” says Tacitus,[63] “that there are no cities inhabited by the Germanic peoples, indeed they do not even tolerate connected dwellings. They live separately and spread apart, wherever there is a spring, a field, or a grove to their liking. They do not locate their villages according to our custom, with adjoining and contiguous buildings. Each one leaves a space around his own house, either as a remedy against the risk of fire or due to a lack of construction knowledge. There is no use of quarry-stones or roof tiles among them; they use ill-shaped material for everything without regard to appearance or taste . . . As a covering everyone has a coarse blanket fastened with a pin, or if that is lacking, with a thorn. Otherwise, they spend entire days unclothed near the fireplace and the fire . . . They also wear the skins of wild animals, etc.”

164. Such was the state of Germania when Trajan was Emperor. How in need of culture and the arts! At long last the Christian Religion introduced the arts and culture there, and it is to this that the Germans owe the fact that they are happy and prosperous, that they live according to a more perfect sort of nature, that they inhabit so many beautiful cities, that they are so distinguished by the great splendor of their republic, expertise of their artisans, and the industriousness and discipline of their intellectuals that there is nothing superior. One would have to be witless or out of his mind to not recognize that all Germany's goods were received due to Christian principles, which, like customs, also changed minds through the remarkable change of circumstances.

165. Thus the Gospel contributed exceedingly to the common good and public happiness. And with it all the goods of nature develop much better and much more durably for human society. However, the libertine Philosophers (if they are worthy of the name of philosophers), only extolling the splendor and glory of natural law, which they do not even understand, conspire to abolish Christian law and divinely inspired Religion. And once it has been removed, all the provinces will necessarily relapse into the chaos of old (for they were once similar to Germania with a wretched assortment of evils and now overflow with an abundance of goods). There is a recent example of this fact before our eyes, that of a territory at the height of flourishing just a few years ago which in this ill-omened time is growing horrifically wild after having been barbarously savaged. But I return to Plato and the Guaraní who, because we were tracking down the origin of their peoples, were the cause of this rather lengthy departure from the main argument.

On Commerce

PLATO

166. No one should import foreign merchandise into the city, Plato says, aside from what is essential, nor should anyone export what the citizens need. Frankincense, purple dye, or anything else that is especially costly, should be brought from abroad no more than the temples' usage requires. Weekly markets for earning money do not occur in the city nor outside of it. Two thirds of the wheat, barley, and other produce, as well as of the brute animals, should be reserved for the provision and sustenance of the inhabitants; only one third should be put up for sale to outsiders, if there are any staying among the citizens for a public purpose or for some inhabitant's private purpose.

CLXVII. Quiquid vendendum sit, in jusso fori loco veneat, tradito statim acceptoque pretio. Praefecti rebus venalibus, et legum Custodes, discant ab viris expertis, quid vitii et doli inesse possit mercibus expositis, deque eo vitio, et dolo moneant scripto cives, figantque in pila, seu columna publica, singularum rerum pretia. Siquis adulterinum quid vendidisse deprehendatur, non modo re vendita (mulctae nomine) privetur, sed tot insuper virgarum plagis vapulet, quot drachmas in mercis pretium petiit, clamante inter verbera praecone causam suplicii.

CLXVIII. Peregrini tantum homines, et advenae, qui boni sint, aut minus mali, caupones sunto, iisque Custodes legum (pretio mercis, et labore, quo merx constitit, juste expensis) aestimationem lucri, quod mediocre sit, edicto definiant. Aediles autem cavento, nequis artificum pro opificio suo plus poscat, quam quanti res valet.

CLXIX. Artifex, qui ad certam diem opus recepit, nec condicto tempore absolvit, quantum valet idem opus, tantum solvito de suo, cogitorque opus illud ipsum gratis facere intra tot dies, quot diebus faciundum spoponderat. Civium nemo aurum, argentumve habeto. Et quoniam nummis opus est, ut heri servis, et conductores operarum his mercedem solvant, apud eos solum nummi sunto, apud alios ne sunto.[64] E mutuata pecunia nemo usuram, sive foenus exigito; neminique item fas esto inhiare intemperanter lucro, quod generosos mores corrumpit. (Lib. V. VIII. XI. *Legg.*)

GUARANII.

CLXX. Guaraniis commercium aliud non erat, quam quo comparabantur res illae, quas regio eorum non fert. Forma commercii haec. Concessum fuerat regio diplomate evehi e triginta oppidis Guaraniorum duodecim millia *arrobarum* (nomen Hispanum est ponderis XXV. librarum, illoque utimur, quod multo expeditius sit ad rem, de qua agimus, declarandam) *Herbae Paraguaycae*.[65] Duodecim autem millium numero in triginta illa oppida diviso, respondent singulis oppidis quadringentae *arrobae*: haec summa, neque amplior, permissa est Indis, ne officeretur fortunis Hispanorum urbis Assumptionis, quorum bona pendent maxime ex *Herbae* commercio. (Scito hic *Herbam* dici recepto nomine: caeterum herba non est, sed sunt tritae frondes ab arbore, imitanti formam Europeae mali aureae.

167. What is to be sold, should be sold at the designated place in the *agora* with the price being accepted right when it is proposed. Superintendents of salable items and Law Guardians should learn from experts about any defect or wrongdoing that could be present in the merchandise for sale and then notify the citizens of the defect or wrongdoing in writing. They should also post the prices of individual items up on a pillar or public column. If someone should be caught having sold something adulterated, not only would he be deprived of the thing sold (as a fine) but on top of that he would be beaten with as many lashes of the switch as drachmas he charged for the merchandise; during the flogging a town crier will proclaim the cause of the punishment.

168. Only resident aliens and foreigners, who are good or only very slightly bad, ought to be salesmen. And the Law Guardians should designate in an edict the calculation of salesmen's profit, which should be moderate (once the cost and the labor corresponding to the merchandise have been fairly calculated). The city magistrates must also take care that none of the craftsmen requests more for his work than what the thing is worth.

169. The craftsman who accepted a job for a given day and did not finish it within the agreed upon time frame must pay out of his pocket however much that same job is worth and must be compelled to do that very same job for free within as many days as he had promised to do it. No citizen ought to have gold or silver. And since there is a need for currency, so that masters and employers can pay the salaries of their slaves and workers, they alone may have cash but not others.[64] No one may demand usury or interest from borrowed money, and likewise it will be impermissible for anyone to covet profit excessively because it corrupts noble habits (*Laws* Books 5, 7, and 9).

THE GUARANÍ

170. The Guaraní had no trade other than that one in which those items their region does not produce were purchased. That type of trade worked as follows: it was conceded by royal decree that twelve thousand *arrobas* (this is the Spanish term for twenty-five pounds in weight, and we use it because it is much more convenient for explaining the matter we are dealing with) of Paraguayan Yerba[65] could be exported from the thirty Guaraní towns. When twelve thousand is divided between thirty towns, it comes out to four hundred *arrobas* per town. This amount, and not more, was allowed to the Indians so as not to hinder the fortunes of the Spaniards of the city of Asunción, whose prosperity depends mainly on the *Yerba* trade. (It should be understood here that the term *Herba* is used in its adopted sense. On the contrary, it is not an herb, but crushed leaves from a tree that resembles the European orange tree.)

CLXXI. Transmissos *Herbae* culeos, jussum illud pondus, pro rata XXX. oppidorum parte, continentes (ubi jam a quaestoribus Regiis discussum lemborum onus fuerat, nequid plus permisso inferretur) culeos, inquam, transmissos in urbem S. Fidei, et Bonasauras vendebant procuratores, qui utrobique in hanc rem destinati erunt. Addebantur autem *Herbae* culeis volumina quaedam telae gossipinae, quae superfuerat post cujusque oppidi usus; manipulorum item sicci tabaci nonnulla vis, bona enim pars oppidanis dividebatur.

CLXXII. Artificum porro lignariorum, et sculptorum, et ceterorum opera, laboresque intra oppida impendebantur, neque eorum quicquam evehebatur foras praeter sacras quasdam icunculas, tornatosque globos pro numerandis B. Virginis MARIAE precibus Rosario descriptis: quippe cum rerum harum in Praetura Paraguayca, et Bonaurensi, et Tucumanica, gravis sit caritas, incitamenta isthaec pietatis gratis dabantur Hispanis civibus, praesertim ruricolis, quibus id munus acceptissimum erat.

CLXXIII. Onustos igitur lembos iis, quas modo diximus, mercibus, agebant secundo amni Parana, et Uruguayco Indi publico commeatu instructi, et quorum, dum aberant, privata praedia communibus operis curabantur; ut esset reducibus sui messis agri. Ceterum procurator Sanfideanus, Bonauriensis, pro se quisque, quid a singulis oppidis accepisset, in rationum libros referebat sigillatim. Vendebat deinde allata, eque pretio solvebat in primis annum tributum Regi; quod autem erat reliqui expendebat emendis rebus, quarum oppida illa indigebant.

CLXXIV. Emebat videlicet artium instrumenta, serras, dolabras, malleos, ascias, secures, cuneos, acus, cultros, forfices, hamos item, et massas coloris pro pictoribus, oleum quoque et salem (quibus caret regio) aliaque id genus, ac omnium maxime telam lineam, sericamque, in vestes sacras, atque aurum textile, ductile, et ceram europaeam ad usus templi, et vinum (vites enim illic non sunt) pro sacrificio. Haec omnia in lembos ad oppida redituros imponebat procurator, perscribebatque seorsum singulis Curionibus, quanti res quaeque constitisset; ut illi recognoscerent a tabulis accepti, et expensi, numquid suo cujusque oppido deberetur; an e contrario (nondum venditis usquequaque mercibus, quae missae fuerant) oppidum ipsum deberet.

171. The transported sacks of *Yerba* containing the dictated weight proportional for the thirty towns (when the weight of the boats had already been examined by royal treasurers, so that no more was brought in than was allowed) these sacks, as I was saying, after having been transported to the city of Santa Fe and Buenos Aires the officials designated for this purpose in each city would sell them. Some cotton fabric, which went beyond that town's needs, would be added to these bags of *Yerba*; likewise, some quantity of bundles of dried tobacco, for a good part was divided among the townsfolk.

172. On the other hand, the artwork and efforts of master carpenters, sculptors, and others were utilized within the towns and none of these was taken abroad except some small sacred icons and lathe-turned beads for counting prayers indicated by the Rosary for the Blessed Virgin Mary; of course, because the high price of these things in the governates of Paraguay, Buenos Aires, and Tucumán was burdensome, these were given for free to the Spanish citizens as an inducement to piety, especially to the rural settlers for whom it was a most welcome gift.

173. In this way, the Indians, equipped with supplies from the public store, drove the boats filled with merchandise, which we have just mentioned, down the Paraná and Uruguay rivers with the current. While they were absent, their private farms were tended with community labor, so that field's harvest would be there for them when they got back. Moreover, the administrator of Santa Fe and that of Buenos Aires, each separately recorded in the account books in detail what he had received from each individual town. He would then sell what they had brought, and from the proceeds he first satisfied the annual tribute to the King; then he spent what was left on buying the things that those towns needed.

174. Namely, he would buy trade-specific tools, saws, mattocks, hammers, carpenter's axes, wedges, needles, knives, shears, and also hooks, as well as masses of pigment for painters, oil, and even salt (which the region lacks), and other things of the like, but above all linen and silk fabrics for sacred vestments, as well as gold for weaving or embroidery, European wax for the use of the temple, and wine for mass (for there are no grapevines there). The administrator would place all these things into the boats headed back to the towns, and he would write out in full for each priest how much each thing had cost, so that they would know from the accounts of what was received and what was spent if something was owed to their town, or on the contrary (when the merchandise that had been sent had not yet been fully sold) if the town itself were in debt.

CLXXV. Nummi inter Guaranios nulli: priscorum more mortalium res illi suas rebus permutabant: qui modus ad simplicitatem naturae propius accedit: *interiores* (Germani) *simplicius,* ait Tacitus, *et antiquius permutatione mercium utuntur.* Pecunia quidem propter exteros potius recepta usu est, quam propter cives, qui, conjuncti loco, et mutuis officiis, alter ab altero accipiebant quondam ultro citroque, quae utilia ipsis vicissim erant. Exteris vero, si pro merce merx semper obtruderetur, descendendum foret ad iniqua pacta, vel certe magno suo incommodo gravia onera in longum saepe iter avehere secum cogerentur: quibus malis obviam itum est ope pecuniae, quam recte vocat Aristotiles[66] κοὶνον μετρὶν communem mensuram, ad quam omnia referuntur, aequata aestimatione mercis et nummi. Atque, opinor, ob ortam e nummis facilitatem in pasciscendo dicta pecunia Graecis est χρεῖμα α χράο, utor, quod in usus commercii aes signatum commodissimum sit.

CLXXVI. Vel ipse Moyses ex institutione divina de annua rerum decima in usus sacros seposita sic cavet: *cum longior fuerit via, et locus, quem elegerit Deus tuus, tibique benedixerit, nec potueris haec cuncta* (frumentum, vinum, oleum primogenita armentorum, et ovium) *portare, vendes omnia, et in pretium rediges, portabisque manu tua, et proficisceris ad locum, quem elegerit Dominus Deus tuus etc.*[67] Ecce hic quodammodo consecratus usus pecuniae.

CLXXVII. Hispani Paraguayci, qui proxime attingunt fines Guaraniorum, commutatione rerum pacta fori exercent. Rarus apud eos usus cusae pecuniae, sine qua tamen felices, vel etiam feliciores sunt (ob eximiam agri fertilitatem, indigenarumque copiam fructuum, et aves plurimas, et feras captu faciles, et optimos pisces ad delicias usque) sunt, inquam, feliciores aliis populis, quibus multum nummorum est, opum naturae parum.

CLXXVIII. Igitur magistratus, quanti res quaeque valeat, edicit publice, idque ex jure indico, quo cautum est: *las monedas de la tierra en Paraguay sean especies, y valgan a razon de seis reales el peso.*[68] Moneta regionis Paraguaycae sunto terrae fructus, resque ipsae speciatim, quarum aestimatio computator in aureum senum argenteorum. Causa statuti hujus fuit, quod tellus illa neque aurum, neque argentum, neque aes gignat, unde cudi pecunia possit.

175. There is no currency among the Guaraní. In the manner of early humans, they exchanged their things for other things, a method that resembles the simplicity of nature. The Germans "living further in the interior," Tacitus says, "carry out the exchange of goods in a very simple and very ancient way." Indeed, money came into use more because of foreigners, than citizens, who, since they were joined together due to their location and mutual obligations, from time to time would accept things that were in turn useful to them, one from another, back and forth. But with foreigners, if a good were to be bartered always for another good, there would be a tendency to acquiesce to unjust agreements, or people would certainly be compelled to carry heavy loads with them on often long journeys to their own great discomfort. The remedy for such problems came through the help of money, which Aristotle rightly calls κoìνον μετρὸν,[66] a "common measure," to which all things are related, once the valuation of the good and the currency has been equalized. And, I suppose, on account of the ease of conducting transactions that arose from currency, the Greeks called money χρεῖμα from χράο, "use," because minted coinage is most convenient for use in commerce.

176. Even Moses himself warns the following about the annual tithe set aside, according to divine instruction, for religious use: "If the road is very long and the place far away, which your god has selected and blessed for you, and you are not able to carry your entire tithe there (wheat, wine, oil, and the firstborn of your cattle and your sheep), you will sell everything, reduce it to its value, and carry it in your hand as you set out for the place, which the lord your God has selected . . . "[67] Behold, here the use of money is, in a way, consecrated.

177. The Spaniards of Paraguay, who are closest to the borders of the Guaraní, carry out their market transactions through the exchange of goods. Among them the use of coined money is rare, without which they are nevertheless happy; or rather they are happier (for the excellent fertility of the soil, the abundance of indigenous fruits, as well as the many birds and beasts that are easy to hunt, and the best fish as far as delicacies go) they are happier, as I was saying, than other peoples who have much currency, but too little of nature's riches.

178. The magistrate, then, will decree publicly how much each thing is worth, and this as established in the Law of the Indies, in which it is decreed, "Let the coins of the region of Paraguay be the produce of the earth, and the amount of each particular good whose value is calculated at one *peso* would be worth six *reales* of silver."[68] The reason for this statute was that that land produces neither gold, nor silver, nor copper from which it would be possible to mint money.

CLXXIX. Rerum igitur aestimatio a magistratu edicitur. Exemplum esto: compositi in manipulos tabaci *arroba* penditur quattuor aureis, quorum singulis seni tantum argentei respondent ex lege illa Indica. *Herbae,* et item gossipii *arroba* aestimatur binis aureis ejusdem generis; bos valet senis aureis. Hinc venditio, et emptio sic fiunt: qui *arrobam* tabaci emit, dat venditori in pretium binas Herbae *arrobas*: vendenti autem bovem traduntur ab emptore ternae *arrobae* gossipii. Minutioris autem rei pactum fit secundum proportionem definitae aestimationis *in arrobam*: atque hinc uni librae gossipii par est pretio libra una *Herbae,* semilibrae vero illius similibra hujus; cum utraque species sit ejusdem pretii publici.[69] His pactis Paraguaycorum Hispanorum similia erant Guaraniorum indorum pacta. Ager meus tuo plus mandiocae extulit, tuus meo plus gossipii; hujus tibi certum pondus do, da tu mihi pondus mandiocae, quod tantidem sit.

CLXXX. Plato pecuniae usum permittit solis heris, et conductoribus operarum, ut mercedem solvant servis, et conductis operis. Inter Guaranios permissioni isti locus non est: praeter enim quam quod servi illic nulli, nemini operae conducendae erant. Suum quisque agrum colebat; et id si nequiret facere ob morbum, causamve aliam, vicini, vel consanguinei vel quos magistratus designabat, vicariam curam agri suscipiebant, accepturi et ipsi vicissim idem auxilii, siquando ab agri sui cultura impedirentur. Domus autem, et publica aedificia sine mercede fiebant et eficiebantur communiter.

CLXXXI. Forum venale apud Guaranios non erat, ideoque Platonis illa cautio, et tot edicta pro rebus vendendis, neutiquam necessaria, sicut legibus nundinariis opus non fuit parvo illi gregi hominum e terrae vastatione superstitum, quos Plato ipse sapienter antea descripsit, ab his enim, simplici naturae modo contentis, omnia ex aequo et bono transigebantur meris rerum permutationibus.

CLXXXII. Nulli itidem in pagis Guaranicis mercatores cauponesque; nam qui ab uno oppido in aliud ibant, aut per praedia commeabant, hospitio communi utebantur, alebanturque gratuito. Domi autem proprii agri frugibus, bubulaque publice data, victitabant, neque empti cibi venalisve mercis indigebant. Quod si e coeli intemperie alicujus oppidi incolis annona defecerat, eis a vicinis oppidis subveniebatur, cum eo, ut redderent tantumdum, ubi ipsis felicior messis obtigisset.

179. As I was saying, the value of things is decreed by the magistrate. Here is an example: an *arroba* of tobacco arranged in bundles is valued at four pesos, each of which corresponds to six silver *reales* according to the Law of the Indies. For *yerba* and also cotton, an *arroba* is valued at two pesos of the same type. An ox is worth six pesos. Sales and purchases happen as follows there: whoever buys one *arroba* of tobacco gives the seller as a price two *arrobas* of *yerba*; to the seller of an ox, however, three *arrobas* of cotton are handed over by the buyer. A transaction for a lesser amount happens according to the proportion of its value in terms of *arrobas*: and so, one pound of *Yerba* is the equivalent in price of one pound of cotton, and a half pound of the one is equivalent to a half pound of the other, since both goods have the same public price.[69] The transactions of the Guaraní Indians were similar to these transactions of the Paraguayan Spaniards. My field produced more yuca than yours; yours more cotton than mine; I give you a certain quantity of the one, you give me whatever quantity is equivalent to the yuca.

180. Plato permits the use of money only to masters and employers to pay their slaves and workers. Among the Guaraní there is no place for such an allowance, because, beyond the fact that there are no slaves, work did not have to be hired out to anyone. Each person cultivated his or her own field; and if unable to do so due to illness or another cause, the neighbors, or relatives, or those whom the magistrate designated assumed substitute care of the field, because they themselves will receive the same help in turn if ever they were prevented from cultivating their own field. Houses and public buildings, moreover, were built and erected by the community without wages.

181. There was no marketplace among the Guaraní; therefore, that precaution of Plato and his many edicts on things being sold were unnecessary, just as financial laws were not at all necessary, just as there was no need for market laws for that small flock of people who survived the devastation of the earth, whom Plato himself wisely described earlier. For, content with nature's simple ways, they reached agreements through pure exchange of goods based on what was fair and honest.

182. Likewise there were no merchants or innkeepers in the Guaraní districts; for those who would go from one town to another or would pass through the farmland would make use of the communal guesthouse and would be fed free of charge. At home they subsisted on the fruits of their own field and the meat that was distributed publicly, so they didn't need purchased food or salable merchandise. But if, due to inclement weather, the harvest had left the inhabitants of some town wanting, assistance would come to them from the neighboring towns, on the condition that they return the same amount when a more favorable harvest should come about for them.

De Peregrinis.

PLATO

CLXXXIII. Civitati, quae cumulandis opibus operam non dat, quorsum exteri? Et quid hi afferent boni? Solet, ait Plato, variarum gentium concursio mores corrumpere; peregrinorumque consuetudo turbat vehementer statum urbis, quod malum Reipublicae, utenti bonis legibus, nocet maxime.[70] Populis autem prave institutis nihil curae est, num eorum senes, adolescentesque pro arbitrio peregrinentur; num e contrario pregrini, vagique aliunde ad eos ventitent. Sed tamen ne cives alio aliquando abeant, fieri prorsus non potest; omnes vero alicunde adventantes urbe nostra penitus excludere, crudele quiddam et arrogans videretur.

CLXXXIV. Sic igitur (ut utrumque malum istud vitetur) de civium peregrinatione, deque peregrinorum admissione statuendum est. Civi nondum nato quadraginta annos nullo modo fas esto peregrinari: privato itidem viro id non liceat, legato publico liceat. Quod si vero legatorum quispiam e peregrinatione rediens disputare ausit contra priscam civitatis nostrae disciplinam, receptasque usu leges, morte mulctator, ne populi pacem, et tranquillitatem urbis, et Reipublicae ordinem evertat. (Quid, quaeso, faceret Plato iis, qui nunc, spretis indigne majorum institutis, revulsisque juris sacrati claustris, totam commovent Europam, vulgusque insanum ad arma cient?)

CLXXXV. Jam vero advenas, qui (more modoque avium nova loca mutantium appetente vere) alias atque alias urbes circumvagantur augendi causa peculii, hos advenas ille, qui cum potestate suburbiis praest, certo in loco extra maenia collocet, et caveat nequid novi moris inducant; nec sinito cum civibus diutius agere, quam quamdiu coget necessitas. Ceterum cum aliquis ad nos publicus legatus venerit, is honorifice excipiatur, et apud urbis primores habitet. (Lib. XII. de Legg.)

GUARANII.

CLXXXVI. Contra Guaraniorum cultores multae multorum fuerunt querimoniae, perinde ac omne hominum genus exosi neminem in oppida admitterent. Dicam paucis quid rei esset. Praetoribus, eorumque legatis, apertum semper iter illuc fuit, itemque militibus, quos contra barbaros, aut tumultuantes vicinos, tribuni Regii secum deducebant. Liber item aditus Antistiti Bonaurensi, et Paraguayco, quoties pro munere oppida suae quisque ditionis lustrare voluit.

On Foreigners

PLATO

183. What use are outsiders for a state that pays no mind to accumulating wealth? What good do they contribute? Contact between different peoples, says Plato, tends to corrupt customs, and interacting with foreigners greatly disturbs the equilibrium of the city, and this evil is most harmful to the Republic employing good laws.[70] Peoples that are ill governed, on the other hand, are not concerned whether their old and their young travel abroad at will, or whether, on the contrary, foreigners and vagabonds from other places regularly visit them. Nevertheless, it is altogether impossible to make it so that citizens don't go here and there periodically; in truth, it would seem somewhat cruel and overbearing to exclude all those coming from elsewhere entirely from our city.

184. Thus (in order to avoid both evils), there must be legislation regarding citizens' travel abroad and the admission of foreigners. For the citizen who is not yet forty years old, traveling abroad is not allowed under any circumstance; likewise, it is not permitted for a private person, only for a public official. But if any of the officials, after returning from travel abroad, dared to challenge the ancient ways of our state and the customary laws, let him be sentenced to death, so that he does not subvert the peace of the people, the tranquility of the city, and the order of the Republic. (What, I wonder, would Plato do with those who throw all Europe into disorder and hasten the insane masses to arms now that our ancestral institutions have been wrongfully rejected and the bulwark of sacred law has been torn away?)

185. When it comes to migrants, who (in the manner of birds moving to new places as spring approaches) rove from city to city in order to earn money, the magistrate in charge of the suburbs should settle these migrants in a place outside the walls and take care that they do not introduce any novel customs. He must not allow them to deal with the citizens any longer than necessity demands. For the rest, whenever any public official should come to us, he would be received with due honors and be lodged among the city's leaders (*Laws* Book 12).

THE GUARANÍ

186. There were many complaints from many people against the Guaraní cultivators, as if they admitted no one to the towns because they hated the entire human race. I shall say in a few words what the fact of the matter was. For the Governors and their envoys, the road there was always open, the same goes for the soldiers whom the royal officers would take with them as a check against barbarians or rebellious neighbors. There was also free access for the Bishop of Buenos Aires or Paraguay, as often as each wanted to examine the towns of his own jurisdiction in an official capacity.

CLXXXVII. Possem equidem ex indice (quem mihi olim confeci contra PAVVIUM Philosophum, mira praedicantem de Curionibus Guaranicis tamquam immanibus instar diri Busiridis exterorum omnium hostibus) longam seriem producere Regiorum ministrorum, Episcoporumque, qui pagos Guaranicos adierunt, redditis sigillatim annis, in quos singulorum adventus incidit: sed quoniam res haec me longius abriperet, id unum hic dixerim, Antistitem Paraguaycum Il. D. Josephum Cajetanum Palavicinum Ordinis S. Francisci oppida Guaranica suae diaeceseos ter lustrasse, annis nimirum MDCCXLIII. et MDCCXLIV. et MDCCXLVII. Cur toties, et adeo frequenter? Quia voluit.

CLXXXVIII. Ad sex autem oppida transparanensia (sunt horum nomina S. MARIA de Fide, S. Ignatius, S. Rosa Limana, S. Jacobus, Ss. Cosmas et Damianus, ac Itapuà, quae omnia, praeter alia, jus sacrum accipiunt ab Episcopo Paraguayco) ad haec sex oppida cuilibet Hispanorum ex urbe Assumptionis, aut aliunde adventanti, quovis mense, et quovis die, aditus patebat, et Hispanos cives ipsemet illic vidi. Praeterea in oppidum Candelariae, quod ad oram citeriorem amnis Paranae situm est, ventitabant etiam Hispani ex urbe Fluentina (*Las Corrientes* vulgo) ut illac merces suas in praeturam Paraguaycam transmiterent. Id ita fieri solitum testes sunt incolae civitatum, quas retuli; iidemque coram inspexerunt, quae esset administrationis Guaranicae forma, haec enim ubique par erat, adeo ut qui oppidum unum viderat, omnia vidisse dicendus, esset.

CLXXXIX. In alia porro oppida, quae media sunt inter Uruguayum flumen et Paranam, inque septem pagos transuruguaycos, privati homines, institoresque (nisi gravis subesset causa) non admittebantur: neque vero erat, cur mercatores eo penetrarent, quandoquidem quae opus sunt Indis, abunde ii ex urbe Bonaurensi onustis lembis, quos supra diximus, sibi, et suis afferebant. Quosvis autem peregrinos intro excipi haud intererat boni communis; non quin sint inter Hispanos multi, quos probes; sed quia si his neque a Praetore missis, neque fide publica munitis, patuisset aditus, patere eumdem necesse fuisset illorum mancipiis, et perfugis nigritis, et vagis hibridis, a quibus quid boni, quaeso, discerent neophyti? Immo vero quid non ab eisdem didicissent mali[71] Plato quidem exteros omnes promiscue urbe recipi, noxium in primis Reipublicae esse (ut est re ipsa) existimat, atque ob id ipsum prohibet.

187. Indeed, from my catalogue (which I once prepared for myself as a check against the Philosopher de Pauw, when he was proclaiming astonishing things about the Guaraní priests as if, like that abominable Busiris, they were monstrous enemies of all outsiders) I could present a long series of Royal ministers and Bishops who visited the Guaraní districts, providing a list of dates on which each arrival took place. But since this would drag me far off course, let me relate just this one instance here: that the Bishop of Paraguay, the Most Illustrious Dr. José Cayetano Paravicino, of the Franciscan Order, visited the Guaraní towns of his diocese three times, in 1743, 1744, and 1747 to be sure. Why so many times and so often? Because he wanted to.

188. Regarding the six towns on the far* side of the Paraná (their names are: Santa María de Fe, San Ignacio, Santa Rosa de Lima, Santiago, Santos Cosme y Damián, and Itapuá, all of which, among others, receive their ecclesiastical law from the Bishop of Paraguay) access to these six towns was open to any Spaniard whatsoever from the city of Asunción or coming from elsewhere, in any month and on any day, and I myself saw Spanish citizens there. Moreover, to the town of Candelaria, which is located on the nearer bank of the Paraná River, Spaniards also used to come regularly from the city Fluentina (*Corrientes* in Spanish), so that from there they could send their merchandise to the Paraguayan governate. The inhabitants of the states that I named are witnesses to the fact that this was customary; and these same men got to observe up close the form of the Guaraní system of government, which was the same everywhere, such that whoever had seen a town could say that he had seen them all.

189. In the other towns further away, which are between the Uruguay and the Paraná rivers, and in the seven districts across the Uruguay, private individuals and peddlers were not admitted (unless there was an important reason). Actually, there was no reason for merchants to go all the way there, seeing that what the Indians needed they would bring for themselves and their families from the city of Buenos Aires in abundance on fully loaded boats, which we mentioned above. In fact it was hardly in the interest of the common good to admit just any foreigners within. This is not because there are not many among the Spanish of whom you would approve. Rather it is because if admission were open to those not sent by the Governor and to those not authorized in an official capacity, it would have been necessarily open also to the enslaved, to blacks seeking refuge, and roving mestizos. And what good, I wonder, would the neophytes learn from these people? On the other hand, what mischief would they not have learned from these same people?[71] Indeed, Plato judges that admitting all outsiders to the city indiscriminately will be, in the first place, harmful to the republic (as in fact it is) and it is for that very reason that he prohibits it.

* i.e., northern.

CXC. Quod si quaeras, cur in sex illa oppida transparanensia liber esset aditus Hispanis, in alia non item, cum vel in omnia admittendi, vel ab omnibus arcendi fuisse videantur; causa est, quod Paraguaycis civibus, ceterisque praeturae illius incolis, cum longissime distent ab aliis urbibus Hispanicis, voluntate Regis Catholici concessum fuit pro ipsorum bono, ut in oppida, quae propius attingunt eorumdem fines, merces suas importarent: haec autem ratio non erat pro aliis urbibus; possunt enim res suas, agrique fructus, facilius vendere seorsum a Guaraniis.

CXCI. De reliquo iis, qui in oppida (ubi permissum erat commercium) ibant, semotum ab Indis diversorium erat, et cum jam merces suas aliis mercibus permutarant, benigne dimittebantur. Nobilibus autem Hispanis, multoque magis Praetoribus, et omnium maxime Antistitibus (hi longe procedentibus obviam Curione, et ejus collega, ac toto magistratu, cum insigni pompa, et effusae laetitiae signis, inter gratulantium Indorum agmina, et festivos Musicorum concentus, ac laetum tinnitum aeris campani e turri sacra, in oppidum, atque adeo in templum deducebantur) nobilibus, inquam, Hispanis, Praetoribusque et Episcopis in Parochi aede hospitium erat, non illud quidem elegans, et magnificum, sed decens, aptumque.

CXCII. Ejusmodi hospites vel in triclinio cum Curione, et ejus collega vescebantur; vel si major erat eorum dignitas, cui non congrueret coenatio communis, in privato eis cubiculo mensa parabatur. Sic cum ad nos venit an. MDCCLXIV. in oppidum S. Ignatii *Guazù* Il. Antistes Emmanuel Antonius de la Torre, illi, illiusque familiaribus epulae seorsum apparatae fuerunt. Atque haec sunt, quae de peregrinis inter Guaranios testis ipse earum rerum possum dicere.

CXCIII. Illud etiam erat secundum instituta Platonis (volentis pro bono publico aliquot aliquando majores natu urbes in alias ire) quod cum ex Europa appulerat Bonasauras novus Praetor, illuc descendebant e singulis oppidis primores Guaraniorum, ut ei, tamquam Regis Catholici personam gerenti, publicum obsequium deferrent, debitamque fidelitatem profiterentur totius nationis nomine. Eidem autem Praetori (siquod bellum instaret) evocanti in auxilium Guaranicas copias, praesto hae aderant ad tria, quattuor, sex millia, ut saepe factum est pro obsidenda Colonia Lusitana, et tum quidem suis stipendiis militabant, ut antea docuimus.

190. But if you should be wondering why the Spanish had free access to those six towns across the Paraná and not to the others as well, when it might seem that they should have been admitted to all or blocked from all, the reason is that the citizens of Paraguay and other inhabitants of that jurisdiction, since they are very far from the other Spanish cities, were granted permission to take their own merchandise to the towns that were closest to their borders, due to the Catholic king's favor and for their own good. This rationale did not apply to the other cities, for they can more easily sell their own things and the produce of their fields, irrespective of the Guaraní.

191. Otherwise, those who went to the towns (where trade was permitted) were lodged separately from the Indians, and after they had finished exchanging their merchandise for other merchandise, they were politely sent away. However, for the Spanish nobility, much more so for the Governors, and most of all for the Bishops (with a long way still to go the Bishops would be met by the priest, his colleague, and all the civic officials with significant pomp and signs of effusive joyfulness amidst an army of rejoicing Indians, the Musicians' festive harmonies, and the happy tolling of the bronze bell from the sacred tower, they would be led into town and right into the church)—as I was saying, for the Spanish nobility, the Governors, and the Bishops, the accommodations in the Parish priest's house were not at all elegant or magnificent but decent and proper.

192. Such guests either ate in the dining room with the Priest and his colleague, or a table was prepared for them in their own room if they had a very high stature that was incongruous with the common dining room. Thus, when the illustrious Bishop Manuel Antonio de la Torre visited us in the town of San Ignacio Guazú in the year 1764, separate banquets were prepared for him and his entourage. And these are the things about foreigners among the Guaraní that I myself am able to tell as an eyewitness to the facts.

193. Another thing that happened according to the instructions of Plato (who wants a few high-born people to go to other cities from time to time for the public good) was that when a new Governor from Europe had landed in Buenos Aires, the Guaraní leaders from each town would go down there to show their public obedience to him, as a personal representative of the Catholic King, and publicly profess the fidelity due to him on behalf of the entire nation. When the same Governor (if there were any threat of war) would call the Guaraní forces to his aid, as many as three, four, or even six thousand would appear on the spot, as often happened to effect a blockade of the Portuguese colony. Indeed, on such an occasion, they performed military service at their own expense, as we explained before.

CXCIV. Neque omittendum hic est arcessitos quondam fuisse Guaranios magno numero ad muniendum monsvideum, extruendamque arcem Bonaurensem, de qua re Regem Catholicum certiorem per litteras fecit Praetor Bruno Mauricius de Zavala cum eximia illorum commendatione. Denique institutam illam apud Guaranios administrationis formam, qua non quivis in omnia oppida peregrini admittebantur, Philippus V. Rex decreto suo ratam habuit an. MDCCXLIII., probavitque morem, quo suis Indi lembis *Herbam Paraguaycam,* concesso pondere XII. millium *arrobarum,* fructusque indigenas in urbem S. Fidei, et Bonasauras devehebant. Sed jam satis de commercio: atque haec quidem si legerit PAVVIUS Philosophus paulo, velim, aequior fiat in Curiones Guaranicos.

De vestibus.

PLATO

CXCV. Vellem scripsisset diserte Plato, quale in civibus optaret vestimenti genus. Quippe cum peregrinationem quibusdam permittat, et vicissim admittat urbe sua quosdam peregrinos, facile erat factu, ut cives visa exterarum vestium forma, eaque probata, suas rejicerent, id quod nunc fieri nimium saepe videmus, unus enim idemque vestimentorum modus vix annum durat; similesque sumus Chamaeleonti, cui proprior color non est, sed eum excipit e colore rei propius eum positae, Idem nobis mos. Si objicitur civium oculis transalpini viri, mulierisve amictus exter (vel si ridiculus sit) id sat est, ut ejus imitandi amor subeat omnium animos; fietve brevi, opinor, inter nos, quod factum olim dicitur a Graecis foeminis, quae septies uno die vestem mutabant majoris cultus causa.

CXCVI. Atqui Plato nihil tam abhorrebat, quam novos mores. Mutatio, inquit, omnibus in rebus, praeterquam in mutanda voluntate a malo in bonum, periculosissima est, ut videre licet in conversa repente coeli temperie, et in venti modo frigidi, modo calidi inconstantia, atque in usu novi cibi, rejecto veteri, inque (quod gravius est) contrariis inter se animi affectionibus, cum quis ardenter amat, quod nuper oderat. Quocirca non modo prisca civitatis jura, et leges mutare vetat, idque ne fiat, diligentissime cavet, sed ne ludos quidem, quibus assuescunt pueri, receptasque publice choreas, et antiquos cantus, variare patitur; quod siquis scilicet a puero instabilis esse coeperit; stabilis dein vir non erit. Proinde poenam statuit in agentes contra firmatum diuturnitate usum probatamque consuetudinem.

194. It must not go unremarked here that the Guaraní were summoned at one point in great numbers to defend Montevideo and to build a fort in Buenos Aires, about which Governor Bruno Mauricio de Zabala informed the Catholic King via a letter that included his utmost commendation for them. Finally, King Felipe V, in a decree issued in the year 1743, ratified that form of governance established among the Guaraní in which foreigners were not automatically admitted to the towns and approved the Indians' practice of transporting the Paraguayan *Yerba*, with the quota set at 12,000 *arrobas*, and indigenous fruits in their own boats to the city of Santa Fe and to Buenos Aires. But enough of commerce; that said, if the Philosopher de Pauw had read these things just a little, I should hope he would be fairer with the Guaraní Priests.

On Clothing

PLATO

195. I wish Plato had written expressly what kind of dress he wanted for citizens. Since he permits foreign travel for some and in turn admits certain foreigners in his own city, it could easily have happened that citizens would reject their own way of dress in favor of what they had seen and liked on outsiders, which is what we see happening all too often today; for one and the same style of dress scarcely lasts a year. We are like the Chameleon, which does not have its own color, but takes it from the object placed next to it; we have the same habit. If a strange garment belonging to a man or woman from the other side of the Alps is placed before the eyes of the citizens (even if it were ridiculous), that is enough for the desire to imitate it to steal into everyone's hearts. Shortly, I think, it will be done among us what it is said was once done by Greek women who changed their clothes seven times in a single day under the pretext of greater refinement.

196. Certainly, Plato loathed nothing so much as new customs. In all things, except when one's inclination is changed from bad to good, he says, change is most dangerous. This can be seen in the sudden change of the weather and in the fickleness of the wind one minute cold, the next hot, as well as in the use of new foods after the old ones have been rejected, and (what is more serious) in the emotional disposition we have toward one another when someone ardently loves what he recently hated. For this reason, he not only forbids changing the old rights and laws of the state (and he is extremely diligent about preventing this from happening), but he also does not tolerate variation in the games to which the children grow accustomed, the dances that are publicly embraced, nor the time-honored songs; because if someone starts out from childhood being unstable, then he will not be stable as a man. Hence, he establishes penalties for those who act contrary to long-established practice and proven convention.

CXCVII. Cur igitur, Plato, vestes non assignas aperte, et sigillatim, ut eaedem semper in Republica sint? Causa forsan est, quod ab aliis alibi ab ipso latis legibus sat constet, temperatissimum atque modestissimum esse debere suorum amictum civium: hos certe omnes, etiam foeminas (quod antea commemoravimus) ad militiam institui vult. Quales autem ille milites informat? A teneris, ait, pueri bello proludant, discantque ab aliis duci, et alios ducere: in hanc rem corpus durent, frenata vitae mollitie et licentia. Temperato viri foeminaeque cibo ac potu utuntor, frigus toleranto; solem aestumque ferunto; strati cubilisque duritiem diligunto; nihil blandi delicative sibi indulgento.

CXCVIII. Ad haec, vis nativa capitis, et pedum corrumpenda non est quaesito extrinsecus tegmine? nam extrema corporis naturali virtute in reliqua, ait membra robur diffundunt: sin vero pedes caputque adscititiis operimentis emollescunt, emollescat pariter necesse est ceterorum artuum vigor. Itaque cives suos vult Plato nudis pedibus incedere, et nudo capite.[72] Hinc tu conjice, quae ejus fuerit mens de vestium genere. (Lib. VII. et XII. de Legg.)

GUARANII.

CXCIX. Guaraniorum vestes tales erant, quales pro Republica sua probaret Plato. Viris femoralia, thorax, subucula. Super haec injiciebant sagulum illud dictum ipsis *Aobacì*, quod membra omnia corporis operiebat, relicto usu brachiorum. Extrema, sive anguli, hujus saguli erant quattuor, quorum bina a tergo ad talos, bina a pectore ad extimas pedum partes defluebant. Simplicius nihil potest fieri. Genus explico, ut rem intelligas.

CC. Extende humi lodicem; hujus in medio scissuram fac sesquipedalem. Eleva eam dein, et caput scissurae immitte. Quid fiet? Mediae lodicis pars collo tenus utrimque armos teget, et brachia: partium aliarum una hinc per humeros descendet ad pedum calcem, altera per pectus ad crura: cum autem pendulas has partes inter se nihil liget, ad latus dextrum laevumque, liber erit usus brachiorum, et manuum.

197. Why, then, Plato, do you not designate the clothing clearly and item by item so that it is always the same in the Republic? Perhaps the reason is that, according to the various laws he has asserted throughout, it is sufficiently clear that his citizens' garments ought to be extremely sensible and modest; certainly, all of these, even the females (which we have recounted previously), he wants to be prepared for military service. And what kind of soldiers is he fashioning? From a tender age, he says, that children play games that are precursors to war and learn both to lead and be led; for in this way they harden the body while lazy and licentious lifestyles are kept in check. Men and women consume moderate food and drink; they will have to tolerate the cold, endure the sun and the heat, be fond of the hardness of their bed and bedding, and indulge themselves in nothing soft or delicate.

198. Moreover, the innate power of the head and feet would have to be corrupted by seeking extraneous coverings, right? For due to their natural vitality the body's extremities, he says, diffuse strength into the rest of the members; but if you weaken the feet and head by adopting coverings, the vigor of the other limbs will necessarily be weakened in equal measure. Thus, Plato wants his citizens to walk around barefoot and bareheaded.[72] From what has been said, you can conjecture what his opinion was about the way of dressing (*Laws* Books 7 and 12).

THE GUARANÍ

199. The garments of the Guaraní were such as Plato would have approved for his Republic. For men: breeches, vest, and shirt. Over these they would throw on that cape they call an *Aovasy*, which covered the whole body, with the use of the arms left free. This cape had four ends or corners, two of which flowed down from the back to the heels and two from the chest to the tips of the feet. Nothing could be simpler. I will unpack the details so that you understand what it is.

200. Spread a blanket on the floor; make a foot-and-a-half cut in the center. Then pick it up and stick your head through the cut. What is the result? Half of the blanket will cover from the neck down to the arms and forearms on either side; one of the other parts will descend from there through the shoulders to the heels of the feet, the other, across the chest to the legs. Since nothing fastens these hanging parts to one another, on the right or on the left, the use of arms and hands will be free.

CCI. Ridiculam dices rem: atqui nec ridicula est, et eadem commodissima ad equitandum, sive quid aliud agendum sit. Sane Hispani vel nobilissimi cum equitant, vel ruri sunt, non alio utuntur illac sago, quod ipsi vocant *Poncho*. Hoc unum interest, quod his multo pretio ejusmodi amictus is constet ob exquisitiorem materiam, intextosque labores: Indis vero suus ille *Aobaci* fiat e tela gossipina (qui mos quoque est Asiae populis ad Malabris, et Cambayae oras, gossipio indutis) tantum pro oppidi primoribus, atque aedituis, aliisque bene de publico meritis addebantur albo colori inter texendum lineae quaedam rubrae caeruleaeve: ceteris unicolor vestis erat: habebantque singuli plus una, ut lavari alternis possent.

CCII. Foeminae praeter interulam utebantur palla sua (*Tupoì*) e gossipio item demissa ad talos usque, quae palla sic eas tegebat, ut nihil nisi facies, et guttur apparerent: omnino modesta vestis erat, et quae vel sacras Virgines deceat. Passos capillos sine taeniis ad tergum rejiciebant. Sed qui mundus earum muliebris? Aures ornabant aeneis inauribus, collum, et manuum carpos varii coloris vitreis orbiculis circumdabant. Haec monilia. Fucus, quo vultum inficerent, apud illas nullus: mos enim faciem tingendi barbararum foeminarum est, Christianarum non est. Palla ea, quam diximus, erat ad templum, publicasque functiones. Domi, et ruri, vestis levior, atque accommodatior ad laborem: ibi capillum crinali theca longiuscula, reticuli instar, includebant.

CCIII. Ceterum e Platonis instituto Guaraniis (si quosdam curae industrioris excipias, quibus tibialia, et petasi erant) nulum capitis, pedumque operimentum, neque de hac re illi laborabant. Praetor tamen, et magistratus ad sollemniores anni dies, utebantur urbano calceamento, subtilibusque tibialibus, ac galeris, et veste reliqua Hispaniensis formae e tela pretiosiore, quae omnia ipsis e publico curabantur: post festum vero diem deponebant vestes istas peregrinas (quae in celebritatem aliam asservabantur apud Curionem) et ad suas redibant. Aeditui, puerique, qui aris ministrabant, calceos induebant, et crurum tegmen praeter ceterum ornatum, quem alibi descripsimus. Sed absoluto sacro ministerio (quasi cultus ille esset ipsis taedio impedimentoque) pedes confestim nudabant.

201. You will call it ridiculous. Well, it is not ridiculous, and this same garment is very comfortable for horseback riding or whatever has to be done. To be sure, the Spanish themselves, even the highest born, when they ride a horse or are in the field, wear no other cloak than this one, which they call a *Poncho*. There is this one difference: that for the Spanish a garment of this type has a high price due to its exquisite material and embroidery, but for the Indians, their *Aovasy* is made of cotton cloth (which is also the custom for the peoples of Asia on the Malabar Coast and Gulf of Khambhat,* who dress in cotton). Only for the leaders of the town, the sacristans, and others serving the public, were red or blue stripes in the textile added to the white color; for the others the garment was monochrome. Each person had more than one so that they could be washed alternately.

202. The women, in addition to an undergarment, wore their version of a dress (*Typói*), made of cotton, which likewise hung all the way down to the ankles, and this dress covered them such that nothing was showing but the face and neck. The dress was quite modest and the sort of thing that would be appropriate even for the Vestal Virgins. They let their hair fall loose, without ribbons, down their backs. But what feminine adornment did they have? They adorned their ears with copper earrings, and they wore glass beads of various colors around the neck and on their fingers. This was their jewelry. They had no rouge to dye their face; for the custom of painting one's face belongs to barbarian women, not Christian women. The dress, which we described, was for church and public functions. At home and in the field, they wore a garment that was lighter and more suitable for labor; there they enclosed their tresses in a longish hair cover, like a net.

203. Otherwise, according to Plato's instruction, the Guaraní had neither head nor foot covering (if you leave aside those with especially active occupations, who had socks and wide-brimmed hats) and they were not troubled by this. The Chief Executive, however, and the civic officials, on especially sacred days of the year, they wore city shoes, fine socks, and caps, as well as the other Spanish-style garments, made with more costly fabrics. All of this was taken care of for them through public resources. After the festival, however, they would take off those foreign garments (which were kept for another celebration at the Priest's house) and return to their own garments. The sacristans and the children who tended the altars, wore shoes and coverings for their legs, in addition to the other attire, which we have described elsewhere. But once the holy service was finished (as if this refinement were irksome and a hinderance to them) they immediately reverted to bare feet.

* On the western coast of present-day India.

CCIV. Clemens Alexandrinus, Platonis premens vestigia, non alia de causa nobis opus esse ait amictu, quam ut corpora contra frigus coelique intemperiem, habita simul modestiae ratione, tegamus, tueamurque: nimio autem cultu, fucataeque lanae splendida tinctura, et quaesito pro vibrandis crinibus artificio, processum, inquit, eo jam est, ut viri quidam foeminis ipsis (quibus se se comendi nullus est finis) effeminatiores evaserint; tantusque obtinuit luxus, ut alienis potius oculis, quam nostrae ipsorum utilitati, forma et usu vestium serviamus.

CCV. Quid vero Clemens ipse de calceis? Optimum, ait, exercitationis genus viro est, nudis (praeterquam si militet, aut iter agat) ire pedibus, id enim et ad sanam corporis habitudinem, et ad facilitatem rei gerendae, operandique confert. Sin autem sine integumento aliquo incedere nequeamus, utendum nobis est (potius quam alio calceamento) socis, sive crepidis, quae quidem multo magis concedendae sunt foeminis utpote natura imbecillioribus. Haec ille.[73]

CCVI. Verum tanta ista in vestitu temperantia, quantam et Plato et Clemens volunt, optari quidem potest; sperari (ut nunc sunt mores, et luxus, quo plebejae foeminae matronas nobiles, matronae nobiles aequare Reginas student) non potest. Rem omnem temperat breviter, et optime D. Thomas, cujus e sententia (cum vestium duplex sit usus, alter, ut corpus tegant, et muniant, alter, ut earum discrimine civium ordines inter se dignoscantur) is in Republica tenendus est mos, et modus, ut suus cuique classi civitatis constet honor debitus. Hinc ille sapienter, *exterior*, ait, *cultus indicium quoddam est conditionis humanae . . . moderatus autem ornatus non prohibetur mulieribus, sed superfluus, et inverecundus, et impudicus.* O quantum hinc mali? Quanta vel in domo Dei ab habitu immodesto scandali materies? Addit Thomas: *nemo vestimenta pretiosa, scilicet excedentia proprium statum, nisi ad inanem gloriam quaerit.*[74] At longius nos Guaraniorum indumenta abduxerunt. Illis, quippe quibus conditione paribus, pares erant vestes, et simplices, eaedemque semper; receptum namque a majoribus morem viri foeminaeque adhuc retinebant.[75]

204. Clement of Alexandria, following in Plato's footsteps, says that we have no need of clothing for any reason other than to cover and defend our bodies against the cold and inclemency of the weather, with consideration taken at the same time for modesty. Yet, due to excessive refinement, the splendid colors of dyed wool, and the sought-after art of curling hair, he says, it is now at such a point that certain men have turned out more effeminate than actual women (for whom there is no end to primping). So much luxury has taken hold that in the form and function of our clothing we are preoccupied with serving the eyes of others rather than our own welfare.

205. But what does Clement himself tell us about footwear? The best type of exercise for a man, he says, is to go about barefoot (unless he is performing military service or on a journey), for this provides for the healthy condition of the body and ease of conducting affairs and working. But if we cannot walk without some type of footwear, we must use (rather than other footwear) slippers or sandals, which are actually far more permissible for women, since they are naturally weaker. This is what he says.[73]

206. Of course it is possible to wish for as much moderation in dress as Plato and Clement want, but it cannot be expected (since the customs and luxury today are such that ordinary women strive to measure up to noble matrons and noble matrons strive to rival Queens). Saint Thomas succinctly and excellently brings the entire matter into balance (since the purpose of clothing is twofold: one purpose is to cover and defend the body; the other is so that through the distinctions in dress the various classes of citizens can be distinguished from one another). In his opinion, in the Republic the custom and fashion must be upheld so that due honor accrues to each class of citizen. Hence, he wisely says: "outward refinement is a sort of index of the human condition . . . Moderate attire is not forbidden to women, but rather what is superfluous, immodest, and lewd." O how much damage comes from that! How much opportunity for scandal even in the house of God comes from immodest dress! St. Thomas himself adds: "No one wears garments that are costly, meaning those that go beyond one's own status, unless he is seeking vain glory."[74] But the garments of the Guaraní have led us rather far off course. They, since of course they were equal in rank, had clothing that was equal, simple, and always the same. For the men and women still retained the habits passed down from their ancestors.[75]

CCVII. Praetor Bonaurensis, qui post indictam exilii legem Curiones Guaranios totum annum (cur tamdiu? norit ipse) in oppidis retinuit, dicitur scripsisse ad illorum praefectum esse rem prorsus intolerabilem a Patribus permitti Indos nudis ire pedibus. Sed hoc erat nodum in scirpo, ut ajunt, quaerere: ac scire vellem, an post exactos tandem veteres Curatores Praetor is, vel novi illuc missi Sacerdotes dederint genti illi calceos, et tibialia? Non, opinor, nam litteris ab urbe Bonaurensi datis scriptum est: *mutato pristinae oeconomiae ordine oppida laborant extrema rerum penuria, ideoque infelices illi incolae, inedia, et nuditate compulsi, elabuntur turmatim alii in ditionem Paraguaycam, alii in fines fluminis Argentei, alii in silvas, quas eorum majores insederant. Templa vero corruunt, et aedes, non resarciendae.*[76] Atqui satius fuisset nudis pedibus oppido Indos retineri, acceptaeque immorari disciplinae, quam addita fame nuditati, vagos per rura, saltusque spargi magna morum labe, magnoque animarum detrimento.

CCVIII. Scilicet in praeturis Bonaurensi, et Paraguayca, et Tucumanica, mos Indorum est non alio ad incedendum uti tegmine, et praesidio pedum, quam quo nascentes a natura donati sunt. Cultores Guaranici indigenas illos excalceatos reperere, et excalceatos eosdem reliquerunt. Vel in ipsa Europa aestatis tempore agricolarum plurimi, nec pauci ex urbis plebe nudis eunt pedibus, quod gratum ipsis sit frui frigidioris terrae tactu, vel minore aestu.

CCIX. Inter Guaranios ver longissimum est, et mitis hiems; usuque ipso ita occallescunt, ut nihil calceamenta desiderent: cur igitur adeo timendum est ne noceat Guaraniis pedum nuditas. Sane Japones capite incedunt fere semper nudo, ac levibus crepidis, sive sandaliis, et nihilo minus diutissime vivunt, vel si hiems saevissima illic sit. Attamen mallem ego (ut verum fatear) a neophytis illis crura et pedes tegi; non quod nudi doleant, sed ut tutiores forent a morsu viperarum, quarum ruri ingens vis. Verum ipsi cum e ferarum corio, ac maxime e Nutriarum molli pelle, munire extrema corporis facile possint, id minus curant.

207. The Governor of Buenos Aires,* who, after the exile order was promulgated, detained the Guaraní priests in the towns for a whole year (why so long? Only he knows), is said to have written to their superior that it was entirely intolerable for Fathers to allow Indians to go around barefoot. But this, as the saying goes, is to seek a knot in a thicket of cattails.† And I would like to know whether, after the former Caretakers were expelled, this Governor or the new Priests sent there will have given those people shoes and socks. I suppose not, for in letters sent from the city of Buenos Aires it is written: "since the old economic system was changed, the towns are afflicted by extreme scarcity of goods, and thus, those unhappy inhabitants, driven by starvation and exposure, escape in bands, some to the jurisdiction of Paraguay, others to the territory of the Río de la Plata, others to the forests, where their ancestors had been based. Indeed, the churches and houses are falling into ruin and not being repaired."[76] Certainly, it would have been preferable to keep the Indians barefoot in their town and to keep up the teachings they had accepted rather than for them to be wandering through the countryside and the woods, hungry and exposed no less, shattered by the great destruction of their customs and the great damage to their souls.

208. The truth is that in the governorates of Buenos Aires, Paraguay, and Tucumán, the Indians' custom when they walk is to not use any covering or protection for their feet other than the one bestowed upon them by nature when they were born. The Guaraní Cultivators found them shoeless and left them shoeless. Even in Europe itself, during summertime, quite a lot of farmers and not a few ordinary people in the city go barefoot, since they are grateful for the enjoyment of touching earth that is cooler or at least less hot.

209. Among the Guaraní, spring is very long, and winter is mild; and through use alone they develop calluses such that they have no desire for footwear at all. Why should there be so much fear that exposed feet are harmful to the Guaraní? To be sure, the Japanese almost always walk bareheaded and with light slippers or sandals, and they are no less long-lived, although the winter there is very harsh. And yet, I would prefer (to be honest) that those neophytes covered their legs and feet, not because being exposed caused them pain, but because they would be safer from snakebites, which are a tremendous danger in the fields. But they, since they can easily protect their bodily extremities with wild animal hides, most of all with the soft skin of otters, they are less concerned about it.

* Francisco de Paula Bucarelli.

† i.e., to seek problems where none exist.

De Magistratibus.

PLATO

CCX. Qui recte, inquit, magistratum gesturi sint, oportet eos ab adolescentia bonis fuisse, moribus. Comitia autem ad deferendum munus publicum benemerentibus in templo habeantur, ibique ferantur suffragia. Qui in pueritia, et juventute, et adulta jam aetate incorruptus fuerit probatusque, is totius civitatis Princeps deligitor, idemque eximio honore et vivus colitor et mortuus.

CCXI. Quot autem futuri sint magistratus, atque eorum officia, sigillatim, accurateque recenset. Sunto, ait, in urbe Praetor, et Aediles, et Quaestores pro sacra pecunia, et Curatores rei agrariae, qui quid ruri fiat, diligenter observent, et siquo derivandae sint aquae, aut alicunde contra arcendae, tempore provideant, et judicent siqua lis, aut rixa colonorum orta fuerit. Sunto item militiae Duces, et Custodes legum. Hos vero, aliosque quos rebus praeficit, nihil privati possidere vult, sed ali contributo a civibus honorario, ita tamen ut ex annuis pro eorum victu sumptibus neque supersit quicquam, neque desit: summum enim, et praestantissimum ipsorum praemium esse debet testimonium conscientiae de administrata sancte, et fideliter Republica.

CCXII. Nemo judicum praefectorumque immunis esto, inquit, a reddendis rationibus de gesto magistratu praeter eos, quorum est extremum judicium ferre de rebus controversis. Jubet autem quotidie ante Solis ortum convenire Sacerdotes (his primas defert) et decem senes ex legum Custodibus, simul cum Censore morum; ut inter se de statu Reipublicae consultent, et quid jubendum, quidve vetandum sit, deliberent.

CCXIII. Singulare vero quiddam est, quod de Judicibus, Medicisque (utrosque enim conjungit) admonet. Malae, ait, et perversae in civitate disciplinae nulla certior fieri conjectura potest, quam si multis Judicibus et Medicis indigeat. Quid enim indignius quam neglecto cultu virtutis, qua sibi quisque recte consulat, et cum aliis juste agat, ad tribunalia confugere? Quanto esset aequius, et melius ita cives vivere, et inter se amare versarique, ut rei eorum componendae causa adeundus judex non esset? Temperato autem homini vix opus medicina est.

On Officials

PLATO

210. The sort of people who would be right to serve as civic officials, says Plato, should have good habits from adolescence. The elections, then, for conferring public office on those who are worthy of it should be held in the temple and the votes should be taken there. Whoever in childhood, adolescence, and now adulthood is uncorrupted and esteemed, he must be selected as chief of the whole state and that same man must be regarded with the utmost honor both while alive and after death.

211. He painstakingly enumerates one by one how many civic officials there ought to be and their duties. There must be, he says, an Urban Warden [ἀστυνόμος], Market Wardens [ἀγορανόμοι], Treasurers [ταμίαι] for the sacred funds, Caretakers of agrarian affairs [ἀγρονόμοι], who can diligently observe what is done in the field and who can anticipate at the right moment whether water has to be diverted or, alternately, has to be kept away from somewhere else, and who can adjudicate if any dispute or quarrel should arise between the farmers. There also must be Military Commanders [στρατηγοί] and Law Guardians [νομοφύλακοι].* He wants these and the others who are in charge of public affairs, to have no private possessions and instead be supported by contributions volunteered by the citizens such that after the annual expenditure for their upkeep there is neither surplus nor deficit. For the highest and most outstanding reward for these officials ought to be the testimony of their conscience that the Republic was administered scrupulously and faithfully.

212. None of the judges or prefects are to be immune, he says, from having to render accounts relating to the office they have held aside from those who must have the final judgment on controversial matters. Moreover, he orders that every day, before sunrise, the Priests (he gives them first place) and ten of the senior Law Guardians meet all together with the Supervisor of Conduct [ὁ περὶ τῆς παιδείας πάσης ἐπιμελητὴς], so that they may consult with one another about the state of the Republic and deliberate on what to command and what to forbid.

213. But there is something extraordinary that he reminds us about judges and doctors (for it pertains to them both). No surer conclusion could be drawn, he says, that the habits in a state are wicked and off course than if there is a need for a lot of judges and doctors. For, what could be more unbecoming than taking refuge in the courts, because the cultivation of virtue has been neglected—that quality by which a person looks after himself properly and conducts his affairs with others justly? How much fairer and better would it be for citizens to live and both love and interact with one another in such a way that a judge did not have to be approached to reconcile their differences! And indeed, a temperate man hardly needs medicine.

* Peramàs draws on the vocabulary of Roman magistracies in an effort to assign Latin equivalents for the Greek terms Plato proposes for his hypothetical officials. Both are provided here.

CCXIV. Mavult idem, siqua controversia orta sit, bonis arbitris rem decidi, quam ad judicium publicum deferri. Qui litigant, inquit, vicinos primum, et amicos, et eos, qui negotii, de quo agitur, experti sunt, adeunto: quod si per illos definiri lis non possit, tum litigatores judicem appellanto. Invehitur dein acriter in rabulas, legulejosque, qui ob avaritiam, vel turpe lucrum, injustis causis patrocinantur. Videtur vero ita velle judicia agitari, expedirique, ut intra annum saltem institutae actionis sententia feratur.

CCXV. Quod ad Medicos attinet, probrum homini est, ait, si opus ipsi sit Medico non ad curanda vulnera, quae forte acceperit, vel ad opitulandum aegrae valetudini, quam contraxerit e coeli intemperie, sed propter morbos ex otio, e desidia, a deliciis, ab ingluvie ortos. Etenim ciborum varietas intemperantiam, et stomachi cruditatem parit; cibus vero simplex temperantiae, ac sanitatis altor, et custos est.[77] (Lib. III. de Repub. lib. VI. XI. XII. de Legg.)

GUARANII.

CCXVI. Magistratus Guaraniorum tot erant, quot esse jubet in oppidis Indorum, et urbibus Hispanis lex Indica. Omnium primi Praetor, ejusque Vicarius (*Teniente de Corregidor*). Urbani consules (*Alcaldes*) duo, et tertius (*Alcalde de la hermandad*) ad rem ruris. Senatores (*Regidores*) quattuor. Praefectus apparitorum (*Alguazil mayor*). Procurator publicus, et scriba.[78] Praeter hos erat Signifer Regius (*Alferez Real*) qui agmine militum stipatus Regis vexillum in maxima oppidi celebritate (cum Divo Praesidi recurrerat sacer dies) inter tympanorum strepitus, cantusque tubarum deferebat ad templum, cujus sub ostium a Curione, ejusque collega, et hospitibus Sacertotibus, qui invitati a vicinis oppidis convenerant, insigni obsequio ob Regis personam, quam repraesentabat, excipiebatur, deducebaturque ad paratam ei sedem selecto in loco. A templo autem (post factum majori caerimonia Sacrificium, habitamque Divi Praesidis laudationem) idem Signifer, eodem comitatu plausuque vexillum ad forum referebat, et locabat in tabulato pro hac ipsa re affabre facto.

214. He also prefers that if a controversy has arisen, the case be decided by good arbitrators, rather than it be brought to a public trial. Those who have the dispute, he says, must first go to neighbors, friends, and those who have experience in the business concerned; if the dispute cannot be resolved by them, then the litigants must appeal to a judge. Plato then fiercely attacks the hacks and hairsplitters who, out of greed or foul avarice, sponsor unjust lawsuits. And he seems to want the lawsuits to be set in motion and expedited such that at least within a year, a sentence is pronounced on the action initiated.

215. With regard to Doctors, it is shameful for a person, he says, if he needs a Doctor not for healing wounds received accidentally or remedying poor health brought on by inclement weather, but because of illnesses that have arisen from leisure, from idleness, from delicacies, or from gluttony. In fact, inconsistency in one's diet breeds intemperance and indigestion; a simple diet, however, is a nourisher and guardian of temperance and health.[77] (*Republic* Book 3 and *Laws* Books 6, 11–12).

THE GUARANÍ

216. The Guaraní had as many officials as the Law of the Indies orders there to be in the towns of Indians and Spanish cities. Of these the primary officials were the Chief Executive (*Corregidor*) and his Lieutenant (*Teniente de Corregidor*). There were two High Magistrates for the city (*Alcaldes*) and a third for rural matters (*Alcalde de la hermandad*). There were four Councilors (*Regidores*), a Chief Constable (*Alguazil mayor*), a Public Treasurer, and a clerk.[78] Beyond these there was the Royal Standard-bearer (*Alferez Real*), who, surrounded by a band of soldiers at the town's biggest festival (when the patron saint's holy day had come around again) amid the din of drums and the blast of horns, would carry the King's banner to the church; at the church door he would be received by the priest, his colleague, and visiting priests, who had been invited to come from the neighboring towns, with extraordinary indulgence for the person of the king, which he represented; and he would be led to a seat prepared for him in a special place. Then from the church (after the Mass had been performed with great ceremony and the praises of the Patron Saint had been pronounced) the same Standard-bearer with the same retinue and fanfare would bring the banner to the town square and place it on a platform ingeniously fashioned for this purpose.

CCXVII. Modus eligendi magistratus erat is. Sub extremum mensem Decembrem, qui eo anno publicis muneribus functi fuerant, deliberabant inter se, qui in proximum annum designandi essent ad oppidi administrationem. Visos prae aliis dignos referebant in album. Nullae ad haec presanda munia (ut assolet) coitiones, nulli motus, nullus ambitus. Scriptum indicem ad Curionem deferebant. Curio siquem sibi probe cognitum, nec merentem, designatum repererat, monebat, ut alium substituerent; idque secundum leges Indicas, quae jubent Parochos interesse Indorum electionibus, ut fiant ordine.

CCXVIII. Calendis Januariis parabantur quaedam ad templi porticum subsellia cum mensa, ubi posita erant insignia magistratuum. Is dies summa agebatur laetitia, festoque apparatu. Curio sedens explicabat primum, audiente circum populo, quae a bono magistratu in publicum bona oriantur, et quae e contrario mala a malo. Designatorum dein nomina legebat, singulique (ut appellati fuerant) in medium prodibant, atque accepta sui muneris tessera, sive symbolo, occupabant sedem ipsis destinatam.

CCXIX. Verum haec creatio magistratuum firma nondum erat; accedere enim debebat consensus Praetoris Bonaurensis, ad quem nomina designatorum mittebantur, ut ipse Regis Catholici nomine auctor electionis fieret. Ceterum Praetor nihil ferme mutabat, sed jubebat, qui delecti fuerant, magistratum gerere. His autem magistratibus attributus erat in aede sacra locus honoratior, ut ab oppidanis penderentur pluris; habebaturque etiam publice major ipsorum ratio in largitione bonorum communium. Eodem illo Calendarum Januariarum die eligebantur aeditui, Aeconomi, fabrorum praefecti, custodes censoresque puerorum, atque alii ad rectum oppidi ordinem. at pro horum approbatione (cum e magistratu non essent) haud requirebatur auctoritas Praetoris Bonaurensis, neque istud ejus intererat.

CCXX. Quotidie Praetor oppidi post sacrum Missae Curionem adibat, et quid eo die maxime fieri oporteret, admonebat, renunciabatque siquid pridie animadversione dignum vel ruri, vel alibi accidisset. Curio, qui stabat pro cubiculi sui janua, quid sibi factu optimum videretur, ostendebat. Tum Praetor egressus foras opus publicum, ubi, et a quibus faciundum esset, indicebat: binis enim diebus laborabant communiter singulis hebdomadis, feria nimirum secunda, et sabbato; praetereaque quoties res aliqua instaret praesentis indigens operae.

217. The way of electing officials was as follows. At the end of December, those who had performed public duties that year determined through deliberation among themselves who should be appointed to govern the town for the next year. They put those who seemed worthy by comparison with others on a register. There were no coalitions to campaign for these positions (as usually happens), no commotion, no intrigue. Once the list was written, they brought it to the priest. If the priest found that someone had been appointed whom he was sure was undeserving, he would advise that they substitute someone else. This is according to the Laws of the Indies, which dictate that the Parish Priests take part in the Indians' elections so that they happen in an orderly manner.

218. On the first day of January, some chairs and a table were set up before the portico of the church, where the insignia of the public officials were placed. This day was most joyful and festive. The priest would sit and first explain, while the people around him listened, what sort of benefits would arise for the public from a good official, and what sort, on the contrary, of evils from a bad one. Then he would read the names of the appointees, and each of them (as they were called) would come into the center and, once the token or insignia of his position was received, take the seat assigned to him.

219. But this appointment of officials was not yet fixed; for it had to have the consent of the Governor of Buenos Aires, to whom the names of those appointed were sent so that he, in the name of the Catholic King, could ratify the election. Otherwise, the Governor changed essentially nothing; he just ordered those who had been chosen to carry out their office. A place of greater honor had been designated for these magistrates in the holy church so that they would be more highly regarded by the townsfolk; and greater consideration for them is taken publicly in the distribution of community goods. On that same first day of January, the sacristans, the Administrators, the superintendent of artisans, the guardians and supervisors of the children, and others necessary for the right order of the town were also elected. But the endorsement of the Governor of Buenos Aires was not required to approve these (since they were not government officials) and he took no part in it.

220. Every day, after Mass, the town's Chief Executive would consult with the Priest and advise him what most needed to be done that day and reported whether anything worth reviewing had happened the day before in the fields or elsewhere. The Priest, who would be standing at the door of his room, would indicate what seemed to him to be the best thing to do. Then the Chief Executive would go outside and announce what public work had to be carried out, where, and by whom. They would perform communal labor two days each week, Monday and Saturday, and beyond that as often as there was some matter requiring immediate attention.

CCXXI. Lites facillime dirimebantur: paucae erant, et de rebus parvis. Si vicini, amicique altercantibus non fecerant satis, uterque jus suum coram Curione exponebat; atque is, cognita causa, quid sibi justum, et aequum videretur, significabat, illiusque stabatur judicio, neque ullis tabulis, et actoribus, tabellionibusque opus erat: tantum testes audiebantur, si res testimonio niteretur.

CCXXII. Timeo, ne hic exurgat scriptor ille Regni Paraguayci, et clamet, hoc, hoc enimvero regium est, hoc est reges esse, judicia facere, sententiam ferre, lites dirimere. Concedo, Regis maxime esse, lites decidere, judicia exercere, sententiam pronunciare. Quid tum inde? An quisquis litem dirimit, Rex est? O bone? Plato rem controversam ad arbitros deferri vult; quod si ab his quidem utrique parti altercantium fiat satis, censet id civibus multo esse melius utiliusque, quam ad judices causam deferri.

CCXXIII. Curiones jam inde ab initio susceptae institutionis Guaraniorum, ab his ultro arbitri, cognitoresque delecti sunt, siquid occurreret rei controversae: illorum judicio pro publica tranquillitate, et pace familiarum stare maluerunt quam suo. Hic nihil regii est: immo vero hic Regis Catholici mens, et voluntas est, qui a Parochis benigne et leniter dissidia Indorum componi optat, atque id ipsum vehementer commendat. Ipsae Hispani regni leges (quas Partitarum vocant) hunc modum litium decidendarum per aequos arbitros approbant.[79] Denique Curiones Guaranici exemplum hac in re secuti sunt S. Francisci Xaverii, qui dissidentium causas Indorum arbiter cognoscebat, et dirimebat, sublata lite ex utriusque partis consensu.[80]

CCXXIV. At enim Xaverio prudentia quaedam coelestis erat; Guaranicus autem Curio et errare poterat, et locum dare justis Indorum querelis. Hoc verum est: atque ut malo ejusmodi obviam iretur, Praefectus sociorum (quem vocabant superiorem Missionum) oppida frequenter obibat, ac siquis oppidanorum quicquam de Curione suo queri vellet, audiebat eum seorsum, et si quidem pro illo ratio et veritas facerent, contra Curionem pronunciabat, et remedium, pro longo usu rei Guaranicae, quo erat ipse excercitatus, opportunum adhibebat.

221. Disputes were resolved very easily: they were few and regarding minor matters. If neighbors and friends had not satisfied the ones arguing, each one would explain his claim to the priest and then he, having become acquainted with the case, would indicate what seemed fair and equitable to him and his judgment would be upheld. There was no need for law codes, no attorneys, and no notaries. Witnesses would be heard only if the matter depended on testimony.

222. I am afraid that author of the *Kingdom of Paraguay* will rise up at this point and exclaim: ah ha! this here is royal, this is what it means to be king: holding trials, passing sentences, resolving disputes. I grant that it is above all the king's place to decide disputes, oversee trials, and pronounce a sentence. And so what? Is whoever resolves a dispute a king? Good grief!* Plato wants the controversial matter brought before arbitrators because he is of the opinion that, if they satisfy both arguing parties, this is much better and more profitable for the citizens than the case being brought before judges.

223. Right from the start when the arrangement with the Guaraní was initiated, they chose the Priests to be arbiters and judges of their own accord whenever a controversial matter came up. In the interest of public tranquility and peace between the families they preferred to rely on the priests' judgment rather than on their own. There is nothing here that belongs to the king; on the contrary, this truly is the intention and the wish of the Catholic King who prefers the Indians' disagreements be settled kindly and gently by the Parish Priests and he strongly recommends this very thing. The Spanish king's very laws (which they call "Divisions" [Sp. *Partidas*]) approve of this way of deciding disputes through impartial arbiters.[79] In the end, in this matter the Guaraní Priests followed the example of Saint Francisco Javier, who as arbiter would become acquainted with cases of disagreements between the Indians and then resolve them by eliminating the dispute through a consensus with both parties.[80]

224. But Javier had a certain heavenly sense of judgment. A Guaraní Priest, on the other hand, could make a mistake and give occasion for just complaints from the Indians. This is true; and so, to combat this kind of problem, a superintendent of the society (whom they called the Superior of the Missions) frequently visited the towns and if any of the townspeople wanted to complain about his Priest for any reason, he would listen to the person privately. If indeed reason and truth were in his favor, he would decide against the priest and apply a remedy that was suitable, according to longstanding practice in the Guaraní culture, with which he himself was well-versed.

* An exasperated, ironic address "Oh good [sir]."

CCXXV. Praeterea tertio circiter quoque anno totius provinciae moderator oppida illa lustrabat, ut gesta ipsius Praefecti, Curionumque recognosceret, statueretque, (salvo Antistum jure) quae pro credito illis animarum ministerio, aptiora ei videbantur. Ne vero id temere faceret, cogebat unum in vicum quotquot Patrum, sine commissae curae neophytorum detrimento, adesse poterant, communicatisque inter se consiliis, quae vel jubenda, vel corrigenda essent ad spirituale temporariumque Indorum bonum deliberabant.

CCXXVI. De Medicis (quoniam quid de his sentiat Plato supra docuimus) dicam brevi. In singulis oppidis quaterni senive Indi id muneris tractabant. Iis (appellabant *Cruciferos* ob Crucem, quam in extrema baculi parte ferebant) cura erat aegros invisendi, monendique Curionem bis quotidie de illorum statu, et siquis forte recens decumberet, ut Sacramenta, et alia Ecclesiae subsidia mature deferret. Cubantes autem Curio ipse, vel ejus collega frequenter adibat, ut ad virtutum excercitationem eos hortarentur; et audirent, si denuo confiteri peccata vellent.

CCXXVII. Interim Curatores illi[81] medicinam gratis faciebant ex natis ibi herbis salubribus, quae multae sunt, et quarum vim explicarunt scriptis Guaranicis Jesuitae quidam hujus rei intelligentes. Quod siquid praeterea cuperent Medici, petebant ab domo Curionis, qui in hunc usum nonnulla sibi comparabat. Ceterum inter Guaranios morbi non multi sunt; ac nisi letales pustulae idemtidem oppida depopulatae fuissent, gens Guaranica binis, vel etiam ternis partibus frequentior esset: sed ea lues ingentem Indis stragem affert, ut supra commemoratum est.

De Legibus.

PLATO

CCXXVIII. Leges, quae virtutis urgendae causa ferri debent, si bonae, et justae sint (quae ipsius legis necessaria conditio est) omnia omnibus pariunt bona. Bona autem duplicia, inquit, sunt, divina alia, alia humana, dependentque humana a divinis: utrorumque oportet a Legislatore rationem in jubendo vetandove haberi; ac de singulis recte et sapienter praecipi (Lib. de Repub. et de Legg. passim).

225. In addition, just about every third year, the Provincial of the entire Province would visit those towns to review the achievements of the superintendent himself as well as the priests and to institute (without violating the Bishops' prerogative) what seemed to him to be particularly fitting for the ministry of the souls that had been entrusted to them. And so that he would not do this haphazardly, he would gather in one village as many Fathers as could attend without compromising their responsibility to the neophytes. Through a mutual exchange of ideas, they would weigh what should be either commanded or corrected for the spiritual and temporal well-being of the Indians.

226. I will briefly say something about Doctors (since we explained above what Plato thinks about them). In each town, from four to six Indians handled this sort of duty. These individuals (they called them *Cruciferos* [Sp. "Cross-bearers"] because of the cross which they carried on the end of their staff) were responsible for looking in on the sick and notifying the priest twice a day about their condition. And if someone young should happen to fall ill, they would see to it that someone brought him the Sacraments and other relief from the Church in time. The priest himself or his colleague frequently visited those on bed rest to encourage them to practice virtue and listen to them if they wanted to confess their sins again.

227. Sometimes those Caretakers[81] would make free medicines from health-promoting herbs native to the place, of which there are many and whose powers certain Jesuits acquainted with such matters described in their writings on the Guaraní. But if the doctors wanted something beyond these, they would ask for it from the house of the priest, who kept quite a few items in stock for this purpose. Otherwise, among the Guaraní there are not many diseases; and if it had not been for the deadly pustules that had depopulated the towns time and again, the Guaraní nation would be more numerous by a factor of two or even three; but this plague visited tremendous destruction on the Indians, as has been recounted above. See *DAG* 18, and especially note 7.

On Laws

PLATO

228. Laws, which should be proposed for encouraging virtue, so long as they are good and just (which is the necessary condition of law itself), bring about all goods for all people. Goods, Plato says, are of two kinds: some divine and others human, and the human ones depend on the divine. It is necessary for both to be taken into account by the Legislator when commanding or forbidding and for precepts to be given justly and wisely about individual matters (*Republic* and *Laws*, frequently).

GUARANII.

CCXXIX. Instituta, quibus regebantur Guaranii, Christiana ante omnia erat lex, quae Platonis, et omnium Philosophorum placita superat infinitis partibus, quippe multo plura aperit, et sancte praecipit de rebus altissimis, atque divinis, quam nova illa et vetus academia, et gravis Stoa, ac tot antiquae Atheniensium scholae, tanta contentione, tantoque naturae, et morum studio extundere valuerunt: erant illa hominum inventa, docta licet, et subtilia: at Evangelium Magistri Dei vox et oraculum est, gymnasiumque verae sapientiae.

CCXXX. Itaque legem Christianam explicabant assidue Guaranici cultores, exercebantque singulis hebdomadis (feriis II. III. IV. et VI.) Catechesi pueros puellasque. Concionabantur autem singulis diebus Dominicis de morum officiis, et laudabant coelestium Herum (cum sacra illorum lux intercurreat) pia facta, quae neophiti pro virili parte imitarentur.

CCXXXI. Concionem in templo habitam repetebat deinde unus e primoribus in atrio Curionis ad viros, ad foeminas vero extra illud senex quidam in idipsum designatus. Atque ego quidem legi justum volumen, quod Indus *Vazquez* dictus (nescio unde cognomen hoc illi haeserit, nam apud Guaranios cognomina Hispanica non sunt, sed sua habent: fortasse ejus familia ab Hispano aliquo e gente *Vazquez* quaedam aliquando beneficia acceperat, ob idque ita appellari coepit) volumen, inquam, legi, quod ille elegantissime scripsit in omnes anni dies Dominicos ex iis quae a Curione suo, vel ejus collega in templo audierat. Attentas nimirum concionanti aures dabat; ac ipse dein domi memor dictorum cuncta stilo suo reddebat.

CCXXXII. Memini praesertim (placuit enim maxime) concionis in Evangelium Dominicae II. post Pascha: *Ego sum pastor bonus.* Pulcherrimus erat is sermo, et explicabat Vazquez disertissime, quae sint partes boni pastoris in oves, et ovium in bonum pastorem. Generatim vero dici potest apparere illo in volumine, quam pulchra, quam dulcis, quam copiosa, et quam elegans sit, si recte tractetur, lingua Guaranica. Vazqueziano isto libro multum ego quondam usus sum. Erat Indus Vazquez ex oppido Laureti.

229. The principles, by which the Guaraní were governed, were above all, Christian law, which infinitely surpasses the maxims of Plato and other Philosophers. To be sure, it righteously offers precepts about the most profound and divine things and reveals much more than that new and old Academy, the weighty Stoa, and so many ancient schools of the Athenians had the capacity to devise from so much effort and such extensive study of the natural world and human behavior. These were discoveries of humans, however learned and subtle; but the Gospel is the voice and oracle of God the Teacher, and it is the training ground for true wisdom.

230. Thus, the Guaraní cultivators were explaining Christian law constantly, and every week (on Monday, Tuesday, Wednesday, and Friday) they would drill the boys and girls in the catechism. They also preached every Sunday about moral duties and praised the pious deeds of the heavenly Masters* (when their sacred day would come around) so that the neophytes would imitate them to the utmost of their ability.

231. One of the leading citizens, a certain elder designated for this purpose, would repeat the sermon given earlier in the church to the men in the Priest's courtyard and to the women outside of it. And what is more, I myself read a whole volume that an Indian called "Vázquez" wrote (I do not know where this surname came from, because among the Guaraní there are no Spanish surnames, instead they have their own; perhaps his family had received some kind of favor at one time from some Spanish person from the Vázquez family and as a result he began to be called that), as I was saying, I read a volume which he most elegantly wrote every Sunday of the year based on what he had heard from his Priest or his colleague in the church. Clearly, he gave an attentive ear to the preacher and then later, at home, mindful of everything that had been said, he rendered it in his own style.

232. I especially remember (indeed, I liked it a great deal) the sermon on the Gospel from the second Sunday after Easter: "I am the Good Shepherd." This sermon was exceptionally beautiful, and Vázquez explained most eloquently what sort of duties the Good Shepherd has toward his sheep and what sort the sheep have toward their good shepherd. In general terms, it can be said that it is evident in that volume how beautiful, how sweet, how rich, and how elegant the Guaraní language is, when used correctly. At one time I got great use from that book by Vázquez. The Indian Vázquez was from the town of [Nuestra Señora de] Loreto.

* i.e., "Patron saints."

CCXXXIII. Ceterum cum ipsemet Christus Dominus aperte dixerit: *qui vos audit, me audit,* fas est Ecclesiae Praepositis, civilibusque Principibus leges (de his enim nunc agimus) condere tamquam adminicula quaedam, et corollaria, innitentia firmo Evangelii fundamento (*aliud enim nemo potest ponere, praeter id quod positum est, quod est CHRISTUS JESUS.*)[82] Quae autem supra *angularem* istum *lapidem* aedificata sint, stabunt immota: siquid vero quis superstruxerit instabili arenae, ubi *descenderit pluvia, et venerint flumina, et flaverint venti,*[83] tota demum fabrica corruat necesse est. Cujus rei quam multa exempla?

CCXXXIV. Inter Guaranios observabantur leges tum Pontificiae e Jure Canonico, tum Episcopales, quas, cum lustrabant oppida, ferebant Antistites, quorum etiam erat Curionum institutio. Parebatur item illis legibus, quas pro Indorum bono tulerunt Reges Catholici; atque id quidem constat auctoritate, qua esse nulla major potest in hac re, Philippi scilicet V. Regis publico testimonio. Audi illum: "cum ex superioribus, inquit, Articulis (*XII sunt*) atque ex antiquis, recentibusque monumentis in Senatu meo recognitis, et pro rei gravitate mature examinatis, factisque insuper certis, manifestum sit, nusquam in Indiis observatum fuisse jus meum regale, et dominium, melius quam in istis Missionibus (*Guaranicis*) neque regium patronatum, et Ecclesiasticam jurisdictionem, alibi sanctius in usum iisse, ut clare constat ex assiduis Episcoporum, Praetorumque lustrationibus, atque e caeca etiam Indorum obedientia, maxime cum a Praetore evocati ad tuendos fines praesto adsunt quaternum, vel senum millium numero, ob haec censui dandum diploma etc." (approbat administrationem illam).

CCXXXV. Quae hic laudat Philippus Rex, ut melius intelligas, explicanda quaedam sunt, tibi fortasse minus nota. Martinus de Barua Praetor Paraguaycus detulit (post Bartholomaeum de Aldunate) Guaranicum nomen ad Regem, atque in accusanda administratione illa liberalis admodum fuit. Philippus Rex, cum de re summi momenti, et fisci quaestu ageretur, jussit quaestionem severe fieri, legavitque an. MDCCXXXII. Joannem Vasquez de Aguero virum strenuum, et peritum juris, et Aulico clarum munere, qui navigans Bonasauras propius omnia cognosceret, referretque ad Indicum senatum. Aguerius, habita jam quaestione, retulit quid e juratis testibus deprehendisset, et causae commentarios, quos prae se misit, secutus dein ipse est remenso Oceano, ut Regem, Senatoresque Indicos de re tota coram doceret.

233. Besides, because Christ the Lord himself expressly said, "he who hears you, hears me," it is divinely sanctioned for authorities of the Church and civil rulers to establish laws (for we are dealing with these now) as auxiliaries and corollaries, supported by the Gospel's solid foundation ("for no one can lay another foundation beyond what has been laid, which is JESUS CHRIST").[82] That which is built on this "cornerstone" will stand steadfast. Whenever someone, on the other hand, builds something on shifting sand, when "the rain falls and the rivers come and the winds blow,"[83] quite all that had been built will necessarily come crashing down. How many examples of this are there!

234. Among the Guaraní, the laws that were observed were sometimes the Pontifical laws derived from Canon Law and other times the Episcopal laws, which the Bishops would bring when they visited the towns. The appointment of Priests was also the prerogative of the Bishops. The Guaraní also obeyed the laws that the Catholic Kings promulgated for the good of the Indians. Indeed, this fact is well established by an authority, which nothing could supersede in this matter, namely, the public testimony of King Felipe (the fifth, of course). Heed his words: "Since it is evident from the preceding Articles (there are twelve)," he said, "as well as from both the old and the recent records reviewed in my Council and carefully examined in accordance with the seriousness of the matter, and other facts besides, that in no place in the Indies has my royal power and dominion been observed better than in those (Guaraní) Missions, and that neither the royal patronage nor the Ecclesiastical jurisdiction have been exercised anywhere else more scrupulously, as is clearly confirmed by the frequent visits from Bishops and Governors; and by the blind obedience of the Indians, especially when they have been called up by the Governor to defend the territory and they arrive on the spot numbering four or six thousand. For these reasons, I judged that this ordinance should be issued. . . . " (He goes on to approve of their system of government.)

235. So that you have a better understanding of what King Felipe is praising here, certain things need to be explained that are perhaps less well-known to you. Martín de Barúa, Governor of Paraguay (after Bartolomé de Aldunate), denounced the Guaraní to the king and he took maximal liberties in rebuking their system of government. Since it was a matter of highest importance and concerned the treasury, King Felipe ordered that the matter be taken seriously and in 1732 dispatched Juan Vázquez de Agüero, a vigorous man, knowledgeable about the law, and famous for his duties at Court, to sail to Buenos Aires to learn everything he could and report back to the council of the Indies. Agüero, once the investigation had been conducted, reported what he had discovered from the sworn witnesses and his notes on the case. He sent these on ahead of himself and then followed, crossing the ocean again, in order to personally inform the King and those on the Council of the Indies, about the whole matter.

CCXXXVI. Interea (ut Rex ipse ait) centum amplius annorum diplomata decessorum Regum, et judicia Praetorum de rebus Guaranicis e regio tabulario prolata sunt, et diligenter excussa. Gaspar Roderius Guaraniorum patronus, priscis novisque auctoritatibus nitens, defendebat nihil in Guaranicis oppidis aut factum fuisse, aut etiam tum fieri, nisi e Regum Catholicorum testata voluntate.

CCXXXVII. Lis haec plus decennio duravit, tanto Senatorum taedio, ut Praeses senatus Indici significarit Joanni Rico, qui procurator nuper e Paraguaya Matritum venerat, satius fore quaestione ista supersedere, nec in recognoscendis tot veterum monumentorum chartis tamdiu immorari. Ad quae ille, immo vero, inquit, optime Praeses, peto quaesoque te, ut neu tu, neu Indici Senatores ab instituta cognitione desistatis, donec decretoria, et secundum jus sententia feratur; ac si quidem Curiones Guaranici peccarunt, poenam luant; sin bene fecerint; ne (quod factum hactenus) molestia posthac afficiantur, vexenturque.

CCXXXVIII. Tandem Rex Philippus, auditis Senatorum suffragiis ad singula accusationis capita, anno MDCCXLIII. mense Decembri decretum fecit XII. Articulis distinctum, cujus summa est ea, quam paulo ante ipsius Regis verbis reddidimus. Jussit autem veterem Guaranicae administrationis formam retineri, nihilque ex ea demi. Integrum Philippi diploma (quod longum valde est) legesis apud Cl. V. Ludovicum Antonium Muratorium in Christianismo felice;[84] apud item Petrum Franciscum Xaverium Charlevoixium, Gallum; in monumentis Historiae Paraguaycae. Atque de hac quidem re satis dictum est.

CCXXXIX. Verum neque Reges, neque Episcopi vetant usquam, ne in urbibus oppidisque, addantur publicis legibus privatae quaedam institutiones, quas locorum conditio, atque usus ipse ostenderint aptas esse informandis populorum moribus. Idcirco Cultores Guaraniorum assidua experientia docti nonnulla inter clientes suos statuerunt, quae conservando bono publico apposita esse cognorant: et haec quidem consulta, sive praescripta, approbantibus, jubentibusque praepositis Provincialibus, compacta erant in librum, quae habebant secum Curiones.

236. In the meantime (as the king himself says) more than a century of ordinances from deceased Kings and opinions from Governors on Guaraní matters were brought forth from the royal archives, dusted off, and diligently examined. Gaspar Rodero, a defender of the Guaraní, relying on old and new records, maintained that nothing had been done in the Guaraní towns or even had taken place at that time, except by the express will of the Catholic Kings.

237. This dispute lasted more than a decade, to such annoyance of the Councilors that the President of the council of the Indies made it known to Juan Rico, the Procurator who had just arrived in Madrid from Paraguay, that it would be preferable to abandon the investigation and not linger too long getting acquainted with the great many pages of old records. To which Rico replied: On the contrary, Your Excellency, Mr. President, I ask, or rather I beseech you that neither you nor the Councilors of the Indies cease the investigation you have begun until a definitive and legally sound sentence should be pronounced. And if the Guaraní Priests failed, let them suffer the penalty, but if they acted properly, they should not be subject to molestation and harassed in the future (which is what happened and continues to happen today).

238. Finally, in December 1743, once the votes of the Councilors on each section of the accusation had been heard, King Felipe issued a decree divided into twelve Articles, whose summary is what we reported a little earlier in the words of the King himself. He therefore ordered that the old form of Guaraní governance be retained and that nothing be taken from it. You may read Felipe's entire ordinance (which is quite lengthy) in *Happy Christianity*,[84] by the famous Ludovico Antonio Muratori and also in the work *History of Paraguay* by Pierre François Xavier de Charlevoix, the Frenchman. Anyway, enough has been said about this matter.

239. But neither Kings nor Bishops ever forbid certain private provisions from being attached to public laws in the towns and cities. The circumstances of the places and actual experience would show whether such provisions were suitable for shaping the habits of the population. For this reason, the Guaraní Cultivators, informed by their ongoing experiences, established among their followers several practices that they recognized as being appropriate for maintaining the public good. Indeed, with the Province's leaders granting their approval and giving the order, these plans or precepts were compiled into a book, and the Priests would carry these around with them.

CCXL. Hunc librum (ut id obiter dicam) legit olim vir quidam clarus militia, et alter quidam, qui Theologus audire vult. Atque ut videas, quam sit hominum varia mens, et diversa voluntas; miles ille magni librum fecit, quod censuerit prudentissima ibi instituta contineri pro religiosa Curionum disciplina, et recto oppidorum ordine: Theologus, contra, id ipsum reputavit audax quoddam molimen, et equi Trojani machinam pro stabiliendo regno nescio quo. Itane vero? Miles regnum non videt, et librum probat; Theologus librum reprobat, et regnum videt? Unde tam contrariae de una eademque re, et de uno eodemque scripto, sententiae? Dicam quid istud sit brevi.

CCXLI. Miles militaribus oculis, quos neque livor, neque amor, neque odium in Guaranicos Curiones turbarat, librum legit, et ratus est cuncta illic recta esse et proba. Theologus bis e Societate ejectus, primum in Europa, dein in America, ardebat ira, ne dicam furore, in eos, qui semel iterumque abs se dimiserant. Hinc vidit, quae nec miles ille, nec Aguerius, nec Philippus V. Rex (quorum supra meminimus) viderant; ac commentus est Regnum Paraguaycum, ut Curiones Guaranici invidia conflagrarent, inimicumque experirentur Jesuitae, quem noluerunt socium et amicum. Opus est posthumum, diciturque auctor vicinus jam morti illud judicio cujusdam religiosi viri permisisse; sed vir ille gravis nihil potuit facere, liber enim ex scrinio, quod indicarat aeger, sublatus jam raptim fuerat, ad editionem scilicet.[85]

CCXLII. Ceterum haud licebat Curionibus Guaranicis novos mores, praeterquam consensu receptos, contentosque illo institutionum libro, inducere: qua re factum est, ut uno modo omnia oppida administrarentur, et rectus ubique locorum constaret ordo sine veteris disciplinae mutatione, quam tantopere oderat Plato, ut dictum est. Quod si morosior quispiam ad ista ipsa privata instituta auctoritatem publicam requirat, haud ea caruerunt Curatores Guaranici, et praefecti Provinciales.

CCXLIII. Quippe Paulus III. Pont. Max. Indicis Soc. operariis concessit, *ut in provinciis remotissimis possent Ecclesias, Hospitalia, et alia pia loca, prout expediens fuerit erigere; ac nunc, et pro tempore erecta reformare . . . et quaecumque statua, et ordinationes desuper necessaria facere, illaque postquam facta fuerint, mutare, alterare, ac illis addere, et detrahere.*[86] Id Pontifex Maximus. Et Rex Catholicus concessionem ejusmodi Jesuitis factam pro Indorum sacris coetibus, sive Ecclesiis (alii *Reductiones,* alii *Doctrinas,* alii *Missiones* vocant) authentico diplomate ratam habuit.[87]

240. This book (if I may say in passing) was read some time ago by a certain famous military man [the pseudonymous "Philosopher La Douceur"] and another man who likes to be called a Theologian [Bernardo Ibáñez de Echavarri]. And so, you can see how varied people's discernment is and how diverse their inclinations. That soldier regarded the book as great because he judged that extremely prudent principles for the religious instruction of the Priests and proper organization of the towns were contained in it. The Theologian, on the other hand, reckoned the very same book to be some audacious undertaking and a Trojan horse mechanism for establishing some sort of kingdom. Really?! The military man sees nothing about a kingdom and approves of the book; the Theologian disapproves of the book and sees a kingdom? Where do such contrary opinions about one and the same thing and one and the same text come from? I will say briefly what it may be.

241. The soldier read the book with military eyes, which neither envy, nor love, nor hatred against the Guaraní Priests had thrown into confusion, and he deemed everything in it to be correct and upright. The Theologian, twice ejected from the Society, first in Europe and later in America, seethed with anger, lest I call it fury, against those who had dismissed him not once but twice. This is why he saw things that neither the soldier, nor Agüero, nor King Felipe V (all of whom we mentioned above) had seen. And so, he contrived the Kingdom of Paraguay, so that the Guaraní Priests would be set ablaze by their unpopularity and the Jesuits would have to contend with as an enemy someone they were unwilling to have as a companion or friend. The work is posthumous and the author, at that point near death, is said to have entrusted it to the judgment of a religious man; but that venerable man could do nothing, for at that point the book had already been carried off hastily from the container, which the sick man had indicated, evidently for publication.[85]

242. Otherwise, by no means were the Guaraní Priests allowed to introduce new customs aside from those authorized by consensus and contained in that book of doctrines. It was done in this way so that all the towns would be administered in the same way and so that right order would endure absolutely everywhere, without alteration to the old system, something Plato hated so much, as has been said. But if anyone more persnickety should inquire after the public authority for those private doctrines, the Guaraní Caretakers and the Provincial superintendents were hardly at a loss for it.

243. Indeed, Pope Paul III granted to the Jesuits laboring in the Indies "that in the most remote provinces they could erect Churches, Hospitals, and other pious places, as would be expedient. And both now and henceforth they could transform what had already been erected . . . and make whatever additional statutes and ordinances were necessary, and then after these had been made, they could change or alter them as well as add to or subtract from them."[86] This is what the Pope declared. The Catholic King also approved a concession of this kind for the Jesuits in support of the Indians' religious communities or Churches (some call them "Reductions," others "Doctrines," and still others "Missions") and ratified it with an authentic declaration.[87]

CCXLIV. Fructus autem ex observatis publicis legibus, et privatis institutionibus, is fuit, ut Guaranii, ex quo illic radices egit Christiana Religio, numquam eam abjecerint, neque aliquod XXX. oppidorum contra aliud conjurarit; sed neophyti omnes inter se fratrum instar amarunt semper, foveruntque mutuis officiis. Quod si tyrannicum (ut obtrectatores administrationis illius volunt) imperium illud fuisset, qua fieret ratione, ut centum quinquaginta annorum (eoque amplius) spatio, conquiescerent misera mancipia (sic enim Guaranios vocat Pavvius) neque quemquam Curionum occiderent, aut male mulctatum fustibus extra fines suos abigerent? Atqui horum accidit nihil, postquam Rochi Gonzalez, Alphonsi Rodriguez, Joannis del Castillo, et Christophori de Mendoza nece institutionis Guaranicae initia quodammodo consecrata sunt. Exinde omnia illic tranquilla, et quieta fuerunt. Plato suae illi Reipublicae, quam vocat divinam, tantum boni tribuit, ut vix timeat oriturum ibi tumultum aliquem, seditionemve, eo quod paternum imperium, quo nullum est justius, et dulcius, in cives suos inducere studuerit.

CCXLV. Idem Plato in rem nostram sapienter dixit: sicui in bene morata civitate (ubi vigil magistratus coercet sontes vi et poenis) multa fuerint manicipia, tutum, dum ibi morabitur, illum fore ob supplicia, quae male agentes manent. Sin autem in desertum aliquem locum, inquit, secesserit cum mancipiis, nihil non ei timendum est, libertatis enim amore conjurabit servum pecus, atque ablato publicae potestatis metu, jugum excutiet, herumque destituet, aut etiam occidet. Audin, Pavvi? Hoc si tibi philosophandi genus placuisset, aliter sensisses de Guaraniis in avio positis loco, et procul ab urbibus Hispanorum, qui eos armorum, et mortis metu a seditione, maleficiisque coercerent.

CCXLVI. Mancipia erant, ais. Esto. Cur igitur numquam in inermem, imbellemque Curionem rebellarunt? Qua dic arte magica senex Sacerdos terna, quaterna, sena Indorum armatorum millia, quot in oppidis quibusdam erant, continuit, ne et ipsum, et ejus collegam solos in sola domo, telis, contis, sudibus conficerent? Non confecerunt autem; filii igitur, non mancipia: sic enim fit, Pavvi, ut patri, vel si in vasta solitudine degat, nihil a numerosa prole metuendum sit: pater est, liberos amat, et alit; ac liberi vicissim patrem colunt, reverenturque. Nobilis quidam Hispanus, cum versatus diu esset inter Guaranios, attenteque observasset, nullam toto die partem quietis esse Curioni satagenti qua spiritualis, qua temporarii clientium suorum boni, haec cum serio apud se reputasset, dixit tandem: non Indi, Curionum mancipia sunt, sed Curiones, Indorum.

244. These were the fruits of the public laws and private doctrines that were observed: from the time when the Christian Religion took root there, the Guaraní have never abandoned it; none of the thirty towns have conspired against another; rather, all the neophytes always loved one another as brothers and fostered a sense of mutual obligation. Because if that empire had been tyrannical (as the critics of that system of government pretend), what explanation could there be for the fact that in the space of a hundred and fifty years (even more than that) the "miserable slaves" (for that is how de Pauw refers to the Guaraní) have been completely at peace and not murdered any of the Priests nor driven one out, after he had been badly beaten with sticks, beyond their territory? But none of these things happened, inasmuch as the beginnings of the Guaraní system were consecrated to some degree by the murder of Roque González, Alonso Rodríguez, Juan del Castillo, and Cristóbal de Mendoza. Since then, everything there has been calm and peaceful. Plato attributes so much good to that Republic of his, which he calls divine, that he is hardly afraid that some rebellion or sedition will arise there, because he took pains to introduce among his citizens a paternalistic form of authority, which is more just and more pleasant than any other.

245. On this very subject of ours, Plato declared wisely: If in a well-mannered state (where the vigilant ruler coerces criminals with force and punishments) there were many slaves, a person's safety, while he remains there, would be a consequence of the punishment awaiting malefactors. But, he says, if someone should withdraw to a deserted location with his slaves, he ought to have more than a little cause for fear. For due to a desire for liberty the enslaved chattel will conspire and, with fear of public control removed, will shake off the yoke and desert or even kill their master. Are you paying attention, de Pauw? If this type of philosophizing had pleased you, you would have thought differently about the Guaraní who were situated in a remote place far from the cities of the Spanish, who would have coerced them with the fear of weapons and death to prevent sedition and crime.

246. They were slaves, you say. So be it. Why, then, did they never rebel against an unarmed, pacifist priest? Tell me, then, with what magical art did an old Priest subdue three, four, or six thousand armed Indians, which is how many there were in some towns, so that with their arrows, spears, and clubs they did not execute him and his companion, all alone in a single house? And yet they did not execute them; they were sons therefore, not slaves. For it just so happens, de Pauw, that there is nothing for a father to fear from his numerous offspring, even if he lives in a vast wilderness. He is a father, he loves his children and nourishes them, and the children, in turn, venerate and respect their father. A certain Spanish nobleman had spent a long time among the Guaraní and had observed attentively that throughout the entire day there is not a moment of rest for the Priest who is occupied with both the spiritual and temporal well-being of his followers, reflecting seriously with himself. When he had thought over his observation in earnest back at home, the nobleman finally said that the Indians are not the property of the priests, but rather the priests belong to the Indians.

De recta disciplina.

PLATO

CCXLVII. Disciplina civitatis firma sit necesse est, si e positis legibus, inter bona divina, suus Deo constet cultus cum pia sacrorum procuratione; inter bona autem humana, si magni a civibus fiat pietas in parentes, et patriam, si sedula, et vigil sit liberorum educatio, si prudens est casta nuptiarum provisio, si mutuus civium amor, si assidua officiorum communio, si rei suae civium singulis justa possessio, si frequens exercitatio operum, quae ab studio virtutis, et recta ratione proficiscuntur. Haec si recte se habeant, recte sit Reipublicae necesse est.

CCXLVIII. Et quoniam optimus urbium status a recta puerorum, et adolescentium institutione pendet, ea erit probatissima omnium disciplina, quae innitatur honesta morum consuetudine, atque aequa animi habitudine erga voluptates, doloresque, ita ut ab initio crescentis aetatis ad mortem usque oderit quis, quae odium merentur, et amet, quae amore digna sunt.

CCXLIX. Id unum est, quod viros probos, et fortes efficit, et utiles Reipublicae; qui autem contrariae horum insistunt viae, magnum sibi malum parant. Sane ruina, ait? Medorum imperii, et Persarum, orta est ab educatione plena licentiae, qua Cyrus, et Darius liberos suos institui passi sunt, ille Cambysem, hic Xerxem, quorum uterque nimia rerum affluentia, immodicisque deliciis, a pueritia corruptus est. (Lib. III. V. etc. de Repub. et II. III. etc. de Legg.)

GUARANII.

CCL. De Guaraniorum disciplina multi multa. Cl. V. Canonicus Bergier Gallus, eruditis ac doctis pro Religione clarus libris, in eo, quem inscripsit: *Certitudo probationum pro Christianismo,* producit,[88] testimonium Comitis Buffonii de recta Guaraniorum disciplina. "Missiones, ait, plures e belluis homines effecerunt, quam victores Principum, exercitus, qui eas armis subjugarunt. PARAGUAYA haud aliter in deditionem voluntariam concessit. Dulcedo, caritas, virtus constanter exercita a Missionariis, barbaros sensim delinierunt, ab eisque pepulerunt diffidentiam, ferociamque. Sua illi sponte stiterunt se se petitum saepe, ut legem docerentur, quae adeo institutioni hominum confert, amplexique ultro ejusdem legis onus, et jugum, in vitae societatem coaluerunt. Quapropter nihil Religioni gloriosus est, quam ab ea mites effectas civilesque gentes ejusmodi?"[89]

On the Correct System of Discipline*

PLATO

247. A state's system of discipline must be steadfast if, in terms of divine objectives, its worship of God along with the pious management of holy matters is to rest upon established laws. In terms of human objectives, on the other hand, the system of discipline must be steadfast if piety toward parents and the fatherland is to be greatly valued by citizens; if the education of children is to be careful and vigilant; if provisioning of weddings is to be prudent and pure; if there is to be mutual love among citizens; if sharing in duties is to be uninterrupted; if individual citizens are to have legitimate ownership of their own property; if the performance of the hard work that comes from a desire for excellence and right reason is to be frequent. If these things are going well, the Republic must necessarily be doing well.

248. And since the optimal conditions for cities depend on the correct instruction of children and adolescents, the most esteemed system of discipline of all will be the one based on honest habits of character and the habituation of the soul to be balanced in relation to pleasure and pain such that from the beginning of childhood right up until death each person will hate what merits hatred and will love what is worthy of love.

249. This is the one thing that makes men upright, strong, and useful for the Republic. However, those who pursue the opposite path, prepare great harm for themselves. To be sure, he says it is their downfall, no? The downfall of the empire of the Medes and Persians arose from an upbringing full of excessive freedom with which Cyrus and Darius allowed their children to be educated; the former did this to Cambyses, the latter to Xerxes, each of whom was corrupted from childhood by an overabundance of possessions and excessive delicacies (*Republic* Books 3, 5, etc. and *Laws* Books 2 and 3).

THE GUARANÍ

250. Much has been said by many people about the system of discipline among the Guaraní. The famed French Canon Bergier, known for his erudite and learned writings in favor of religion, in one entitled "The Certainty of the Evidence for Christianity,"[88] brings in the testimony of Comte de Buffon on the correct system of discipline among the Guaraní. "The missions," he says, "made more humans out of beasts than did the victorious armies of the Princes, which subjugated them with weapons. PARAGUAY agreed to a surrender that was nothing other than voluntary. The gentleness, charity, and virtue constantly practiced by the Missionaries gradually calmed the barbarians down and drove from them their mistrust and ferocity. Often, they came of their own accord to ask to be taught the law, which is so useful for human institutions. Then because they embraced the burden and the yoke of this same law voluntarily, they came together into a civil society. For this reason, nothing is more glorious for Religion than the fact that through it nations of this kind have been made calm and civilized?"[89]

* *Disciplina* here refers both to the disciplined civic system and the practices of education and habituation that perpetuate it.

CCLI. Haec e celebri Buffonio Cl. Bergier. Sed idem alibi[90] egregie pugnans pro Religione demonstrat quantum ex hac generatim derivatum boni sit in ethnicos, vindicatque ab Haereticorum calumniis sacros Novi Orbis operarios cum aliarum provinciarum, tum Guaranicae regionis, laudato eorum zelo ac sollicitudine pro amplificando JESU CHRISTI regno. Ne autem rem istam studio partium urgere videatur, appellat vel testem, vel judicem, martialem Philosophum Ladouceur,[91] qui converso in stilum, et calamum gladio stat acriter pro cultoribus Guaranicis, ejus argumenta, quae Bergier in medium affert, sunt sex, e quibus ego bina dumtaxat delibabo.

CCLII. Si Germani, inquit Ladouceurius, Sacerdotes (idem dic tu de Galliis, de Italis, de Hispanis) non zelo Religionis, fideique Catholicae causa, sed ut opes cogerent, quas in aliorum usus Romam mitterent, navigabant in Americam, amentissimi omnium hominum, expertesque sensus communis fuisse dicendi prorsus sunt. Quid enim? Objectabant suum illi caput saepe apertis mortis periculis; nullam habebant in oppidis quietis partem; magistri erant; Catechistae erant; pastores erant; et Indorum bona partim spiritualia, partim temporaria, non intermisso usquam labore, procurabant. Illis autem vel aulam fuisse, vel luxum, vel regia commoda, vel vestem magnificam, ne adversarii quidem eorum dicunt.[92]

CCLIII. Miseram igitur Guaranici cultores, operarii vivebant vitam, idque pro Europaeis Jesuitis (sic enim ferunt) ditandis. At id, quaeso, quis credat? Quid veri habet simile? Neminem certe illorum redire vidimus in Germaniam, qui, post haustas tot aerumnas, otio hic et partis divitiis frueretur; novimus neminem, qui vel auri lamellam e Paraguayca regione secum attulerit. Quam vero diversa ratio institoriae societatis Angelicae in Oriente Curatoribus? Hi postquam aliquot annos sua, et suorum, inter Indos negotia gesserunt, properant tempestive in Angliam reverti, ut cum pleno suo illo peculio domi suae tranquille, delicateque vivant. Reliquum ergo est, ut Guaranii Sacerdotes vel stolidissimi omnium mortalium fuerint, qui ad alios locupletandos immania mala perferrent, vel ut mero divinae gloriae studio, et salutis alienae desiderio, illuc navigasse, et inter rerum aspera neophytos suos instituisse censeantur.

251. The famed Bergier quoted this from the celebrated Buffon. But elsewhere[90] he himself, fighting brilliantly on behalf of Religion, demonstrates how much good for the pagans in general has been derived from Religion and defends the religious laborers of the New World from the malicious charges of the Heretics, not only from the other provinces, but also from the region of the Guaraní, praising the zeal and care they put into enlarging the kingdom of JESUS CHRIST. And so that he does not seem to be pressing the matter out of partisanship, he appeals to a soldier, "le Philosophe La Douceur," as a witness or a judge,[91] who enthusiastically champions the Guaraní cultivators with his sword transformed into a pen and writing. He has six arguments, which Bergier reproduces for his audience, and of these I will pluck out just two.

252. If the German Priests, says La Douceur (you can say the same of the French, the Italians, and the Spanish), did not sail to America due to Religious zeal and the cause of the Catholic faith, but instead so that they would amass riches, which they would send to Rome for the benefit of others, then they must be designated as the stupidest of all humans and totally devoid of common sense. Why? They often exposed their own lives to obvious mortal perils; in the towns, they had not a moment of rest; they were teachers; they were Catechists; they were shepherds; and with never-ending labor they tended to both the spiritual and temporal well-being of the Indians. Not even their enemies claim that they had a palace, or luxury, or royal comforts, or magnificent clothing.[92]

253. It was an exhausting life that the Guaraní cultivators and laborers led, and all this (so they say) to enrich the European Jesuits. Who, I ask, would believe that? What plausibility does it have? Certainly, we have not seen a single one of them return to Germany in order to enjoy leisure and his share of the riches now after imbibing so many hardships; we know of no one who has brought with him from the region of Paraguay even a flake of gold. Indeed, how different is the calculation for the Caretakers in the English huckster society in the East? After they have conducted their affairs and those of their order among the Indians for several years, they hasten to return to England when the time is right so that they can live peacefully and luxuriously at home with their savings full. Therefore, all that remains is that the Guaraní Priests were either the most brutish of all mortals because they suffered immense harm in order for others to be enriched or rather, out of pure zeal for divine glory and a desire for the salvation of others, they thought it worthwhile to sail there and educate their neophytes despite the adversity of doing so.

CCLIV. Alterum argumentum Ladouceurii Philosophi est. Si Curionum Guaraniorum gubernandi modus erat autocraticus, durusque et tyrannicus, qua factum est causa, ait, ut barbari recens e silvis educti, assuetique nativae libertati, eos patienter tulerint? Cur in nota latibula non refugerunt excusso jugo? Certe Aethiopes, abrepti in servitutem, circumspiciunt undique fugam, subducuntque se se, si possunt, ab eos abducentium manibus. Et vero Curionibus illis nullus erat Europaeorum exercitus, qui Indos, si tumultuarentur, contineret. Haec miles Philosophus, cuius cetera argumenta de hac re videsis loco, quem diximus, novae Encyclopaediae.

Quid de Guaranica disciplina senserit
Philosophus Raynal

CCLV. Philosophus is in suis illis de Indico commercio libris non poterat non meminisse Guaraniorum, quandoquidem his una cum Hispanis Paraguaycis Herbae mercimonium est. Pone autem factum, quod homini supra quam credi potest libero, audacique, stomachum non moverint Curiones Guaranici. Stomachum moverit dixi? Immo vero miris eos effert laudibus praesertim ob institutam bonorum communionem, quae proxime, inquit, accedit ad auream naturae simplicitatem. De reliquo administrationem illam vocet, et THEOCRATICAM, nec male id quidem, si eo nomine intelligit timore DEI, et amore, Indorum animos ad virtutis cultum, civilemque disciplinam, excitari solitos a Curionibus, eorumque collegis. Sane nihil ibi freqentius audiebatur, quam Dei nomen, Dei sanctitas, Dei lex, et legem servantibus Dei praemia, violantibus autem poenae a Deo. Illum ipsum agrum communem, unde viduis, et aegris, puerisque victus curabatur, apellabant Indi TUMPAMBAE, Dei rem; singulorum vero privatos agros ABAMBAE, hominis rem, ut supta docuimus.[93]

254. The Philosopher La Douceur's other argument is: If the Guaraní Priests' way of governing was autocratic, harsh, and tyrannical, he says, what caused the barbarians to patiently tolerate them, despite having been recently led out of the forests and being accustomed to freedom from birth? Why did they not flee back to their familiar refuges given that their yoke was shaken off? Certainly, the Ethiopians,* dragged off into slavery, look everywhere for a way to escape and free themselves, if they can, from the hands of those who abducted them. To be sure, those Priests had no army of Europeans to subdue the Indians if they rebelled. This is what the military Philosopher says, whose other arguments about this matter you can see in the part of the new *Encyclopedia* we mentioned.

What the Philosopher Raynal Thought about the Guaraní System of Discipline

255. In his books on commerce in the Indies this Philosopher could not fail to make mention of the Guaraní, since they share with the Spanish a trade in Paraguayan *Yerba*. Indeed, consider the fact that the Guaraní Priests did not turn the stomach of a spirited man who is fond of liberty beyond what could be believed. Turn his stomach, I said? Quite the contrary, he exalts them with marvelous praise, particularly on account of the community of goods they had established which, he says, comes closest to the gold standard of nature's simplicity. In other respects, he calls that system of government THEOCRATIC, and this is not entirely wrong, if by that term he means that the Priests and their colleagues used the fear of GOD, and his love as well, to urge the Indians' souls toward the cultivation of virtue and civic discipline. To be sure, nothing was heard there more frequently than the name of God, the holiness of God, the law of God, and the rewards reserved for those who keep God's law, and the punishments that come from God for those who violate it. That same community field from which sustenance was provided for widows and the sick as well as for children, the Indians called it *Tupâmba'é*, "God's property," while they called everyone's private fields *Avamba'é*, "human property," as we explained above.[93]

* i.e., enslaved Africans.

CCLVI. Erat igitur quodammodo THEOCRATICA Guaraniorum administratio, sive disciplina. Hanc vidit, et probavit Ill. D. Josephus de Peralta Ordinis Praedicatorum. Adiit ille pro munere an. MDCCXLI. oppida suae dioeceseos Bonaurensis. Exin datis ad Philippum V. Regem litteris VI. Idus Jan. an. MDCCXLIII. sic narrat, praeter alia: "e triginta his Doctrinis XVII. pertinent ad hanc dioecesin Bonaurensem, XIII. Ad Paraguaycam. Cum lustrassem jam oppida omnia meae ditionis, ivi ad administrandum Sacramentum Confirmationis in aliquot oppida dioeceseos Paraguaycae, cum id a me petisset collegium Canonicorum illius Ecclesiae, Sede vacante . . . Dicam quae vidi oculis meis, ac manibis meis contrectavi . . . Moerens inde discessi, et pio animi sensu sic plenus, ut quotidie gratias agam Deo, quod ita gentibus illis benedicat . . . . Mihi erat gaudio inexplicabili templa cernere, et cultum divinum, et pietatem in sacris functionibus, et elegantiam ornatumque altarium, et magnificentiam, qua illic Deo sacrificatur, addito singularis artis cantu." Explicat deinde minutatim, qui ordo in oppidis esset, agitque de *Abambae*, privatis scilicet Indorum agris, et de *Tupambae*, id est Dei agro, pro publicis impensis, de *Herbae* item Paraguaycae XII. millibus *arrobis*, et refert quos in usus expendatur pretium ipsius *Herbae* etc. Has litteras Rex Philipus (qui earum meminit in decreto de re Guaranica) edi in lucem voluit, et saepe illae typis commissae sunt.[94] Atque haec quidem Il. Peralta.

CCLVII. Quod ad Raynalem Philosophum attinet, vellem reputasset apud se eam rerum Communionem, quam tantopere laudat, non ab solo naturae ductu, effatisve saecularis Philosophiae, sed e lege Christiana, sacrisque documentis petitam fuisse. Nam quid nos docent *Actus Apostolorum* de primaevis Christianis? *Multitudinis credentium erat cor unum, et anima una, nec quisquam eorum, quae possidebat, aliquid suum esse dicebat, sed erant illis omnia communia . . . nec quisquam egens erat inter illos.*[95]

CCLVIII. Haec legerant Curatores Guaranici, atque hinc quoque hausere illum regendi Neophytos modum, qui tribus magnis viris (praeter eos, quorum sanguine irrigatus, ut dictum est, ager ille laetissimam fidei, et virtutum messem extullit) tribus, inquam, viris magnis maxime debetur Marcello Lorenzanae, Antonio Ruiz de Montoya, et Francisco Diaz Tano.

256. Accordingly, the system of government, or system of discipline, of the Guaraní was THEOCRATIC to a degree. The most illustrious José de Peralta, of the Order of Preachers, saw this and approved of it. In 1741 he went, in an official capacity, to the towns of his diocese of Buenos Aires. Later, in a letter sent to King Felipe V on January 8, 1743, he recounts, among other things, the following: "Of these thirty Doctrines, seventeen belong to this diocese of Buenos Aires, and thirteen to that of Paraguay. After I had visited all the towns of my jurisdiction, I went to administer the Sacrament of Confirmation in some towns in the Paraguayan diocese, because the college of Canons of that Church had asked it of me due to the Seat being vacant . . . I will tell what I saw with my own eyes and touched with my hands . . . It grieved me to leave that place; my soul was brimming with a sense of piety such that every day I thank God for blessing those communities thusly . . . It was a source of an inexplicable joy to me to see the churches, divine worship, and piety in carrying out holy tasks, as well as the elegance and ornamentation of the altars and the magnificence with which sacrifices to God are performed there, topped off by singing of an unparalleled caliber." Then he describes in great detail the order that existed in the towns and discusses the *Avamba'é*, meaning the Indians' private fields, the *Tupâmba'é*, that is, God's field for public expenses, and also the twelve thousand *arrobas* of Paraguayan *Yerba*. He also mentions what the money from that *Yerba* is spent on, etc. King Felipe (who makes mention of it in the Cédula on the Guaraní question) wanted this letter to be published, and it was reprinted often.[94] And this is what the most illustrious Peralta has to say.

257. Concerning the Philosopher Raynal, I should have liked him to have reflected on the fact that Community ownership, which he praises so much, had not been achieved by the impulse of nature alone nor by the axioms of secular Philosophy, but from Christian law and sacred writings. For what do the *Acts of the Apostles* teach us about the original Christians? "The multitude of believers had a single heart and a single soul, and no one said that any of the things he had was his own. Instead, all things were common among them . . . and not one among them went without."[95]

258. The Guaraní Caretakers had read these things and derived from them that way of governing the Neophytes, which is most of all due to three great men (aside from those whose blood irrigated the land, as the saying goes, that sprouted a most abundant harvest of faith and virtues), as I was saying, three great men: Marciel de Lorenzana, Antonio Ruiz de Montoya, and Francisco Díaz Taño.

CCLIX. Lorenzana, qui primus fuit ad Paranam gentis Guaranicae cultor (eo missus ab Episcopo urbis Assumptionis Paraguaycae Il. D. Reginaldo Lizarraga Ordinis Dominicani, et regio Praetore Fernando Arias)[96] quadriennio Theologiam Compluti audierat a Francisco Suarez Doctore Eximio. Montoya praestantis vir ingenii, ac peritissimus linguae Guaranicae, prout ejius editae typis lucubrationes ostendunt, Indos ad Guairam in oppida coegit. Diaz Tanius, consultissimus, Juris Hispani Indici, et sacrarum legum (extat illius M. S. *De Indo converso* sanequam doctum, et eruditum) bis ab America Matritum, et Romam venit, ut Regis Catholici, et Pontificis Maximi auxilium imploraret pro Neophytis Guaranicis (quos inter plurima egit, et passus est) contra immanium Mammalucurom maleficia.

CCLX. Ars autem pia, qua triumviri isti ferae gentis colla leniter subdiderunt suavi legis Christi jugo repetenda est (quamquam de hac re nonnihil jam supra diximus) ex iis quae Petrus Joannes Maffejus narrat[97] gesta a P. Emmanuele Nobrega Lusitano ejusque sociis, in convertendis Brasilicis Guaraniis. Pulcher locus est, et qui docet Indicos Operarios, qua ratione barbarorum animos, cum auxilii coelestis ope, sibi concilient.

CCLXI. „Doctrinae, ait Maffeius, Christianae capita, certasque precationes, ut assolet, Brasilice vertunt. Dehinc vicos, et tuguria paullatim obire; modestia, comitate, beneficiis obligare sibi homines omnium aetatum; ac simul de rebus divinis dicere per se ad populum incipiunt. Mirificos insolita praedicatio motus animorum effecit in rudi tenebrisque involuta barbarie; satisque apparebat, cum alia, tum praesertim, quae de omnipotentia et infinitate Dei disserebantur, ingenti cum admiratione aeque a viris ac mulieribus accipi . . . post diuturnam institutionem, qui maxime idonei ad baptismum evasere, vitali fonte lustrati, cumque unica uxore, certis dimissis, rite conjuncti sunt."

259. Lorenzana, who was the first cultivator among the Guaraní people in Paraná (he was sent there by the Bishop of the city of Asunción in Paraguay, the Most Reverend Reginaldo de Lizárraga of the Dominican Order, and by Governor Hernando Arias),[96] he studied Theology for four years under Francisco Suárez, Extraordinary Doctor, in Alcalá de Henares. Montoya, a man of outstanding talent and extremely skilled in the Guaraní language, as the publications of his candlelit labors show, collected the Indians in Guayrá into towns. Díaz Taño, well-versed in the Spanish Law of the Indies and in Canon Law (his exceptionally learned and erudite manuscript, "On the Indian Convert," still exists) came twice from America to Madrid and then to Rome to implore the Catholic King [Felipe IV] and Pope [Urban VIII] for help on behalf of the Guaraní Neophytes (among whom he labored and suffered very much) against the malefactions of the monstrous Mamelukes.*

260. However, the pious art, by which that triumvirate gently led the necks of a wild people under the agreeable yoke of Christ's law, must be sought (although we have already said a little about this above) in the deeds that Giovanni Pietro Maffei[97] recounts were done by Father Manuel da Nóbrega of Portugal and his companions to convert the Guaraní of Brazil. It is a beautiful passage, and it shows the method by which those Laboring in the Indies, thanks to heavenly support, win the souls of the barbarians over to their side.

261. "They translate into Brazilian the main points," says Maffei, "of Christian doctrine and certain prayers, as is customary. From there, they visit the villages and shelters, a few at a time; with modesty, kindness, and favors they bind people of every age to themselves; and at the same time, they begin to speak to the people explicitly about divine matters. The unfamiliar preaching effected a marvelous spiritual stirring in a backward land of barbarism enveloped in darkness. It was clear enough that everything else, but especially what was discussed about the omnipotence and infinity of God, was accepted with tremendous wonderment by both men and women equally . . . after extensive training, those most suitable hastened to baptism and were washed in the fountain of life and married to a single wife in a religious ceremony after the others had been sent away."

* i.e., slave raiders.

CCLXII. „Infantes primum quam plurimos in tutum recipere (sicui forte ante usum rationis obeunda sit dies) et salutari summi Pastoris nota insignire festinant. Patres dein matresque familias precibus, promissis, blandimentis adducunt, ut puerilem aetatem ac sobolem sibi in disciplinam dent. hosce postmodum ipsos, et cibo et crepundiis paulatim illectos, omni arte mansuefaciunt, nec poenitendus fuit labor. Siquidem et tradita facile accipiebant, et retenta fideliter grandioribus natu quotidianae consuetudinis et linguae beneficio per otium inculcabant; et suo ipsi exemplo sensim ceteros a nefariis atque impuris moribus avertebant. Parentes interea (ut est etiam improbis ipsa per se virtus amabilis) filiorum obsequio, sobrietate, cultu, doctrina laetari eosque ultro ad proficiendum accendere: ac tantus erat Chistianae institutionis amor, ut pii catechismi carminibus ac beatis vocibus JESU et MARIAE, litora, campi, luci perstreperent."

CCLXIII. Haec ille, quae, quamvis paulo longiora, ideo exscibere voluimus, quod non tam hic quid actum a Nobrega, ejusque sociis sit in Brasilia, quam quid egerint in Guaranica regione gentis illius cultores, describere Maffejus quodammodo videatur. Antistes fluminis Januarii (quae dioecesis contermina Guaraniis est) Il. D. Laurentius Hurtado de Mendoza: "testis sum, ait, linguae usu Guaranicae, et grandi atque Apostolico zelo, et tolerantia multorum et gravium laborum, retulisse eum (*Montoyam*) et ejus socios maximum cum maxima Dei gloria animarum fructum in convertendis ethnicis illis, quos barbaros antea et silvestres non solum instituunt divina fide, sed etiam Christiana politia in eximium Dei, et Regis obsequium." Et ne solis verbis, sed factis ipsis rem hanc probet, addit se se praefecisse in officina quadam saccari Brasilicis operis neophytum unum e discipulis Guaranicorum Sacerdotum, qui ceteros dulci illi labori addictos mysteria Religionis edoceret.[98]

CCLXIV. Igitur administrationis Guaranicae auctores valebant ingenio, valebant animi eruditione; sed non tam vis, et industria artis humanae, et scientiae (quamquam et haec magni facienda est operariis Indicis) quam lux Evangelii, dux eis et fax fuit ad mirabilem illam regiminis formam stabiliendam. Ita, Raynal, est, e Christi doctrina praeceptisque bonum publicum petendum est, non e recentium Philosophorum (quorum tu unus es) commentis pestilentibus.

262. "First they hurry to bring as many infants as possible to safety (in case any should happen to die before possessing the use of reason) and to mark them with the supreme Shepherd's sign of salvation. Then, with prayers, promises, and flattery they persuade fathers and mothers to give their offspring and its childhood to them for training; after a while they skillfully tame these very children, who were gradually enticed by food and rattles; and the work was not unsatisfying. Since, indeed, they would easily learn what was taught and what they retained they faithfully instilled in their elders in their leisure time mediated through their customs and language. By their own example they were themselves gradually turning the others away from abominable and impure habits. Meanwhile, the parents (since virtue is intrinsically agreeable even to the wicked) were delighted by their children's obedience, reasonableness, culture, and instruction and of their own accord fanned the flames of their progress. In fact, the love for Christian education was so great, that the shores, the fields, and the woods resounded with the songs of the pious catechism and the blessed cries of 'JESUS' and 'MARY.'"

263. This is what Maffei has to say; and we wanted to write it all out, although it is somewhat long, because in a certain way he seems to be describing not so much what was done by Nóbrega and his companions on that occasion in Brazil, as what the cultivators of that nation set in motion in the Guaraní region. The Bishop of Rio de Janeiro (which is a diocese adjoining the Guaraní), Rev. Lourenço Hurtado de Mendonça, says, "I am a witness that through the use of the Guaraní language, great, Apostolic zeal, and endurance of much hard labor, he (*Montoya*) and his companions returned the maximum harvest of souls together with the maximum glory for God in converting those pagans. They prepared these forest-dwelling former barbarians for exceptional obedience to God and King not only through divine faith, but also Christian state." And so that he may prove this not with words alone but with actual deeds, he adds that in a particular sugar mill he himself put a neophyte, one of the pupils of the Guaraní Priests, in charge of the Brazilian laborers so that he would instruct the rest of those devoted to that sweet labor in the mysteries of Religion.[98]

264. Accordingly, the authors of the Guaraní system of government were strong in terms of their ingenuity and knowledge of the soul; but it was not so much the force and industry of the humane arts and sciences (although those laboring in the Indies had to esteem these as well) as it was the light of the Gospel that served them as a guiding beacon in establishing that wonderous form of governance. Thus, O Raynal, it is from the teachings of Christ and his precepts that the public good must be sought, not in the pestilent contrivances of modern-day Philosophers (which includes you).

CCLXV. Quippe Evangelium politicae felicitatis (qui finis est societatis civilis) firmissimum praesidium est, adjectis ab eo fabricae legis naturalis per se imbecilli novis eijsdemque validissimis munimentis, et propugnaculis, quae ab hominum coetibus arcent; quidquid turbare potest rectum rei communis ordinem. Atque is quidem ordo id exigit, ut tales sint cives, quales esse debent erga Deum, erga se ipsos, erga socios, quibuscum vivunt, quae tria perfectam hominis vitam et conditionem continent. Ecce hic tibi summam doctrinae Christianae, cui si applices docilem et humilem animum (nam *sapientia quae de sursum est* non revelatur superbis sed *parvulis*) disces profecto nihil omissum in divina evangelii institutione, quod urbes beatas efficiat.

CCLXVI. Passim ibi magister Deus concordiam et pacem civium praedicat (*beati pacifici*).[99] *Pacem habete inter vos*[100] passim mansuetudinem, qua fit, ut cum aliis pacifice vivamus (*beati mites*)[101] passim misericordiam, qua sine mansuetudo sterilis est (*beati misericordes*)[102] passim recti et aequi amorem, quo et a malo abstinemus, et bonum sequimur (*beati, qui esuriunt, et sitiunt justitiam*)[103] passim tolerantiam in flebili ac adversa rerum sorte ne desperemus, passim tranquillitatem animi in paupertate, ne fracti calamitatibus, et cupiditate ditescendi, alii ab aliis, boni publici damno, disjungamur (*beati, qui lugent: beati, qui persecutionem patiuntur: beati pauperes spiritu*).[104]

CCLXVII. Quam vero diligenter consulit in Evangelio Christus singulorum bonis, et securitati? (*non homicidium facies, non adulterabis, non facies furtum, non falsum testimonium dices.*)[105] Quam sollicite urget, ut suum cuique statim reddatur? (*esto consentiens adversario tuo cito . . . non exies donec reddas novissimum quadrantem.*)[106] Quam studiose pactis cavet? (*quicumque te angariaverit mille passus, vade cum illo et alia duo.*)[107] Quam enixe commendat sinceritatem et candorem in agendo, ne Respublica mendaciis fraudibusque turbetur? (*sit sermo vester est, est: non, non.*)[108] Quam aperte usuram, et foenus vetat, ut turpe lucrum resecet? (*mutuum date, nihil inde sperantes.*)[109]

265. Surely the Gospel is the staunchest protection for political happiness (which is the goal of civil society) because to the framework of intrinsically weak natural law, it adds new and yet very robust fortifications and bulwarks, which separate groups of people from the things that can disturb the right order of the community. And indeed, this order demands that just as they must behave toward God, so should citizens behave toward one another and toward the companions with whom they live. For these three things preserve the perfect conditions for human life. Behold here the essence of the Christian doctrine, and if you should apply yourself to it obediently and humbly (for "the wisdom that comes from above" is revealed not to the proud, but "to little children") you will undoubtedly learn that nothing that would make cities fortunate has been omitted in the gospel's divine system.

266. Everywhere there, God the teacher proclaims the harmony and peace of the citizens ("blessed are the peacemakers").[99] "Have peace among yourselves"[100]—gentleness at every step, which makes us live in peace with others ("blessed are the meek");[101] mercy at every step, which is barren without gentleness ("blessed are the merciful");[102] love for what is right and just at every step, through which we abstain from evil and follow good ("blessed are those who hunger and thirst for justice");[103] patience in tearful and adverse circumstances at every step, so that we do not despair; peace of mind in poverty at every step, lest, shattered by calamities and the desire for growing rich, we become disengaged from one another, to the detriment of the public good ("blessed are those who mourn; blessed are those who suffer persecution; blessed are the poor in spirit").[104]

267. Indeed, how diligently Christ shows concern in the Gospel for the goods and security of individuals! ("You shall not commit murder," "you shall not commit adultery," "you shall not commit theft," "you shall not bear false witness.")[105] How carefully he urges that everyone is given his due straightaway! ("Find agreement with your adversary quickly... because you will not get away until you have paid your last penny.")[106] How zealously he protects agreements! ("Whosoever compels you to walk a mile, go with him another two.")[107] How earnestly he recommends sincerity and candor in dealings so that the Republic is not disturbed by lies and frauds! ("Let your 'yes' be a 'yes' and your 'no' a 'no.'")[108] How clearly he forbids usury and interest to curtail profiting in an unseemly manner! ("Lend, expecting nothing in return.")[109]

CCLXVIII. Quam idem nos severe revocat a nocendo, ut non manus solum ab injuria temperemus, sed oculos etiam a libidine (*omnis, qui viderit mulierem ad concupiscendum eam, jam moechatus est*),[110] et aures ab obtrectatione, et linguam a conviciis, et contumelia (*qui dixerit fratri suo, raca, reus erit concilio, qui autem dixerit, fatue, reus erit gehennae ignis*)[111] et a verbis etiam otiosis, quae nec loquenti prosunt, nec audienti (*omne verbum otiosum, quod locuti fuerint homines, reddent rationem de eo in die judicii*)[112] et mentem a temeraria suspicione, et cor a pravis desideriis (*a corde exeunt cogitationes malae, homicidia, adulteria, fornicationes, furta, falsa testimonia, blasphemiae; haec sunt, quae coinquinant hominem*).[113] Quam sancte et provide castas ac stabiles esse nuptias vult; ut rem, et bona, et educationem prolis, aucturae civitatem, firmet? *Quod Deus conjunxit, homo non separet. Quicumque dimiserit uxorem suam, etc.*

CCLXIX. Ad haec, quam stricte jubet, ne laesi laedamus, sed potius laedentibus bene ultro faciamus? Quam crebro denunciat, ut detentis carcere, ut esurientibus, ut sitibundis, ut aegris, ut peregrinis, ut nudis opitulemur? Quam graviter inculcat liberis amorem et obsequium in parentes, servis observantiam et fidelitatem in heros, Regi subditis, et Principi obedientiam, et venerationem in Regem, et Principem; divitibus liberalitatem in pauperes, omnibus denique cultum, et pietatem, et religionem (sine quibus civilis status stare non potest) in Deum, idque verbis adeo planis, atque ita appositis similitudinibus exemplisque, ut vel infima plebs quid praecipiatur intelligat. Quo autem cuncta civium in cives officia generatim complecteretur, ea velut in compendium redegit brevi hac sententia: *quaecumque vultis, ut faciant vobis homines, et vos facite illis: haec est enim lex.*[114] O lex? O divina lex, quae hominum civitates coelestium civium beatae Reipublicae similes reddis?

268. How severely he calls us back from causing harm so that we restrain: not only our hands from lawlessness, but also our eyes from lust ("everyone who shall have looked at a woman so as to covet her, has already committed adultery");[110] our ears from disparagement; our tongue from insults and affronts ("Whoever shall have called his brother, '*raca*,'* will be in danger from the Council. Whoever shall have called him, 'fool,' will be in danger from hell's fire"),[111] and likewise from careless words that benefit neither the speaker nor the hearer ("Every careless word, which men shall have said, they will account for on the day of judgment");[112] our mind from rash suspicion; and our heart improper desires ("from the heart come evil thoughts, murder, adultery, fornication, theft, false witness, blasphemy; these are what contaminates humankind").[113] How solemnly and providently is his wish that marriages be chaste and stable, in order to secure the property, goods, and upbringing of offspring who will increase the citizenry? "What God has joined together, let not humans put asunder." "Whoever will have sent his wife away . . . " etc.

269. Furthermore, how strictly does he order us not to harm when we have been harmed, but instead to spontaneously do good unto those harming us? How frequently does he declare that we should bring aid to those held in prison, to the hungry, to the thirsty, to the sick, to the itinerant, and to the naked! How seriously does he instill love and compliance toward parents in children; attentiveness and fidelity toward masters in servants; obedience and veneration toward the King and Prince in subjects of the King and Prince; generosity toward the poor in the rich; and finally, in all he instills worship, piety, and reverence toward God (without which the political state cannot endure). And he did it with such plain words and such suitable comparisons and examples, that even an ordinary person of the lowest rank would understand what is prescribed. And so that all the duties citizens have toward citizens would be embraced universally, he rendered them, as if in summary, with this brief sentence: "Whatever you want people to do unto you, do unto them. For this is the law."[114] O law! Oh, divine law, you who make the states of humankind similar to the blessed Republic of heavenly citizens!

* Aramaic *reka* for "empty-headed."

CCLXX. Adde huc, quod doceamur in Evangelio verae virtutis naturam cum spe certa aeterni praemii, si pii, et justi fuerimus; cumque minis inevitabilibus poenae aeternae, si injusti, et impii. Adde, quod ostendatur illic nobis, quasi intento digito, quid ab ira, quid a superbia, quid ab ambitione, quid ab impudicitia, ceterisque animi pestibus timere debeamus, propositis simul in singula horum vitia opportuno remedio, et prudenti cautione. Adde, quod internam opem, et valida e coelo auxilia det omnibus Christus ipse ad implenda ea, quae jubet, atque id quidem nemini praestare possunt legislatores alii. Adde demum, quod certa inibi aperiatur via, resereturque modus, quo, siquis peccarit, amicitiam divinam recuperet, eaque recuperata, melior et sibi, et aliis civibus fiat. Philosophi, utpote profani legis naturalis interpretes, cum quid culpae quis admiserit, in media illum veniae desperatione destituunt, neque quidquam suggerunt, quo admissa deleat, et resurgat a lapsu. Ergo Respublica desperatis reis plena erit; resipiscentibus, spe impetrandae veniae asylum non erit.

CCLXXI. Explicui, Raynal, quae sit vera THEOCRATIA. Haec est una, quae Rempublicam justam, et tranquillam, et felicem reddit: neque alia fuit opus lege, et doctrina, ut populos illos Guaraniorum a barbarie ad civilem cultum, a licentia vitae ad pudicos mores, a desidia inerti ad laborem, et curam agri, a silvestri et ferino victu ad humaniores epulas, a belli furore ad pacis otia, a vago errore ad sedem stabilem, a connubio incerto ad certas nuptias, a rudi consuetudine ad artes utiles, ab inscitia rerum omnium ad coelestem sapientiam, a Satanae servitute ad Christi libertatem lenibus officiis, et divinae opis praesenti auxilio, traducerent praecones divinae philosophiae.

CCLXXII. Restat, ut ab Raynali me tandem expediam, singulare ejus de administratione Guaranica argumentum expendere. Casu scripsit de oppidis illis sub ipsum jussi exilii tempus. Norat cultores Guaranicos ab aliis dici Regis Catholici jura fideliter tueri, et augere; ab aliis contra, non Regis, sed suam eos rem agere, et quaesisse sibi clandestinum quoddam regnum. Atqui adest, inquit, jam dies, qui ostendet palam, utrum istorum de illis judicium verum sit. Si jussi illinc abire Jesuitae, parent, abeuntque pacifici, neque Indos ad arma instigant; bene est: fideles erant, curabant rem Regis, non suam. Sin autem abitioni resistunt, et oppida turbant, et vim parant; perduelles erant, curabant rem suam, non Regis, regnum usurparant.

270. Add to this that in the Gospel we are taught the nature of true virtue including the reliable expectation of eternal reward if we are pious and just; and the unavoidable menace of eternal punishment if we are unjust and impious. Add that he indicates to us there, as if with finger outstretched, what we ought to fear from anger, pride, ambition, shamelessness, and the other plagues of the soul, indicating at the same time for each of these vices the prudent precaution and opportune remedy. Add that Christ himself gives everyone the internal resources and effective heavenly support for implementing what he commands; and indeed, this is something that no other legislator can provide for anyone. Add, finally, that right there a reliable path is revealed, and a way is opened up, by which, if someone has sinned, he can regain divine friendship, and once it has been regained, he is made better both for himself and his fellow citizens. Philosophers, as profane interpreters of natural law, when someone admits some guilt, they leave him out in the open with no hope of forgiveness and do not suggest anything with which he might erase his crimes and rise up from his fall. Therefore, their Republic will be full of desperate criminals; there will be no asylum for those coming back to their senses and no hope of obtaining forgiveness.

271. I have explained, O Raynal, what a true THEOCRACY would be. This is the one thing that renders a Republic just, peaceful, and happy. No other law or doctrine was necessary for the heralds of divine philosophy to lead those Guaraní populations from barbarism to a civic culture, from a licentious life to demure customs; from unproductive idleness to labor and management of the fields; from a wild diet fit for beasts to dishes more suited to humans; from the fury of war to the respite that comes from peace; from aimless wandering to a stable residence; from unreliable coupling to reliable marriages; from unrefined habits to useful arts; from ignorance of everything to heavenly wisdom; from Satan's slavery to the freedom of Christ, all of which they accomplished through light obligations and the ready support of divine aid.

272. Before I can at long last rid myself of Raynal, it remains to weigh his unique argument about the Guaraní system of government. He happened to write about those towns just after the exile was ordered. He knew that the Guaraní cultivators were said by some to be faithfully defending and increasing the authority of the Catholic King; on the contrary, by others they were said to be acting for their own benefit, not for the King's, and to be seeking a clandestine kingdom of sorts for themselves. But now, he says, the day is upon us which will show plainly which of these two judgments about them is true. If the Jesuits, after having been ordered to depart, make ready and leave peacefully, without inciting the Indians to take up arms, then all is well: they were faithful; they were looking after the king's interests and not their own. If, however, they resist departing, agitate the towns, and make ready for violence, then, they were public enemies; they were looking after their own interests, not the King's; they had usurped his kingdom.

CCLXXIII. Non quaero, Raynal, quae, et quanta huic tuo argumento vis insit: poterant siquidem sine ulla Curionum culpa Guaranii tumultuari, illorumque exilio obsistere, neque audire suadentes otium, quantumvis aliis illos in rebus reverentur, et amarent. Nam quoties in Europa plebs, et mobile vulgus, mota seditione, virorum gravium, et Sacerdotum, quos ceteroqui diligit, consilia et monita de debita Principi obedientia, respuit, et pergit insanire?

CCLXXIV. At stemus, Raynal, praesagitioni isti tuae philosophicae. Arbiter tu ipse sis, et judex. Et ne diutius animi pendeas, scito Curiones Guaranios nihil omnino exilium impedisse, totumque annum (quod nusquam in ceteris Hispani imperii provinciis tum accidit) postquam lex illa lata est, hortati Indos sunt qua privatim, qua e loco superiore, ut quiescerent, ut se se voluntati Regis submitterent, et omnia, mutatis etiam Parochis, sperent. Sic est. Franciscus Bucarelius duodecim ipsos menses distulit (Laurentius illum Balda Sociorum Guaranicorum praefectus ardentibus litteris nequicquam stimulabat, ut veniret, ut se se quam primum, et suos cura liberaret) distulit, inquam, Bucarelius ex oppidis Curatores evocare, et alios secundum voluntatem Regis submittere. Totum vero istud tempus impensum eis est in Indorum parandis animis, donec tandem adfuit Bucarelius ipse, ac, nemine contra hiscente, abierunt illinc, datis successoribus, Jesuitae. Tu, Raynal, hinc, quod malis infer; nisi forsan annuum spatium nimis breve fuisse existimaris ad concitandos Neophytorum animos, omnesque aditus occludendos, ne inde Curiones amoverentur.

Alia aliorum judicia de disciplina Guaranica.

CCLXXV. Gallus quidem scriptor, *siquis est*, ait, *felix populus, is non alibi quam in Paraguaya est. Indutus, nutritus, apte occupatus, et re praesenti contentus, debetne Indus solicitus esse, quid superfluo fiat?*[115] Verum si auctor is, partium liber ut de se ipse profitetur, contentos ait Guaranios re presenti, quasi nihil privati habuerint patresfamilias, rem plane ignorat, nam *Abambaae* proprium uniuscujusque praedium erat, cujus fructum sibi et suis servare in posterum poterat. Sin autem quaerens *quid superfluo fiat*? intelligi vult post impensas ex *Tupambae*, sive agro communi, in aegros, et viduas, et pueros, et necessaria instrumenta in oppidi usus, *superfuisse* aliquid; errat rursus, nihil enim supererat, et aliquando etiam deerat.

273. Raynal, I am not trying to probe the strength of your argument. In truth, the Guaraní could have, through no fault of the Priests, become agitated and obstructed their exile instead of heeding those recommending calm, even though in other matters the Guaraní respected and loved the Priests. For, how many times in Europe did ordinary people and the fickle crowd, when sedition was afoot, reject advice and warnings about the obedience due to the Prince offered by authoritative men and Priests, whom they otherwise esteem, and persist in their insanity?

274. But let us linger, Raynal, on that philosophical prescience of yours. You yourself should be arbiter and judge. And so that you are not held in suspense any longer, know that the Guaraní Priests did nothing at all to impede the exile, and for an entire year after that law was promulgated (something that never happened in the Spanish empire's other provinces at the time), they encouraged the Indians both privately and from the pulpits, to remain peaceful, to submit to the King's will, and trust completely in the new Parish Priests.* And so, it is. Francisco Bucarelli put it off for twelve whole months (Lorenzo Balda, Superior of the Guaraní Jesuits, was urging him in vain with fiery letters to come as soon as possible to liberate him and his priests from their anxiety) Bucarelli, as I was saying, put off recalling the Caretakers from the towns and submitting the others to the King's will. Indeed, this entire time was devoted to preparing the Indians' souls, until finally Bucarelli himself appeared and, without anyone uttering a peep in opposition, the Jesuits departed, with their successors already designated. You, Raynal, can infer what you will from this; unless, perhaps, you judge a year to have been too brief a space of time for exciting the spirits of the Neophytes and blocking off all the entrances, so that the Priests would not be removed from there.

How Others Judge the Guaraní System of Discipline

275. Indeed, a French writer [Simon-Nicholas Henri Linguet] says: "If there is any population that is happy, it is none other than the one in Paraguay. Dressed, nourished, suitably occupied, and content with their present circumstances, should the Indian be concerned about what happens with the surplus?"[115] But if this author, free of partisanship, as he professes himself to be, says that the Guaraní are content with their present circumstances, as if the heads of the families had nothing in private, he is clearly ignorant of the circumstances. For, each one of them had his *Avamba'é*, his individual plot of land, the fruits from which he could save for the future for himself and his family. But if in asking the question he means for "what happens with the surplus?" to be understood as "was there anything left over" from the *Tupâmba'é*, or communal field, after the expenditures for the sick, the widows, the children, and the instruments necessary for use in the town; he is mistaken again, for nothing would be left over, and there would even be a deficit sometimes.

* After the Jesuit expulsion in 1767, Franciscans, Mercedarians, and Dominicans each took over the administration of a third of the Guaraní-Jesuit communities of Paraguay.

CCLXXVI. Rectius rem explicat anonymus Anglus, qui librum edidit de *Paraguayae rebus*.[116] Hic, desipimus, inquit, Europaei, cum Curiones Guaranicos reprehendimus. Cur vero? quia nobis optanda est potius sors illa, quae sine ulla vi ullisve impendiis, Guaraniorum genti contigit. Eorum in oppidis singuli laborant pro omnibus, et omnes pro singulis. Non vendere, non emere opus illis est, et tamen unicuique nec ementi, nec vendenti cuncta ad manum sunt, ut commode Vitam toleret: suppetit nimirum cibus ipsis, et vestis, et domus, et animi institutio, et medicina corporis e publico. Europaei, si pecunia desit, deesse sibi omnia rentur, et dolent: at Guaranii (quamvis illis aurum, argentumque non sit, et numis careant) quotidie usu sentiunt illud priscis dictum: *dii laboribus omnia vendunt*. Pro sexus, et aetatis, ac virium conditione, laborant; numquam tamen labore opprimuntur. Nesciunt delicias, neque affluunt rebus supervacaneis; sed non propterea sit, quin tam illi beati sint, quam nostrum opulentissimi. Quippe felix, non cui multum est, sed cui parum satis est. Haec Guaraniorum conditio.

CCLXXVII. Sic ille, fortassis eo res Guaraniorum melius, quam alii, norat, quod Angli ob diuturnam commorationem Bonisauris (ubi permissu Regis Catholici aedes, et collegium institorum habuerunt pro vendendis Nigritis) Guaranios illuc saepe descendentes viderint, et quae apud eosdem esset disciplina, ab Hispanis, qui pagos illos adierant accuratius didicerint.

CCLXXVIII. Hallerius, qui magnum sibi in republica litteraria nomen peperit, non modo instituta Guaranica eximie laudat, eaque componit cum aureo felicis aetatis saeculo ob miram incolarum aequalitatem, bonorumque communionem. Sed etiam disciplinae illius auctores vindicat ab obtrectatorum querelis.[117] Montesquieus autem suo illo in opere de natura, et ratione legum, Guaraniorum vivendi modum magnifice commendat.[118]

CCLXXIX. Quid multa? Recentissimum (ne te aliis onerem) testimonium accipe. Antonius Fridericus Buschingius quinis (non minus) paginis amplae formae de origine progressuque Guaranicorum oppidorum disserit, ita narrationem orsus:[119] *Paraguaya* adeo in Europa celebris ob tantam vicissitudinem illorum Jesuitarum, de quibus tot fabulae et sparsae, et creditae hoc extremo sunt tempore . . . Pergit inde et meminit *Regis Nicolai*, cujus nomine inscriptum vidisse se nummum ait, additque commentum hoc tale esse, ut aliquando Europaeis pudori futurum sit advertisse aures tam impudenti ineptaeque calumniae.[120]

276. An anonymous Englishman [Edmund Burke] explains the situation better in a book he published, *News from Paraguay*.[116] Here he says, we Europeans are being foolish, when we find fault with the Guaraní Priests. Why? Because that fate, which befell the Guaraní people without any violence or any expense, should be the one we most desire. Individuals in the towns work on behalf of everyone, and everyone works on behalf of each individual. They have no need for selling or buying, and yet for each and every non-buyer and non-seller everything is at hand to sustain Life comfortably. Without a doubt, they have on hand food, clothing, housing, education for the soul, and medicine for the body, all at public expense. Europeans, if they lack money, reckon that they lack everything and are despondent; but the Guaraní (although they do not have gold or silver and lack currency) experience every day that maxim of the ancients: "The gods sell us everything for our labor." They labor according to their sex, age, and the level of their physical strength. However, they are never oppressed by labor. They do not know delicacies, nor do they have an abundance of superfluous possessions. But this does not make it so that they are any less blessed than the richest among us. Naturally, the one who is happy is not the one who has much but the one for whom little is enough. This is the condition of the Guaraní.

277. So says that writer, who perhaps was more familiar with Guaraní matters than others because of the fact that the English, due to their long-term residency in Buenos Aires (where, with the permission of the Catholic King, they had houses and a commercial association for selling Blacks), they would frequently see the Guaraní going down there, and they would hear in more detail about their teachings back home from the Spanish, who had visited those districts.

278. Haller, who made a great name for himself in the republic of letters, not only offers exceptional praise for the institutions of the Guaraní, but he also compares them to a golden age of the happy life, due to the marvelous equality of citizens and their community of goods. But he also defends the authors of that regime from the complaints of their detractors.[117] Montesquieu, too, in his work on the nature and the theory of laws, offers a magnificent recommendation of the Guaraní way of living.[118]

279. Why go on? Take the most recent testimony (so as not to burden you with the others). Anton Friedrich Büsching discusses the origin and development of the Guaraní towns for no less than five large-format pages. He began his account thus:[119] *Paraguay*, so famous in Europe due to the many vicissitudes of those Jesuits about whom so many fictions have been spread and in these recent times believed . . . He then goes on and makes mention of "King Nicolas," whose name, he says, he saw engraved on a coin; and he adds that this contrivance was such that at some point having lent an ear to such shameless and inept chicanery will be a source of shame for Europeans.[120]

CCLXXX. Quod porro ad initia attinet quaesitae illius gentis opus fuisse ait et Martyrum constantia, et Angelorum patientia in educendo e silvis, et retinendo, instituendoque inconstantis ferique populi grege. Quid vero fieret in oppidis fuse dein narrat, et de disciplinae genere non dubitat dicere neophytos Guaranicos a Curionibus regi solitos, ut pater filium regit, ut magister docet discipulum. Sed eo lapsus Buschingius est, quod autumet fuisse Indorum numerum, cum illinc exacti sunt Jesuitae, ad trecenta millia, quam summam posuit etiam Argonauta ille Bougainville, qui minus errare debuit, quandoquidem Bonisauris rem nosse facilius potiut; edidissent enim illi, si rogasset, Regii quaestores e tabulis vectigalium publicis verum Guaraniorum censum, qui anno MDCCLXVII. ad centum millia capitum non ascendit. Sunt et alia quaedam, quae corrigas, in Buschingiana descriptione. Id tamen auctori tam longe ab America scribenti benignius condonandum est.

CCLXXXI. Dicet hic mihi forte quispiam: laudatores rerum Guaranicarum profers, vituperatores non profers. Numne nulli sunt? Immo sunt fere innumerabiles, praesertim extremi temporis, cujus meminit paulo ante Buschingius, postquam videlicet buccinator quidam classicum cecinit ob disturbatum ab Indis Guaranicis foedus limitum, e quo Lusitani (tradita pro septem oppidis cisuruguacis Colonia Sacramenti) aureos sibi montes spoponderant. At pro thesauro (victis tandem Indis) carbonem, ut ajunt, reperere, seu, ut ipsorum Lusitanorum unus non insulse dixit, *coiros* tantum et *cornos*, id est, *coria* et *cornua*: et certe abundabant illic utraque, cum quotidie multa boum capita mactarentur in singulis oppidis pro dividenda communiter bubula.

CCLXXXII. Per id igitur tempus, quo Guaranii omnia tentabant (ut sua cuique patria dulcis est) ne avitis finibus expellerentur, Aeolis ille (Carvallium volui dicere)

> . . . Cavum conversa cuspide montem
> Impulit in latus: ac venti, velut agmine facto,
> Qua data porta ruunt, et terras turbine perflant . . .
> Eripiunt subito nubes coelumque diemque
> Treucorum ex oculis, ponto nox incubat atra.

280. Moreover as regards the initial phase of searching for those people, it required, he says, the perseverance of Martyrs and the patience of Angels to lead the flock of fickle and wild people out from the forests, to keep them in one place, and to indoctrinate them. Then later he pours forth a description of what was done in the towns; and with reference to the type of discipline they had there, he does not hesitate to say that the Guaraní neophytes were used to being governed by the Priests as a father governs his son, as a master teaches his apprentice. But Büsching is mistaken in that he asserts that the Indians, when the Jesuits were expelled from there, numbered close to three hundred thousand. This is the sum that Argonaut Bougainville cited as well, but he should have erred less, since in Buenos Aires it was easier to learn the facts. For the King's treasury officials, if he had asked, would have produced, based on the public tax records, the true census of the Guaraní, which did not reach one hundred thousand in the year 1767. There are still a few other things one might correct in Büsching's description. But an author writing at such a distance from America deserves a rather generous pardon.

281. But here someone will perhaps tell me: "You cite those praising Guaraní affairs but not those condemning them. Are there none?" Certainly, and they are almost innumerable, especially in recent times, which Büsching made mention of a little earlier, since evidently a certain trumpeter sounded the alarm on account of the Guaraní Indians breaking the boundary treaty, in which the Portuguese had negotiated mountains of gold for themselves (Colonia del Sacramento was exchanged for the seven towns on this* side of the Uruguay River). But (in the end, when the Indians were defeated) instead of treasure they found, as they say, coal, or as one of the Portuguese said saltily, just *coiros* and *cornos*, that is, "hides" and "horns." Both are certainly abundant there since each day several head of cattle were slaughtered in each town for the communal distribution of meat.

282. And so, during this time when the Guaraní were trying everything (since everyone's homeland is held dear) to keep from being expelled from their ancestral territory, that famous Aeolus (Carvalho, I mean):

> . . . struck the hollow mountain on its side
> with his trident upturned: and the winds, as if in a battle line,
> flowed forth from the new made door, and blew across the lands . . .
> Suddenly, clouds snatch away the sky and its light
> from the eyes of the Trojans; dark reclines across the sea [Vergil *Aeneid* 1.81–83, 88–89].

* i.e., eastern.

Haud aliter medio hoc saeculo immanis quaedam tempestas volitantium hinc et illinc libellorum in res Guaranicas exorta est, quam magnae undique tenebrae consecutae sunt. Equidem, siqui posthac probarint falsa esse, quae de administratione illa posui, et mox ponam, non recusabo, quin eos irasci merito Curatoribus Guaranicis profitear. Interim patienter ferant nostra, si libenter nequeunt. At me longius provexit suscepta explicatio disciplinae Guaraniorum:[121] redeo illuc jam, unde discessi.

De suppliciis.

PLATO

CCLXXXIII. Norat Plato, ubi homines sunt, quantumvis bonae sint leges, et recta disciplina, et prudens ac vigil magistratus, fieri non posse, quin multi frenum mordeant, recalcitrentque: Quapropter ea omnium optima Respublica est, non in qua sontes nulli sint (nusquam enim hujusmodi civitas, et coetus mortalium est) sed ubi, siquid a quopiam peccatur, confestim reus corripitur, ne pravo exemplo cives alii corrumpantur. Atque hinc poenarum necessitas; quarum nulla, inquit, mali causa est, sed e contrario justa criminum animadversio efficit alterutrum, vel ut melior, vel saltem ut non tam sit malus qui punitur.

CCLXXXIV. Itaque nullum in Republica scelus impunitum, ait, esto; sed aut ignominia, aut plagis, aut carcere, aut mulcta, aut exilio, aut morte, qui culpam admisit (prout erit quisque meritus) plectitor. Explicat deinde sigillatim, qua quodque facinus poena vindicandum sit. In nullos autem severior est, quam in impios, et sacrilegos (quibus quid fieri vellet supra docuimus) et in patriae hostes, seditiososque, et in parricidas, et in eos, qui sibi mortem consciscunt, quos quidem deserto in loco ad extremos regionis fines sine ullo prorsus honore sepeliri jubet, aut etiam projici inhumatos, nisi quis forte servus sit (non liber civis) qui eos humet. (Lib. IV. de Repub. Et IX. De Legg.)

No different, in the middle of this century, an immense tempest of sorts arose, one made up of booklets on Guaraní matters flying here and there; and everywhere a great darkness has followed it. Certainly, if afterward someone should prove what I have asserted about that system of government and what I will assert shortly to be false, I will not object to confessing that they are rightly angry with the Guaraní Caretakers. In the meantime, would that they endure our claims patiently, if they cannot do so cheerfully. The explanation of the Guaraní system of discipline that I undertook has carried me rather far off course.[121] I return now to where I left off.

On Punishments

PLATO

283. Plato was aware that where there are human beings, no matter how good the laws are, how correct the system of discipline, and how prudent and vigilant the civic officials, it cannot but happen that many bite down on the bit and kick back. For this reason, the best Republic of all is not one in which there are no criminals (for nowhere is there a state or gathering of mortals like this), but one where, if someone commits some kind of sin, the culprit is immediately reproached, so that the other citizens are not corrupted by the improper example. And from this arises the need for punishments, none of which, he says, is for the sake of the evil. On the contrary, attending to crimes in a just way achieves one of two things: the one who is punished is either better or, at least, not so bad.

284. Thus, in the Republic let no crime, he says, go unpunished; instead let the one who has committed a crime be punished (according to what he deserves) with dishonor, with lashes, with jail, with a fine, with exile, or with death. He then explains one by one which punishments have to compensate for which crimes. However, on none is he more severe than on the impious and sacrilegious (above we explained what he wants to be done with them), on the enemies of the fatherland and seditionists, on parricides, and on those who kill themselves. He orders that these last ones be interred in a solitary place at the extreme edge of the territory without any honor at all; or even that they be cast out, unburied, unless it happens to be a slave (not a free citizen) who buries them (*Republic* Book 4 and *Laws* Book 9).

GUARANII.

CCLXXXV. E Platonis poenis binae tantum apud Guaranios usu receptae erant, carcer nimirum, et verbera. Et nequis miretur de adhibitis illic virgis, poena haec decreta olim fuit divino instinctu in reos a *Moyse: sin autem,* inquit, *eum qui peccavit, dignum viderint* (judices) *plagis, prosternent, et coram se facient verberari. Pro mensura peccati erit plagarum modus.*[122] In Novo orbe mos is obtinuit pro Indis, et in Philippinis etiam insulis idem fit: nam Sinas apud quos cum insigni crudelitate cives crebro vapulant, non moror. In Europa etiam contra quosdam sontes vibratur scutica, sed rarius.

CCLXXXVI. Ceterum haud opus fuit illic Platonis severitate in impios, et parentum percussores, inque inimicos patriae, eosque qui sibi manus inferunt; scelera enim haec inter Guaranios inaudita erant. Levioris culpae rei vel certis flagri ictibus, vel carcere, qui in foro erat, et unde vinctos quotidie deducebat custos ad Sacrum Missae, plectebantur. Quod siquis crimen aliquod mortis dignum admisisset, cautum erat, ut anno uno arctis vinculis, iteratisque idemtidem plagis, et praeparco cibo, maceraretur; post annum vero extruderetur oppidi finibus, qua iter brevius est in Hispanorum urbes.

CCLXXXVII. Hic miras tragoedias excitat (ut abripi oestro solitus est) scriptor *Regni Paraguayci.* Videte demum. O Hispani, et tandem aliquando cognoscite, quo vos habeant loco Curiones Guaranici. Qui omnium sceleratissimi, qui capitalia ausi, qui immedicabiles sunt, hos illi amandant ad urbes vestras tamquam ad foeda facinosorum hominum receptacula, ubi pares cum paribus vivant. Huccine decus, et sanctum, et inclytum Hispanorum nomen recidit? . . . Haec ferme ille. Sed o bone? o Theologe (nam Theologum te esse nos doces magnifica illa tui praedicatione YO THEOLOGO SOI) pone paulisper iram, neque Hispanos patres, et plebem, frustra instiges in Curiones immerentes.

CCLXXXVIII. Ego te (quando sacra sic doctrina praestas) consulo usus exordio sapientis illius foeminae Thecuitidis ad Davidem Regem: *ancillae tuae erant duo filii, qui rixati sunt adversum se in agro, nullusque erat, qui eos prohibere posset, et percussit alter alterum, et interfecit eum, et ecce consurgens universa cognatio adversus ancillam tuam dicit: trade eum, qui percussit fratrem suum, ut occidamus eum.*[123] Hoc digno moerentis matris exemplo, et pio dolore, compello te pro Guaraniis, qui quamvis amarent inter se fratrum more modoque, humanae conditionis, et naturae labilis expertes non erant.

285. Of Plato's punishments only two had been put to use among the Guaraní: without a doubt, they were jail and flogging. And in case anyone is shocked at rods being employed there, long ago this penalty was decreed for the guilty by Moses on the basis of divine inspiration: "if they (the judges) have seen that the man who sinned is deserving of lashes, they will make him lie down and cause him to be beaten in front of them. The means of lashing will be commensurate with the sin."[122] In the New World this custom was prevalent among the Indians and the same happens in the Philippine Islands. I do not linger on China where citizens frequently get beatings with remarkable cruelty. In Europe against certain criminals, a whip is also brandished, though more rarely.

286. As for the rest, there was hardly any need there for Plato's severity toward the impious, parent murderers, enemies of the fatherland, and those who inflict self-harm; for these crimes were unheard of among the Guaraní. Less consequential offenses were punished with a fixed number of strokes from the scourge, or with jail, which was in the town square and every day the guard would lead them, bound, from there to Mass. But if anyone had committed some sort of crime worthy of death, care was taken that for one year he would be worn down by tight chains, beatings that were repeated time and again, and extremely little food; after a year, he would be forced out from the town's territory, in the direction of the shortest path to the Spanish cities.

287. Here, the author of the *Kingdom of Paraguay* (accustomed, as he is, to getting carried away by frenzy) whips up a bewildering tragedy: "Just look, oh Spaniards, and recognize at long last where the Guaraní Priests have got you! The most criminal of all, those guilty of capital crimes, those who are incurable, they banish them to your cities, as if to a foul reservoir for villains, where they live as birds of a feather.* Has the dignity and holy and renowned name of the Spanish fallen to this!" This is basically what he has to say. Good grief!† Some Theologian! (For, you show us that you are a Theologian in that magnificent sermon of yours: "I AM A THEOLOGIAN" [Sp.]) Set aside your anger for a brief while so that you do not speciously incite the Spanish fathers and the ordinary people against the Priests, who do not deserve it.

288. I look to you (since you evidently excel in holy doctrines) for what to do with the beginning of the wise Tekoan woman's speech to King David: "Your slave had two sons, who quarreled with one another in the field. There was not a single person who could keep them in check, and then, one struck the other and murdered him. And lo! all the relatives are rising up as one against your slave and saying, 'Hand over the one who struck his brother so that we may kill him.'"[123] I charge you to respond to this worthy example of a grieving mother and her pious pain in the context of the Guaraní, who, although they love each other in the tradition and manner of brothers, were not exempt from the slippery nature of the human condition.

* Lit. "equals among equals."

† An exasperated, ironic address "Oh good [sir]."

CCLXXXIX. Audi ergo me, et dubium animi doce. Neophytorum unus, irae impotens, inter rixandum occidit ruri tribulem. Occisor intercipitur a praetore, qui illum intrudit in carcerem. Quid fiet hic, o Theologe? Indus praetor nihil molitur majoris momenti sine consilio Curionis, idque e mente animoque est Regis Catholici. Dicetne Curio adeunti ipsum praetori, i, occisorem occide? id meruit. Non, opinor, sed benigniora respondebit cum Davide ad precantem illam Thecuitidem: *non cadet de capillis filii tui super terram.*[124]

CCXC. Praeter enim quam quod praetori jus vitae necisque in oppidanos non est, Curioni ipsi sacris est vetitum minis, ne se se causae sanguinis ulla parte immisceat: sin aliter, et certum hominem re, vel etiam nutu, ad mortem designet, cadit gradu suo, vel (ut vos Theologi dicitis) sit irregularis: nefasque ei deinceps est divina mysteria (quae administros suos volunt quam mitissimos) tractare, nisi sancte expiatus in pristina templi munia, araeque ministerium restituatur.

CCXCI. Interea percussor ille culpam luit, vapulat saepe, rigida inedia atteritur, umbraque et squalore carceris contabescit, ut scilicet alii a maleficiis deterreantur, recte nam ait ille: *oderunt peccare mali formidine poenae.* Sed jam lapsus est annus. Homicidam diutius detineri onus foret admodum grave custodiae praeposito, qui ei adstiturus assidue serviturusque est: atque ipse alioquin reus alendus esset e publico. Quod si domum remitteretur, ut sibi victum quaereret, libereque cum suis ageret, id non fieret sine plurium, et maxime occisi consanguineorum offensione. Illud restabat unum, ut mitteretur in exilium. Esto, inquis (neque enim adeo crudus es, ut capite illum plecti a praetore, cui id non licet, velis) mittatur in exilium; sed cur Hispanas urbes versus? Hispanorum odio. Meliora quaeso; non hac, mihi crede, sit causa.

289. Now hear me out, and then make your doubts known. One of the neophytes, powerless over his anger, kills a fellow tribesman during a quarrel out in the countryside. The killer is intercepted by the Chief Executive, who throws him into prison. What is to be done here, o Theologian? The Indian Chief Executive undertakes nothing of major importance without consulting the Priest; and this is in accordance with the designs and the sensibilities of the Catholic King. Will the Priest say to the Chief Executive coming to him: 'Go, kill the killer? He deserves it.' No, I don't think so. Rather, he will respond more benignly as David spoke to that Tekoan woman making the entreaty: "Not one hair from your son's head will fall upon the ground."[124]

290. For, apart from the fact that the Chief Executive does not have authority over life and death among the townspeople, it is forbidden, subject to holy threats, for a Priest to himself become mixed up with any aspect of a blood trial. If in any other way he should mark a particular person out for death in a case, even with just a nod, he loses his standing or (as you Theologians say) he would become "irregular." In which case it is thereafter impermissible for him to conduct the holy mysteries (which require ministers to be as mild as possible) unless he has undergone holy expiation and is restored to his former duties for the church and altar service.

291. Meanwhile the assailant purges his guilt, he is beaten often, worn down by strict starvation, and is gradually consumed by the darkness and squalor of prison, so that, naturally, others are deterred from wrongdoing. For he who said "Bad men hate sinning because they are fearful of punishment"* was right. And already the year has passed. For the murderer to be detained any longer would be a very heavy burden for the person charged with his custody. For he must constantly watch over and serve him; what is more, the culprit himself would have to be fed from community resources. Because if he were sent back home, to procure food for himself and to carry about freely with his family, it would not be without offending many, and especially the relatives of the one killed. There was just one option left: for him to be sent into exile. So be it, you say (for you are not so cruel that you would wish for him to be capitally punished by the Chief Executive, who does not have that power), let him be sent into exile. But why to the Spanish cities? Out of hatred for the Spanish? I am looking for something better. Trust me that this is not the cause.

* Henry de Bracton modifying Horace.

CCXCII. Iterum audi. Si reus in barbarorum silvas protruderetur, viveret freni omnis expers, et barbarico more, proculque a sacris, proculque a Sacerdotibus, evaderetque e Christiano ethnicus, aut etiam (ut assolet, qui praeceps ferri coepit) ethnicis ipsis pejor, gravi injuria violatae Religionis. Atque huc attinet, quod cum pro Hebreae Reipublicae sontibus varii generis supplicia jussu Numinis edixerit Moyses, nusquam in quemquem sanxit poenam exilii e finibus Israeliticis. Cur id? quia cum in sola Judaea verus esset Dei cultus, siquis inde penitus excluderetur, foret ei occasio quaedam labendi in idololatriam; quae erat pia Davidis querela adversus illos, qui instigato in ipsum Saulis odio, compulerant eumdem vagari per exterorum fines: *ejecerunt me hodie*, ajebat, *ut non habitem in haereditate Domini, dicentes: vade, servi diis alienis.*[125]

CCXCIII. Accommoda istud sonti Guaranio, quo de agimus. Si in greges circumvagantium barbarorum, densosque lucos secederet, e contubernio exlegis gentis in vitia sensim, et animi perniciem, nullo retinente, rueret: sin vero contenderet in urbem aliquam Hispanorum, exemplo bonorum civium mores fortasse mutaret, et resipisceret. Sacerdotes quidem viventi adessent morientique. Quod si (ut *perversi difficile corriguntur*) aliquid morte dignum denuo admitteret, Praetor Hispanus, cui id licet, extremo illum supplicio afficeret, et tunc tandem veteris culpae, et novae pro merito poenam penderet. Ex his vide, o Theologe (siquidem nulla illinc contumelia in Hispanos redundabat, sed gloria quodammodo et laus, quod ab ipsorum consuetudine bonum homini scelesto peteretur) quam tu temere accuses Curiones Guaranicos, et quam hi nusquam inconsulto progressi sint.

CCXCIV. Ad extremum, Guaranicae administrationis modus, miti illa reorum animadversione, sesquisaeculum recte atque tranquille retentus argumento est majore poenarum severitate opus illic non fuisse. Lustraturus olim publica auctoritate oppida Guaranica Senator amplissimus Joannes Blazquez de Valverde, secum adduxit Indum quemdam advenam, qui professus fuerat, se auri venas, quas ad Uruguayum amnim exercebant Guaranii, ostensum ire: hunc Indum (cum nusquam venae illae apparerent, neque ullum earum extaret vestigium, ac praeterea affirmarent metallicae rei periti, qui senatori ipsi aderant, terram illam gignendo auro aptam non esse) delusus Blazquius tamquam falsum Indicem, et causam tot impensarum ea in expeditione factarum, suspendio, post bis centum flagri plagas, addicendum censuit lata e jure sententia.[126] V. Kal. Octobr. an. MDCLVI.

292. Listen again. If the culprit were simply thrust out into the forests of the barbarians, he would live free of any yoke, according to barbarian customs, far from the sacraments, and far from the Priests; he would turn from a Christian into a pagan, or (as usually happens when someone is starting to get carried away) something even worse than the pagans, due to the serious injury caused by having violated his Religion. And here it is relevant that when Moses published punishments of various kinds for the criminals of the Hebrew Republic, based on the commands of the Divine Will, he never sanctioned anyone with the penalty of exile from Israel's territory. Why was that? It was because, given that true worship to God existed only in Judea, if anyone were barred from there completely, it would furnish a sort of opportunity for him to lapse into idolatry. And this was David's pious complaint against those who, after instilling in him a hatred of Saul, compelled that same man to wander through the territories of outsiders. "They have driven me out today," he said, "so that I should not have my share in the Lord's inheritance, telling me: 'Go, serve other gods'?"[125]

293. Apply this to the Guaraní criminal we are discussing. If he were to withdraw into the dense groves and among the flocks of roving barbarians, little by little from dwelling together with lawless people he would rush toward vice and his soul's peril with no one to hold him back. But if he were to set out for any of the Spanish cities, through the example of good citizens perhaps he would change his habits and come back to his senses. Indeed, Priests would be there for him while he lives and when he is dying. But (given that "the twisted are difficult to set straight")* if he were to commit some crime worthy of death again, the Spanish Governor, who does have that power, would condemn him to the ultimate penalty. At that point, he would finally pay the penalty for the old crime and the new one as deserved. Indeed, no affront flowed back onto the Spanish from this, rather glory and praise to a certain degree, since it was good that was being sought for the heinous person via the customs of these very people. See from these details, O Theologian, how blindly you accuse the Guaraní Priests and how they have never proceeded recklessly.

294. At last, maintained justly and peacefully for a century and a half, the moderation of the Guaraní system of government, with its mild punishments for culprits, serve as an argument that there was no need there for punishments of greater severity. One time, Juan Blázquez de Valverde, most honorable *Oidor*,† went to visit the Guaraní towns on state business, and with him he brought an Indian from elsewhere, who had promised that he was going to show him the veins of gold that the Guaraní were exploiting along the river Uruguay. Deceived (since those veins never appeared, nor was there any trace of them, and moreover metals experts, who accompanied the same *Oidor*, also confirmed that that land was not suitable for yielding gold), Blázquez judged that this Indian be sentenced to hanging after two hundred blows with the scourge, for being a false Informant and the cause of the great many expenses incurred in that expedition. This sentence was permitted by law.[126] September 27, 1656.

* *Ecclesiastes* 1:15.

† In overseas Spanish *audencias*, the *Oidor* was a judge with expansive administrative powers.

CCXCV. Erat tum Guaranicorum Sociorum praefectus Franciscus Diaz Tanius (quem supra laudavimus). Is tristem indi illius sortem miseratus, oravit, obsecravitque Blazquium Judicem, ut mortem condonaret homini infelici, qui in istud falsi indicium non sua sponte descenderat, sed impulsu heri, quondam sui.[127] Valuere preces, et lenius cum illo actum est citra necem. Equidem haec Diaz Tanii viscera misericordiae multo malim induere, quam cum scriptore Regni Paraguayci declamatorem agere, vel abjecta Sacerdotali mansuetudine actorem esse cuiquam in quemquam mortalium secures, ferrum, rotas expediendi.

De funere et coemeterio.

PLATO

CCXCVI. Plato (quo erat ingenio) omnia Rempublicam spectantia complexus mente, de sepulcrorum etiam situ, et de funere cavit, ne sumptuosiora essent, neu sordidiora, quam civem ingenuum decet; sed modus servaretur. Nullum, ait, in agro ad culturam apto sepulcrum fiat: neque enim par est mortuos officere vivorum alimentis. Elatio autem functi fato, nec citius acceleretur, nec protrahatur diutius, quam quanto opus est tempore, ut sat constet, eum vere mortem obiisse. Atque id quidem de corpore: namque animus, inquit, noster immortalis est, solutisque terrenis vinculis ad deos evolat, actae vitae, operumque, rationem redditurus: quo in judicio bonis quidem fiduciae, et gaudii, locus erit, malis contra terroris, et infelicitatis extremae, quippe quibus illic nullum aliunde auxilium futurum est.

CCXCVII. In funerum pompa moderatus esto sumptus. Ad sepulturam ejus, qui maximi census sit, non amplius quam quinque minae impenduntor; tres vero, si secundi sit census; duae, si tertii; una, si quarti. Aequum autem est eos civium publicis ornari laudibus, qui vel corporis robore, vel dotibus animi, praeclara quaedam atque ardua gesserunt pro Republica, quique sancte, et constanter legibus paruerunt: atque haec quidem sollemnis laudatio parentalibus virorum, feminarumque virtute praestantium communis esto. (Lib. IV. VII. XII. de Legg.).

GUARANII.

CCXCVIII. Ut Guaraniorum vita, et victus simplex erat, ita et funus sepulcrumque. Viri omnes foeminaeque tela tecti gossipina (ut Hebraei olim sindone) efferebantur ritu Christiano. Pueris puellisque major in feretro ornatus, festivoque sacri aeris tinnitu sepeliebantur. Ceterum digna commemoratu est forma coemeterii. Hoc ad alterum templi latus erat, aeque ac templum ipsum longum, sed paulo latius.

295. Francisco Díaz Taño (whom we praised above) was the Superior of the Guaraní Jesuits at that time. Feeling sorry for the sad fate of that Indian, he begged and beseeched Judge Blázquez to refrain from the death penalty for that unfortunate man, who had sunk to providing false information, not of his own free will, but at the instigation of his former master.[127] These entreaties were effective, and he received more lenient treatment, short of death. Certainly, I would much prefer to clothe myself in the tenderness of Díaz Taño's mercy, than to play declaimer along with the author of the *Kingdom of Paraguay*, or, with priestly gentleness cast aside, become the agent responsible for preparing the executioner's axe, the sword, or the wheel for any mortal whatsoever.

On Funerals and Cemeteries

PLATO

296. Because his mind embraced everything relating to the Republic (given his great ingenuity), Plato was also concerned about funerals and the location of graves, that they be neither more extravagant, nor shabbier than befits a native citizen; rather that moderation be observed. Let no sepulcher be built, he says, in a field suitable for cultivation; for it is not fair for the dead to interfere with the sustenance of the living. The carrying out of one who died a natural death should be neither hastened, nor drawn out more than the period of time necessary for it to be determined that the deceased has truly died. Indeed, this is just what concerns the body; for our soul, he says, is immortal and, once the earthly bonds have been dissolved, it flies toward the gods to give an account of the life lived and its deeds. And in that court of justice, for the good there will be occasion for confidence and joy, but by contrast for the bad there will be one of terror and extreme unhappiness, since no support from anywhere will come to them in that place.

297. Let the expenditures on funeral processions be moderate. For the burial of one in the highest census category, let not more than five *minae* be spent; but three, if he is in the second category; two, if in the third; and one, if in the fourth. It is certainly fair to exalt with public praises those citizens who, with either their bodily strength or spiritual gifts, have done distinguished and challenging things for the Republic and those who have obeyed the laws scrupulously and consistently. And indeed, let these solemn eulogies of men and women who are outstanding in terms of their virtue take place publicly at the *Parentalia* festivals (*Laws* Book 4, 7, and 12).

THE GUARANÍ

298. Just as life and the means of living among the Guaraní were simple, so too were funerals and burial. All men and women would be covered with a cotton cloth (like the Hebrews' *sindōn* in times past) and carried out for burial according to Christian ritual. The decoration on the bier was more substantial for boys and girls, and they were interred to the festive ringing of the church bell. Otherwise, the layout of the cemetery is worth recording. It was located on the other side of the church and was equally as long as the church itself but a little wider.

CCXCIX. Totum coemeterium divisum erat in partes quattuor: tumulabantur enim viri separatim foeminaeque, separatim pueri puellaeque. Quattor autem illae partes, quae inter se pares erant, discriminabantur iterum quasdam in areas, quarum singulae dena, duodenave corpora capiebant. Sursum vero et deorsum, atque in latera quoquoversus, aditum euntibus aperiebant directi calles, quos longa utrimque serie leniter obumbrabant alternis immistae malis aureis palmae virentes. Ad margines autem minorum arearum eminebant satae nardi, quibus ne innascerentur herbae inutiles, curabant foeminae, solitae circum loca, ubi suos sepultos norant, flexis genibus orare.

CCC. Totum coemeterii ambitum tegebat protenta porticus cum peristylio, ut possent, qui sacris caerimoniis humandorum cadaverum intererant vel ab imbri, vel a sole defendi. Sacellum ibi quoque structum pulchre; et Crux stabat sublimis, Christianae post mortem spei sacrum signum, et pignus. Itaque si rei inscius locum illum adires (binae erant portae, altera parieti adhaerens templi, altera forum versus, atque hujus quidem fores non solidae, sed cancellatim striatae, ut intro pateret aspectus) si adires, inquam, illuc rei ignarus, crederes, non te sepulcra (nulla enim apparebant usquam nuda ossa, nullum mortui vestigium corporis) subire, sed viridarium aliquod: nam ut nihil triste oculos offendebat, sic nec foetor nares: immo vero (si tepidum esset tempus, ut ibi fere semper est) omnia suaviter flagrabant tot nardorum, aurearumque malorum odorifera vi. Atque ipse situs coemeterii, cujus pars postica vergebat ad agros, purgatioribus auris perflabatur, quo etiam fiebat, nequid graviter spiraret.

CCCI. Jam vero cum (adstante Sacerdote linteato, funebresque preces fundente) mandabatur corpus aperto tumulo, humusque injicebatur, tum demum erumpebat (nam antea siluerant) foeminarum planctus (quem Guaranii *Guaju* vocant) interque flendum recensebant illae mortui laudes, memorabantque, quae pro oppido fecerat, quaequae facturus esset, si perrexisset vivere. Ah! (exempli causa) siquis immature obierat expolitioris mentis, fuisset is quondam, ajebant gementes praeficae, Ludimagister, Aeconomus, Musicae praefectus, Senator, Consul, Regius vexillifer, Praetor: haec enim munera maximae apud eos laudis erant et gloriae. Lamenta autem illa tot interjectionibus, tot reconditis, exquisitisque fandi formulis efferebant, ut nullus in Guaraniorum lingua esset locus difficilior ad discendum.

299. The entire cemetery was divided into four parts. For men were entombed separately from women, and boys and girls separately from these. These four parts, which were equal to one another, were divided again into discrete areas, each of which could accept ten or twelve bodies. Up and down and in every lateral direction, straight footpaths provided access for those walking; in long rows on either side of these paths verdant branches interspersed with oranges provided gentle shade by turns. Along the edges of the smaller parcels, spikenard that had been planted stood prominently. So that weeds did not spring up, these parcels were cared for by women, who made a habit of praying while kneeling where they knew their family members were buried.

300. A colonnade provided shelter around the entire perimeter of the cemetery so that those who attended the sacred ceremonies accompanying the inhumation of corpses could be protected from the rain and the sun. There was also a beautifully built chapel there; and a cross stood aloft, a sacred marker and pledge of Christian hope after death. Thus, if you were entering that place unaware of what it was (there were two doorways, one on the wall of the church, another toward the square, and the doors of the latter were not solid, but had lattice-like openings, so that the inside is open to view), as I was saying, if you were going in without knowing what it was, you would believe you were coming upon some kind of orchard rather than graves (no exposed bones were visible anywhere, nor any trace of a dead body). This was so that nothing sad would offend the eyes, nor stench offend the nose. Moreover (if the climate were temperate, as it almost always is there), everything sweetly blazed with the fragrant intensity of so many spikenards and oranges. Even the site of the cemetery itself, the back part of which was situated along the fields, was ventilated by cleansing breezes, making it so that it would not emit a disagreeable odor.

301. Moreover, while the body was committed to the open tomb and earth was thrown upon it (with the Priest standing there clothed in linen, pouring forth the funeral prayers), not until then would the women's lamentations (for they had previously remained silent) burst forth (which the Guaraní call *guahu*). Between their tears they would recount the praises of the deceased and remembered what he had done for the town and what he would have done had he kept on living. Ah! if someone with a particularly refined mind had died prematurely (for example), the wailing women leading the lamentations would say that he would have been Schoolmaster, Administrator, Music Director, Councilor, High Magistrate, Royal Standard-bearer, or Chief Executive! For these positions were considered the highest praise and glory among them. Those lamentations were offered up with so many exclamations, so many recondite and elaborate formulas of speech, that there was no aspect of the Guaraní language more difficult to learn.

CCCII. Denique, si cujus insignia fuerant merita in publicam rem, is in templo seorsum sepeliebatur, qui honos et plurimi ab indis fiebat, et accendebat ceteros ad consectandam virtutem; semper enim, et ubique gentium, attributae vita functis laudes, et decreta a majoribus praemia, ut columnae, ut illustrior tumuli locus, ut statuae, ut arcus, ut alia ejusmodi, incitamento vivis fuerunt ad praeclare agendum, studendumque recti aequique officiis, quo et ipsi post mortem idem sibi decus pararent, pergerentque vivere in perenni civium memoria, et gratis animis.

Epilogus institutae comparationis.

CCCIII. Ecce tibi, quae de administratione Guaranica collata cum Platonis Republica dicere habuimus. Erant quidem plura, quae huc adduci possent; sed nos specimen dumtaxat quoddam dare rei voluimus; atque id ipsum, quod dedimus, haud deerit fortasse, qui nimis longum putet. Verum defensioni nobis esto idem Plato, quem secuti sumus, ait enim de longa, aut brevi dicendi scribendique forma, quemquam angi ineptam prorsus sollicitudinem esse: quippe non brevissima, aut longissima, sed optima (sive brevia sint, sive longa) eligenda prudenti viro, vel dicat, vel scribat, sunt.

CCCIV. Quod si Aristoteles magni magistri sui stilum, ut redundantem in Republica, carpsit, fecit id immerito, ut ego quidem sentio. Certe Orator summus, et Philosophus, Tullius, Platonis, non Aristotelis dicendi genus probavit, secutusque est intractandis rebus Politicis, ut sat liquet e particula, quae extat, somni Scipionis.

302. Finally, if one's record of public service had been extraordinary, that person would be interred separately, in the church, an honor held in the highest regard by the Indians, one which kindled the others to pursue virtue. Always and everywhere in the world, praises given to the deceased for how they lived and rewards decreed by the elders, such as columns, a more distinguished tomb location, statues, arches, and other such things have served as an inducement for the living to behave admirably and to be eager to carry out their duties correctly and justly, so that in this way they might prepare the same honor for themselves after death and thereby keep on living in the eternal memory and grateful hearts of citizens.

Epilogue to the Comparison Performed

303. Here is what I had to tell you about the Guaraní system of government set in juxtaposition with Plato's Republic. There were certainly many more things that could be added here. But I just wanted to give some proof of the matter, and yet there will almost certainly be someone who thinks that what I have presented is too long. But let Plato himself, whom I have followed, serve as my defense; for he says that it is an utterly senseless concern for anyone to feel tormented about speaking and writing at length or briefly; of course, a judicious man must choose, whenever he speaks or writes, not what is shortest or longest, but what is best (whether short or long).

304. And if Aristotle reviled the style of his own great master in the *Republic* as redundant, he did it without merit, in my opinion. Of course, the greatest Orator and Philosopher, Cicero, approved of Plato's rather than Aristotle's way of speaking and followed suit in his exposition of political questions, as is clear from the little bit of the *Dream of Scipio* that is extant.

CCCV. De reliquo, cum auctor elegantissimus Joannes Baptista Noghera administrationem Guaranicam laudarit, eamque praetulerit Reipublicae Platonicae, operae pretium erit eximia ipsius de Indis illis sensa pro epilogo huc transcribere. Agens contra liberiores Philosophos de bonis, quae Religio Christiana Orbi terrarum peperit, "me, ait, presertim rapit ad se recentissimum exemplum. Integra atque adeo innumerabilis natio est, quae (sibi ipsa vix prius sat cognita) perpetuum cum vicinis gerebat bellum, et bellum ita dirum, et atrox, ut victi non praeda solum, sed cibus etiam victorum essent. Ubi autem Religio Christiana eo penetravit, egitque ferali in regione radices, ecce tibi in oppida coeunt palabundi antea hominesne an ferae? Et tamen hi, depositis inimicitiis, nunc inter se ritu fratrum observant, ac colunt, aliisque alii adversis in rebus opem ferunt, caritate sic conspicua, insignique, ut barbari finitimi tanta morum conversione obstupefacti, id de novis Christianis dicant, quod de priscis dixisse ethnicos narrat Tertullianus:[128] en ut isti invicem amant, paratique sunt pro aliis alios vitam ponere. Quae autem prior se se subdidit Christo tribus, ea aliam dein exemplo suo ad illum trahit, atque e gentibus indole, et more variis unus coalescit populus, cui cor unum, et unus spiritus est, spiritus pacis, spiritus innoventiae, spiritus caritatis. Quocirca e crudelium antehac ferarum, immaniumque antropophagorum plurimis turmis una jam constat RESPUBLICA MULTO ILLA MORIBUS MELIOR, MULTOQUE FELICIOR, QUAM EA, CUJUS SIBI IMAGINEM ET MEMBRA FINXIT PLATO."

CCCVI. "Nemo non videt haec me dicere de populis Paraguaycis. Neque est cur hoc nomine commoveantur Philosophi liberiores, remque istam cum fastu ad fabulas rejiciant. Etenim sunt nobis testes locupletissimi, qui illuc penetrarunt data opera, oculisque hauserunt, quae de iis oppidis praedicamus: sunt incorruptorum Praetorum idem testantium litterae: sunt tabulae utriusque magistratus sacri profanique: atque hi quidem omnes circumspectissimi erant, ne vel sibi imponi sinerent, neu ipsi aliis imponerent. Et vero idem est doctorum virorum judicium, nec solos dico Muratorios, sed etiam Montesquievos, Buffonios, et Hallerios, quorum verba hac de re ita omnibus nota sunt, ut opus non sit, huc ea producere." Haec ille.[129]

305. As for the rest, since the most elegant author Giovanni Battista Noghera praised the Guaraní system of government and preferred it to Plato's Republic, it will be worthwhile to transcribe here, as an epilogue, his exceptional thoughts about those Indians. Countering the libertine Philosophers regarding the benefits that the Christian religion has provided for the entire world, he says: "A very recent example particularly captivates me. There is a nation so large that it is ignorant of its own extent, which (almost as soon as it encountered its other parts) was perpetually waging war with its neighbors, and the war was so terrible and savage that the conquered were not only their conquerors' plunder but also their food. However, when the Christian Religion penetrated there and took root in that beastly region, lo and behold the former wanderers—were they men or beasts?—are coming together to form towns. And, their enmity set aside, they now regard each other in the manner of siblings, and they even respect one another and help each other in adversity with such a striking and remarkable charity that the neighboring barbarians, dumbfounded by the change of behavior, say about the new Christians what Tertullian reports the pagans said about the first Christians:[128] 'Look how these people love each other and are prepared to lay down their lives for each other.' Moreover, the tribe that first submitted itself to Christ then through its example attracts another tribe to Christ, and out of races varied in disposition and customs, a single people with a one heart and a one spirit coalesces: a spirit of peace, a spirit of innocence, a spirit of charity. Wherefore, out of so many hordes of formerly savage beasts and monstrous cannibals, now stands THIS ONE REPUBLIC MUCH BETTER IN TERMS OF ITS BEHAVIOR AND MUCH HAPPIER THAN THE ONE WHOSE PARTS AND OVERALL FORM PLATO FASHIONED."

306. "Everyone sees that I am referring to the peoples of Paraguay. There is no reason why the libertine Philosophers should be upset by this name and arrogantly reject this matter as nonsense. Because I have the most reliable witnesses, who took pains to make it all the way there and drank in with their eyes all that I proclaim about these towns: there are letters of honest Governors that give the same testimony; there are public records from both the ecclesiastical and secular magistrates: and all of them were extremely circumspect men who would not allow themselves to be deceived nor would they deceive others. And certainly, the judgment of learned men is the same; and I am not only referring to the writings of Muratori but also those of Montesquieu, Buffon, and Haller, whose words about this issue are so well-known by everyone that it is not necessary to reproduce them here." These are the things Noghera said.[129]

APOSTROPHE

Ad liberiores Philosophos.

CCCVII. Post absolutam comparationem Guaranicae administrationis cum Republica Platonis, siquis recentium Philosophorum (qui more veterum Atheniensium qui *ad nihil aliud vacant nisi aut dicere aut audire aliquid novi*)[130] me forte rogarit censeamne fieri posse quicquam illius formae simile in Europa? Potuit olim, nunc non potest, respondero. Potuit tum, cum Europaei ante cultas artes, positasque urbes, turmatim vivebant, atque ita vagabantur, ut parum, aut nihil different a gentibus Americanis. Nunc autem non potest, quandoquidem rerum Europaearum ordo politicus tot jam abhinc saeculis plane mutatus est.

CCCVIII. Guaranii, ubi primo eos adiere sacri cultores, ita agebant inter se pari conditione usi pro domo rudibus tuguriis, atque pro cibo piscatu, et venatione, agrique et silvae fructibus, ut facile, siquid melius proponeres, aliam illos in partem (favente Deo) flexurus esses traducturusque a gravi penuriae statu ad uberem copiae sortem, idque ne ipsis quidem invitis Caciquiis, quorum victus, et vitae ratio, dispar non erat miseris clientium rebus, relicta eis in bello auctoritate quadam, et imperio levissimo.

CCCIX. His tu si pares divideres agros, si parem laborem et facilem indiceres, si paria tecta strueres, si civilem cultum, si commoda, si vestem largiorem, si liberaliores epulas curares, si Orphei instar eosdem sensim mansuefaceres, si utilibus artibus erudires suavi et leni modo (*humanitatis* enim *dulcedo*, ait Valerius Maximus, *barbarorum ingenia penetrat*) si ita, inquam, communi illorum bono consuleres, ultro ea gens omnis grates tibi maximas ageret tamquam patri optimo, atque e superis sedibus delapso divinitus genio propitio.

CCCX. Quod si quondam in Europa (quod narrat Aristoteles)[131] Oenotriae Rex palantes inter Scyllaceum et Lamedicum sinum indigenas agriculturam docuit (erant prius vagi pastores) illisque leges posuit, allexitque ad communia eos convivia; Regi isti Oenotrio ita prudenti haud difficile fuisset infelix illud hominum genus ad parem fortunarum modum leniter pertrahere.

307. Now that the comparison between the Guaraní system of government and Plato's Republic is complete, if any of the modern-day Philosophers (who, after the manner of the ancient Athenians, "spend their time doing nothing but talking about and listening to whatever is novel")[130] by chance asks me whether I think something similar to that form of government could be instituted in Europe, I shall answer: "Once upon a time it was possible, but it is not now." It was possible back when Europeans, before the arts were cultivated and cities established, wandered about in such a way that they hardly, if at all, differed from the people in America. Now, however, it cannot happen, since the political organization of European affairs, so many centuries hence, has been completely changed.

308. The Guaraní, when the holy cultivators first approached them, lived on equal terms with one another, using simply made shelters for housing, and relying on fishing, hunting, and the fruits of the field and forest for their food. It was such that, if you were to propose something better, you would easily (God willing) turn them in the opposite direction and transfer them from a state of severe penury to a condition of productivity and abundance. And not even the Caciques themselves would be resistant to this; for their nourishment and manner of life and was not unlike the unfortunate situation of their followers, although in war a certain degree of authority and the slightest of powers was reserved for them.

309. If you were to divide the land equally for them, assign them easy and equal labor, build equal dwellings, if you were to provide civilized living arrangements, comforts, sufficient clothing, an abundance of food, if, just like Orpheus, you were to tame them gradually, if you were to teach them the finer points of the useful arts in a pleasant and gentle manner (for Valerius Maximus says, "the sweetness of humanity penetrates the minds of the barbarians"), if, as I was saying, you were to look out for their common good in this way, that entire nation would render unto you the greatest thanks, as if to the father above or to the propitious spirit of a divinity descended from its lofty realm.

310. But if at one time in Europe (as Aristotle tells it)[131] the King of Oenotria [Italus] taught agriculture to the Indigenous peoples dispersed between the Scylletic and Lametic gulf* (who were originally wandering shepherds), set down laws for them, and enticed them to have communal meals, it would have been by no means difficult for that Oenotrian king, wise as he was, to gently draw that unhappy group of people to the same degree of fortune [as the Guaraní].

* The Gulf of Squillace and the Gulf of Saint Euphemia along either side of the Calabrian peninsula (present-day Italy).

CCCXI. Idem fere potuit fieri ibi, ubi nunc CAPUT ORBIS est, cum Ausonidum sic exiguae erant opes, et *rara domorum tecta* (*quae nunc Romana potentia coelo aequavit*) ut hospes Aeneas *pauperis Evandri* angustum subiens larem, locatus sit *solio effulto foliis, et pelle Libystidis ursae,* pro copia scilicet parvi tum Regis, qui (Caciquium diceres) *Tyrrhena pedum* circumdabat *vincula plantis, demissa ab laeva pantherae terga retorquens.*[132]

CCCXII. Nam si dinastae hujusmodi tenuibus clientibus benigne suasisses bonorum aequalitatem, probassent eam utique, quippe qui antea assueti caprino lacte, et nucibus castaneis, et parca leguminum dape duram vitam vivere. Idem dictum esto de priscis Gallis, Hispanisque, quibus informis quidam et absurdus fuit agendi modus, asperque victus, et labor durus.

CCCXIII. Cornelius Tacitus de veteri Germania disserens, non tam Germanorum, quam Indorum in America videtur mores describere: accipe haec paucula. *Coeunt,* inquit, *nisi quid fortuitum et subitum acciderit, cum aut Luna inchoatur, aut impletur* (eadem in idem rei momenta Lunae servant Indi). *Quoties bella non ineunt, non multum venatibus, plus per otium transigunt dediti somno ciboque* (is Indis mos piger). *Litterarum secreta viri pariter ac foeminae ignorant* (par Indorum inscitia). *Diem noctemque continuare potando nulli probrum* (ne Indis quidem istud probro est). *Potui humor ex ordeo aut frumento, in quandam similitudinem vini corruptus* (sic *Chicha* sit, Indicae deliciae). Haec ille generatim de priscae Germaniae gente.

CCCXIV. De Fennis autem (quos dubitat Germanis an Sarmatis adscribat) refert speciatim: "mira feritas, foeda paupertas: non arma, non equi, non penates; victui herba, vestitui pelles, cubile humus. Sola in sagittis spes, quas inopia ferri ossibus asperant, idemque venatus viros pariter ac foeminas alit, passim enim comitantur, partemque praedae petunt. Nec aliud infantibus ferarum imbriumque suffugium, quam ut in aliquo ramorum nexu contegantur: huc redeunt juvenes, hoc senum receptaculum. id beatius arbitrantur, quam ingemere agris, illaborare domibus, suas alienasque fortunas spe metuque versare." Hi Fennis mores, hi mores ferme Indis Americanis.

311. Almost the same thing could have happened in what is today the CAPITAL OF THE WORLD,* when the Ausonians† had such minimal resources and "rare were the rooftops" ("which Roman power has now made equal to the heavens"), that Aeneas, entering "poor Evander's" simple house as his guest, was situated "on a throne of leaves and the skin of a Libyan bear," in accordance with the wealth of the then minor king (you might call him a Cacique), who "used to wrap the soles of his feet in Etruscan thongs and tossed back the panther's hide hanging down from his left shoulder."[132]

312. For, if you had kindly advocated an equality of goods to the humble followers of such a princelet, they certainly would have accepted it, since before they were accustomed to goat's milk, chestnuts, and enduring the hard life with a frugal diet of vegetables. Let the same be said about the ancient French and Spanish whose way of operating was unorganized and absurd: rough fare and hard labor.

313. Cornelius Tacitus, while discussing ancient Germania, seems to describe the customs not so much of the Germans as those of the Indians in America. Consider just a few examples: "they assemble," he says, "except in the case of a sudden emergency, either when the Moon is new or when it is full" (the Indians observe these same phases of the Moon with the same purpose). "When they are not waging war, they do not spend much time hunting, they spend more of their time at leisure, devoted to sleep and food" (the Indians have that idle habit also). "Men and women are equally ignorant of the secrets of writing" (on par with the Indians' incomprehension). "No one considers spending an entire day and night in drinking a disgrace" (this is not a disgrace for the Indians either). "A liquid for drinking is made of barley or other grain and fermented into something resembling wine" (just as with *Chicha*, an Indian delicacy). This is what Tacitus says in general about the people of ancient Germania.

314. However, regarding the Fenni in particular (whom he is not sure whether to connect with the Germans or Sarmatians), he says: "bewildering savagery, foul poverty: no weapons, no horses, no household gods; grass for food, hides for clothing, the ground for a bed. Their only hope lies in their arrows, which, for lack of iron, they tip with bone. And so, hunting nourishes men and likewise women; for they accompany the men everywhere and insist on their share of the kill. Their young have no other refuge from beasts and storms other than sheltering under some tangle of branches. This is where the young return and the old take refuge. They consider this more fortunate than grunting in the fields, working on houses, or alternating between hope and fear in contemplating their own and other men's fortunes." These were the customs of the Fenni, and these are very nearly the customs of the American Indians.

* i.e., Rome.

† i.e., Romans.

CCCXV. Postquam vero crevit paulatim Europaearum nationum cultus, constititque communi consensu legum vis, et auctoritas principum, horum auspiciis ductuque, e parvis initiis magnam sibi fecerunt populi privatam rem et publicam, auctique sunt divitiis et gloria domi militiaeque, divisis procerum et plebis classibus, e quibus rectus ordo, et felicitas Reipublicae pendet.

CCCXVI. Sed tamen communio rerum, et par omnium sors in Republica, est, ais, optima. Optima est? Quid si ne induci quidem generatim potuit, post Adae lapsum, in genus humanum, prout sunt hominum diversae animi, et corporis dotes, diversa ingenia, diversi rei tuendae, augendaeque labor conatusque? At id non disputo: unum illud contendo post factam vel industria vel casu rerum divisionem velle quempiam aequatam civium sortem, tantumdem esse ac velle in urbes revocare tristem et horridam publici mali confusionem confusioni illi similem, qua

> unus erat toto naturae vultus in Orbe,
> quem dixere Chaos, rudis indigestaque moles,
> nec quicquam nisi pondus iners, congestaque eodem
> non bene junctarum discordia semina rerum.[133]

At leges, inquies, modum, et mores civium temperare poterunt. Ne id quidem, obsistent quippe certatim populus patresque.

CCCXVII. Fac Petrum, cum Romam pauper, vili veste, nudis pedibus, ingressus est, genti patriciae, et Senatoribus, et Aedilibus, et militum tribunis, et Augurum collegio, et Consulibus, atque adeo Imperatori ipsi, suadere palam coepisse, ut abolitis honorum titulis, et revulsis praediorum terminis, allatisque in medium domesticis opibus, opumve pretio, omnia cum plebe communicarent, et pari conditione viverent. Quid dic tum fieret? Haec si Petrus statim proposuisset, putasset Senatus Poplusque Romanus advenisse sibi e Graecia discipulum Platonis, jussissetque male affectum verbis navigare eum in Cretam, quando pro Cretentibus, non pro Quiritibus Rempublicam ille suam adumbrarat.

315. But, after the refinement of European nations gradually took hold, both the power of the laws and the authority of princes was established through general consent. Under their auspices and guidance, from modest beginnings, the populations made great private and public spheres for themselves. They grew in wealth and glory at home and on the battlefield. The noble and common classes of people were divided, and it is upon this that right order and the happiness of the Republic depends.

316. But still, community ownership and the equal allotment of everything in the Republic is, according to you, the best. Is it the best? What if, after Adam's downfall, this could not be introduced generally into the human race, given that humans have varying physical and spiritual endowments, their talents are varied, their levels of inclination and exertion for defending and increasing their property are varied. But I do not dispute this; I only contend one thing, that after the division of property has been made, either intentionally or by chance, there will be someone who wants the lots of citizens to be equalized, and this would be just like wanting to summon back into the cities that sad and horrible confusion of public evil similar to the confusion in which:

> The world over, Nature had but one face,
> what we call Chaos: a raw and undefined mass,
> nothing but inert matter, and all in the one place were
> discordant atoms of things poorly fitted together.[133]

But the laws, you will say, will be able to temper the citizens' manner and conduct. Not at all; the people and the nobles will certainly resist.

317. Imagine that Peter, when he entered Rome, poor, shabbily dressed, barefoot, had begun to recommend publicly to the patricians, the Senators, the Aediles, the legionary officers, the College of Augers, the Consuls, and even the Emperor himself that, once the honorary titles were abolished, estates' property lines were removed, and domestic property, or the cash value of that property, was made public, they would share everything with the plebs and live on equal terms. Tell me, what would happen then? If Peter had proposed these things all of a sudden, the Senate and the Roman People would have thought that one of Plato's disciples had come to them from Greece, and they would have ordered the man, ill influenced by his teacher's words, to sail to Crete, since Plato had outlined his Republic for the Cretans and not for the Quirites.*

* i.e., Romans.

CCCXVIII. At enim idem Petrus multo difficiliora Romanis persuasit; utique, sed ut Christi discipulus, ejusque Vicarius. Et quae persuasit? Quae nimirum natura ipsa, et recta dictat ratio, quaeque hominis sublime genus a ferina turpitudine discernunt. Quod si populum patresque sancta sensim mysteria et quae supra sensus sunt, docuit, ea certis, et publicis prodigiis (quibus sana mens refragari non potest) et divina auctoritate sanxit, confirmavitque. Verum omnia esse omnibus paria e naturae praeceptis non est, neque id Deus umquam pro recta civitatum forma ab humano genere postulavit. Immo in metatione illa terrae promissae voluit divisionem fieri quam diligentissime minutissimeque *in funiculo distributionis: quam dividetis,* ait, *vobis sorte. Pluribus dabitis latiorem, et paucis angustiorem. Singulis, ut sors ceciderit, ita tribuetur haereditas. Per tribus, et familias possessio dividetur.*[134] Quin vero, facta jam agrorum divisione, familiae arte, vel pretio, plura sibi adquirerent (dummodo in eadem tribu) et ditescerent prae aliis, vetitum lege non fuit: atque adolescens ille, qui *omnia* alioquin *mandata servarat,* dicitur *habuisse multas possessiones.*[135]

CCCXIX. Hierosolymis quidem, atque Alexandriae, communio bonorum inter Christianos inducta est, sed id ipsis sponte volentibus, ut de pretio venditi agri dixit diserte Petrus ad subdolum Ananiam: *nonne manens tibi manebat, et venumdatum in tua erat potestate*? Adde huc, quod aequalitas illa ad certum dumtaxat piorum numerum pertinuit, non ad ceteros cives; ad solo videlicet Apostolorum discipulos in urbe sancta, et ad Essenos, quos ex Alexandrinis S. Marcus instituit.

CCCXX. Doctor gentium Paulus commonens Timotheum Episcopalis officii[136] haud id exigit, ut praecipiat divitibus divitiis cedere, sed eisdem recte uti, ac *bene agere, et facile tribuere*; neque heris usquam denunciat servos manumittere, ac pares sibi facere; sed *justum* illis et *aequum praestare.*[137] Per se autem ipse Onesimum, fugitivum mancipium, Philemoni cum commendatitiis litteris restituit, nec petiit, ut eum libertate donaret, sed haberet, utpote jam frugi factum, et Christianum, tamquam filium, concessa fugae venia.[138]

318. But that same Peter convinced the Romans of things far more difficult. Granted, it was as a disciple of Christ and as his Representative. And of what did he convince them? Of what nature itself and right reason truly mandate, and of what distinguishes the lofty human race from the baseness of wild animals. But if he taught the people and the nobles about the sacred mysteries and what is beyond the senses little by little, he confirmed them by means of sure and manifest wonders (which a sane mind cannot contest) and rendered them inviolable through divine authority. However, that everything is equal for everyone, is not one of nature's precepts, nor did God ever require this from humankind as the right form for states to take. What's more; in measuring out the promised land he wanted the division to be made as carefully and precisely as possible "as measured by the cord of apportionment": "'which you shall divide,' he said, 'among yourselves by lot. You shall give a larger portion to the many, and a lesser portion to the fewer. Inheritance shall be given to each exactly as his lot shall fall. The possession shall be divided by the tribes and the families.'"[134] In truth, once the division of the land had been made, there was no legal prohibition against families acquiring more for themselves either through skill or purchase (as long as it was done within the same tribe) and some became richer than others: and that adolescent who otherwise "respected all the commandments" is said to "have had many possessions."[135]

319. For instance, in Jerusalem and Alexandria the community of goods was also introduced among the Christians, but only for those who wanted it of their own free will, as Peter very clearly told the deceitful Ananias, in relation to the profit from the field he had sold: "While it remained in your possession, was it not your possession? And after it had been sold, was it not still under your control?" Add to this that this equality only pertained to a select number of pious people, not to the rest of the citizens; that is to say, only to the disciples of the Apostles in the holy city, and to the Essenes, those of the Alexandrians whom St. Mark taught.

320. Paul, Teacher of Gentiles, when he reminds Timothy of his Episcopal duties,[136] he by no means demands that Timothy order the rich to forfeit their riches, but rather that they use them properly and that "they do good and give easily"; nor does he ever order masters to free their slaves let alone make them their equals; but rather "to provide for them what is just and equal."[137] Moreover, he himself gave Onesimus, a fugitive slave, back to Philemon with a letter of recommendation, and he did not ask Philemon to grant him his freedom, but that he consider him like a son, forgiving him for having fled, since Onesimus had become an honest man and a Christian.[138]

CCCXXI. Idem olim Athenis mysteria Religionis docens illius Reipublicae patres, illud praeter alia divino instinctu dixit: *ex uno homine omne genus hominum fecisse Deum habitare super universam faciem terrae, et definisse statuta tempora, et terminos habitationis eorum.*[139] De communione vero bonorum, quam norat a pio fidelium coetu jam usu receptam Hierosolymis, nihil significavit, idque cum dissereret apud Areopagitas, quibus ea res minus accidisset nova, cum sat scirent quantopere commendata fuisset a cive suo Platone aequatio fortunarum.

CCCXXII. Et vero isthaec Platonica rerum communio, et par omnium modus, quantas, et quam graves secum difficultates affert? nusquam certe ex hujusmodi institutis ulla adhuc civitas constitit, nec, ut conjectare licet, constitura umquam est. Vel ipse aequatae sortis auctor nobis, velim, explicet, qua fiet ratione, quod jussit. Nempe in civium domibus impari saepe sunt numero domesticorum capita. Est, qui plurimos habet liberos, est qui pauciores, est qui nullum. Si bona feceris paria, minus foecundo viro suppetet sat alimentorum, foecundiori non suppetet; infoecundus autem affluet rerum omnium copia: et tamen secus fieri recta poscit ratio, patri scilicet familias, qui plures sustulit filios plura publice deberi (quod aucta prole Rempublicam auxerit) quam alii sterili, cujus domus plane vacua est.

CCCXXIII. Inter cives iterum (ut anima praestat corpori, et pedibus caput) varii sint gradus et ordines necesse est, nisi forte malis cives omnes (exempli causa) magistratus esse, omnes senatores, aut e contrario omnes fabros, omnes agricolas. Jam vero, qui altiori in loco est, ei oportet largior fiat sumptus, nec fieri poterit, si pares sint opes. Quid? quod, sicuti contra justitiam est meritis aequales inaequalibus affici praemiis, ita et contra eamdem est inaequalia promeritos praemiis aequalibus remunerari? Sine aequalibus autem inaequalibusque partibus, vel membris, consistere nequit rectus ordo, qui est (ut sapienter docuit Augustinus) *parium impariumque rerum sua cuique tribuens dispositio.*

321. One time, in Athens, while that same man* was teaching the mysteries of Religion to the nobles of that Republic, among other things he said the following with divine inspiration: "from a single man God created the entire human race to populate the whole surface of the earth. He determined fixed time periods and the boundaries of their habitation."[139] But about the community of goods, which he knew was already put into practice by a pious group of the faithful in Jerusalem, he made no mention, although he discussed it among the Areopagites,† whom the matter would have struck as less novel, since they were well aware of how highly the equalization of fortunes had been recommended by their fellow citizen, Plato.

322. As for that Platonic concept of community ownership and everyone having an equal measure of all things, how many and how serious are the difficulties it brings along with it? Certainly, nowhere up to now, has any state consisted of institutions of that sort, nor, if I may conjecture, will one ever be so constituted. I wish that the inventor of this theory of equalized lots, would himself explain to us by what procedure his orders could be carried out. Without a doubt, the family head count in the homes of citizens is not usually equal. There are those who have a great many children, those who have fewer, and those who have none. If you make it so that the goods are equal, the fertile man will hardly have enough provisions, the very fertile man will not have enough; the infertile man, on the other hand, will be flush with an abundance of all things. And yet, right reason demands that it be the other way around; naturally, the public is indebted far more to the head of the household who has raised a great many children (because he has increased the Republic through increased production of offspring), than it is indebted to the other man, who is sterile and whose house is completely empty.

323. Again, among citizens (just as the soul is superior to the body and the head to the feet), the existence of different degrees and ranks is necessary, unless perhaps you prefer all the citizens to be (for example) magistrates, all senators, or conversely all artisans or all farmers. Therefore, there ought to be a greater expenditure on whoever is in a higher position, and this could not happen if everyone's resources are equal. Why? Because just as it is an affront to justice when equally deserving people are honored with unequal rewards, in the same way, is it not an affront to the same principle when people who are not equally deserving are presented with equal rewards? Certainly, without equal and unequal segments, or members, there can be no establishment of right order, which is (as St. Augustine wisely taught) *the distribution which allocates things equal and unequal, each to its own place* [*City of God* 19.13].

* Paul.

† Members of the Areopagus, an elite judicial council made up of former Athenian officials that was among the most prestigious and powerful institutions in Athens.

CCCXXIV. Ceterum ille idem Plato summi ingenii Philosophus, qui tantum tribuit arti Musicae (ut alibi diximus) ad rectam adolescentium educationem, vel ex ipsa Musica debuit discere sine honorum, et graduum discrimine aequam in republica disciplinam esse non posse. Nam qui erit symphoniae concentus, si par canentium sit vox? quaeve harmonia ab Organo pneumatico, si aequales sint tibiae, et tubi, neque alius alio major, alius alio crassior? Apage barbarici melos modi. Ita est, e vocibus paribus, e paribus tibiis, non gratus nascetur auribus sonus, sed inconditus, et rudis strepitus, ac murmur intolerabile.

CCCXXV. At quorsum tenuia nobis, et levia exempla, cum graviora, et sanctiora suppetant? *In magna,* ait Doctor gentium, *domo non solum sunt vasa aurea et argentea, sed et lignea et fictilia.*[140] Respublica instar est domus magnae, in qua nobilibus (quorum alii aliis illustriores sunt) respondent vasa aurea et argentea ab opifice fabrefacta; secundo autem civium ordini, et plebi, quae manu laborat, similia sunt vasa lignea et fictilia.

CCCXXVI. Illud vero ejusdem Pauli quam pulchrum? *Corpus unum est, et membra habet multa . . Si dixerit pes: quoniam non sum manus, non sum de corpore: num ideo non est de corpore? Et si dixerit auris: quoniam non sum oculus, non sum de corpore: num ideo est de corpore? Si totum corpus oculus, ubi auditus? Si totum auditus, ubi, odoratus? Nunc autem posuit Deus membra unumquodque eorum in corpore sicut voluit.*[141] Hoc audiant, hoc intelligant liberiores Philosophi, providente Deo fieri, ut alii in Republica *oculus* sint, ut Rex, magistratus, nobiles: alii *auris,* qui juste praecipientis vocem audiant, et pareant, ut pleb, ut vulgus: alii *pes,* et *manus,* ut artifices, qui, dum ordo supremus bono, et felicitati publicae invigilt, vi corporis, et opere impleant, quae ad pacem, ad tranquillitatem, ad rem communem spectant.

CCCXXVII. Sed ecce tibi exsurgit contra nobiles (ut plebi palpet, eaque ad perturbandam Rempublicam utatur) nescio quis, ac malis, quae ex bonorum, et ordinum aequalitate oriri argumentamur, obviam iri posse contendit, si Magnates, si Duces, si Comites, si Equites non sint, si honoris insignia deleantur: tum enim pares inter se cives paribus erunt opibus. Quid? nobiles ne sint in Republica? Hoc vere sapientum, et Philosophorum, dixit adhuc nemo. Vel inter barbaros Americanos, quorum res communis admodum informis est, nobilitatis gradus non desunt, nec praemia iis, qui prae aliis fortiter agunt in bello, tuenturque suae tribus agros, et silvas, ac tribum ipsam promovent. Inter Guaranios autem Christianos retentus est gradus, et dignitas Caciquiorum, quorum nostro tempore erant quingenti, ut dictum jam antea est.

324. As for the rest, that same Plato, Philosopher of highest intellect, who assigned so much importance to the art of Music (as I said elsewhere) for the correct upbringing of young people, from that very music, he ought to have learned that without distinctions of degree and value, the system in the Republic cannot be fair. For, what sort of harmony will a symphony have if the singers have the same voice? And what sort of harmony would come from a pneumatic organ if the reed pipes and flue pipes were the same, and some were not longer than others, some not thicker than others? Be gone, barbarian-style melody! So it is; the sound born from equal voices and from equal instruments will not be pleasing, but rather a jumbled and unrefined din, and indeed an intolerable rumbling.

325. But why give weak and trivial examples, when more serious and more august ones are at hand? "In a grand house," the Teacher of the Gentiles says, "the tableware is not only gold and silver, but also wood and ceramic."[140] The Republic is like a grand house, in which the artisan-made gold and silver tableware corresponds to the nobles (some of whom are more illustrious than others); and the wood and ceramic tableware is similar to the second rank of citizens and the plebs, who do manual labor.

326. And Paul himself put it rather nicely: "The body is a whole and it has many members . . . if the foot should say, 'Since I am not the hand, I am not of the body,' is it therefore not of the body? And if the ear should say, 'Because I am not the eye, I am not of the body,' is it therefore not of the body? If the whole body were the eye, where would hearing occur? If the whole were hearing, where would smelling occur? But now God has set the members, every one of them, in the body according to his wishes."[141] The libertine Philosophers ought to pay attention to this and understand that through God's foresight it happens that some in the Republic are an *eye,* such as the king, the magistrate, the nobles; others such as the plebs and the masses, who hear and obey the voice of one ruling justly, are an *ear;* others are a *foot* or a *hand,* such as the artisans, who, so long as supreme order watches over the public good and happiness, with bodily strength and effort execute that which aims at peace, tranquility, and the commons.

327. But lo and behold, someone or other rises up against the nobles (to cajole the plebs and use them to throw the Republic into chaos) and contends that if the Magnates, Dukes, Counts, and Knights did not exist and if the honorific distinctions were erased, it would be possible to avoid the evils, which I argue arise from the equality of goods and classes; for then, all the citizens will be equal in relation to one another by virtue of their wealth being equal. What? Should there be no nobles in the Republic? In fact, up until this point not one of the sages or Philosophers has said this. Even among the American barbarians, whose notion of the commons is very rudimentary, degrees of nobility are not lacking, nor are rewards for those who conduct themselves bravely in war on behalf of the others, and defend their tribe's fields and forests, and promote the tribe itself. Among the Christian Guaraní the rank and official dignity of the Caciques, who numbered five hundred in my time, was retained, as has already been mentioned.

CCCXXVIII. Ne sint rursus in civitate tituli nobilitatis? Ubi tum grata beneficiorum memoria in eos, qui rebus praeclare gestis, vel providis consiliis, vel sumptis armis, vel partis victoriis, vel acceptis vulneribus, patriam defenderunt, amplificaveruntve? Ubi justitia, si concessos ob merita honores, et cum honoribus auctas juste opes, per vim auferas? Inhumanitas id ferina est, rabies est, furor est: neque odium istud in nobiles ab eo differt vecordi, et insano Ephesiorum veterum decreto: *nemo de nobis unus excellat.*[142]

CCCXXIX. Praestantia virorum illustrium, et nobilitas orta ab egregiis factis maximus omnium stimulus civi bono est de Republica benemerendi, ob collatum enim dignis honorem studet dignitate praeeuntes aemulari. Sane heroica illa de Gethaeo gigante victoria, quae toti Israelitarum populo salutem peperit, ab speratae nobilitatis laude, secundum Deum, profecta est. Audiit generosus adolescens illud: *virum, qui percusserit eum, ditabit Rex divitiis magnis et filiam suam dabit ei, et domum patris ejus faciet absque tributo in Israel.*[143] Tot illis et tam praeclaris accensus praemiis animum colligit, it, pugnat, vincit. Quod si tam laeta spes, et nobile calcar deforent, an fuisset David ad tantum certamen descensurus, nescio.

CCCXXX. Itaque si nobiles in Republica necessarii sunt (ut sunt) opes etiam iis majores sint, quam plebeis, necesse est. Et quidem apud Hispanos inter regni primores illi censentur, quos ipsi vocant RICOSOMES, id est dites homines, decet enim nobilem simul ditem esse, ita tamen, ut divitiis rite utatur, et *bene agat*, et *facile tribuat*, ut supra e D. Paulo docuimus. Atque id quidem multo valet magis in summo Reipublicae moderatore, cui nisi fiscus sit, urgere bonum publicum, ac benemerentes, et praemio dignos vel ob praestantem doctrinam, vel ob militarem gloriam, vel ob eximiam divini, humanique juris peritiam, vel ob insignem fandi, et agendi prudentiam, vel etiam ob singularem industriam et dexteritatem in aliqua arte utili, liberaliter habere (ut debet) non poterit.

CCCXXXI. Neque huic formae rem publicam administrandi officit communio illa bonorum nascentis Ecclesiae: nam ea non fuit generalis pro omnibus lex, sed sanctissimi illius coetus sublime quoddam decus, et mirus vivendi modus, et status quidam virorum perfectorum, quem Christus quondam proposuit adolescenti illi, cujus alibi meminimus: *si vis perfectus esse, vade, vende, quae habes, et da pauperibus, et habebis thesaurum in coelo, et veni sequere me.* Quod vero attinet ad cives, qui minus alta sequuntur, aequum est divisis eos rebus, et agris uti, ne jurgia, et lites sint, quemadmodum Abrahamo, et Lotho factum est, quamvis ejusdem essent stirpis, et amarent inter se.

328. Should we go back to there being no titles of nobility in the state? Where, then, will the grateful memory of benefactions reside for those who defended the fatherland or even amplified it through heroic deeds, prescient counsel, taking up arms, bringing about victories, and suffering wounds? Where will the justice be, if you forcibly take away honors awarded for merit and the wealth justly amassed alongside those honors? This is inhumanity fit for animals! It is madness! An outrage! This hatred of yours for the nobles is no different from that crazy and absurd decree of the ancient Ephesians: *let no one among us, not even one, stand out.*[142]

329. For the good citizen, the preeminence and nobility of illustrious men, born from their extraordinary deeds, is the greatest of all inducements to living in a way that is worthy of the Republic. To be sure, it is with an eye to the honor conferred on the worthy that he is eager to emulate those who are leading the way in terms of their rank. Indeed, that heroic victory over the giant from Gath, which secured the safety of the entire Israelite population, was brought about, according to God's will, by the esteem for renown, which David hoped to win. The noble-minded teen heard that "the king will enrich the man who slays [Goliath] with great riches, give him his daughter, and make his father's house free from taxation in Israel."[143] Inspired by so many outstanding rewards, he gathered his courage, he went, he fought, he won. But absent such cheerful aspiration and such noble incitement, I do not know whether David would have engaged in so great a contest.

330. Thus, if nobles are necessary in a Republic (as they are), they must necessarily have greater wealth than the plebs as well. In fact, among the Spanish the men whom they call *RICOS OMES*, that is "rich men," are counted among the leading men of the kingdom, for a nobleman ought to likewise be rich, provided that he uses his wealth properly, he both "does good" and "gives easily," as we explained above with reference to St. Paul. And this applies all the more to the highest ranking manager of the Republic, who, were it not for the privy purse, could not encourage the public good; more to the point he could not (as he ought) be generous to the worthy and those deserving of rewards, be it for their outstanding learning, their military glory, their utmost expertise in divine and human law, be it for their remarkable eloquence, their prudent conduct, or even their unique diligence and aptitude for another of the useful arts.

331. The nascent Church's community of goods is not at odds with this way of administering the Republic: for it was not a general law for everyone, but a sort of lofty distinction for that most holy community—a marvelous way of life and indeed a state of righteous men, which Christ on a certain occasion proposed to that young man, whom I have mentioned elsewhere: "if you want to be righteous, go, sell everything you have and give it to the poor; you will have a treasure in heaven—come, follow me." But as it pertains to citizens, who pursue less lofty goals, it is fair that they make use of property and lands that have been divided up, so that there are no altercations or disputes, as happened with Abraham and Lot, although they belonged to the same lineage and loved each other.

CCCXXXII. Haud tamen, quod aequalia nunc omnibus bona non sint, propterea cessatum est a provida egentium cura; successere enim primaevae rerum communioni certa, et firma vel in necessitatem, vel in utilitatem privatorum civium praesidia. Primum horum est Antistitum, et Clericorum opes, ac reditus, qui sunt pauperum patrimonia. Atque is est veluti publicus Ecclesiae fiscus. Quo autem singulis quibusque malis per species subveniretur, instituta ubique locorum sunt nosocomia, orphanotrophia, Xenodochia, periclitantium puellarum, maleque nuptarum asyla, et infantium, quos vel a pudore, vel a paupertate, parum piae matres abjiciunt, receptacula, et ne amentium quidem et furiosorum omissa est benigna custodia, admisto metu, ne noceant.

CCCXXXIII. Ad haec, sunt sacri virorum coetus, qui pueros gratis elementa litterarum, et mysteria Religionis docent, sunt pia Parthenia, quae eiisdem rebus puellas erudiunt magno Reipublicae bono. Sunt, praeter communes Academias, Religiosi homines, qui grammaticam, qui Philosophiam, qui Theologiam, qui officia virtutum sine pretio tradunt. Sunt, qui domi quosvis excipiunt aegros, ac lecto, et cibo, et medicinis fovent. Et quoniam recentes a morbo multa circumstant salutis discrimina, sunt etiam, qui convalescentes privatim curant. (Ordo is Bethleemitarum nomine in America ortum habuit.)

CCCXXXIV. Sunt, qui insanabili affectos lue, quibus possunt commodis, recreant, et tristi levant sorte. Sunt, qui temere vagantes per urbem, et sordidatos orphanos colligunt, et tecto, et veste donant, et victu alunt, et rerum coelestium cognitione, et honestis moribus imbuunt. Sunt, qui captivos et a gravi jugo, et a periculo abjurandae fidei, magna mercede redimunt. Sunt, qui praeternavigantes a piratarum insidiis paratoque maleficio, armata classe defendunt. Sunt, qui moribundis, etiam peste aflatis, extrema auxilia deferunt, ad id ipsum nuncupato sacramento devoti. Sunt, qui ruricolas, quibus minor audiendi verbi divini, disciplinaeque animi percipiendae, occasio est, sponte sua adeunt, et Cathechisino instituunt, et rite jam expiatos *exhortantur, ne in vacuum gratiam Dei recipiant.*[144]

332. However, although goods are not equal for everyone today, this hardly means that there is a deficiency in forward-thinking care for those in need; for the primitive concept of community ownership was succeeded by sure and constant assistance for private citizens whether relating to necessity or utility. The first of these is the wealth and, what's more, the revenue of the Bishop and the Clergy, which are the patrimony of the poor. Moreover, it is as if the Church's purse were public. And so that by this means specialized relief would be available for each and every kind of evil, hospitals have been established everywhere, as have orphanages, indigent hostels, places of refuge for girls in danger and those badly married, and shelters for infants, whom insufficiently pious mothers have abandoned either out of shame or poverty; not even the benign confinement of the insane and deranged has been forgotten, despite the fear that they might cause harm.

333. In addition to these, there are holy associations of men who instruct children for free in literacy and the mysteries of Religion; there are also pious associations of Virgins, who educate the girls in the same subjects for the greater good of the Republic. In addition to the regular Academies, there are Religious people who teach grammar, Philosophy, Theology, and the duties of virtue, all without charge. There are those who take on sick people of all kinds in their homes and provide them with a bed, food, and medicine. And since the recently recovered straddle the border between sickness and health, there are also those who privately care for the convalescent. (The Order of Bethlehemite Brothers had its origin in America.)

334. There are those who invigorate people afflicted with incurable diseases by means of whatever comforts they can offer, lifting them up from their sad lot in life. There are those who round up people aimlessly wandering the city and the shabbily clad orphans and provide them with clothes and a roof, nourish them, and imbue them with an awareness of heavenly matters and honest habits. There are those who at great cost release people who are captives not only from the burdensome yoke but also from the danger of repudiating their faith. There are those who with an armed fleet defend sailors from the ambushes and calculated criminality of pirates. There are those who give the ultimate assistance to the dying, even to those in the throes of plague, committed to this task by a sacred oath. There are those who voluntarily approach the people of the countryside, who have the least opportunity to hear the divine word and receive a spiritual education, and they instruct them in the Catechism and, the ones duly atoned, "they urge them not to receive the grace of God in vain."[144]

CCCXXXV. At infinitus sim, si cuncta persequar quae vel pro bono fidelium, vel etiam infidelium (quod amplius est) promovendo, aut pro avertendis publicis privatisque malis, inventa sunt pia subsidia, ut communionem rerum quodammodo suppleant, et quidem thesaurus inexhaustus est pro miseris divini Magistri denuntiatio illa, et oraculum: *Amen dico vobis, quamdiu fecistis uni ex his fratribus meis minimis, mihi fecistis.*[145] Hinc felicitas pauperum: hinc etiam divitum infelicitas, si pauperibus necessaria negent, audient, enim olim: *quamdiu non fecistis uni de minoribus his, nec mihi fecistis.*[146]

CCCXXXVI. I, licet, totoque vagatus terrarum orbe circumspice, num alicubi (exceptis provinciis Christianis) quicquam hujusmodi institutorum sit. Nusquam vestigia tantae in commune beneficentiae caritatisque reperies. Joannes Petrus Maffejus, magnificus ceteroqui Sinarum laudator, ad extremum non dubitat dicere: *totius humanitatis multis in rebus videntur expertes.*[147] Atque hi sunt illi, quos Philophi liberiores, ut Christi religionem deprimant, ad insaniam usque commendant. De Japoniis autem (hi secundum Sinas politica re ad orientem Solem praecellunt) idem historiarum Indicarum scriptor post recensita eorum bona, non minora addit mala: "praegnantes foeminae, ait, partum haud raro medicamentis abigunt, idque Bonziis auctoribus ac magistris (*adeo boni sunt religionis illius antistites*) vel etiam editos in lucem infantes, alendi taedio inopiave, crudeliter injecto praefocant pede. Egentibus, aegrotis aut peregrinis publica et gratuita diversoria nulla. Sub dio pernoctant, miseramque trahentes animam deserti ab hominibus vel ipsa die sanantur, vel extincti morbo, abjiciuntur in sterquilinium. Eo majore cum approbatione Japonii Christianam caritatem erga destitutos, et calamitosos, itemque sepulturae ac funerum instituta mirantur."[148] Haec ille. Quae omnia, ut contraria propius et invicem composita magis eminent, Religionis, quam nos docuit Deus Homo, sanctitatem, et excellentiam quam maxime praedicant.

335. But I would go on forever, if I were to set forth the entirety of the pious subsidies for promoting the good among the faithful and even among the unfaithful (who are the majority), or for averting public and private evils—subsidies devised to fill in, in a way, for community ownership. Indeed, the divine Teacher's declaration and oracular pronouncement is an inexhaustible treasure: "I say 'Amen' to you, inasmuch as you have done it to the least of my brethren, you have done it to me."[145] Hence the happiness of the poor, and hence too the unhappiness of the rich, if basic necessities are denied to the poor, they will then hear: "inasmuch as you did it not to one of those less fortunate, you did it not to me."[146]

336. Go ahead and scour the whole Earth to see whether there is any other place (aside from the Christian provinces) that has any institutions like these. Nowhere will you find traces of such beneficence and charity for all. Giovanni Pietro Maffei, otherwise a magnificent panegyrist of the Chinese, does not hesitate to state in the end: "in many things they seem to lack all humanity."[147] And these are the ones whom the libertine Philosophers laud, to the point of absurdity, in order to belittle the religion of Christ. About the Japanese (the ones out toward the rising sun who, according to the Chinese, excel in politics) the same author of the *Histories of the Indies*, after enumerating their good qualities, adds their not insignificant bad ones: "the pregnant women," he says, "not infrequently end their pregnancy using medicine, with *Bozu** for authorities and instructors in this matter (*that's how good the priests of that religion are*), alternately, either because of poverty or an aversion to raising them, they even cruelly suffocate newborn infants by stomping on them. There is no free, public lodging for the needy, the sick, or the itinerant. They spend the night in the open air; drawing in each miserable breath, abandoned by fellow human beings, they either heal due to the passing of time or they are destroyed by their illness and cast onto the dung pile. That is why the Japanese marvel approvingly at Christian charity toward the destitute and those down on their luck; that, and they marvel at the burial and funeral traditions."[148] This is what Maffei says. All these things, since the differences are more prominent when things are arranged side by side, proclaim as clearly as possible the moral purity and excellence of Religion, which God as Man has taught us.

* A Buddhist priest.

CCCXXXVII. Redeo jam ad comunionem pristinam bonorum. Eam certos in coetus hominum foeminarumque inducere haud difficile est, sequunturque etiamnum primaevos illos christianos viri quamplurimi Religiosi, Sacrataeque Virgines, quibus omnia communia sunt: victusque id genus, et paris sortis aequatio, si rite servetur, magnarum virtutum fons et origo sunt. Sed vivendi hunc modum ad omnes civium ordines extendi optandum quidem esset, sperandum non est. Fac (rei, quam supra egimus, exemplo utimur) ut delicatae matronae pro publico bono neant (ut Guaraniae nebant Indae) quae vel pro paranda liberis veste edignantur fusum tractare. Fac, nobiles communem agrum una cum privato colant (ut Guaranii viri colebant) qui vix sua praedia revisunt, ne tantisper domestico careant otio, urbanisque deliciis.

CCCXXXVIII. Quae cum ita sint, siquis liberiorum Philosophorum contenderet in Europam transferre Guaranicam administrationem, turpiter erraret, pessimeque (ut nunc sunt res) de Republica mereretur, turbato rerum omnium ordine, confusisque civium classibus, et officiis. Vel sola rogatio, et proposita quondam lex de dividundis, regundisque aliter agrorum finibus, quantum in discrimen (nisi obstitisset tribuni plebis conatui Marcus Tullius Consul)[149] Romanam Rempublicam adduxerat? At vero nihil mali, et boni plurimum ortum est inter optimos neophytos ex institutione illa approbata a Rege Catholico: neque ullis ibi litibus, querelisque, et discordiae locus erat: ac praeterea cavebatur, ut e bonis communibus, quod e proprio agro forte alicui deerat, suppleretur.

CCCXXXIX. Illud huc addo, ne inter ipsos quidem Guaranicos eam boni publici oeconomiam retineri diutius posse, nisi XXX. illa oppida mutuo sustentent, et fulciant se se. Etenim ad res multas alii aliis indigent, ideoque reciproca caritate subveniant sibi alternis necesse est. Urbs Lais, ejusque cives misere olim perierunt. Causam quaeris? eam reddit divinus auctor: *Sexcenti,* inquit, *viri . . . percusserunt eos in ore gladii urbemque incendio tradiderunt, nullo penitus ferente praesidium, eo quod procul habitarent a Sidone, et cum nullo hominum haberent quidquam Societatis, ac negotii.*[150]

337. But I return now to the pristine community of goods. Introducing it into particular groups of men and women is not difficult; even now, a great many Religious men and Consecrated Virgins, among whom everything is shared, follow those early Christians: this type of life and the equalization of lots, if duly observed, are the source and origin of great virtues. But although it would be desirable for this way of life to be extended to all classes of people, it is beyond hope. Imagine (I use as an example what I suggested above) delicate matrons, who would not deign to work the spindle even to prepare clothes for their children—imagine them weaving for the good of the community (as the Guaraní women would do). Imagine the nobles, who scarcely visit their own estates so as not to miss out on the slightest bit of domestic leisure and urban delight—imagine them cultivating a communal field beside a man with no office or title (as the Guaraní men would do).

338. Given that this is how things are, if any of the libertine Philosophers tried to transfer the Guaraní system of government to Europe, he would make a horrible mistake and (as is now the case) would deserve the Republic least of all because the order of everything would be disturbed and the social classes and their civic duties would be thrown into confusion. A single legislative proposal, along with the law it set forth about dividing up and redrawing the boundaries of lands, had thrust the Roman Republic into such crisis (or would have if Cicero, as Consul, had not opposed the attempt of the Tribune of the Plebs)?[149] But certainly, among the best neophytes, nothing bad and actually quite a lot of good came out of that arrangement, which the Catholic King approved. There was no occasion for disputes, complaints, or discord there. As for the rest, care was taken that whatever someone might happen to lack from their own field would be provided from the communal goods.

339. To this point I will add that this economy of public goods is not sustainable for very long even among the Guaraní themselves, except for the fact that those thirty towns sustained and supported each other. For in many matters, they need each other, and therefore it is necessary for them to assist one another by means of reciprocated charity. There was a city called Laish, whose citizens once died horribly. Do you want to know the cause? The divine author explains it: "Six hundred men," he says, "ran them through with sharp swords and burnt down their city, with absolutely no one to bring them aid, because they dwelt far from Sidon, and had no fellowship or business with a single person there."[150]

CCCXL. Atque id quidem agmen illis fatale civibus revocat mihi in memoriam Chacenses barbaros, qui trajecto saepe amni Paraguayo in magnas redegerunt angustias oppida Guaraniorum quattuor S. Mariae de Fide, S. Jacobi, S. Rosae Limanae, et S. Ignatii Guazu. In hoc ego quondam eram, cum Abiponum, seu Guaicuruorum (utros nescio) praedatorum cuneus ita proxime ad oppidum accessit, ut oppidani raptim arma ceperint, et aditus omnes occuparint. Tristissimus ille mihi dies fuit: procella tamen ferae gentis daeseviit tum in oppidum S. Jacobi. Ob hos igitur grassatores, causasque alias, quas explicare hic opus non est, nisi Guaranii, qui longe ab urbibus Hispanis positi sunt, inter se ament, et benigne foveant, actum de eis erit: quod malum Deus Optimus Maximus avertat.

FINIS COMMENTARII

CCCXLI. De Europae provinciis (quoniam de iis mihi sermo est) id unum dixerim, siqua gravis mutatio administrationis pristinae in illas induceretur, novi ordinis modum, diversumque rerum, et legum systema, felicitati populorum, et civili societati ruinam ac cladem allaturum fore; haud secus, quam annosae virentisque arboris si vivas radices reseces. Quapropter parendum nobis est divino illi oraculo: *ne transgrediaris terminos antiquos, quos posuerunt patres tui.*[151] Quippe quae aequa, et prudens a majoribus nostris instituta fuit forma Reipublicae, longo corroborata usu, servanda sancte est, neque susque deque vertenda, *beatior* enim *erit*, si sic permanserit, ut alia de re agens monet nos Doctor gentium.[152]

CCCXLII. Huc pertinet viri perquam eruditi solida dissertatio, cui titulum fecit *Lasciamo star le cose come stanno*, id est: Eunto res, ut eunt. Discernit ille quidem de disciplina Ecclesiastica, sed argumento nostro res tota congruit maxime, cum vere Philosophiae, et recepti dudum moris prudentum consensu, eadem utrobique sit ratio. Sapienter D. Thomas, "habet, ait, ipsa legis mutatio, quantum in se est, detrimentum quoddam communis salutis, quia ad observantiam legum plurimum valet consuetudo, in tantum quod ea, quae contra consuetudinem fiunt, etiamsi leviora, de se graviora videantur. Unde quando mutatur lex, diminuitur vis constrictiva legis, in quantum tollitur consuetudo: et ideo nunquam debet mutari lex humana, nisi ex aliqua parte tantum recompensetur communi saluti, quantum ex ista parte derogatur . . . Unde dicitur a Jurisperitis, quod in rebus novis constituendis evidens debet esse utilitas, ut recte recedatur ab eo jure, quod diu aequum visum est."[153]

340. And indeed, this assault, which was fatal for those citizens, reminds me of the barbarians of the Chaco, who, frequently crossing over the river Paraguay, caused great anguish for four Guaraní towns, Santa Maria de Fe, Santiago, Santa Rosa de Lima, and San Ignacio Guazú. I was in the last of these once when a strike force of Abipones or Guaicuruan looters (I am not sure which) approached the town, causing the townsfolk to immediately take up arms and block all the entrances. That was the saddest day I ever experienced; the whirlwind caused by these wild people then ravaged the town of Santiago. Because of these roving pillagers, as well as other reasons not necessary to explain here, if the Guaraní, who are situated far away from Spanish cities, do not love and generously support each other, it will be their downfall. May god almighty stave off that evil.

End of the Treatise

341. Regarding European nations (since my discourse is about them) I would like to say only one thing: if any serious change to the original system of government were introduced in these nations, a measure of reorganization or a different system of laws and of handling property, it would usher in calamity and ruin for the happiness of the populace and for civil society—no different than if you were to cut off the living roots of a long-established, flourishing tree. Wherefore we must comply with this divine prophecy: "Thou shall not pass beyond the ancient bounds, which thy forefathers have set."[151] Since the form of Republic that is fair and wise had been established by our ancestors and ratified through its long use, it ought to be scrupulously preserved and not turned upside down, for "it will be more blessed" if it remains thus, as the Teacher of the Gentiles cautions, though in connection with another matter.[152]

342. Pertinent here is the thorough dissertation of an exceedingly learned man [Zaccaria], entitled, *Lasciamo star le cose come stanno*, that is: "Let things be as they are." He is of course examining Church teachings, but the whole of what he says fits perfectly with my argument, because, in fact, Philosophy and the customs previously authorized by the consensus of judicious men both have one and the same rationale. St. Thomas wisely says: "The change of law in and of itself is in a certain way detrimental to community well-being: because custom is especially robust when it comes to the observance of laws, to such an extent that things done contrary to custom, even trivial matters, are seen as rather serious. Consequently, when a law is changed, the law's binding power is diminished, to the extent that the custom is destroyed. And for this reason, human law should never be changed unless the degree of damage inflicted on community well-being from one aspect of the change is proportionately compensated for in some other aspect . . . Wherefore the Jurists say that in establishing new laws, their utility ought to be evident, so that there is an orderly retreat from the law which has long been seen as fair."[153]

CCCXLIII. Haec vera sunt: videant proin ii, qui nihil veterum institutorum salvum, et integrum volunt, an isto novarum rerum studio *evidentem* sequantur *utilitatem*. Evidentem utilitatem? Immo vero pernicies evidens boni publici rectique ordinis (ut viri cordati clamant) oritura est, atque oriri jam pridem coepit. Gallicus conventus e liberiorum placitis Philosophorum conatus est nova statuta, formamque aliam in regnum inducere. Quid, quaeso, boni accidit? quae inde consecuta est populi felicitas? Res toti nota Europae est. Quantum o mali! quanta fortunarum eversio! quanta perturbatio familiarum! quantum sanguinis innocentis effusum! quae rixae! qui facinosorum hominum furor! quot latrocinia! quot ausa sacrilega! quam inverecunda impietas! quam detestabilis morum licentia! quam vecors juris omnis aequique abrogatio! quam moesta publicae privataeque securitatis conditio! Agis modo domi tuae cum tuis nulli mortalium noxius, et momento post, ni pareas prava jubentium dictis, indicta causa, in patibulum ageris, et pendes tumultuantis et armatae plebis victima. Truncatum dein caput, et laniata membra ferali spectaculo per forum viasque raptantur. At cur nomina obscura queror! Regi ipsi, regiaeque stirpi quietis esse non licet: coguntur solio exscendere, coguntur domo fugere, coguntur latere, coguntur trepidare, coguntur convicia insani vulgi audire, coguntur... sed quis sat explicet quae coacti sunt pati, et patiuntur etiam num?

CCCXLIV. Veniet profecto tempus, veniet, cum tantae vel insaniae, vel crudelitatis, vel perfidiae, seros immanium parentum avorumque nepotes pudebit. Sed haec cultae alioquin nationis non tam peccata sunt, quam efferi partus insanientis philosophiae. O Philosophi! o exleges Philosophi! Illud possum vere dicere, et contenta voce, quam omnes intelligant, profiteri, ne inter quidem barbaros Paraguaycos, Tobas, Guaycuruos, Abipones, Mbayas, aliosque, hujusmodi inhumanitatis exempla videri. Saeviunt, sed in hostes; trucidant, sed in bello; praedas abigunt, sed solo ab extero. Inter se vero ejusdem tribus, ejusdemque contubernii familiae, amant, et sibi parcunt, et tranquillius vivunt, quam Europaei quidam populi philosophicae libidini, et libertati, tamquam impatiens freni equus, penitus mancipati. O tempora! O mores! Sed finis sit.

343. These things are true: So, let those who want none of our ancient institutions to remain safe and intact see whether in their zeal for revolution they are pursuing "evident utility." Evident utility? Or is it peril for the public good and right order that is evident (as men of understanding proclaim) and about to arise; in fact, this is already starting to happen. As a result of the libertine Philosophers' maxims, the French Assembly has tried to introduce new statutes and a different form of government into their kingdom. What good, I ask, comes of this? What happiness for the people follows from it? The result is known through the whole of Europe. O how much evil! What a great reversal of fortunes! What a great disruption of families! What a lot of innocent blood spilt! What quarrels! What a frenzy of villains! How many robberies! How many reckless acts of sacrilege! How shameless the impiety! How abominable the libertinage! How insane the abrogation of every fair law! How deplorable the condition of both public and private safety! One minute you are in your own home with your family not bothering a living soul, and the next minute, unless you obey the perverse commands of those giving orders, without a hearing, you are led to the gallows, and hanged, the victim of armed and rebellious plebs. Then your severed head and mangled limbs are dragged off through the roads and the town square in a beastly spectacle. But why am I lamenting those whose names are obscure! The king himself and his royal progeny are not free to be at peace; they are being forced to get up from the throne, forced to flee their home, forced to hide, forced to tremble in fear, forced to listen to the insults of the insane masses, forced . . . but who could properly explain what they have been compelled to endure, and what they are enduring even now?*

344. There will come a time, it will surely come, when the grandchildren of monstrous parents and grandparents will belatedly feel ashamed of such insanity, cruelty, and perfidy. But these are not so much the sins of an otherwise refined nation, as they are the savage offspring of a philosophy gone mad. O Philosophers! O lawless Philosophers! I can truly say and profess in a vehement voice, for all to understand, that not even among the barbarians of Paraguay, the Tobas, Guaicurú, Abipones, Mbayás, and others, have examples of this sort of inhumanity been seen. They become violent, but against their enemies; they kill, but in war; they pillage, but only abroad. Among themselves, however, those of the same tribe, those of the same family, living under the same roof, love and forgive each other; they live more peacefully than certain peoples of Europe who are thoroughly enslaved to philosophical lust and libertinage, just like a horse chafing at the bit. O the times! O the customs. Let this be the end.†

* Indeed, the French king, Louis XVI, had already been executed on January 21, 1793, just a few months before the publication of this book.

† The combination here of widely quoted exclamations from Ciceronian speeches serves to dramatize the author's dismay at the present state of affairs.

NOTES

1 Plato bina scripsit opera de gubernandi modo, alterum cui titulus est RESPUBLICA, sive de JUSTO, et constat X. libris, alterum, quod de LEGIBUS inscribitur, et habet libros XII. Ex utroque nos opere sensa Platonis sparsum sequimur, non verba, nec ordinem.

2 Haec ratio digna Philosopho est: nam societas urbana poscit, ut cives inter se ament, non amabunt autem nisi inter se noscant, noscendi vero opportuna occasio est cum eunt in templum, aut ab eo abeunt, et locus ipse communione sacri cultus animos conjungit, eosque movet ad praestandam opem iis, qui egent, ut nascente Ecclesia in Agapis fiebat. At, dicet aliquis, agere etiam inter se cives, et nosse possunt in theatro, in ludis publicis in foro. Verum id: sed theatrum Zelotypiae, et impuro amori: ludi publici rixis, et contentioni: forum litibus et dolis expositum magnopere est: adde ortam inde morum corruptionem; qua excitantur odia, contracteque amicitiae dissolvuntur: religiosa autem templi frequentia vitiis istis aditum obstruit.

3 Lycurgus Lacaedemoniorum, et Cretensium legislator interdixit civibus usu auri, et argenti.

4 Haec XXX. oppida amplo nimis vocabulo urbes vocat Rev. adm. S. P. Magister F. Thomas Maria Mamacchi in opere eruditissimo *Originum et antiquitatum Christianarum* tem. II. lib. II. ubi Guaraniorum mores laudat. Sed *oppida* illa, non urbes erant, et oppida perpetuo adpellarunt omnes sacri Antistites, Praetoresque regii, qui eadem saepe lustrarunt.

5 Elegantia, et artificium Guaranicae linguae robur addit opinioni eorum, (inter quos censendus est Plato in Cratylo) qui dicunt linguas non hominum inventa esse, sed donum singulare hominibus datum a Deo. Qua enim ratione barbari per se ipsi progressi fuissent a nudo litterarum sono ad syllabas, a syllabis autem ad vocabula, a vocabulis vero ad discrimina nominum, et pronominum et ad utrorumque affectiones, ut aliud proprium sit aliud appellativum, aliud fixum, aliud mobile aliud, comparans, aliud superlatum? Etc. quo item, modo verborum definissent vim, primum, substantivi, quod omnia pervadit, deinde activi, et passivi, et neutrius, post, impersonalis, et meditativi, et frequentativi, horum autem omnium varios modos, et diversa tempora; atque infinita alia, sine quibus perfecta lingua stare non potest?

Dominicus Bandiera, cultor olim Chiquitorum Indorum, quibus plena artificii lingua est, ac certa quadam sui parte locupletior cumulatiorque, quam quae Gracis, et Latinis fuit, re hac veluti, stupefactus scripsit fieri id omnino non posse, nisi initium a Deo repetatur, ut in Turri babelica: idem ipse de reliquis Indorum linguis censet. Et vero si inter silvestres homines perfecta typographia ars reperta fuisset, id non sine miraculo factum diceremus; cur igitur non idem dicimus de linguis? Stat pro hac sententia cum Claudio Duret, et aliis Laureutius Hervas *Idea Universi* etc. tom. XXI. art. I. IV. V. ubi erudite admodum agit de linguis Americanis.

6 Recte id; crescit enim populus vel propter amoenitatem loci, et salubritatem, vel propter foecunditatem gentis, vel propter civium concordiam, vel propter diuturnam ab externis bellis cessationem.

NOTES

1 Plato wrote two works about governance, one carries the title either of *Republic* or *On the Just* and consists of ten books, the other, which he wrote on *Laws*, has twelve books. In each work I shall follow Plato's notions scattered throughout, not his words or his order.

2 This is reasoning worthy of a Philosopher: for an urban society asks that its citizens like one another, but they will not like one another unless they get to know one another; it is indeed a fine opportunity for them to get acquainted when they are coming and going from the temple, and in communion of the sacred cult the place itself joins souls and moves them to offer help to those in need as it was at the Agape Feast in the early church. But someone will say, citizens can also interact and get to know one another in the theater, at the public spectacles in the forum. This is true: but the theater is especially open to jealousy and impure love; the public spectacles to quarreling and strife; the forum to lawsuits and fraud: add to this the corruption of customs arising from there; in which enmities arise and, on a contracted scale, friendships are dissolved; religious assembly at a temple, however, impedes the development of these very vices.

3 Lycurgus, the Lawgiver of the Spartans and Cretans, forbade citizens from using gold and silver.

4 The Very Reverend Master of the Sacred Palace, Brother Tommaso Maria Mamachi, refers to these thirty towns by the overly grand term "cities" in his most learned work *Christian Origins and Antiquities* (Vol. 2, Bk. 2) where he praises the habits of the Guaraní. But these "towns" were not "cities," and all the Bishops and Royal Governors, who often examined them, always declared them to be "towns."

5 The elegance and refinement of the Guaraní language adds strength to the belief of those (among whom Plato in the *Cratylus* must be counted) who say that languages are not the inventions of men but rather a unique gift given to men by God. For, by what faculty could people with no language, on their own, have passed from the bare sound of letters to syllables, let alone from syllables to words, and then from words to distinctions between nouns and pronouns and the relationships between the two, namely that one is proper, and another is common, one is fixed and another variable, one is comparative and another superlative, etc.? Likewise, how could they have determined the force of verbs, first of the substantive, which pervades all things, then of the active, and the passive, and the middle, then the impersonal, and meditative, and frequentative, and the various modes and diverse tenses of all these, and infinite other details without which a language cannot be complete?

A former cultivator of the Chiquitano Indians, who have a language that is full of refinement and to some extent richer and more complete than what the Greeks and Latins had, Domenico Vandiera, as if frightened by this fact, wrote that it was not at all possible unless the language's origins were derived from God, as in the tower of Babel; and he is of the same opinion about the other languages of the Indians. And certainly, if the art of typography had been found completely developed among men living in the jungle, we would say that this had not been accomplished without a miracle. Why then do we not say the same about languages? Along with Claude Duret and others, Lorenzo Hervás supports this sentiment in *Idea of the Universe* (volume XXI, article I, IV and V) where he deals with American languages quite eruditely.

6 He is right about this. For the population grows due to the pleasantness and wholesomeness of the site, the fecundity of the race, the harmony of the citizens, or long-term abstention from external wars.

7 Quantum haec lues ibi saviat, hinc argue. An. MDCCXXXII in triginta oppidis Guaranicis erant e Parocborum tabulis capita hominum 144252. Biennio post extincti sunt pustulis minoribus (*Sarampion* vocant Hispani) 18773. Anno autem MDCCXXXVII. e pustulis majoribus (*Variolis*) interierunt 30000. praeter alios aliis morbis sublatos. Atqui pestilentia haec brevi illac temporum intervallo recrudescit. Hinc opida alias frequentia, alias infrequentia sunt, Quamquam paucitatis oppidi S. Laurentii, quod omnium minimum diximus, alia aliunde fuit causa, tumultus nimirum ille, quo septem pagi Cisuruguayci (e quibus unus Laurentianus est) iussa migrationi e foedare Lusitano restiterunt: tum enim multi et occisi, et dissipati sunt. De isto foedere, et de jure, quo civibus (cum id exigit bonum publicum) abire e sede pristina in novam sedem praecipi possit, agit graviter Cyriacus Morelli, Socius olim Paraguaycus *De Rudimentis juris Naturae, et Gentium* lib. II. disp. VIII., §11.

8 De Nat. Deor. lib. II.

9 IV. Regg. e IV. V. 10.

10 Videsis Bened. XIV. opus de Festis in festo Corporis Christi, atque ejus epistolam ad Episcopos de templi cultu etc. utrobique Ecclesiam Guaraniorum laudat, et probat.

11 Litteras has Philippi V. Regis scriptas V. Kal. Januar. an. MDCCXLIV. reddit Petrus Francis. Xav. Charlevoixius Gallus in documentis, qua adjecit historiae Paraguaycae.

12 Vide *Dicionarium Antiphilosophicum* P. Nonnot tom. III. Verb. *Passions.* Nempe Philosophi liberiores, Atheique laudant magnopere passiones animi, amoremque sui. Cur id? quia cum mysteria Religionis negent, nolintque corruptam esse a primaeva labe hominum naturam, ab hac nihil pravi irritamenti oriri contendunt, excluduntque (quod consequens est) divini necessitatem praesidii et gratiae. Sed bellua sit oportet qui belluinos sibi inesse appetitus non norit, nec sentiat, se se ab nimio sui amore, et impatientibus freni affectionibus in malum, et vitia trahi, a quibus nemo liber evadit, nisi ope divina imbecillis arbitrii viribus addita. Seneca Philosophus passim affectiones animi, tamquam omnis mali fontem, frenandas predicat. Vide epist. CXVI.

13 *Recherches philosophiques sur les Americains* tom. I. pag. 81.

14 *Histor. de la India Occidental.* Decad, I. Cap. 19.

15 Platonica haec aequalitas bonorum, rerumque communio, nequedum stetit ulla in Republica, neque usquam gentium stabit. Quippe hominum ingenia varia sunt, et vires corporis, animique dotes inaequales; quo fit, ut qui sollicitior sit, prudentiorque in re quaerenda, alio inerti, et stolido, abundet magis. Atque hinc etiam orta sunt discrimina divitum pauperumque; et dominorum servorumque. Quod si nascente Ecclesia in piorum coetu communio ejusmodi, et aequalitas perfecta fuit id factum est singulari ope Spiritus Sancti, qui doctrinam Christi tam eximio exemplo illustrare voluit, ut ad eam alios aliosque alliceret, et vero fideles illos *magnificabat populus, et magis augebatur credentium in Domino multitudo virorum, ac mulierum* (Act. AA. c. V. vv. 13. et 14.) Quin et ipse Hebraeorum disertissimus Philo attonitus re mira, et sancto vivendi genere plebis Alexandrinae Marco praeceptore, librum de communione illa bonorum scripsit.

7 Deduce from the following how much this plague raged there. In 1732, according to the parish records, there were 144,252 individuals in the thirty Guaraní towns. Two years later 18,773 were extinguished due to smaller pustules (which the Spanish call "Sarampión" [measles]). In 1737, however, 30,000 were lost due to larger pustules ("Variolis" [smallpox]), besides those taken down by other diseases. So it is that this plague breaks out again there after brief intervals of time. Hence, at one time towns are well-populated and at others less so. However, the cause of the smallness of the town of San Lorenzo, which we said was smallest of all, was something else entirely; without a doubt it was that uprising, in which the seven districts on the eastern border of Uruguay (of which one is that of San Lorenzo) resisted the migration ordered by a Portuguese treaty; on that occasion many were either killed or dispersed. About this treaty and about the law whereby it is possible for citizens to be ordered (when the public good demands it) to leave their original site to go to a new site, Domingo Muriel, a former Paraguayan Companion, treats authoritatively in *Elements of Natural Law and the Law of Nations* 2.7.2.

8 *On the Nature of the Gods* 2 [1.4].

9 *4 Kings* 4:5 [*2 Kings* 4:10].

10 See Benedict XIV's work *On Holy Days* on the feast of Corpus Christi, and his letter to the Bishops on the church's ritual, etc.; in both places he praises and approves of the Guaraní Church.

11 The Frenchman Pierre François Xavier de Charlevoix included this letter from King Felipe V written 5 January 1744 in the documents he added to his *History of Paraguay*.

12 Look under "passions" in volume three of the *Anti-philosophical Dictionary* [*corr. Philosophical Dictionary of Religion*] by Father [Claude-Adrien] Nonnotte. Of course, the libertine Philosophers and atheists zealously praise the passions of the soul and self-love. Why is that? Because when they deny the mysteries of religion and object to human nature having been corrupted by original sin, they maintain that no improper stimulus arose from this, and consequently exclude the necessity of divine protection and grace. But it must be a beast who does not recognize the bestial appetites that exist within himself and does not feel that by his excessive self-love and unbridled inclinations he is himself drawn toward evil and vices from which no one comes out free unless divine aid augments our feeble willpower. The Philosopher Seneca often proclaims that the inclinations of the spirit must be restrained on the grounds that they are the source of every evil. See his *Epistle* 116 [114].

13 *Philosophical Research on the Americans* vol. 1, pg. 81.

14 *History of the West Indies* 1.19.

15 This Platonic equality of goods and community ownership has not yet succeeded in any Republic, nor will it ever succeed anywhere in the world. To be sure, people's natural talents are varied, and their bodily strengths and spiritual properties are not equal. As such, it will happen that if someone should be more engaged and more prudent in seeking out property, he would have greater abundance than another who is unproductive and stubborn. From here too arise the differences between rich and poor and between masters and slaves. And if in the nascent church there was such a community and perfect equality in the company of the pious, this was achieved by the unique ability of the Holy Spirit, which desired to illustrate the doctrine of Christ with an example so extraordinary that it would attract a variety of people toward it. Certainly, the people highly esteemed those faithful, and the multitude of men and women who believed in the Lord increased even more (*Acts* 5:13–14). Indeed, Philo himself, the most learned of the Hebrews, touched by this astonishing fact and by the Alexandrian people's holy way of living with Mark as their teacher, wrote a book on that community of goods.

Verum ea civium aequalitas ad retinendam Religionem necessaria non erat, et cessavit paulatim, successitque bonorum communioni modus plane alius, quo inopum vitae, et victui consuleretur. Certe humana providentia ordinem illum paris omnium conditionis statuere non potest ob rationes, quas redemus sub hujus commentarii finem. Unum hic addo (quandoquidem nunc ubique locorum perstrepunt insanae illae voces *aequalitas, rerum communio, par sors*) eo incumbendum esse novis Philosophis, ut quam maxime vigeat Christiana Religio, haec enim sola mores illos olim piae multitudini inspiravit, et eosdem etiam nunc inspirat tot Religiosorum virorum coetibus. At id impiae genti ingratum auditu est.

16 *Mina Attica major* pendebat centum et sex aureos nostros cum aurei quadrante. (Joan. Mariana *de ponderibus et mensuris c.* VIII.) Atque hinc liquet quam vellet Plato cives suos etiam ditissimos tenui esse censu.

17 Bougainville Gallus in descriptione navigationis, qua terrarum Orbem circumiit, ponit (ex eoque retulerunt Ephemerides Romanae, ac Florentinae) fuisse in oppidis Guaranicis collegium quoddam adolescentularum, quae variis oppificiis operam navabant sub magisterio seniorum foeminarum. In istud collegium, sive gyneceon (*CONATIGASU* nomine) quod baerebat aedi Parochi, ab hujus domo erat internus aditus. Quam multa, quam paucis!

Vidit id Argonauta ille? non vidit, nam navis ejus constitit Monsvideano in portu, qui distat a primo Guaraniorum oppido centumquinquaginta, eoque amolius, leucis. Audiit ergo ab aliis, et hi quidem adeo periti erant, ut vel nomen rerum, de quibus narrabant, prorsus nescirent: nam Domus nulla Guaraniis dicitur *CONATIGASU,* sed *COTIGUAZU,* idest domus ampla, quod haec aliis ampiior esset.

Haec autem domus non erat *adolescentularum,* sed viduarum, quibus vel parentes deerant, vel cognati, apud quos honeste habitarent. Hae viduae de publico alebantur; nec varia illis artificia, sed una nendi ars; neque eisdem magistrae seniores foeminae, sed anus quaedam, quae illarum mores regebat. Nusquam porro in oppidis Guaranicis hospitium istud conjunctum erat cum aede Parochi, sed ab hac satis superque separatum, neque eo iri poterat nisi publica et patente via. Quod si Parocho, vel ejus collega illuc forte eundum esset, ut aegrae alicui sacramenta ministraret, ibant simul cum Parocho, vel ejus collega aeditui, et unus ex Indis medicis. Narro quae vidi.

Sed multo validior ratio est pro refutando indigno isto commento, quod nauta Bougainville legentibus obtrudit. Ebiscopi graves Episcopi, quorum unus fuit meo tempore Il. D. Emmanuel Antonius de la Torre, qui tres circiter menses moratus est cum Parocho Joanne Emmanuele Gutierrez in oppido S. Rosae, graves, inquam, Episcopi Il. Faxardo Trinitarius, Il. Peralta Dominicanus, Il. Palos Franciscanus, hi, aliique, qui Guaranica oppida lustrarunt, permisissent umquam aedi Curionis adjunctum seminarium adolescentularum, et cum intimo aditu? Ubi pudor! ubi bonae odor famae!

At quid argumentis opus? Res propalam est. Curant oppida nunc Religiosi viri variorum ordinum, commeant illuc innumerabiles Hispani, hi dicant, sit ne uspiam haerens domui Parochi, et non publice ab ea sejunctam aedes viduarum *COTIGUAZU.* Licet hic exclamare: quot in Viatorum commentariis fabulae? Quot item excerptae a Viatoribus nugae in Ephemeridibus? Plato certe hujusmodi Ephemeridas in gravi illa sua Republica non probabat.

But this equality among citizens was not necessary to maintain the religion, and gradually it ceased, and an entirely different way of sharing goods took its place, in which care should be taken for the life and subsistence of the poor. In fact, human providence cannot, for reasons that we will report at the end of this treatise, institute that arrangement of equal circumstances for all. On this matter I would just add (especially now when those maddening voices are raising a ruckus about "equality," "community ownership," "parity of fortune" all over the place) that it is incumbent upon the new Philosophers that the Christian religion should flourish as much as possible since it alone once inspired those customs among a pious multitude and even now inspires the same among so many companies of religious men. But this is unpleasant for impious people to hear.

16 The greater Attic *mina* weighed 106.25 of our gold pieces. (See Juan de Mariana, *On Weights and Measures*, ch. 8 [*corr.* ch. 7, p. 44].) From this it is clear how much Plato wanted his citizens, even the richest, to have meager property.

17 The Frenchman Bougainville, in the description of his voyage that circled the globe, he relates (and it's from this that the Roman and Florentine newspapers draw their accounts) that in the Guaraní towns there was a sort of college of young girls, who labored diligently at various handicrafts under the direction of older women. Into said college, or "women's center" (called CONATIGASU), there was a secret entrance from the priest's house which was right beside it. What a lot there is in so few words!

Did that Argonaut see it? No, he did not; for his ship stopped in the port of Montevideo, which is one hundred and fifty leagues, if not more, from the first Guaraní town. Thus, he heard about it from others, men so knowledgeable that they were utterly ignorant of the name of the things they were describing. For, among the Guaraní there is no house called CONATIGASU, but COTYGUASU, meaning "big house," since it is bigger than the others.

However, this house was not for young girls, but for widows, who lacked parents or other relatives with whom they could live respectably. These widows were supported from public resources; and they did not engage in a variety of crafts, just the art of weaving. Nor did they have older women as directors, rather they had an elderly woman who would manage their routine. Never, by the way, in the Guaraní towns was this lodging connected with the parish priest's house, but rather it was separated more than enough from the house, and it was not possible to go there except by a street that was public and wide open. And if by chance the parish priest or his companion had to go there to administer the sacraments to some sick woman, sacristans and one of the Indian doctors would go together with the parish priest or his companion. I describe what I have seen.

But there is a much stronger argument for refuting that shameful gossip, which the sailor Bougainville foists on his readers. Bishops, serious Bishops (of which one in my time was the Hon. Manuel Antonio de la Torre who stayed for almost three months with the Parish Priest Juan Manuel Gutiérrez in the town of Santa Rosa) serious Bishops, I repeat, like the Hon. Fajardo, a Trinitarian; the Hon. Peralta, a Dominican, the Hon. Palos, a Franciscan, these and others who examined the Guaraní towns, would never allow a seminary for young girls attached to the priest's house, and with a super-secret passageway? Where's the decency! Where's the odor of a good reputation?

But what need is there for arguments? The matter is clear. Religious men of various orders now look after the towns and countless Spaniards pass through there. Let them say whether there is anywhere a house for widows, *COTYGUASU*, stuck onto a priest's house and not separated from it by public spaces. One may well exclaim: how many lies are there in the travelers' chronicles?! Likewise, how much nonsense excerpted by travelers is in the newspapers?! Plato certainly did not approve of such newspapers in his serious Republic.

18 In Republica Hebraeorum statutum a Deo fuit pro bono ordine: *indigens, et mendicus non erit apud vos.* Ne essent autem jussit Moyses tertio quoque anno decimam agrorum seponi ad alendos pupillos, viduasque, etc. (Deuter. c. XIV. vv. 28. 29.) Praeterea lege cautum est, ut singulis septenniis vacaret tellus a possessorum cultura, et quaestu, idque in bonum indigentium. *Sex annis, ait, seminabis terram tuam, et congregabis fruges ejus. Anno autem septimo dimittes eam, et requiescere facies, ut comedant pauperes populi tui.* (Exod. c. XXIII. vv. 10. 11.)

Atque huc, opinor, pertinet, quod Heliodoro misso a Rege Seleuco, ut efferret e templo, et addiceret fisco, indicatam ipsi vim summam pecuniae, respondit cum sacra obtestatione Onias Pontif. Max. deposita esse haec, et *victualia viduarum, et pupillorum et.* (II. Mach c III. v. 10.) Heliodoro autem, cum jussae rapinae insisteret, male res cessit, exceptus enim est a sessore quodam terribili, et a pari juvenum divinitus apparentium, plagis maximis. Quo utinam exemplo alii saperent.

19 Quiddam simile rei agrariae Guaraniorum fuit olim in Hispania, atque etiam nunc est. Ecce tibi quid narrat Cyriacus Morellius, gravis auctor. "De Vettonum et Vaccaeorum agris ait Julius Frontinus: *ager est mensura comprehensus, cujus modus universus civitati est assignatus, sicut in Lusitania Salmaticensibus, aut in Hispania citeriore Palentinis, et in compluribus provinciis.* Id communionis hodiedum observatur, nominatim apud Tamamenses, qui agri Salmantini coloni sunt et in communia pascua pecus et armentum immittunt pro rata. Arvorum etiam communium subigit, colit, et seminat unusquisque colonorum pro libitu, ea tamen lege, per binos deputatos, ne cultus privatus communitati praejudicium et nocumentum paret, et post messem ad usum, et dominium communitatis revertatur." Haec ille (*de Rudimentis Juris Nat. et Gent.* lib. 1. disp. VIII. §1.)

Auctores Trevultiani agentes de libro, cui titulus est: *Entreten d' un European avec un Insulaire de Dumocale,* ajunt (apud eumdem Morellium) Stanislaum Regem induxisse apud Lotaringios suos id moris, ut certus agri modus ab indigenis communiter coleretur, fructus autem ex agro isto in horreum publicum inferretur, ut inde (cum sterilitas messem falleret, corrumperetve) toti populo subveniri posset . . . (Mem. de Trev. an. 1753. vol. I. tom. 207. art. 10. pag. 226.)

Ubi sunt agri vacantes haud esset difficile partem illorum communiter arari, et coli, et meti, unde post indigenti turbae necessaria praeberentur, ac colonis (quando messis eos defecisset) mutuum daretur semen. Hic foret optimus *Monspietatis.* Neque ejus rei labor gravis. Paucorum (quo tempore opus cultura est) dierum vice per annum ab oppidanis, descriptis a magistratu, ager ille exerceretur. Quod si quis per se (quia dives, vel nobilis) nollet laborem subire, posset illuc operas mittere suo nomine, et aere. Utilitas autem in omnes redundaret, nam cum miseris succurrendum sit e Christi praecepto, atque ex ipsa etiam naturae lege, communis ille agri fructus cunctorum esset erga pauperes stips, et eleemosyna. Inter Guaronios non solum ager publicus pro publicis impensis colebatur, sed omne etiam pro communi re opus communiter fiebat, et tamen abunde otii suppetebat Indis, ut praedio quisque suo, et suis rebus privatim consuleret.

20 Ant. Gabut in vita S. Pii V. apud Bolandianos tom. I. mensiis Maj die V.

21 Lib. 1. de Augmentis Scient.

22 Ad. Galat. c. II. v. to.

23 I. Petri c. II. v. 2.

18 In the Republic of the Hebrews, it was decreed by God on behalf of public order: "there shall be neither an indigent nor a needy person among you." And so that there would not be any, Moses ordered that every three years a tenth of the produce of the field be set aside to feed orphans and widows, etc. (*Deuteronomy* 14:28–29). Moreover, it was decreed by law that every seven years the land would rest from the cultivation and profit of its owners, and this would be for the benefit of the indigent. "For six years," he says, "you will sow your land and reap its fruits. But in the seventh year you will leave it and let it rest, so that the poor of your people may eat" (*Exodus* 23:10–11).

And it was a reference to this, I think, that when Heliodorus was sent by King Seleucus to forcibly remove a certain sum of money himself from the temple and deposit it in the royal treasury, the high priest Onias responded to him with a sacred entreaty that these monies had been deposited for "the nourishment of widows and orphans," etc. (2 *Maccabees* 3:10). However, the matter ended badly for Heliodorus because he had pressed on with the plunder as commanded. For he received many blows from a rather terrible horseman and a pair of young men who appeared miraculously. If only others would learn from that example.

19 Something similar to the agrarian system of the Guaraní once existed in Spain and it exists yet today. Behold what Domingo Muriel, a serious author, relates: "Regarding the lands of the Vettones and the Vaccaei Julius Frontinus says: lands are divided by measurement, a portion of which is designated as collective for the entire polity, just as in Lusitania among the Salamancans, or in Spain among the Palencians in Nearer Iberia and in many other provinces. This type of communalism is observed to this day, specifically among the people of Tamames, who are settlers from the Salamancan countryside and who send their flocks and herds into the communal meadows by turns. Each one of the colonists also plows, tends, and sows in these common fields as they please, under the law, however, enforced by a pair of deputies, that private cultivation does not cause any damage or nuisance to the community, and that after the harvest it should be restored to the use and domain of the community" (*Elements of Natural Law and the Law of Nations* 1.8.1).

Authors from Trévoux, discussing a book entitled *Entretien d'un Européen avec un insulaire du Royaume de Dumocala* [*Conversation between* a *European and an Islander of Dumocale*], say (according to Muriel again) that King Stanislaus introduced among his Lotharingians the custom that a certain portion of the land would be cultivated communally by the Indigenous people, and moreover the fruits of that land would be deposited in a public silo so that when fruitlessness damages or corrupts the harvest, there could be aid for the entire populace (*Memoirs of Trévoux,* 1753, vol. 1, tom. 207, article 10, page 226).

Where there are vacant fields, it would not be difficult to plow, cultivate, and harvest a portion of them communally, from which necessities could later be supplied to the indigent throng; and seeds could be loaned to the colonists, if ever the harvest failed them. This would be the best Mount of Piety. And the labor for this endeavor would not be burdensome. In shifts of a few days a year, during the period when there is a need for cultivation, this land would be worked by citizens appointed by the magistrates. But if someone (because he is rich or noble) did not want to submit to the labor himself, he could send paid laborers in his stead. Indeed, the utility would redound to everyone, for according to Christ's precept and natural law itself it is necessary to suffer alongside the unfortunate; that communal fruit of the land would be a small offering and alms for the community's poor. Among the Guaraní, not only was that public land cultivated for public expenses, but all work done for the community was done communally; and yet there was an abundant supply of free time for the Indians so that each could tend to his own farm and private interests.

20 [Giovanni] Antonio Gabuzio in the *Life of St. Pius V* in the Bollandists' [*Acts of the Saints*], Vol. I. May 5.

21 *On the Advancement of Learning,* Book 1.

22 *Galatians* 2:10.

23 1 *Peter* 2:2.

24 Fuit, qui autumarit Platonem non de vera feminarum communione, sed de metaforico quodam amore, et mutua benevolentia civium inter se locutum fuisse; verum res clarior est, quam ut celari fictis tropis, et umbris possit.

Marsilius Ficinus supra modum studiosus maximi Philosophi non negat agi ab eo de vera communicatione, conaturque rei invidiam minuere; sed *laterem*, ut ajunt, *lavat*. Dicendum omnino est Platonem hic errasse: licet enim vulgo divinus audiat, homo erat. Aristoteles, ejus discipulus, communionem istam foeminarum esse probat contra bonum commune argumentis octo validissimis (Lib. II. Pollitic.) quae argumenta explicat D. Thomas in scholiis ad eum Aristotelis locum.

25 Epist. CXX.

26 Isaiae c. V. v. 20.

27 Effrenes philosophi (ut eorum unus Rosseau ipsis exprobat) in definienda lege naturali, id est, in aperiendis recte vivendi fontibus, sibi non constant, pugnantesque inter se alii alia docent. Quos, quaeso, sequemur? Bayle ipse, qui impiorum fax quodammodo et dux est, non dubitat affirmare: *siquando philosophia ita dominabitur, ut nemo alia approbet sensa, quam quae clare sua ipsi ratio dictet; et inducat animum e propriae dumtaxat rationis ductu vitam agere, sine dubio humanum peribit genus.* (Litt. Crit. in hist. Calv.) Sane magnifici isti legis naturalis laudatores, eo demum relabuntur, ut alii fatum adstruant, alii hominem e mera materia conflent, et cum belluis componant, alii prorsus Athei sunt. Itaque (quod prius dicta consequitur) sola Religio divinitus inspirata verum justi, et injusti; boni et mali discrimen ostendere potest, et mentis errores discutere, et mores regere.

28 Aristoteles aetatem ad matrimonium in foeminis censet esse annum duodevicesimum; in viris autem sextum et tricesimum. (Lib. 7. politic.) quo loco interpres D. Thomas tempus istud approbat; de aetate vero duodecim annorum in puellis, et quattuordicim in adolescentibus, id inquit, jura concedunt, quia jam tum natura valida est; sed non (addit) determinat lex illud tempus optimum esse, aut melius alio ad matrimonium. Hanc Thomae doctrinam scriptor Regni Paraguayci non legerat, nec vidit neminem in Europa injicere religionem Parochis, aut parentibus: quod puellas non statim anno duodeno, et pueros anno quaterdeno (nisi quid mali praesentis id cogat facere) ad matrimonium vocent.

Paulus Zachias Medicus Innocentii X. Pontif. Max. docet aetatem nuptiis commodissimam in viris esse annum tricesimum, in foeminis decimum octavum. (Lib. I. tit. I. q. 6. a num. 38. et lib. IV. tit. II. q. 4.)

Cornelius autem Tacitus laudat in hac re mores veterum Germanorum: *sera*, inquit, *juvenum venus, eoque inexhausta pubertas: nec Virgines festinantur; eadem juventa, similis proceritas. Robora parentum liberi referunt.* Certe connubia nimium festinata vel nulla sequitur proles, vel imbecillis, et tumulo proxima; ideoque familiae saepius herede carent ob praecox herede desiderium.

29 Vide disserentem de hac re Cyriacum Morelli (*In rudim. Juris Nat. et Gent.* lib. II. disp. II. § I.)

30 Lycurgus lege vetuit, dotem dari viris, ut ii sine ullo respectu acceptae pecuniae, alteriusve rei, uxores in officio liberius continerent.

31 Juvenal. Satyr. VI.

32 Idem satyr. II.

33 De parentum vita et moribus sapienter praecipit Graecus Plutarchus: ante omnia, inquit, debent parentes nihil peccando, omniaque pro officii ratione agendo, evidens se se liberis exemplum praebere, ut in eorum vitam tamquam in speculum intuentes a turpibus dictis factisque abstineant. (Lib. de liberis educandis.)

24 There was one who believed that Plato was not speaking about the actual sharing of women, but of a certain metaphorical love and mutual benevolence of citizens toward each other; however, the matter is clearer than one that could be concealed by figured tropes and shadows. Marsilio Ficino, zealous beyond measure for the greatest Philosopher, does not deny that Plato means a literal sharing and tries to diminish scandalousness of the matter; but, as they say, "he is washing a brick" [i.e., wasting his time]. It absolutely must be said that here Plato made a mistake; for although popularly called "divine," he was human. Aristotle, his disciple, proves with eight very strong arguments that this practice of sharing wives is contrary to the common good (*Politics* Book 2), arguments that St. Thomas explains in his commentary on that section of Aristotle.

25 *Epistle* 120.

26 *Isaiah* 5:20.

27 The unbridled philosophers (as one of them, Rousseau, reproaches them), in defining natural law (i.e., in revealing the sources of living correctly) do not agree and they fight among themselves, each teaching different things. Who, I ask, shall we follow? Bayle, who is a sort of instigator and leader of the impious and does not hesitate to assert that "if ever philosophy were so powerful that no one would accept ideas other than those their own reason clearly dictated to them but would induce the will to conduct life according to the commands of its own reason, without doubt the human race would perish" (*General Critique of Maimbourg's History of Calvinism*). Truly these magnificent panegyrists of Natural Law are backsliding to the point that some are building on fate, others fashioning the human being from mere matter and comparing it with beasts, and others, in a word, are atheists. Thus (as follows from what has been said before), only divinely inspired Religion is able to show us the reality of the just and unjust and the distinction between good and evil, to shatter the mind's delusions, and regulate our habits.

28 Aristotle judges the age of marriage for women to be eighteen years; thirty-six for men (*Politics* Book 7). Interpreting that section, St. Thomas approves of that timeframe; but he says the law allows it from the age of twelve for girls and fourteen for boys, because nature is already able at that point; but (he adds) the law does not determine that that time is the best or better than another time for the marriage. The author of the *Kingdom of Paraguay* had not read Thomas's doctrine, nor did he see anyone in Europe impose this religious duty on the parish priests or parents because they did not call girls to marriage immediately at twelve and boys at fourteen (unless some evil is at hand to compel it to happen).

Paolo Zacchia, physician to Pope Innocent X, teaches that the most opportune age for marriage is thirty for men and eighteen for women (1.1.6.38ff. and 4.2.4).

Cornelius Tacitus, in turn, praises the customs of the ancient Germans on this subject: "sex comes late," he says, "for young men and therefore their virility is unexhausted; neither do virgins rush; they have the same experience of youth and have a similar tall stature. Children reproduce the strength of their parents." Certainly, in a marriage that was too hasty either no offspring follows, or one that is feeble and close to the grave; and for this reason, families often lack an heir on account of the premature desire for one.

29 See Domingo Muriel discussing this matter in *Elements of Natural Law and the Law of Nations* 2.2.1.

30 Lycurgus legally prohibited dowries to be given to men, so that they would be more likely to voluntarily keep their wives in that role without any regard for the money received or for any other reason.

31 Juvenal *Satire* 6 [14.31–33, 40–41, 44–49, 70–74].

32 Juvenal *Satire* 2 [6.239–240].

33 Regarding the life and habits of parents, the Greek Plutarch wisely instructs: "First of all," he says, "parents must, by not sinning at all and by doing everything with a consideration for duty, offer themselves as a clear example to their children so that their children look upon their parents' life as if looking into a mirror and abstain from foul words and deeds" (*On the Education of Children* [14a]).

34 Separatio virorum foeminarumque in templo, sua utrisque parte destinata, fieri consuevit sub initia nascentis Ecclesiae, eamque restituere conatus est (quo erat zelo pro domo Dei) S. Carolus Borromaeus: ac re ipsa in quibusdam dioecesis Mediolanensis oppidis viri seorsim et foeminae in aede sacra consistebant; qui mos duret ne adhuc, nescio.

Josephus Hebraeus scribit sejunctionem istam sexus utriusque a Deo fieri iussam in augusto illo templo Hierosolymitano. (De bel Judaic. lib VI. c. 6.)

Idem cautum est Hispanorum Regum lege, Juri Indico inserta: *Los Jueces no consientan, que los hombres esten entre las mugeres,* id est ne judices permittant viros inter foeminas consistere.

35 Non solum impedita Guaranica ratio numerandi, sed et absurda, et barbara videbitur quibusdam Europaeis At hi meminisse debent, ut maxime apud nos Arabum beneficio artis arithmeticae creverit facilitas, tamen etiamnum vel a doctis viris ad explicandam corporis magnitudinem latitudinemve adhiberi solitam mensuram *cubiti, ulnae palmi, digiti, pedis,* quod non multum, opinor, differt ab illa Guaraniorum forma.

Neque vero hinc trahi argumentum potest contra elegantiam, et artificium, quod supra laudavimus, linguae Guaranicae; facilis enim responsio est, nempe eum Indos illos Arithmetice modum habuisse, qui satis esset ad simplex, et naturale vivendi, agendique genus, quod sectabantur; quorsum nam ipsis vel subtilitas Algebrae, vel Arabicae supputationis multiplex usus?

36 Pono Callaicam linguam distinctam a Castellanica, quod ab hac illam diversam esse contendat, et probet Bened. Hieronymus Feyjoo, Callaicus ipse. (Theatr. Critic. tom. I. dissert. 15.)

37 Jus Indicum. Tit. I. lib. VII. leg. 18.

38 Aeneid. lib. XII.

39 Judic. c. XX. v. 16.

40 Judic. c. III. v. 15.

41 Philo. lib. de Agricult.

42 M. F. Quintil. *Instut.* lib. I. c. 10.

43 M. Tullius *de legibus* lib. II.

44 Joannem Vasseum eximie laudat ab optima in Guaranios Indos inducta Musica Julius Cordara, quem vide (Hist. S. I. lib. VI. n. 216.)

45 Cattaneì litteras edidit Cl. V. Ludov. Ant Muratorius, adjecitque eas operi suo *Christianismi felicis.*

46 E Musica Guaranica nihil quidem detraxisset optimus vates P. Franciscus Grimaldi, qui de puero Musicen docendo ita eleganter canit: (*De Vita oeconomica* lib. II.)

Dum digiti faciles, dum vox magis apta canendo est,
    Et canat, et tenero pollice pulset ebur.
Sic est: occulta trahimur dulcedine cantus,
    Et gens ad numeros nata modosque sumus.
Scilicet ad mores cantus facit: otia virtus
    Hinc sua perpetuo fessa labore trahit.
Fingendis puer apta canat mihi moribus: unde
    Et curis animum tristitiaque levet.

47 Serm. II. contra luxur.

48 D. Pau. (in Encyclop. V. America) scribit de Americanis: *pauci corpore defecti, quod apud eos, ut olim apud Lacaedemonios; barbarus sit mos pueros perdendi, quos distortio aliqua membrorum inutiles reddit, ut sibi cibum quaerant venando, piscandoque.*

34 The separation of men and women in church, with a section designated for each, began to be used at the very beginning of the nascent Church, and Saint Carlo Borromeo tried to restore it (according to his zeal for the house of God); and for that reason, in certain towns of Milanese diocese the men and the women would stand apart in the sacred shrine. I do not know whether this custom lasts until.

The Hebrew Josephus writes that this separation of the sexes from one another was ordained by God in the venerable Temple of Jerusalem (*The Jewish War* 6.6 [5.5]).

The same was ordered by the Law of the Spanish kings, inserted in the Law of the Indies: "Los Jueces no consientan, que los hombres esten entre las mugeres," i.e., judges must not allow men to be among women.

35 To certain Europeans the Guaraní way of counting will seem not only cumbersome but absurd and barbaric. But they ought to remember that especially among us, facility in the art of arithmetic comes thanks to the Arabs. However, even today, the traditional measurement of the forearm, the arm, the palm, the finger, and the foot are employed by learned men for explaining the magnitude and width of the body. And this, I think, is not much different from the Guaraní method.

Nor can there be drawn from this an argument against the elegance and ingenuity of the Guaraní language, which we praised above. For the response is simple: obviously those Indians had the type of Arithmetic that was sufficient for the simple and natural way of living and working that they pursued. What would be the point for them in the subtlety of Algebra or the versatility of Arabic computations?

36 I consider the Galician language to be different from Spanish because Benito Jerónimo Feijóo, himself a Galician, argued and proved that the one is different from the other (*Universal Critical Theater* 1.15).

37 *Law of the Indies* 1.7.18.

38 *Aeneid* Book 12 [verses 823–825, 833–835].

39 *Judges* 20:16.

40 *Judges* 3:15.

41 Philo *On Cultivation* [9].

42 Quintilian *On Oratorical Education* 1.10[.12, 13, 15, 16].

43 Cicero *On Laws* 2.

44 Giulio Cordara highly praises Jean Vaisseau for having introduced the best music to the Guaraní Indians, on which see his *History of the Society of Jesus*, Book 6n.216.

45 The renowned Ludovico Antonio Muratori published Cattaneo's letters and appended them to his own work, *Happy Christianity* [p. 60].

46 There is nothing in the music of the Guaraní that the excellent poet Father Francesco Grimaldi could disparage. He sang elegantly on teaching children music as follows (*On the Life of the Householder* Book 2):

When fingers are agile, and voice more suited to singing,
let him sing and with his tender thumb strum the lyre.
That's right: we are drawn in by the song's hidden charm
and we are a people born for rhythms and harmonies.
Singing obviously shapes our habits; and virtue,
wearied by perpetual labor, takes its rest from there.
Let the child sing to me of the things good at shaping manners; whereby
it relieves the soul of concerns and sadness.

47 Sermon 2 *Against Luxury*.

48 De Pauw (in the *Supplement to the Encyclopedia* Book 5 "America") writes about the Americans: "few are defective in body because among them, as previously among the Spartans, there exists the barbarous practice of discarding children who, due to a distortion of limbs, were rendered useless for seeking their own food through hunting and fishing."

Hic te volo, Pavi, et rogo, an mos informes partus necandi esse possit Americanis, apud quos non nascuntur foetus informes? De hac re testis ego, qui non exiguam Americae Meridionalis partem vidi; testis Ciriacus Morellius, qui plures, quam ego, illius provincias percurrit (Vide *Rudim. Juris Nat. et Gent.* lib. II. disput. III. § I.) testis D. Fourcoy, qui librum edidit, quo physicae educationis modum, quem ab Americanis (septemtrionalibus opinor) didicisse se se profitetur, stabiliri oportere contendit apud matres Europaeas, quod ille consilium non daret nisi proba animadvertisset quam Indi pueri et sine vitio corporis nascantur et sine labe artuum educentur. (Ex Ephemer. Roman. an. 1780. n. 49)

49 Pulchre in hanc rem Grimaldius vates: (loc. cit.)

Quis dubitet, quin prima bonae sit cura parentis,
Lactis ut infanti sedula praestet opem?
Scilicet ejusdem est, prima qui munera vitae
Tradidit, ut vitae pabula prima ferat.
Hinc minor in matrem reverentia: cujus amorem
Lacteolo sensim combibit ore puer.

Pulchrius in idem argumentum Favorinus apud Gellium: "quod est, ait, hoc contra naturam imperfectum ac dimidiatum matris genus, peperisse, ac statim ab se se abjecisse? aluisse in utero sanguine suo nescio quid quod non videret, non alere nunc suo lacte, quod videat jam vivens, jam hominem, jam matris officia implorantem?"

50 Lacedaemones, et Cretenses e legibus Lycurgi habebant convivia publica, sed soli viri.) Aristoteles Politic. lib. II.) Quippe volebat severus ille Legislator prandere patresfamilias palam, ne cujusquam, vel opes, vel intemperantia in occulto essent. Equidem ad sanctiorem causam refero, quod in benemoratis coenobiis omnes simul, et eisdem obsoniis vescuntur in communi triclinio ut nimirum temperatiores sint, liberique a parando sibi cibo, diutius vacent rebus spiritualibus.

51 *De Mandiocae cultura* etc. Edit. Romae an. 1781. Huic carmini alterum addidit *de cultura boum in Brasilia,* et tertium *de cultura herbae Nicotianae.* Omnia lectu dignissima.

52 2. 2. quest. 169. art. 4. *de Modestia*

53 Vergil. Ecl. VIII.

54 Epist. VII.

55 Testes hujus rei Americanae matres, quae sine ferri usu non nent solum belle, et scite, sed pulchre etiam telas texunt, facto e cannis textorio praelo mirae simplicitatis.

56 Homines in societatem vitae, civitatisque convenire secundum instinctum naturae humanae est: singuli enim hominum, aut etiam familiae seorsum agentes plurimis et ad utilitatem corporis, et ad animi institutionem disciplinamque necessario carerent. Ut autem debitus Dei amor, et cultus ex ipsa hominis intelligentis vi, et intima proprietate descendit, coeuntibus multis in vitae societatem, officia religionis multo melius, mutuis civium exemplis, et praefectorum jussis, constant, curanturque: atque ob id ipsum voluntas Dei est populos communiter vivere, addito (ut in praesenti rerum ordine filiis Adae coeleste regnum Deus destinat, et *vult omnes homines salvos fieri*) fine supernaturali.

I wish you were here, de Pauw, so that I could ask: Could the custom of killing malformed newborns exist among the Americans, where no malformed offspring were born? On this matter I, who saw a not insignificant portion of South America, am witness. Another witness is Domingo Muriel who traversed more of its provinces than I (See *Elements of Natural Law and the Law of Nations* 2.3.1); another is de Fourcroy, who published a book in which he contends that it would be beneficial among European mothers to establish the mode of physical education, which he professes that he himself learned from the Americans (North Americans, I think), which he would not advise unless he had seen proof of how Indian children are born without bodily defect and are brought up without failing strength. (From the *Roman Newspapers* n. 49 in 1780.)

49 On this matter the poet Grimaldi put it beautifully (loc. cit.):

> Who would doubt that the good mother's primary concern
> would be to furnish a wealth of milk for her tireless infant?
> To be sure, it is the duty of the same mother, who bestowed
> life's first gifts, to bring forth life's first nourishments.
> Hence the young boy is in awe of its mother and he gradually
> imbibes her love with his milk-white mouth.

Favorinus made this same argument rather beautifully in Gellius's *Attic Nights* [12.1.6]: "For," he said, "what unnatural, imperfect, and halfway sort of mother is it to have given birth and at once cast it aside from herself? To have nourished in her womb with her own blood an I-don't-know-what, which she could not see, and not to feed now with her own milk what she sees, now alive, now human, now crying for a mother's duty?"

50 The Spartans and the Cretans, according to the laws of Lycurgus, held public meals, but only the men (Aristotle *Politics* Book 2). For that severe legislator wanted the heads of the household to eat in public, so that neither the abundance nor the intemperance of anyone would be hidden. I attribute to a holier cause the fact that in well-mannered monasteries everyone eats the same food at the same time and in a communal dining room, no doubt so that they are more moderate and, because they are free from having to prepare food for themselves, they can devote more time to spiritual matters.

51 *On the Cultivation of Yuca*, etc., published in Rome in the year 1781. To this poem he added another *On the Cultivation of Cattle in Brazil* and a third *On the Cultivation of Tobacco*. All are very worth reading.

52 *On Modesty* 2.2.169 Reply to Objection 4.

53 Vergil *Eclogues* 8

54 *Epistle* 7.

55 American mothers are witness to this fact, for without using any iron they not only spin excellently and expertly but also weave fabrics beautifully, with a textile press made from reed that is of astonishing simplicity.

56 Human beings, by their very nature, enter into social and civic partnerships. For if they did things separately, individual humans and even individual members of families would unavoidably lack many things for the benefit of the body and for the disposition and training of the spirit. Given that the love and worship owed to God derives from the human intellect's potency and profound peculiarity, when many people come together to form a social partnership, religious obligations endure and are served much better thanks to the examples citizens provide for one another and the prescriptions of those who preside over them. For this reason, it is the will of God that the peoples live communally—adding the supernatural goal that in the present order of things, God intends the heavenly kingdom to be for the children of Adam and wants all men to be saved.

57 Cornelius Tacitus eam de priscis Germanis formam societatis refert, quae proxima naturali regimini est: *Reges,* inquit, *ex nobilitate, duces ex virtute sumunt. Nec Regibus infinita, aut libera potestas; et Duces exemplo potius quam imperio, si prompti, si conspicui, si ante aciem agant, admiratione praesunt.* Nec dicere omisit Tacitus de eorumdem Germanorum religione; hujus enim populis omnibus vel etiam maxime barbaris semper cura fuit (major minorve pro gentis feritate.) *Caeterum,* ait, *neque animadvertere, neque vincire, neque verberare quidem nisi sacerdotibus permissum: non quasi in poenam nec ducis jussu, sed velut deo imperante, quem adesse bellantibus credunt.*

58 Lege caput X. Geneseos.

59 I. Regg. c. XIII vv. 16. 21. 22.

60 Error de negato *R.* Brasilicis Indis, nasci potuit, quod Guaranica gens numquam *R.* duplicet, velut antiquissimi Romanorum nusquam litteram aliquam geminabant, et ajebant *opidum* pro *oppidum*. Nec vero defuisse Guaraniis *L.* et *F.* mirum est. Nam vel cultiores linguae aliquot carent elementis. Hebraea omnium prima habet dumtaxat litteras XXII., Latina XXIII, Graeca caeteris copiosior XXIV. aucto Alphabeto, quod ab Hebraeis acceperunt.

61 Maffej. lib. II. Histor. Indic.

62 Joann. Petrus Maffejus Histor. Indic. lib. XV.

63 C. Cornel. Tacitus de morib. German.

64 Lycurgus usum pecuniae civibus suis generatim prohibuit. Vates Iuvenalis corruptam veteris Romae disciplinam et gravitatem studio quaesitae pecuniae attribuit: (Satyr. VI.)

> Prima peregrinos obscoena pecunia mores
> Inculit, et turpi fregerunt saecula luxu
> Divitiae molles.

65 De *Herba Paraguayca* sic disserit Pavvius Philosophus. Dederunt, ait, Curatores Guaranici (Jesuitae) operam, ut undique locorum eradicaretur arbor illa (unde *Herba* sit) praeterquam e ditione sua, ubi unice merx haec pretiosa deinceps proveniret. Cavebant autem maxime, ne quod foras efferretur semen, quo e semine educi arbor illa posset; frondesque ipsas ita pinsebant, commiscebantque adjecta nescio qua re, ut dignosci ab ementibus verum arboris genus nequiret.

Hinc Curatorum illorum insanae divitiae, quandoquidem *Herbae arroba* valuit aliquando aureis tricenis senis (*trente six piastres fortes.*) Annua autem venditio erat librarum ad quattuor milliones, quibus parandis occupabantur an. 1756. tercenta millia Indorum praeter Aethiopas, qui tamen multi non erant... Omitto alia (ut de impensis in fabricas, et officinas, ubi *Herba* conficiebatur) quae addit Pavvius tanto digna Philosopho. (Tom. II. a pag. 411. ad pag. 415.)

Haec autem omnia quam sint vera, tu ipse, lector, judicato e sequentibus propositionibus, quarum testes appello Urbis S. Fidei, et Assumptionis Paraguaycae cives, aliosque praeturae illius Hispanos incolas, qui rem hanc probe norunt.

I. Arbor *Herbae Paraguaycae* publica illic est; ac sponte sua provenit in desertis silvis *Maracayù, Monday, Yeyù, Aracay, Mbaeverà,* alibique, quas in silvas penetrant, cum volunt Hispani omnes, et Indi. Ea autem loca longissime distant ab XXX. oppidis Guaranicis, neque ullus ibi Jesuita erat... Pavvius ait ab Jesuitis extirpatum undique (praeterquam ex suis oppidis) id genus arborum, ut ipsi uni. et soli *Herbam* colerent.

57 Cornelius Tacitus, speaking about the ancient Germans, reports on the same form of association, which is closest to the natural state of governance: "Kings," he says, "begin from nobility, leaders from excellence. The kings do not have infinite and free power; the leaders lead by example rather than by command. If they are energetic, if they are conspicuous, if they fight in front of the battle line, they lead because they are admired." Tacitus does not neglect to speak about the religion of those same Germans. For all people always have a concern for this —even the most barbarous (more or less depending on the savagery of the people). "But none but the priests," he says, "are permitted to chastise, restrain, or beat the others, and that not as a punishment nor at the command of the leader, but as if by the command of God whom they believe aids the warriors."

58 Read *Genesis* 10.

59 1 *Kings* [1 *Samuel*] 13:16, 21, and 22.

60 The mistake about denying that the Brazilian Indians had the letter "R" could have been born from the fact that the Guaraní people never double their "R" just as the earliest Romans never duplicated any letter and said "*opidum*" instead of "*oppidum*." Indeed, it is not remarkable that the Guaraní actually did lack the "L" and the "F." For even very elegant languages lack certain letters. Hebrew, first of all, only has 22 letters, Latin has 23, and Greek, richer than the others, has 24, since the Alphabet they took from the Hebrews was augmented.

61 Maffei *Histories of the Indies*, Book 2.

62 Giovanni Pietro Maffei *Histories of the Indies*, Book 15.

63 Gaius Cornelius Tacitus *Germania* [16–17]

64 Lycurgus generally prohibited the use of money by his fellow citizens. The poet Juvenal attributes ancient Rome's corrupted discipline and authority to a zeal for acquiring money (*Satires* 6):

> First of all, filthy money introduced foreign customs,
> and with its repulsive luxury dainty affluence
> dashed our age into pieces.

65 Philosopher de Pauw discusses *Paraguayan Yerba* as follows: "The Guaraní Caretakers (the Jesuits)," he said, "made an effort to eradicate that tree (which is the source of *Yerba*) from everywhere except from the lands under their authority, so that this precious merchandise would then come exclusively from there. Moreover, they took the utmost care that the seed was not taken abroad, so that the tree could not be produced from the seed; they crushed the leaves themselves and mixed them with I don't know what additive such that the actual species of tree could not be discerned by the buyers.

Hence the insane wealth of these Caretakers, since an *arroba* of *Yerba* was at one time worth thirty-six gold pieces (*trente six piastres fortes [Fr.]*). The amount sold annually was four million pounds, the preparation of which in 1756 occupied three hundred thousand Indians, not counting the Ethiopians, of whom there were not many anyway . . . " I pass over the other things de Pauw adds (such as the expenditures on factories and workshops where the *Yerba* was processed), which are worthy of a philosopher such as him (Vol. 2 pp. 411–415).

You, reader, must judge for yourself the truth of all this from the following propositions, for which I call as witnesses the citizens of Santa Fe and Asunción del Paraguay, and other Spanish inhabitants of that governorate, who are thoroughly familiar with this matter:

1. The tree of the Paraguayan *Yerba* is a public matter there; and flourishes all on its own in the deserted jungles of Mbaracayú, Monday, Jejuí, Acaray, Mbaeverá, and elsewhere, and any Spaniard or Indian can enter these jungles as they like. Moreover, these places are extremely far from the 30 Guaraní towns, and there were no Jesuits there . . . de Pauw says that this species of tree was eradicated by the Jesuits from all over (except from their own towns), so that they could cultivate *Yerba* all by themselves.

II. Ad parandam *Herbam* nulla est opus fabrica, nullis officinis, ideoque impensae in hanc quidem rem nullae. In mediis illis silvis carpuntur arborum frondes; hae semiustulatae coguntur in scrobem subitaneo factam opere. Inde postea acervus ille frondium detritarum immittitur in culeos e bovilo corio. Culei devehuntur venum in urbes Hispanorum, Ecce tibi hic tota conficiendae *Herbae* ratio, et ars . . . Pavvius nescio quas fabricas, officinasque comminiscitur instar aerearum turrium, castellorumque, quae famoso Heroi *Quixotio della Mancha* passim occurrebant, facessebantque novo illi Herculi non leve negotium.

III. Commercium *Herbae Paraguaycae* commune est Hispanis viris Villaricianis, et Curuguatiensibus, et civibus Assumptionis, quae urbs praetoria est. Hi omnes per flumen Paraguayum, quot volunt *Herbae* culeos, et quoties volunt, devehunt in urbem S. Fidei (quae adjacet Paranae amni, in quem Paraguayus influit) et Bonasauras. . . . Pavvius ait, Curiones Guaranios arrogasse sibi monopolium *Herbae,* quam (ne dignosci posset, unde fieret) ignota cujusdam materiae adjectione commiscebant cavebantque summopere nequod foras semen efferretur. O lepidum caput novi Philosophi!

IV. Guaranicis oppidis solum permittebatur venum exponere XII. millia *arrobarum,* idest, quadringentas *arrobas* singulis oppidis, quae erant numero triginta. Vectigalium autem redemptores, et Regii ministri excubabant, nequid amplius inferretur a lembis Guaraniorum . . . Pavvius ait Curiones Guaranicos quotannis vendere solitos quattuor milliones librarum.

V. Pretium *Herbae* crassioris, et rudioris (*Yerba de palos* vulgo) erat binum aureorum in singolas *arrobas* pretium vero *Herbae* minutioris, et purgatioris (*Caamini*) ternum, vel quaternum aureorum: Quod si alterutrius maejor erat aliquando caritas: primum *Herbae* genus venibat binis et semis, vel trinis aureis, alterum quinis circiter. . . . Pavvius ait Herbae arrobam veniisse nonnumquam sex et triginta aureis (*trente six piastres fortes.*) Euge, Pavvi, est quo ditescas brevi. I Bonasauras, edic te pro singulis *arrobis* daeturum aureos duodecim. Guaraniorum nemo, nemo Paraguaycorum civium non tibi *Herbam* ultro vendet, Tu emptam venum expone non aureis tricenis senis (quod nimium mihi crede est) sed vicenisquinis: redibunt tibi tum lucro e singulis *arrobis* undeni aurei. Quid vis amplius?

VI. *Herbae* devectio ex urbe Assumptionis (haec urbs illius emporium est, Villariciani enim et Curuguantienses cives eo Herbam suam deferunt, ut inde Bonasauras transmittatur) erat ferme centum triginta millium *arrobarum* quotannis; ut auditus est olim dicere ex publicis rationum tabulis Praetor Assumptionis Jacobus Sanjust (quem novi.) Ab Guaranicis autem oppidis exportabantur (ut dictum est) XII. millia *arrobarum.* Sed cum iter longissimum sit, et magnarum impensarum, fiebat, ut civibus Paraguaycis puri parum lucri restaret; Guaraniis vero, cum a singulis oppidis quadringenta dumtaxat *arrobae* venderentur ne unus quidem aureus in capita respondebat. . . . Pavvius ait vel e sola *Herba* inaestimabiles divitias cogi a Curionibus Guaranicis.

VII. Census ex omnibus triginta oppidis Guaranicis erat plerumque minor (ut constat ex tabulis quas habeo) centum millibus, idque inclusis censu pueris, puellis, matribus, viris, senibusque. Unus hoc saeculo (ut alibi docuimus) annus felicior fuit aucto vehementer numero: at ne eo quidem anno omnium census ascendit ad centum quinquaginta millia. Anno autem jussi exilii fuerunt censi 88864 . . . Pavvius ait, in sola paranda *Herba* an. 1756. occupata fuisse a Curionibus Guaranicis tercentum millia Indorum (viros, opinor, vult dicere, seclusa imbelli turba.) Si illis ergo addas pueros, et puellas, et matres, quanta erit cunctorum summa? Et vero hic, Pavvi, non capio, cur *trecenta millia Indorum* pararint dumtaxat in singulos annos *quattuor milliones librarum.* Indulgentiores fuerint Curiones in imperando Indis labore necesse prorsus est.

2. To prepare *Yerba* there is no need for factories or workshops; so, the expenditures on that are zero. The leaves of the trees are collected from trees in the middle of the forest; slightly singed by fire, the leaves are collected into a makeshift trench. From here, the pile of broken-down leaves is then put into cowhide sacks. These bags are carried away for sale in the cities of the Spanish. Behold, here is the entire method and art of processing *Yerba* . . . de Pauw is dreaming up who knows what factories and workshops like the towers and fortresses made of air that frequently appeared to the famous hero Don Quixote and occasioned no slight labor for that new Hercules.
3. The trade in Paraguayan *Yerba* is common to the Spaniards of Villarrica, Curuguaty, and the citizens of Asunción, which is the seat of the governorate. They all carry away however many bags of *Yerba* they like as often as they like down the Paraguay River to the city of Santa Fe (which is on the banks of the Paraná River, into which the Paraguay flows) as well as to Buenos Aires. de Pauw says that the Guaraní Missionaries acquired a monopoly of *Yerba* for themselves, which (so that it would be impossible to discern where it came from) they mixed with an unknown additive of some sort and took all precautions so that the seed was not carried abroad. What a clever mind the new Philosopher has!
4. The Guaraní towns were only permitted to export twelve thousand *arrobas* for sale, that is, four hundred arrobas for each town, which were thirty in number. Tax collectors and royal ministers were on alert so that no more was taken from the Guaraní boats. de Pauw says that Guaraní Priests were used to selling four million pounds each year.
5. The price of the thicker and coarser *Yerba* (commonly called *Yerba de palos*) was two strong pesos per *arroba*, while the price of the finest and most refined *Yerba* (*ka'amini*) was three or four strong pesos: and if the cost of either was greater at some point, the first type of *Yerba* would reach two and a half or three pesos, and the other around five. de Pauw says that sometimes an *arroba* of *Yerba* reached thirty-six strong pesos (*trente six piastres fortes [Fr.]*). Bravo, de Pauw! What a way to get rich quick! Go to Buenos Aires and announce that you will pay twelve strong pesos per *arroba*. Absolutely any Guaraní or Paraguayan citizen will willingly sell you the *Yerba*. Then you put your purchase up for sale not at thirty-six pesos (which, believe me, is too much) but at twenty-five; eleven strong pesos per arroba will then come back to you as profit. What more do you want?
6. The downstream transport of *Yerba* from the city of Asunción (that city is a trade center for it, since citizens of Villarrica and Curuguaty take their *Yerba* there to be transferred to Buenos Aires) was about 130,000 *arrobas* annually, as the Governor of Asunción, Jaime Sanjust (whom I met), was once heard reporting from public accounting records. 12,000 *arrobas* (as has been said) were exported from the Guaraní towns. But since the journey was exceptionally long and very costly, it happened that little net profit was left over for the Paraguayan citizens; indeed, for the Guaraní, since each town sold only 400 *arrobas*, the yield was not even a single strong peso per person. de Pauw says that from *Yerba* alone the Guaraní Priests amassed incalculable riches.
7. The census of all thirty Guaraní towns was for the most part less than 100,000 (according to the records I have), and that is with the boys, girls, mothers, husbands, and elderly included in the census. In this century there was (as we have explained elsewhere) one quite fruitful year when the population increased dramatically; but even in this year the total census did not rise to 150,000. In the year that exile was decreed, 88,864 were counted in the census. de Pauw says that in 1756 there were 300,000 Indians employed by the Guaraní Priests just in the preparation of *Yerba* (I suppose he means men, with the mob of noncombatants excluded). So, if you add the boys and girls and mothers to these, how much will the sum of them all be? And on that point, de Pauw, I cannot grasp why 300,000 Indians would prepare only "4,000,000 pounds" per year except that the Priests would have to have been rather indulgent in the labor they demanded of the Indians.

VIII. In oppidis Guaranicis ne unus quidem erat Aetiops . . . Pavvius ait ad conficiendam *Herbam* adjunctos Indis Aetiopas quosdam, *non tamen* (addit) *multos,* atque hoc extremum sine ulla dubitatione verum est, nam ubi nullus est, multi non sunt.

Ex his octo propositionibus quae omnes verae sunt, et quarum appello iterum testes Sanfideanos, et Paraguaicos cives argue tu, quam explorata, et quam sincera, retulerit Pavvius de *Herbae Paraguaycae* commercio, e quo immensas sibi divitias accumulabant Curiones Guaranici.

Qattuor et viginti circiter anni sunt, ex quo scripsit illustris quidam Presul consuesse quotannis mitti a sociis Paraguaycis ad Socios Romanos unum aureorum millionem e redditu *Herbae.* Quid dicam? Miror sane, sed non tam irascor Illm̃o illi Sacrorum Antistiti, quam Pavvio, Pavviique similibus, qui falso praedicando immensas divitias ex *Herba Paraguayca,* vel optimis alioquin viris imponunt.

Millio unus aureorum e toto simul *Herbae* mercimonio pluribus pluribusque annis non provenit civibus Villaricianis, Curuguatiensibus, et Paraguaycis, quantumvis vendant quotannis centum triginta circiter *arrobarum* millia: demenda enim sunt (ut dixi) graves impensae longissimi itineris. Quid fiet igitur e solis duodecim millibus *arrobarum* transvectarum in urbem S. Fidei, et Bonasauras ex oppidis Guaranicis? quippe ex his oppidis millio ille Romanus extraendus est, quandoquidem collegia *Herbam* non habebant.

Adde huc Guaranica oppida condi coepisse an. 1610.: ab hoc anno ad annum jussi exilii 1767. abierunt anni 157. totidem igitur numero milliones aureorum ex *Herbae* proventu transmissi fuisse Romam dicendi tibi erunt: ego autem rogo, quid actum sit de tot millionibus? Num in aliquam illi altam caveam profundae fossae abditi: custoditique sunt pro thesauro Jesuitico? sed de his hactenus.

66 Aristotel. Nicom. IX. I.

67 Deuter. c. XIV. vv. 24. 25.

68 Jus indic. Tit. XXIV lib. IV. leg. 7. Aureum, qui ex hac lege aestimatur senis tantum argenteis; vocant Paraguayci cives *PESO HUECO,* id est vacuum, sive non solidum. Solidus autem aureus valet in America octo argenteis; idem in Europa, aucto pretio, valet argenteis denis.

69 Cyriacus Morelli recte monet Paraguaycos fructus *Herbam, tabacum, mel, frumentum Indicum,* sive *Maiz,* induere ex lege illa pecuniae conditionem modumque, ob idque de eis perinde censendum, decernendumque esse in praetura Paraguayca, ac de veris nummis. Extra vero praeturam illam reputantur ea ipsae terrae munera, ut mera merx, seu ut fructus venales, qui veneunt, ementurque quanti potest juste. Atque hinc fit sex argenteos esse legitimum et publicum pretium aurei Paraguayci ficti, seu non solidi. Duo autem argentei, qui aureo isti accrescunt Bonis auris in *Herbae* venditione sunt pro impensis evectionis, quam gravem reddit difficultas trecentarum leucarum partim per flumen Paraguayum, partim per amnem Argenteum, ac praeterea damnum saepe parit ipsa navigiorum debilis moles, qua evenit ut corrompatur interdum *Herba,* vel etiam naufragio pereat: (Legesis ipsum Morellium *de Rudim. Juris Nat.* et Gent. lib. 1. disput. XI. §. 2. ubi plura affert scitu digna de commercio Paraguayco.)

70 Nocet peregrinorum consuetudo 1. quia cum fastidium ferme nobis generent ea, quibus assuevimus, ad nova in allis visa ultro ferimur. 2. nocet quia naturae ipsius impetu (ut videre licet in pueris) ad immitandum propensi sumus, atque ex alio in aliud facile mutamur, ideoque exteros mores plerumque probamus, et imitamur. 3. nocet, quia cum aliae atque aliae vestium, et utensilium, formae usu inducuntur, magna fit jactura rei familiaris, ac saepe jejunium familiae indicitur, ut supersit aliquid in peregrinum cultum. 4. nocet, quia ut utentem ornatu novi generis aequare possis, fraudibus non parcis, nec dolis, si opes domi non sunt; et negas mercedem operariis, et mercatoribus acceptae mercis pretium. 5. nocet ob alias causas, quas non libet hic persequi.

8. In the Guaraní towns there was not a single Ethiopian. de Pauw says that to process the *Yerba* some Ethiopians were added in with the Guaraní—"not many anyway" (he tacks on). At last, here is something that is without any doubt true, for where none exist, there are not many.

From these eight propositions, which are all true and for which I again call as witnesses the citizens of Santa Fe and Paraguay, see for yourself how well investigated and how sincere are the things that de Pauw has reported about the trade of *Paraguayan Yerba*, from which Guaraní Priests accumulated immense wealth for themselves.

It is some twenty-four years since that most illustrious Prelate wrote that Jesuits of Paraguay used to send each year to the Jesuits of Rome one million strong pesos from the *Yerba* income. What can I say? I am rather shocked but not so angry at that most illustrious Bishop as at de Pauw and the likes of de Pauw, who through false assertions attribute immense wealth from the *Paraguayan Yerba* to otherwise excellent men.

One million strong pesos from the entire Yerba trade over many, many years does not reach the citizens of Villarrica, Curuguaty, and Paraguay, even if they were to sell about 130,000 *arrobas* per year; for significant expenses must be subtracted (as I have said) for the very long journey. What then will become of the mere 12,000 *arrobas* transported to the cities of Santa Fe and Buenos Aires from the Guaraní towns? Obviously that Roman million would have to be extracted from these towns, given that the company did not have *Yerba*.

Add to this that the Guaraní towns began to be founded in the year 1610; from that year until the year exile was decreed in 1767, 157 years passed. Thus, just as many millions of strong pesos from Yerba sales will have to have been said to have been transmitted to Rome. And so, I ask, what was done with so many millions? Were they hidden away in some huge cavity of a deep pit and guarded as a Jesuit treasure? Anyway, enough about that.

66 Aristotle *Nicomachean Ethics* IX.I.

67 *Deuteronomy* 14:24–25.

68 *Law of the Indies* 4.24.7. The peso, which according to this law is worth just six silver *reales*, is what the Paraguayan citizens call the *peso hueco*, meaning "empty" or "not whole." A whole peso is worth eight silver *reales* in America; the same in Europe, with an increased value, is worth ten silver *reales*.

69 Domingo Muriel rightly reminds that the products of Paraguay *Yerba*, tobacco, honey, Indian wheat, or *Maiz*, according to that law, assume the status and value of money and on account of this it is necessary in the province of Paraguay to assess and judge them just like real currency. But outside that province, these gifts of the earth itself are considered to be simple merchandise or salable produce, which go for sale and are bought at whatever fair price can be had. And from here it comes that six *reales* is the legitimate and public price of the pretend, "not whole," Paraguayan peso. But, the two reales that are added to the peso for the sale of *Yerba* in Buenos Aires are for the cost of transportation, which is rendered burdensome due to the difficulty of traveling three hundred leagues part by the Paraguay river, part by the Rio de la Plata, not to mention the loss often brought about by the weak structure of the ships, due to which it happens that sometimes the *Yerba* rots or is even lost due to shipwreck. (You may read Muriel himself, *Elements of Natural Law and the Law of Nations* 1.11.2, where he brings up many things worth knowing about Paraguayan trade.)

70 Interacting with foreigners is harmful 1) because, since things that have become familiar usually generate contempt among us, we are drawn automatically toward the novelties we see in others. 2) It's harmful because due to our natural instincts (as may be seen in children) we have a propensity to imitation, and what's more we switch from one thing to another easily; therefore, we generally try out and imitate the customs of outsiders. 3) It's harmful because when more and more types of clothing and paraphernalia come into use, it produces a major drain on the household finances and often the family goes hungry so that something is left over to spend on foreign luxury. 4) It's harmful because in order for you to measure up to someone using the new-fangled trappings, you don't stop short of fraud or deception, if there aren't the resources at home; and you deny workers their wages and merchants the payment for merchandise received. 5) It's harmful for other reasons that I prefer not to go into here.

Generatim de Peregrinis ait optime Seneca "Peregrinatio notitiam dabit gentium, novas tibi montium formas ostendet, inusitata spatia camporum, et irriguas perennibus aquis valles . . . caeterum neque meliorem faciet, neque saniorem . . . Quamdiu quidem nescieris quid fugiendum, quid petendum, quid necessarium, quid supervacuum, quid justum quid honestum sit, non erit hoc peregrinari, sed errare. Etc." (Epist. CIV.)

71 Cl. V. Antonius de Ulloa, inclitum Hispanis nomen ab ingenio, et arte Matematica "firmitas, ait, PP. Societatis in prohibendis Hispanis, Indis, Hibridisque oppidorum aditu multarum adversus eos calumniarum occasio fuit; sed prohibendi causas nemo cordatus non videt. Quippe, si aliter fieret, Indi, qua sunt morum innocentia, perfectaque docilitate, qui unum in coelo Deum, unum in terra Regem norunt, et quibus imbibitum animo est, nihil a suis pastoribus pravum, nihil non sanctum ipsis tradi, et qui alioquin ignorant injustitiam, vindictam, et caeteras humanarum perturbationum pestes, brevi degenerarent," Haec ille in *Relat. Histor. itineris in Americam meridialem.* Sed de negato Hispanis aditu, quem ponit generatim, excipienda sunt sex illa oppida, quae diximus.

Locupletior rei ejusdem testis est Il. D. Petrus Faxardo Ord. SS. Trinit. qui oppida Guaranica dioeceseos suae Bonaurensis lustravit. Post lustrationem scripsit ad Philippum V. Regem, et "lustratis, inquit, saepe eorum Missionibus testor nusquam rerum ordinem vidisse me aptius constitutum . . . Revera Missionarii cavent, ne Indi frequentent Hispanos, nec temere cavent consuetudinem innocentibus exitialem, qua vitae licentia, et corrupti mores inolescerent . . . Certe commercium Hispanorum pestis Indorum est." (Has Il. Faxardi litteras datis 20. Maj an. 1721. vide apud Charlevoixium Hist. Parag. lib. V. edit. Venet. lat. an. 1779. cum adjecto scholio ab interprete, et continvatore ejusdem historiae.)

72 Dura alicui videbitur haec Platonis disciplina; sed durior fuit Lycurgi, qui sanxit adolescentes omnes una solum veste uti toto anno, nec alium alio ornatius indui; vescive opimius: quin etiam sine pulmento vitam eos tolerare jussit, idque inter agri labores, quousque viri jam facti urbe admitterentur. Hinc robusti illi, et fortes bello Lacaedemones.

73 Paedagog. lib. II. cc. 10. et 11.

74 2. 2. 169. art. I. qui est de ornatu corporis, et modestia

75 Esset hic locus dicendi aliquid de Indis aliis Americanis, qui, contra ac Guaranii, paene nudi incedunt. Cyriacus Morelli quaerit, an sit de jure naturae hominem veste uti? In hanc rem refert sensa P. Benedicti Stattler Germani e Soc. J. qui ait (Eth. Univ. p. 2. s. 2. c. I. de cura corporis pag. 172. et 176.) partes obscoenas tegere idoneo vestimenti genere gravis, et generalis officii debitum esse (post Adae lapsum) inter omnes homines. Vide eumdem Morellium, qui ex Stattlero ipso sententiae hujus rationes dat. (*De Rud. Juris Nat. et Gent.* lib. 1. disp. VII. §.)

Regarding foreigners, in general, Seneca says it best: "Travel will offer knowledge of other nations; it will reveal to you the peculiar shapes of mountains, unfamiliar expanses of fields, valleys fed by year-round waters . . . But it will make you neither better nor more sound . . . Indeed, as long as you are ignorant of what should be avoided and what sought, what is necessary and what is superfluous, what is right and what is honorable it won't be traveling, merely wandering. Etc." (*Epistle* 104).

71 The illustrious Antonio de Ulloa, a name famous among the Spanish for his genius and mathematical knowledge, says: "the firmness of the Jesuit Fathers in prohibiting the Spanish, the Indians, and Mestizos from accessing the towns was the cause of many false accusations against them. But no prudent person fails to see the reasons for the prohibition. Furthermore, if it had been done differently, the Indians would fall into decline in short order, given that they are characterized by the innocence of their customs and their complete openness to learning, they recognize a single God in heaven and a single King on earth, their spirits have drunk in the idea that nothing transmitted to them by their shepherds is improper or unholy, and they are otherwise unacquainted with injustice, vengeance, and the other plagues that cause upheaval among humans." This is what he says in his *Historical Account of the Voyage to South America*. But regarding access being denied to the Spanish, which he describes as categorical, those six towns that we mentioned must be excepted.

A very credible witness to this fact is the Illustrious Pedro Fajardo, a Trinitarian, who visited the Guaraní towns of his diocese of Buenos Aires. After the visit, he wrote to King Felipe V and said: "Having visited their Missions many times, I bear witness that nowhere have I seen a more fitting organization of affairs established . . . In truth, the missionaries take care that the Indians do not interact much with the Spanish, and not without reason they guard against interactions that are harmful to the innocent, since a licentious lifestyle and corrupt customs would become ingrained . . . Certainly, dealing with the Spanish is a plague for the Indians." (For these letters from the illustrious Fajardo dated May 20, 1721, see the Latin edition of Charlevoix's *History of Paraguay*, Book 5, published in Venice in 1779 with the commentary attached by the translator [i.e., Muriel] who added onto his history.)

72 Plato's teachings on this will seem harsh to some. But Lycurgus's were harsher; he ordained that all adolescents wear just one outfit throughout the entire year, and one not dressing more ornately than the other or eating more sumptuously; moreover, he even ordered that they tolerate going without food even while laboring in the fields, until such time as they had become men and could be admitted to the city. This is why the Spartans were so vigorous and strong in war.

73 *Paedagogus* 2.10–11.

74 2.2.169.1, which is about bodily attire and modesty.

75 This would be the place to say something about other Indians of America, who, unlike the Guaraní, walk about almost naked. Domingo Muriel wonders whether humans wearing clothing is derived from natural law. On this matter he mentions the sentiments of Father Benedikt Stattler, a German Jesuit, who says (*Universal Christian Ethics* 2.2.1, "On the Care of the Body," pp. 172 and 176) that it is a serious responsibility common among all humans (after the fall of Adam) to cover one's obscene parts with a suitable type of garment. See Muriel himself, who, relying on Stattler, gives the reasons for this opinion (*Elements of Natural Law and the Law of Nations* 1.7).

Nostra memoria piratae fluminis Paraguay Indi Payaguaae, genus hominum impudens inita cum Hispanis pace, urbem Assumptionis penitus nudi (usi sunt instar piscium sub acquis paene vivere) subibant. Id vehementer offendit prestantissimum Praetorem Raphaelem de Moneda, qui edixit, proposita poena, ne quis illorum urbem adiret, nisi inhonesta corporis modeste tectus. Ut autem Moneda non verbo tantum edicebat, sed serio urgebat edicta metu supplicii gens caeteroquin inverecunda paruit tum quidem: sed cum praetura jam abiisset Moneda, paulatim Paraguaye ad ingenium redibant. Quapropter P. Michel Crespo Lopez acerime e loco superiore declamavit id neque ferri, neque permitti ullo modo posse, quod civibus esset gravi scandalo.

76 Has litteras 23. Mart. an. 1774. datas reddit Continuator Charlevoxii inter historia documenta pag. 595.

77 Optime simplicis victus bona, et gulae mala explicat Hispanus Seneca. (Epist. XCV.)

78 Cum Guaranii haec publica munera olim non habuerint, ne nomina quidem munerum habuere: ideo ad illorum lingua indolem quaedam Jesuitae vocabula finxere. *Corregidor, Poroquaìtara*; qui agenda jubet. *Regidores Cabildoiguara,* qui ad concilium, seu senatum pertinent. *Alguazil mayor Ibiraruzu,* primus inter eos, qui manu virgam praeferunt. *Alferez, Aobebè rerequara,* is, cui vexilli cura est. *Escribano* Quatìaapohara: Scriba, qui scribit. Ipsi Scripturam non norant, sed a pictura, quam rudi quodam modo norant, scripturae nomen accomodarunt; *Aiquatìa* enim Guaranicum est Latinum *pingo*. Regem vocarunt *Mburubichabete,* qui superiorum maximus est. Atque haec quidem nomina jam inde ab initio aditae regionis inducta illuc sunt: ea enim ponit in Lexico Guaranico, edito Matriti an. 1610., P. Antonius Ruiz de Montoya, qui e primis Cultorum Guaranicorum fuit, et lingua peritissimus.

79 Part. III. t. 4. leg. 23. *Jueces avenideros son de dos maneras* etc. Videsis Thomam Sanchez in Decalog. lib. VI. cap. 13. n. 66. et 67.

80 Daniel Bartoli *dell' Asia* lib. V. pag. 425.

81 Hi *Cruciferi* (quorum ars ab usu magis, quam a librorum studio pendebat) respondent (si parva licet componere magnis) *PARABOLANIS* illis, qui heroicis temporibus Alexandriae, alisque in urbibus, decreto publico, nec sine magno praemio, aegris Christianis ministrabant. De eis meminit Honorii et Theodosii lex *PARABOLANI.* (Cod. lib. I. tit. III.)

82 I. ad Corinth. c. III. v. II.

83 Matth. c. VII. v. 27.

84 Christ. felic. parte II.

85 Continuator, et interpres latinus Petri Fran. Xav. Charlevoixii Galli respondet sigillatim ad objecta scriptoris hujus pro Regno Paraguayco. Edit. Venet. an. 1779. a p. 579.

86 Paulus III. P. M. Constit. *Licet debitum*. 18. Oct. an. 1549.

87 Philippus III. Rex Cath. diplomate dato in S. Laurentii 5. Septemb. an. 1620.

88 Parte II. c. X. §. III.

89 Buffon Histor. nat. tom. VI.

90 In nova Encyclop. tom. I verb. America. artic. *Theologia.*

91 De l'Amerique et des Americains. edit. Berlini an MDCCLXXI.

In my memory, the Payaguaes Indians, the pirates of the Paraguay River, a shameless sort of humans, after entering into a peace with the Spanish, came to the city of Asunción entirely naked (they enjoyed living mostly underwater like fish). This violently offended the most distinguished Governor Rafael de la Moneda, who issued an edict with a penalty set forth that none of them should approach the city unless modestly covered with respect to the disgraceful parts of the body. But since de la Moneda's edict was not just talk but rather he seriously enforced it, the otherwise immodest people, for fear of punishment, complied at least for then. But once de la Moneda had left office, little by little the Payaguaes returned to their natural inclination. For this reason, Father Miguel Crespo López harshly declaimed from his high position that anything that would be a serious scandal for the citizens could neither be tolerated nor permitted in any way.

76 Charlevoix's successor [i.e., Muriel] published this letter sent March 23, 1774, among his historical documents on page 595.

77 The Spaniard Seneca excellently explains the benefits of simple nourishment and the evils of gluttony (*Epistle* 95).

78 Since the Guaraní did not have these public offices previously, they did not have names for the positions either. Thus the Jesuits, in accordance with the native quality of the Guaraní language, invented certain words: *Corregidor—Poroquaitara,* one who dictates what has to be done; *Regidores—Cabildoyguara,* those who belong to the council or senate; *Alguazil Mayor—Yvyrarusu,* chief among those who brandish a rod in their hands; *Alferez—Aoveve rerekuara,* one who takes care of the flag; *Escribano—Kuatia apohara*—the clerk, who writes. They did not know about writing, but they adapted a word for writing from painting, which they knew about in a rudimentary way. For *aikuatia* in Guaraní is *pingo* ["I paint"] in Latin. They called the king *Mburuvichavete,* which means "the greatest of the superiors." And so those words were introduced from the time when the region was first approached. For, Fr. Antonio Ruiz de Montoya, who was one of the first Guaraní Cultivators and extremely skilled in the language, put them in his *Guaraní Lexicon,* published in Madrid in 1640.

79 *Part* 3.4.23. "Mediating judges are of two types," etc. See Tomás Sánchez in *Ten Commandments* 6.13.66–67.

80 Daniello Bartoli *Asia* Book 5, page 425.

81 These *Cruciferos* (whose art depended more on experience than on the study of books) correspond (if the small can be compared with the great) to the famous PARABOLANI, who, in the heroic times of Alexandria and in other cities, would minister to sick Christians by public decree and not without great reward. The *Law of Honorius and Theodosius* makes mention of them: PARABOLANI (Codex 1.3).

82 *1 Corinthians* 3:11.

83 *Matthew* 7:27.

84 In Part 2 of *Happy Christianity*.

85 The one who continued the work of Pierre François Xavier de Charlevoix and translated it into Latin [i.e., Muriel] responded one by one to the objections of this man, the author of the *Kingdom of Paraguay*. See the Venice edition of 1779 on page 579.

86 Pope Paul III issued the *Licet debitum* on October 18, 1549.

87 The Catholic King Felipe III in a declaration issued in San Lorenzo on September 5, 1620.

88 Part 2, Chapter 10, Section 3.

89 Buffon *Natural History*, vol. 6 [*corr.* vol. 3, pp. 506–507].

90 In the new [*Methodical*] *Encyclopedia,* the first volume of the series on *Theology,* under "Americans, America."

91 [Bonneville, Zacharie de Pazzi de], *On America and Americans* published in Berlin, 1771.

92 Pace hic Philosophi Ladouceurii dixerim, non deesse, qui magnificentiam regiam, atque exquisitas delicias Curionibus Guaranicis attribuunt. Gallicus liber (editus an. 1712.) sic habet: Presbyterium (idest Curionis aedes) Aularum magno numero distinctum est cum aulaeis, et fictis, pictisque simulacris. Prestolantur foris oppidani egressurum Curionem, qui eos audiat. Amplae illic apothecae, in quas indi laboris sui fructus inferunt. Reliquam domum atria valde multa occupant, et viridaria, et famulorum conclavia. Quae quidem omnia complectuntur spatium sexaginta jugerum, sive sex millia perticarum quadratarum, muro undique circumducto. Haec liber ille.

Et tu ad haec quid Ladouceuri? An non id totum regium est? non luxus? non dignus Craeso apparatus? non domus voluptuaria? Enimvero non palatium modo, sed urbem pro aede dicendus est habuisse Curio Guaranicus. Sed Gallum fabulatorem omittamus.

Illud scio (et olim praesens vidi) in aede Curionis Guaranici nullas fuisse aulas, nulla picta fictave simulacra (si quasdam excipias Divum imagines rudis operis appensas in cubiculo ad excitandam pietatem) nullum viridarium, sed hortum unum pro colendis oleribus, nullas famulorum cellas, cum non alius Indorum, quam senex janitor, ibi habitaret, et dormiret, nullam superiorem contignationem, cum omnia plano solo inaedificata essent, nullum murum praeter maceriam horti, et parietem, qui Curionis atrio praetentus erat instar claustri domus religiosae, ne cui foeminae illuc aditus pateret.

Atria erant duo, unum pro Curionis, et ejus collegae, hospitumque cubiculis, sex unoquoque ulnarum, ac pro gymnasio Musicorum, et apotheca, qua fructus agri communis (non praedii, quod sibi patresfamilias colebant) condebantur in usus publicos. Atrium alterum continebat fabrorum officinas, et pars ejus erat pro macello, ubi bubula viritim dividebatur ex oppidi armento. Horum autem aedificiorum, simul cum horto, ambitus (quoad ejus recordari possum) erat octoginta ulnarum circiter. Appello testes viros illos religiosos, qui illic nunc habitant. En tibi quo reciderunt *sexaginta illa jugera, sive sex millia perticatum quadratarum* impostoris inepti.

Cl. Bougainville certam mensuram non ponit contentus dicere domum Curionis *vastam* esse. Sitne vasta jam satis explicui. Illud addit ridicule: Curionem semper foras egredi equo, et magno comitatu? Quid? Egrediturne Curio ad invisendos agros, et ad Sacramenta administranda, etiam equo? Egreditur etiam equo ad vicina oppido sacella? Immo vero et Curio, et ejus collega ibant semper pedibus ferentes manu baculum, cui Crux superne erat, nisi si quando longum iter susciperent. Quaenam vera suis illa magni comitatus pompa? Dicam: cum ad ades Indorum eundum erat Curioni, vel ejis collegae, pro sacro ministerio (alia causa non ibant) binos afferebant secum comites alterum, cui egrorum cura erat, alterum ex aedituis. (Soli enim nunquam domo egrediebantur, ut religiosos viros decet.) Sin autem peregre proficiscendum duo item Indi, etiam ipsi equo vecti, Curionem, vel ejus collegam comitabantur.

Atque hinc satis coniici potest quam recte posuerit auctor Moralis Practicae (tom. III. Pag. 67.) adem Curionis Guararnici esse arcem munitissimam. Praeclara profecto, et eximia artis arx, quam Sacerdos unus, et ejus collega, et senex Indus Ianitor, tria capita, contra sex Indorum armatorum millia noctu defendebant.

93 De Tupambae, et Abambae Guaraniorum disserit Cyriacus Morellius eoque rem melius explicat, quod inter ipsos Guaranios olim versatus sit. (De Rudim . Juris Nat. et Gent. lib. l. disp. VIII. S, 2.)

92 With the Philosopher La Douceur's pardon, I must say here that there is no lack of those who attribute royal magnificence and sought-after delicacies to the Guaraní Priests. A French book (published in 1712) holds as follows: "The Presbytery (that is, the Priest's house) is divided into a large number of halls with tapestries, statues, and paintings. Outside, the townspeople stand ready for the priest to come out to hear them. There are ample storehouses there to which the Indians bring the fruits of their own labors. A great many patios, orchards, and servants' quarters take up the remainder of the house. All of this is encompassed in a space of sixty arpents, or six thousand square rods, with a wall surrounding it on all sides." So says that book [*Memoir Concerning the Establishment of the Jesuit Fathers in the Spanish Indies* by Moïse-Augustin Fontanieu].

And you, La Douceur, what do you say to this? Is not all this royal? Not luxury? Not splendor worthy of Croesus? Not a house filled with pleasures? Certainly, the Guaraní Priest must be declared to have had not only a palace but a city for his home. But let us set aside the French fabulist.

This I know (and once saw in person) that in the house of the Guaraní priest there were no halls, no paintings or sculptures (unless you count certain simply made images of Saints, which were hung in the bedroom to excite piety), no orchard, but a single garden for growing vegetables; there were no cells for the servants, since no Indian lived and slept there except an old porter; there was no upper story, since everything was built on one level; no wall other than the garden fence and a partition that had been placed in the Priest's courtyard as an enclosure for the religious living space so that the entrance to it would not be accessible to any women.

There were two courtyards; one was for the bedrooms of the Priest, his colleague, and guests, each of six *varas* [approx. 16 ft] per side, as well as for the musicians' school and the storeroom, in which the fruits of the community field were stored for public use (not those of the farm, which each householder cultivated for himself). The other courtyard contained the craftsmen's workshops and part of it was used as a butcher's shop, where meat from the town's herd was distributed to each person individually. The area occupied by all these buildings, together with the garden (as far as I can remember), was about eighty *varas* [approx. 220 ft] per side. I appeal to those religious men who live there now as witnesses. Behold! How that inept impostor's "sixty acres, or six thousand *perche carrée*," shrink back.

The famed Bougainville does not specify any measurement and is content to say that the Priest's house is vast. Now I have sufficiently explained whether it was vast. But he adds this ridiculous detail: that the priest always goes out on horseback and with a large retinue?! What?! Did the priest go to visit the sick and administer the sacraments on horseback as well? He also went on horseback to the small sanctuaries neighboring the town? No indeed! Both the priest and his colleague always went on foot carrying a staff, on top of which was a Cross, except when they undertook a long journey. Pray, is there any truth to that pomp of the "great retinue"? Let me tell you: when the Priest or his colleague had to go to the homes of Indians for sacred ministry (they did not go for any other reason) they would take with them two companions, one was charged with care for the sick and the other was one of the sacristans. (For they would never leave the house alone, as befits religious men.) But if travel abroad was necessary, likewise two Indians, who were themselves also riding horses, would accompany the Priest or his colleague.

And so, from this it can reasonably be concluded how rightly the author of *Moral Practice* (Vol. 3, p. 67) alleged that the house of the Guaraní Priest was "a heavily fortified citadel." It is an absolutely splendid and state-of-the-art citadel, which a single Priest, his colleague, and an old Indian porter —three people—can defend at night against six thousand armed Indians.

93 Domingo Muriel discusses the *Tupâmba'é* and *Avamba'é* of the Guaraní and he explains the matter better due to the fact that he once lived among the Guaraní (*Elements of Natural Law and the Law of Nations* 1.8.2).

94 Auctoritate litterarum Il. Peralta usus novissime est Cl. V. Maximus Mangold Doctor Theologus tom. I. Reflexionum in R. P. Alexandri a S. Joanne. De Cruce Carmelitae excalceati continuationem histor. Eccles. Claudii Fleurii. Pagg. 446. 447. 448. edis, Augustae Vindelicorum an. 1783.

95 Act. AA. C. IV. vv. 32. 34.

96 Petrus Fran. Xav. Charlivoix Histor. Paraguay. lib. VI. sub. init.

97 Pet. Joan Maffej, Histor. Indic. lib. XV.

98 In approbatione Gramatices, et Lexici linguae Guaranicae editi a P. Montoya an. 1640. Matriti.

99 Matth. c. V. v. 9.

100 Marc. c. IX. v. 49.

101 Matth c. V. v. 4.

102 Matth. c. V. v. 7.

103 Matth. c. V. v. 6.

104 Matth. c. V. vv. I. 5. 10.

105 Matt. c. XIX. v. 18.

106 Matth. c. V. v. 25.

107 Matth. c. V. v. 41.

108 Matth. c. V. v. 37.

109 Luc. c. VI. v. 35.

110 Matth. c. 5. v. 28.

111 Matth. c. V. v. 22.

112 Matth. c. XII. v. 36.

113 Matth. c. XV. vv. 19. 20.

114 Matth. c. VII. v. 12.

115 Histor. Impartiel des J. MDCCLXVIII. A. S. M. le Roy de Pruse.

116 Conversus est is liber in linguam Germanicam, et recusus Hamburgi an. 1768.

117 Traite sur divers sujets interessants de politique et de morale §. III. pag. 120.

118 L' esprit des Lois. cap. VI. pag. 40. et 41.

119 Novae Geographiae tom. XXXIII. edit. Venet. apud Ant. Zatta. an. 1781. Art. Governo de Buenos Ayres. §. Paraguay.

120 Adeo famosus fuit NICOLAUS I.: ut Ripert de Monclar Procurator generalis Aquensium Conventus, sive Parlamenti, in Scholiis ad suam contra Jesuitas actionem (Nota XXXVI) non dubitarit asserere, novi istius Regis Paraguayci potentiam eo devenisse, ut si tres quattuorve annos firmare opes suas sineretur, verendum esset, ne omnes ille Europae Principes e solio deturbatum veniret. Risum teneatis amici. Immo vero lacrymis digna res est. Bonus procurator docebat Aquenses de periculis numquam futuris e Novo Orbe. Atqui multo ille melius eosdem monuisset de imminente jam jam totius regni Gallici occasu, et ruina, idque non a Nicolao I.

121 Guaraniis solatio fuit Carolus III. Rex, qui foedus illud limitum, a decessore suo Fernando VI. initum, voluit irritum esse: Guaranii autem ex ejus voluntate oppida sua retinuerunt, hodieque retinent.

122 Deuter. cap. XXV. v. 2.

123 Lib. II. Regg. c. XIV. vv. 6. et 7.

124 Ibid. v. 11.

125 Lib. I Regg. c. XXVI. v. 9.

94 Most recently, the famed Doctor of Theology Maximus Mangold made use of the authority of the most illustrious Peralta's letter in the first volume of *Reflections on Alexander's Continuation of Claude Fleury's Ecclesiastical History*, pp. 446–448, published in Augsburg in 1783.

95 *Acts* 4:32 and 34.

96 Pierre François Xavier de Charlevoix *History of Paraguay*, near the beginning of Book 6.

97 Giovanni Pietro Maffei *Histories of the Indies*, Book 15.

98 In approving the grammar and lexicon of the Guaraní language, published by Father Montoya in Madrid in 1640.

99 *Matthew* 5:9.

100 *Mark* 9:49.

101 *Matthew* 5:4.

102 *Matthew* 5:7.

103 *Matthew* 5:6.

104 *Matthew* 5:1, 5, and 10.

105 *Matthew* 19:18.

106 *Matthew* 5:25.

107 *Matthew* 5:41.

108 *Matthew* 5:37.

109 *Luke* 6:35.

110 *Matthew* 5:28.

111 *Matthew* 5:22.

112 *Matthew* 12:36.

113 *Matthew* 15:19–20.

114 *Matthew* 7:12.

115 *Impartial History of the Jesuits*, [published in] 1768 for His Majesty, the King of Prussia.

116 The book was translated into German and reprinted in Hamburg in 1768. [An excerpt of Burke's *An Account of the European Settlements in America* (London, 1757–1758) was published anonymously in German as "Nachricht eines Engländers von Paraguay und den Jesuitischen Missionen" in *Neue Nachrichten von den Missionen der Jesuiten in Paraguay und von andern damit verbundenen Vorgängen in der Spanischen Monarchie.*]

117 [Georg Ludwig Schmid], *Treatises on Various Interesting Subjects of Politics and Morals*, §. 3. p. 120.

118 *The Spirit of the Laws* ch. 6, pp. 40–41.

119 *New Geography* vol. 33, [a Tuscan translation] published in Venice by the press of Antonio Zatta in 1781. See the section on Paraguay in the article titled "The Government of Buenos Aires."

120 "NICOLAS I" was so famous that Ripert de Monclar, *Procureur général* for the Assembly, or Parlement, of Aix-en-Provence, did not hesitate to assert in the *Notes* appended to his proceedings against the Jesuits (Note 36) that the power of that new King of Paraguay reached the point that if he had been allowed three or four more years to solidify his influence, there was a fear that he would come to dethrone all the Princes of Europe. Hold your laughter, my friends. Indeed, this is a matter worthy of tears. The good Procureur was teaching Aix-en-Provence about dangers from the New World that were never going to happen. And he would have done much better to warn the same men about the now imminent downfall and ruin of the entire French kingdom, a thing not brought about by Nicolas I.

121 King Carlos III was a comfort to the Guaraní, for he wanted to invalidate that treaty about the boundaries, agreed to by his predecessor Fernando VI. And so, through his will, the Guaraní retained their towns and retain them today.

122 *Deuteronomy* 25:2.

123 2 *Kings* [2 *Samuel*] 14:6–7.

124 Ibid. 14:11.

125 *1 Kings* 26:9 [1 *Samuel* 26:19].

126 Hanc Blazquii sententiam secundum acta causae reddit Gallus Charlevoixius inter documenta. Hist. Parag.

127 Is erat Christophorus Ramirez de Fuenreal, qui jam jam moriturus, quae dixerat de venis auri ad Uruguayum revocavit coram testibus.

128 Tertul. Apolog. c. XLIX.

129 Riflessioni sulla Filosofia del bello spirito pars. I. Rifles. 10.

130 Act. AA. c. XVII. v. 21

131 Aristot. Politic. lib. VI.

132 Aeneid. lib. VIII. Scio Virgilium licentia hic usum poetica, sed scio item memorem hic eum fuisse praecepti illius: *ficta voluptatis causa sint proxima veri:* quo sine poeta bonus erit nemo.

133 Ovid. Metamorph. lib I. sub initium.

134 *Num.* cap. XXXIII. v. 54.

135 *Matth.* c. XIX. v. 22.

136 *Ad Timoth.* I. c. VI. v.18.

137 *Ad Colossens.* c. IV. v.1.

138 *Epist. ad Philemonem.*

139 *Act. AA.* c. XVII. v. 29.

140 *Paul. II. ad Timoth. c.* XII. v. 20.

141 Idem I. ad Corinth. c. XII. a v. 12. ad 18.

142 *Tullius Tuscul.* V. v. 36.

143 *Lib. I. Regg.* c. XVII. v. 25.

144 *D. Paul. II. Corint.* c. VI. v. 1.

145 *Matth.* c. XXV. v. 40.

146 *Ibid.* v. 46.

147 *Joan. Petr. Maffej Histor. Indic. lib. VI.*

148 Idem lib. XII.

149 Extant M. Tulli Orationes tres de Lege agraria in P. Servillum Rullum Tribunum plebis, quem vehementer exagitavit, quod novis rebus studeret, coegitque tandem ab instituta rogatione desistere.

150 *Lib. Judic.* c. XVIII vv. 27-28.

151 *Proverb.* c. XXII v. 28.

152 *D. Paul. I. ad Corinth.* c. VII. v. 40.

153 *D. Thom.* t. 2. quest. 79. a. 2.

126 Among the documents in his *History of Paraguay*, the Frenchman Charlevoix cites the sentence Blázquez gave based on the trial records.

127 This was Cristóbal Ramírez de Fuenreal, who when he was about to die recanted in front of witnesses what he had said about veins of gold along the Uruguay River.

128 Tertulian, *Apology*, 49 [*corr.* 39.7].

129 *Reflections on the Philosophy of the Beautiful Spirit* part 1. Reflection 10.

130 *Acts* 17:21.

131 Aristotle *Politics* Book 6 [7.1329b].

132 *Aeneid* Book 8. I know that Vergil is using poetic license here, but I also know that he was mindful here of that famous precept: "Fictions meant to amuse should be close to reality"—without which no poet will be good.

133 Ovid *Metamorphoses* I, at the beginning.

134 *Numbers* 33:54.

135 *Matthew* 19:22.

136 *1 Timothy* 6:18.

137 *Colossians* 4:1.

138 *Epistle to Philemon.*

139 *Acts* 17:29.

140 2 *Timothy* 12:20.

141 *1 Corinthians* 12:12–18.

142 Cicero *Tusculan Disputations* 5.36.105.

143 *1 Kings* [*1 Samuel*] 17:25.

144 2 *Corinthians* 6:1.

145 *Matthew* 25:40.

146 *Matthew* 25:46.

147 Giovanni Pietro Maffei *Histories of the Indies*, Book 6.

148 Giovanni Pietro Maffei *Histories of the Indies*, Book 12.

149 Regarding the agrarian Law there are three surviving Orations by Cicero against Publius Servilius Rullus, Tribune of the Plebs, whom Cicero attacked viciously, because of that man's zeal for revolution, and forced to abandon his intended proposal.

150 *Judges* 18:27–28.

151 *Proverbs* 22:28.

152 *1 Corinthians* 7:40.

153 St. Thomas [Aquinas] 2.79.2 [*corr.* 2.97.2].

BIBLIOGRAPHY

EDITIONS AND TRANSLATIONS

Peramàs, José Manuel

1793 *De Vita et Moribus Tredecim Virorum Paraguaycorum*. Ex typographia Archii, Faenza.

1946 *La República de Platón y los guaraníes*. Translation and notes by Juan Cortés del Pino; preface by Guillermo Fúrlong. Emecé Editores, Buenos Aires. [Spanish]

1994 *Guaranica: De Administratione Guaranica Comparata ad Rempublicam Platonis Commentarius*. Translation by Stelio Cro. Symposium Press, Hamilton, Ontario. [Italian]

2004 *Platón y los guaraníes*. Translation by Francisco Fernández Pertíñez and Bartomeu Melià; preface and notes by Bartomeu Melià. Centro Estudios Paraguayos "Antonio Guasch," Asunción. [Spanish]

2018 *Peramás y su obra: Jesuitas y gauchos en el Rio de la Plata*. Translation and notes by Stelio Cro. Editorial Académica Española, Saarbrücken. [Spanish]

SELECT BIBLIOGRAPHY

Arbo, Desiree

2016 The Uses of Classical Learning in the Río de la Plata, c. 1750–1815. PhD dissertation, University of Warwick, Coventry.

Armani, Alberto

1994 *Ciudad de dios y ciudad del sol: El "estado" jesuita de los guaraníes 1609–1768*. Fondo de Cultura Económica, Mexico City.

Astorgano Abajo, Antonio

2004 La biblioteca Jesuítico-Española de Hervás y su liderazgo sobre el resto de los ex jesuitas. *Hispania sacra* 56 (113):171–268.

Austin, Shawn Michael

2020 *Colonial Kinship: Guaraní, Spaniards, and Africans in Paraguay*. University of New Mexico Press, Albuquerque.

Avellaneda, Mercedes

2014 *Guaraníes, criollos y jesuitas: Luchas de poder en las Revoluciones Comuneras del Paraguay; Siglos XVII y XVIII*. Editorial Tiempo de Historia, Asunción.

Batllori, Miguel

1966 *La cultura hispano-italiana de los jesuitas expulsos: Españoles, hispano-americanos, filipinos, 1767–1814*. Gredos, Madrid.

Berg, Hans van Den

2010 *Con los yuracarees (Bolivia): Crónicas misionales (1765–1825)*. Iberoamericana, Madrid.

Bertrán Quera, Miguel

1984 *La pedagogía de los jesuitas en la Ratio Studiorum: La fundación de colegios; Orígenes, autores y evolución histórica de la Ratio; Análisis de la educación religiosa, caracterológica e intelectual*. Universidad Católica del Táchira, San Cristóbal, Venezuela.

Bonomo, Mariano, Rodrigo Costa Angrizani, Eduardo Apolinaire, and Francisco Silva Noelli

2015 A Model for the Guaraní Expansion in the La Plata Basin and Littoral Zone of Southern Brazil. *Quaternary International* 356:54–73.

Brumbaugh, Michael

2021 Utopia Writes Back: José Manuel Peramás on the Limits of Republicanism. In *Brill's Companion to Classics in the Early Americas*, edited by Maya Feile Tomes, Adam J. Goldwyn, and Matthew Duquès, pp. 50–72. Brill, Leiden.

Burgés, Francisco, and Roberto Tomichá Charupá

2008 *Francisco Burgés y las misiones de Chiquitos: El Memorial de 1703 y documentos complementarios*. Instituto Latinoamericano de Misionología, Editorial Verbo Divino, Cochabamba.

Bustamante, Francisco

2001 Guaranies y Jesuitas en la provincia paraquaria segun las crónicas de Montoya, Cardiel y Peramás (siglos XVII y XVIII). PhD dissertation, University of Florida, Gainesville.

Campana, Paola

2021 *Con ogni diligenza corretto e stampato: Stampatori, librai e cartari a Faenza dal XV al XVIII secolo*. Polaris, Faenza.

Caturelli, Alberto

1992 Ciudad platónica y cuidad cristiana en el Nuevo Mundo: El pensamiento de José Manuel Peramás. *Verbo* 310–302:17–33.

Cerno, Leonardo, and Franz Obermeier

2013 Nuevos aportes de la lingüística para la investigación de documentos en guaraní de la época colonial (siglo XVIII). *Folia histórica del nordeste* 21:33–56.

Cid Labra, Patricia L., and Leonardo Casini

2021 La Pontificia Universidad de San Javier: Agente de transformación de la sociedad panameña. *Congreso Nacional de Ciencia y Tecnología—APANAC*, doi.org/10.33412/apanac.2021.3075.

Cornelli, Gabriele

2016 Platão e os Guaranis: Utopias transatlânticas na obra De Administratione guaranica comparata ad Rempublicam Platonis commentarius de José Manuel Peramás. In *Cosmópolis: Mobilidades culturais às origens do pensamento antigo*, edited by Gabriele Cornelli, Maria do Ceu Fialho, and Delfim Leão, pp. 35–46. Coimbra University Press, Coimbra.

2017 El comunismo de Platón y de los Guaraníes: Observaciones sobre el *De Administratione guaranica comparanda ad Rempublicam Platonis commentarius* de José Manuel Peramás. *Avatares filosóficos* 4:81–91.

Costa Oller, Francesc

2018 *L'extraordinària vida dels germans Peramàs*. Francesc Costa Oller, Mataró.

Cruz Freire, Pedro

2013 Joaquín de Peramas: Un ingeniero militar en América. In *Barroco iberoamericano: Identidades culturales de un imperio*, edited by Carme López Calderón, María de los Ángeles Fernández, and Inmaculada Rodíguez, vol. 1, pp. 375–388. Andavira Editora, Santiago de Compostela.

2016 Fort San Carlos de Barrancas: Power and Control in the Gulf of Mexico and Southern America. In *From Colonies to Countries in the North Caribbean: Military Engineers in the Development of Cities and Territories*, edited by Pedro Luengo Gutiérrez and Gene A. Smith, pp. 23–38. Cambridge Scholars Publishing, Newcastle upon Tyne.

Cunninghame Graham, R. B.

1901 *A Vanished Arcadia: Being Some Account of the Jesuits in Paraguay, 1607 to 1767*. W. Heinemann, London.

Dainville, François de

1978 *L'éducation des jésuites: XVIe–XVIIIe siècles*. Minuit, Paris.

Donato, Clorinda

2014 The Politics of Writing, Translating, and Publishing: New World Histories in Post-Expulsion Italy; Filippo Salvatore Gilij's 1784 *Saggio di Storia Americana*. In *Jesuit Accounts of the Colonial Americas: Intercultural Transfers, Intellectual Disputes, and Textualities*, edited by Marc André Bernier, Clorinda Donato, and Hans-Jürgen Lüsebrink, pp. 50–80. University of Toronto Press, Toronto.

Estenssoro, Juan Carlos

2015 Las vías indígenas de la occidentalización: Lenguas generales y lenguas maternas en el ámbito colonial americano (1492–1650). *Mélanges de la Casa de Velázquez* 45(1):15–36.

Feile Tomes, Maya

2015a Further Points on Peramás: An Erratum and Two Addenda. *International Journal of the Classical Tradition* 22(3):383–389.

2015b News of a Hitherto Unknown Neo-Latin Columbus Epic, Part I: José Manuel Peramás's *De Invento Novo Orbe Inductoque Illuc Christi Sacrificio* (1777). *International Journal of the Classical Tradition* 22(1):1–28.

2015c News of a Hitherto Unknown Neo-Latin Columbus Epic, Part II: José Manuel Peramás's *De Invento Novo Orbe Inductoque Illuc Christi Sacrificio* (1777). *International Journal of the Classical Tradition* 22(2):383–389.

2018 The Angel and Ameri(c)a: Performing the "New World" in José Manuel Peramás's *De invento Novo Orbe inductoque illuc Christi sacrificio* (1777). In *Changing Hearts: Performing Jesuit Emotions between Europe, Asia, and the Americas*, edited by Yasmin Haskell and Raphaele Garrod, pp. 121–145. Brill, Leiden.

Feile Tomes, Maya, and Bram van der Velden

n.d. *Columbus Sails in the 1770s: A Late Iberian Epic on the Discovery of the New World; Translation and Commentary of José Manuel Peramás's "De Invento Novo Orbe Inductoque Illuc Christi Sacrificio" (1777)*. Bloomsbury, forthcoming.

Ferrante, Florencia

2021 Una obra italiana para la independencia novohispana: Estudio de una traducción al español de "Le lettere americane" de Gianrinaldo Carli. *1611: Revista de historia de la traducción* 15.

Foucault, Michel

1984 Des espace autres. *Architecture mouvement continuité* 5:46–49.

Friedrich, Markus

2008 Circulating and Compiling the Litterae Annuae: Towards a History of the Jesuit System of Communication. *Archivum Historicum Societatis Iesu* 77:3–39.

Fúrlong, Guillermo

1921 La imprenta jesuítica de Córdoba (1763–1767). *Estudios* 20:241–249, 346–357.

1925 Un gran humanista de la época colonial José Manuel Peramás. *Estudios* 29:377–382.

Fúrlong, Guillermo (editor)

1952 *José Manuel Peramás y su diario del destierro (1768)*. Librería del Plata, Buenos Aires.

Ganson, Barbara Anne

2003 *The Guaraní under Spanish Rule in the Río de la Plata*. Stanford University Press, Stanford.

2016 Antonio Ruiz de Montoya, Apostle of the Guaraní. *Journal of Jesuit Studies* 3(2):197–210.

Garavaglia, J. C.

1999 The Crises and Transformations of Invaded Societies: The La Plata Basin (1535–1650). In *The Cambridge History of the Native Peoples of the Americas*, vol. 3, *South America*, pt. 2, edited by Frank Salomon and Stuart B. Schwartz, pp. 1–58. Cambridge University Press, Cambridge.

Guasti, Niccolò

2009 Rasgos del exilio italiano de los jesuitas españoles. *Hispania sacra* 61(123):257–278.

2019 Los jesuitas españoles expulsos y la educación de las élites italianas (1767–1815). *Espacio, tiempo y educación* 6(2):79–97.

Guzmán, Augusto

1969 Los Peramás y el Curitu. In *La tradición en Cochabamba*, edited by Hector Cossio Salinas, pp. 357–364. Editorial "Los Amigos del Libro," Cochabamba.

Hudde, Hinrich

1983 Griechisches Ideal und südamerikanische Wirklichkeit: Zu José Manuel Peramás' Vergleich zwischen Platons Staatsschriften und dem "Jesuitenstaat" in Paraguay. *Lateinamerika-Studien* 13(1):355–367.

Imbruglia, Girolamo

2017 *The Jesuit Missions of Paraguay and a Cultural History of Utopia (1568–1789)*. Brill, Leiden.

Jackson, Robert H.

2019 *Regional Conflict and Demographic Patterns on the Jesuit Missions among the Guaraní in the Seventeenth and Eighteenth Centuries*. Brill, Leiden.

2021 *Jesuits in Spanish America before the Suppression: Organization and Demographic and Quantitative Perspectives*. Brill, Leiden.

Lee, Kittiya

2014 Language and Conquest: Tupi-Guarani Expansion in the European Colonization of Brazil and Amazonia. In *Iberian Imperialism and Language Evolution in Latin America*, edited by Salikoko S. Mufwene, pp. 143–167. University of Chicago Press, Chicago.

Lugon, Clovis

1949 *La république communiste chrétienne des Guaranis (1610–1768)*. Editions ouvrières, Paris.

MacCormack, Sabine

1999 Ethnography in South America: The First Two Hundred Years. In *The Cambridge History of the Native Peoples of the Americas*, vol. 3, *South America*, pt. 1, edited by Frank Salomon and Stuart B. Schwartz, pp. 96–187. Cambridge University Press, Cambridge.

Maeder, Ernesto J. A.

1992 *Misiones del Paraguay: Conflictos y disolución de la sociedad guarani (1768–1850)*. MAPFRE, Madrid.

1996 *Aproximación a las misiones Guaraníticas*. Ediciones de la Universidad Católica Argentina, Buenos Aires.

2013 *Misiones del Paraguay: Construcción jesuítica de una sociedad cristiano guaraní (1610–1768)*. ConTexto, Resistencia.

Mateos, Francisco

1960 Un manuscrito inédito del P. Bernardo Recio. *Missionalia hispánica* 17:137–193.

Melai, Fabrizio

2011 I gesuiti del Paraguay espulsi in Italia: Mitologia politica e sociologia dell'esilio. PhD dissertation, Scuola Normale Superiore, Pisa.

2020 The Impossible Dialogue between Plato and Epicurus: José Manuel Peramás's *Commentarius* on the Paraguayan Missions. In *Transnational Perspectives on the Conquest and Colonization of Latin America*, edited by Jenny Mander, David Midgley, and Christine D. Beaule, pp. 35–46. Routledge, New York.

Melià, Bartomeu

1981 El "modo de ser" guaraní en la primera documentación jesuítica (1594–1639). *Revista de antropologia* 24:1–24.

2003 *La lengua guaraní en el Paraguay colonial*. Centro de Estudios Paraguayos Antonio Guasch, Asunción.

2015 El buen vivir se aprende. *Sinéctica* 45:1–12.

Meruvia Balderrama, Fanor

2000 *Historia de la coca: Los Yungas de Pocona y Totora (1550–1900)*. Plural Editores, La Paz.

Molas i Ribalta, Pedro

1973 *Societat i Poder Polític a Mataró 1718–1808*. Caixa Laietana, Mataró.

Monteiro, John

1999 The Crises and Transformations of Invaded Societies: Coastal Brazil in the Sixteenth Century. In *The Cambridge History of the Native Peoples of the Americas*, vol. 3, *South America*, pt. 1, edited by Frank Salomon and Stuart B. Schwartz, pp. 973–1023. Cambridge University Press, Cambridge.

Morales, Martín

1998 Los comienzos de las Reducciones de la Provincia del Paraguay en relación con el Derecho Indiano y el Instituto de la Compañía de Jesús: Evolución y conflictos. *Archivum Historicum Societatis Iesu* 67:3–130.

2010 ¿Guaraníes? No, aqueos. Una lectura de la obra de José Manuel Peramás, "La República de Platón y los Guaraníes." In *Los jesuitas formadores de ciudadanos: La educación dentro y fuera de sus colegios, siglos XVI–XXI*, edited by Perla Chinchilla, pp. 205–244. Universidad Iberoamericana, Mexico City.

Müller, M.

2011 Pater Karl Haimhausen und die bayerischen Jesuiten in Chile im 18. Jahrhundert. In *Bayern in Lateinamerika: Transatlantische Verbindungen und interkultureller Austausch*, edited by Peter Claus Hartmann and Alois Schmid, pp. 195–236. C. H. Beck, Munich.

Neumann, Eduardo

2015 *Letra de indíos: Cultura escrita, comunicação e memória indígena nas Reduções do Paraguai.* Nhanduti Editora, São Bernardo do Campo.

Neumann, Eduardo, and Guillermo Wilde

2014 Escritura, poder y memoria en las reducciones jesuíticas del Paraguay: Trayectorias de líderes indígenas en tiempos de transición. *Colonial Latin American Historical Review* 19(3):353–380.

Orta Nadal, Ricardo

1953 *Un aspecto de la historiografía y etnología jesuíticas del litoral: La idea de cultura en José Manuel Peramás*. Universidad Nacional del Litoral, Santa Fe, Argentina.

Recio, Bernardo

1947 *Compendiosa Relación de la Cristiandad de Quito*. Consejo Superior de Investigaciones Científicas, Madrid.

Rodríguez-Alcalá, Carolina

2010 Apuntes para una historia de la escritura en guaraníel estatuto y la circulación del texto en las misiones jesuíticas. *Scriptura* 21–22:9–32.

Romanato, Gianpaolo

2010 I gesuiti delle "Reducciones" dal Paraguay all'Italia: José Manuel Peramás. In *La presenza in Italia dei gesuiti iberici espulsi: Aspetti religiosi, politici, culturali*, edited by Ugo Baldini and Gian Paolo Brizzi, pp. 113–123. CLUEB, Bologna.

Sarreal, Julia J. S.

2014 *The Guaraní and Their Missions: A Socioeconomic History*. Stanford University Press, Stanford.

Silverman, Daniel Enrique, and Marina Garone Gravier

2021 *Laudationes Quinque* (1766): History, Materiality, and Graphic Technology of the First Jesuit Printed Work in Córdoba, Argentina. *Diseña* 18:3–22.

Storni, Hugo

1980 *Catálogo de los jesuitas de la Provincia del Paraguay (Cuenca del Plata), 1585–1768*. Institutum Historicum S.I., Rome.

Suárez, Marcela Alejandra (editor)

2005 *José Manuel Peramás, Laudationes Quinque. Cinco alabanzas al muy ilustre Sr. Dr. Ignacio Duarte y Quirós, fundador del Colegio de Monserrat de Córdoba en América. Edición bilingüe anotada.* Biblioteca Nacional, Buenos Aires.

2017a At iam satis est de rebus guaranicis: La digressio etnográfica en el Annus Patiens de José Peramás. *Folia histórica del nordeste* 28:13–27.
2017b La traducción italiana del Annus Patiens del P. Peramás: Reescritura, manipulación e imagen de un original. *Circe, de clásicos y modernos* 21(2).

Telesca, Ignacio, and Alejandra Vidal (editors)
2021 *Historia y lingüística guaraní*. Editorial Sb, Buenos Aires.

Tomichá Charupá, Roberto
2002 *La primera evangelización en las reducciones de Chiquitos, Bolivia, 1691–1767: Protagonistas y metodología misional*. Editorial Verbo Divino, Cochabamba.

Vega, Fabián R.
2018 La dimensión bibliográfica de la reducción lingüística: La producción textual jesuítica en guaraní a través de los inventarios de bibliotecas. *Nuevo mundo, mundos nuevos*, https://doi.org/10.4000/nuevomundo.73946.

Velema, Wyger, and Arthur Weststeijn
2018 *Ancient Models in the Early Modern Republican Imagination*. Brill, Leiden.

Whitehead, Maurice
2015 On the Road to Suppression: The Jesuits and Their Expulsion from the Reductions of Paraguay. In *The Jesuit Suppression in Global Context*, edited by Jeffrey D. Burson and Jonathan Wright, pp. 83–99. Cambridge University Press, Cambridge.

Wilde, Guillermo
2001 Los guaraníes después de la expulsión de los jesuitas: Dinámicas políticas y transacciones simbólicas. *Revista Complutense de Historia de América* 27:69–106.
2009 *Religión y poder en las misiones de Guaraníes*. Editorial Sb, Buenos Aires.
2014 Adaptaciones y apropiaciones en una cultura textual de frontera: Impresos misionales del Paraguay Jesuítico. *História unisinos* 18(2):270–286.
2018a Jesuit Missions and the Guarani Ethnogenesis: Political Interactions, Indigenous Actors, and Regional Networks on the Southern Frontier of the Iberian Empires. In *Big Water: The Making of the Borderlands Between Brazil, Argentina, and Paraguay*, edited by Jacob Blanc and Frederico Freitas, pp. 54–80. University of Arizona Press, Tucson.
2018b Missions' Past and the Idea of Return, between History and Memory. In *The Oxford Handbook of the Jesuits*, edited by Ines G. Županov, pp. 1–39. Oxford University Press, New York.

Zantop, Susanne
1997 *Colonial Fantasies: Conquest, Family, and Nation in Precolonial Germany, 1770–1870*. Duke University Press, Durham, N.C.

NAMES AND WORKS CITED IN *DE ADMINISTRATIONE GUARANICA*

Citations are to section numbers (§) in the *De Administratione Guaranica.*

ANCIENT AUTHORITIES

POST-ANTIQUE AND EARLY MODERN AUTHORITIES

Membership in a religious order has been noted with the following abbreviations: CO (Oratorians), CRSP (Barnabites), OCD (Discalced Carmelites), O. de M. (Mercedarians), OFM (Franciscans), OM (Minims), OP (Dominicans), OSB (Benedictines), OSsT (Trinitarians), and SJ (Jesuits).

Burke, Edmund (1729–1797), *An Account of the European Settlements in America* (London, 1757–1758), §276

Büsching, Anton Friedrich (1724–1793), *Nuova geografia* (Venice, 1773–1782), §6, 279–281

Cardiel, José, SJ (1704–1781), *"De moribus Guaraniorum,"* published as an appendix to the Latin translation of Charlevoix's *Historia Paraguajensis* (Venice, 1779), §5, 65, 94

Charlevoix, Pierre François Xavier de, SJ (1682–1761), *Historia Paraguajensis* (Venice, 1779), §5, 25n11, 189n71, 238, 241n85, 259n96, 294n126

Cordara, Giulio, SJ (1704–1785), *Historia Societatis Iesu* (Rome, 1750), §87n44

Echavarri, Bernardo Ibáñez de, ex SJ (1715–1762), *El reino jesuítico del Paraguay* (1762), §61n28, 62, 64, 222, 240–241, 287–295

Feijóo y Montenegro, Benito Jerónimo, OSB (1676–1764), *Teatro crítico universal* (1726–1739), §79n36

Fontanieu, Moïse-Augustin de (1662–1725), *Mémoire touchant l'établissement des pères jésuites dans les Indes d'Espagne* (n.p., 1712), §252n92

Fourcroy de Guillerville, Jean-Louis de (1717–1799), *Les enfans élevés dans l'ordre de la nature* (Paris, 1774), §96n48

Gabuzio, Giovanni Antonio, CRSP (1551–1621), *De vita et rebus gestis Pii V. Pont. Max.* (Rome, 1605), §52n20

Gerson, Jean Charlier de (1363–1429), "Sermo contra luxuriam dominica III adventus" in *Opera Omnia: Opera Moralia* (Antwerp, 1706), §94

Grimaldi, Francesco, SJ (1680–1740), *De vita oeconomica* (1738), §88n46, 97n49

Herrera y Tordesillas, Antonio de (1549–1625), *Historia general de los hechos de los castellanos en las Islas i Tierra Firme del Mar Océano* (Madrid, 1601–1615), §40

Hervás, Lorenzo, SJ (1735–1809), *Idea dell' universo* (Cesena, 1778–1787), §15n5

Insaurralde, José, SJ (1663–1730), *Ara poru aguĩyey haba* (Madrid, 1759–1760), §111–112

Linguet, Simon-Nicholas Henri (1736–1794), *Histoire impartiale des Jésuites* (Madrid, 1768), §275

Maffei, Giovanni Pietro, SJ, (1536–1604), *Historiarum Indicarum* (1588), §154–156, 161, 260–263, 336

Mamachi, Tommaso Maria, OP (1713–1792), *Originum et antiquitatum christianarum*, vol. 2 (Rome, 1750), §15n4

Mangold, Maximus, SJ (1722–1797), *Reflexiones in R. P. Alexandri A S. Joanne de cruce carmelitae excalceati continuationem historiae ecclesiasticae Claudii Fleurii Abbatis* (Augsburg, 1783), §256n94

Mariana, Juan de, SJ (1536–1624), *De ponderibus et mensuris* (Toledo, 1599), §43n16

Melo, José Rodrigues de, SJ (1723–1789), *De rusticis Brasiliae rebus* (Rome, 1781), §120

More, Thomas (1478–1535), *Utopia* (Louvain, 1516), §48

Montesquieu (1689–1755), *L'esprit des lois* (Geneva, 1748), §6, 278, 306

Muratori, Lodovico Antonio [secular clergy] (1672–1750), *Il cristianesimo felice nelle missioni del Paraguay* (Venice, 1743), §5, 88n45, 238, 306

Muriel, Domingo, SJ (1718–1795), *Rudimenta juris naturae et gentium* (Venice, 1791), §18n7, 50n19, 63n29, 96n48, 179n69, 189n71, 206n75, 207n76, 241n85, 255n93

Noghera, Giovanni Battista, SJ (1719–1784), *Riflessioni su la filosofia de bello spirito* (Bassano, 1767), §305–306

Nonnotte, Claude-Adrien, SJ (1711–1793), *Dictionnaire philosophique de la religion* (Avignon, 1772), §37n12

Pauw, Cornelius de (1739–1799), *Recherches philosophiques sur les Américains* (Berlin, 1768); and "Amérique," *in Supplément à l'encyclopédie* (Amsterdam, 1776), §39–41, 96n48, 121, 149, 170n65, 187, 194, 244, 245, 246

OTHER NAMES

Michael Brumbaugh is Associate Professor of Classical Studies and Core Faculty at the Stone Center for Latin American Studies at Tulane University. His work examines political thought in ancient Graeco-Roman literature and the ways in which such literature featured in subsequent political discourses from the Hellenistic era to the early modern period. He is especially interested in examining these dynamics in contexts where diverse wisdom traditions and sources of authority collide. His first book, *The New Politics of Olympos* (2019), investigates Greek discourses of power, authority, and kingship leveraged in Egypt as Macedonian rulers sought to construct new political regimes out of existing Hellenic, Persian, and Egyptian traditions. Brumbaugh's work on the Graeco-Roman tradition in South America began in 2008 and has been generously supported by major grants and fellowships from the Loeb Classical Library Foundation, the National Endowment for the Humanities, and Tulane University. In connection with the present volume on the Guaraní and Plato, he is working on a closely related monograph project that interrogates early modern engagement with Mediterranean antiquity and its political modalities in the context of reform movements during the so-called Age of Revolutions (1775–1848), particularly in Europe and the Americas.

TEXTS *from the* EARLY AMERICAS

Dumbarton Oaks, Trustees for Harvard University, Washington, D.C.

Texts from the Early Americas presents English translations of archival and printed texts from the early Americas, with a particular focus on primary sources in Indigenous languages and Latin. Bilingual editions preserve the original text alongside the English translation, ensuring their accessibility to both scholars and general readers. The original texts and translations are accompanied by short introductions that provide information about the context in which the primary sources were generated. The series includes a range of textual genres, including historical, administrative, and missionary sources of both Indigenous and non-Indigenous authorship.

Further information on Pre-Columbian Studies publications can be found at www.doaks.org/publications.

Josep Manuel Peramàs, *A Treatise on the Guaraní System of Government in Comparison with Plato's Republic (1793)*, edited and translated by Michael Brumbaugh